T0351778

DISTANT VOICES: SKETCHES OF A SWEDENBORGIAN WORLD VIEW is the sixth volume in a series of publications exploring Swedenborg's place and influence within the history of ideas. Other titles in the series include *Gardens of Heaven and Earth* by Kristin King (2011); *Philosophy Literature Mysticism: an anthology of essays on the thought and influence of Emanuel Swedenborg*, ed. Stephen McNeilly (2013); *The Grand Theme and Other Essays* by Anders Hallengren (2013); *Imaginal Landscapes: reflections on the mystical visions of Jorge Luis Borges and Emanuel Swedenborg* by William Rowlandson (2015); *New Jerusalem: the good city and the good society* by Ken Worpole (2015); and the forthcoming *Medicine, Mysticism and Mythology: Garth Wilkinson, Swedenborg and Nineteenth-Century Esoteric Culture* by Malcolm Peet. In *Distant Voices: Sketches of a Swedenborgian World View* John Haller focuses specifically on Swedenborg's influence on key figures of the nineteenth and twentieth century including Henry James, Sr, Ralph Waldo Emerson, Charles Fourier, Albert Brisbane, Thomas Lake Harris, J J G Wilkinson, James Tyler Kent, Charles Bonney, Ralph Waldo Trine, D T Suzuki, Paul Carus and Herman C Vetterling. Although linked by a common theme of social reform and the desire for a better society, each chapter can also be read as a self-contained essay.

DR JOHN S HALLER, JR, emeritus professor of history and medical humanities at Southern Illinois University Carbondale, has written on subjects ranging from the history of race and sexuality to medicine, pharmacy and spirituality. His most recent books include *The History of American Homeopathy: From Rational Medicine to Holistic Health Care* (2009); *Swedenborg, Mesmer, and the Mind-Body Complex: The Roots of Complementary Medicine* (2010); *The History of New Thought: From Mind Cure to Positive Thinking and the Prosperity Gospel* (2012); and *Shadow Medicine: The Placebo in Conventional and Unconventional Medicines* (2014). He is former editor of *Caduceus: A Humanities Journal for Medicine and the Health Sciences* and, until his retirement at the end of 2008, served for eighteen years as vice-president for academic affairs for the Southern Illinois University system.

Distant Voices:
Sketches of a Swedenborgian
World View

essays on Henry James, Sr and Ralph Waldo Emerson;
Charles Fourier and Albert Brisbane; Thomas Lake Harris;
J J G Wilkinson and James Tyler Kent; Charles Bonney
and the World's Parliament of Religions; Paul Carus and
Herman Vetterling; Ralph Waldo Trine; and D T Suzuki

Distant Voices:
Sketches of a Swedenborgian World View

essays on Henry James, Sr and Ralph Waldo Emerson;
Charles Fourier and Albert Brisbane; Thomas Lake Harris;
J J G Wilkinson and James Tyler Kent; Charles Bonney
and the World's Parliament of Religions; Paul Carus and
Herman Vetterling; Ralph Waldo Trine; and D T Suzuki

by

John S Haller, Jr

The Swedenborg Society
20-21 Bloomsbury Way
London WC1A 2TH

2017

Typeset at Swedenborg House.
Printed at T J International, Padstow
Book design and artwork © Stephen McNeilly

Published by:
The Swedenborg Society
Swedenborg House
20-21 Bloomsbury Way
London
WC1A 2TH

ISBN 978-0-85448-202-3
British Library Cataloguing-in-Publication Data.
A catalogue record for this book is available from the British Library.

ACKNOWLEDGEMENTS

The two individuals to whom I am most indebted are Stephen McNeilly, the Swedenborg Society's Executive Director, for his support and wise counsel, and James Wilson, the Society's Assistant Editor and Secretary to the Society's Advisory and Revisions Board, for his meticulous reading and careful editing. His many comments and suggestions resulted in what I hope will be a useful contribution to the scholarship surrounding Swedenborg's influence on Western and Eastern thought. I also wish to express my personal thanks to the Society's publishing assistants Mala Gattney Hyde and Oliver Hancock; the librarians and staff of Morris Library of Southern Illinois University Carbondale; the Swedenborgian House of Studies Library and Archives; Stanford University Library; University of Michigan Library; Google Books; and JSTOR. Equally important, I am grateful to my wife, Robin, who offered both encouragement and criticism in her numerous readings of my drafts. Those errors of fact or interpretation that remain are mine alone, and for them I take full responsibility.

CONTENTS

FOREWORD

Devin Zuber

I n 1743, in the midst of a life-changing existential crisis, the natural scientist-turned-mystic Emanuel Swedenborg (1688-1772) bought a large property on the island of Södermalm, a district in southern Stockholm. The buildings (a main house, kitchen and servant's quarters, and a summerhouse) were arranged around a spacious and elaborate garden that occupied most of Swedenborg's plot of land on Hornsgatan 43. Over the next three decades, whenever Swedenborg was at home and not residing abroad (as he frequently had to do while undertaking the publication of his heterodox theology in London or Amsterdam), the former assessor of mines avidly tended to his green space, growing all manner of flowers and edible foodstuffs. Swedenborg's garden was particularly remarkable for the extraordinary number of rare specimens that he collected and grew from the 'new' world of North America, including mulberries, pod-bearing trees, buttonwoods, flowering dogwoods, corn, peas and various sorts of melons.

Swedenborg's garden has intrigued several generations of writers and scholars who have found in its layout and details many suggestive metaphors for Swedenborg's theological projects.[1] As an allegory for his ideas, the 'horticulture' contained in Swedenborg's thinking often proved to be too exotic for the Lutheran soil of his native Sweden, and his theology would ultimately come to find a much more fertile reception in distant American climates during the 'long' nineteenth century. Around 1850, the presence of Swedenborgian ideas was so persistent and pervasive among various American forms of popular esotericism—such as mesmerism and spiritualism—that Ralph Waldo Emerson could marvel in his journal how 'This Age is Swedenborg's'.[2] The abundance of American specimens in Swedenborg's garden, thus, appropriately adumbrates the later flourishing that his ideas would come to have across North America, as savants like Emerson germinated the seeds of his theology into productive forms of Transcendentalism, alternative medicinal systems, philosophical pragmatism, communitarianism and New Thought—to name but a few of the many fruits, some of them admittedly strange, that Swedenborg's ideas helped to generate.

In *Distant Voices: Sketches of a Swedenborgian World View*, John Haller usefully provides a kaleidoscopic perspective on the converging, overlapping figures who took up these Swedenborgian seeds and dispersed them across the broad landscape of nineteenth-century American thought and culture. Though some of the twelve primary figures he dexterously sketches were definitively planted in soils elsewhere—such as Charles Fourier in France, James John Garth Wilkinson in London, or D T Suzuki in Japan—it was within the medley of American spiritual and philosophical eclecticism that their respective readings of Swedenborg came to most fully flower. Fourier's theories, arguably, came to their fullest realization within the Swedenborgian phalanxes that cropped up across the United States in the antebellum period. Wilkinson's writings, while largely neglected in his own England, were warmly read and received by Emerson, Thoreau and others in New England. Suzuki's critical role as a harbinger of Zen Buddhism for the West reached its acme when he was residing in New York City in the 1950s and becoming a de facto spiritual advisor to the Beat writers Jack Kerouac and Allen Ginsberg, and the avant-garde composer John Cage.

When we compile Haller's intellectual and biographical sketches together and process them one after another, a little like the proto-cinematic flipbooks of the late nineteenth century that were once so popular, a moving picture of the liveliness and vitality of Swedenborg's ideas becomes animated, as concepts like 'correspondence' and 'use' flicker from one field into another: from Wilkinson's homoeopathy into the pragmatism of William James and Charles Sanders Peirce, the social reform of Albert Brisbane into Ralph Waldo Trine's New Thought. All of these cases presented,

Haller argues, eloquent alternatives to the reigning rationalist materialism of the Enlightenment, even as each and every one of the persons in his sketches fully 'accepted science and admired evolution'.

As far-flung as some of the figures appear to be from one another, 'flipping' and collating these sketches reveals a dense ecology of (inter)relations. Henry James, Sr was intimately befriended with James John Garth Wilkinson, and their long transatlantic correspondence produced some of their best mutual thinking and writing. James, Sr further financed several of Wilkinson's endeavours and helped him to obtain a graduate certificate from the Hahnemann Homeopathic Medical College in Philadelphia. In Wilkinson's spacious (if rented) home near Hampstead Heath in London, a steady retinue of houseguests and friends passed through who also recur in the pages of this book: Brisbane, Emerson, Hugh Doherty, John Morell and Thomas Lake Harris. Later, Harris would establish himself in Sonoma County north of San Francisco as both a leader (perhaps cultish) of a new religious movement, and a savvy vintner—the 'Robert Mondavi of his day',[3] as he has been coyly called—at precisely the same time that Herman Vetterling to the south of San Francisco, in the mountains above Santa Cruz, was beginning to publish *The Buddhist Ray*, the very first Buddhist journal in the United States that was 'Devoted to Buddhism in General and to the Buddhism in Swedenborg in Particular', as each issue announced in its header. Among the early readers of *The Buddhist Ray* was almost certainly a young D T Suzuki in Japan, a lay student of the Zen master Shaku Soyen who had attended the 1893 World's Parliament of Religions in Chicago organized by Charles Bonney and other Swedenborgians; thanks to Soyen's connections, Suzuki would later live for a period of time with Paul Carus in LaSalle, Illinois. Carus's signally important work in the nascent field of comparative religions, in turn, catalyzed the syncretism of the emerging New Thought movement, and one of New Thought's leading exponents, Ralph Waldo Trine—named after none other than Ralph Waldo Emerson—glommed onto Swedenborg as 'one of the most remarkable and valuable men who ever lived in the world'.

With such dense interpenetrations of ideas, coteries and various shifting associations, it makes less sense to speak of a singular, lineal direction of influence when it comes to Swedenborg's ideas, and more of a rhizomatic (in the Deleuzian sense) horizontal outgrowth of different Swedenborgian hybridities.[4] One essential aspect of this network of Swedenborgian adaptations was—in spite of American culture functioning as a hub for its dispersal—the profoundly transcultural dimensions of its circuitry, the ways Hindu and Buddhist concepts 'migrated', in Haller's phrasing, along the courses of Swedenborgian thought between East and West. Long before D T Suzuki had proclaimed Swedenborg was a 'Buddha of the North', in a by now famous anecdote from the 1950s that Haller recounts very well, the French novelist Honoré de Balzac had already detected the post-Christian, interreligious radical nature of Swedenborgian spirituality. In the 1830s, precisely at the same time that Emerson was beginning to devour volume after volume of Swedenborg and to formulate his first publication *Nature* (1836), a text that would quickly become the manifesto for American Transcendentalism, Balzac claimed that Swedenborg was a 'Bouddha chrétien', who 'undoubtedly epitomises all the religions'.[5] His titular character in the novel *Louis Lambert* (1832) further explains: 'Swedenborg borrowed from Magianism, Brahmanism, Buddhism, and Christian mysticism all the truth and divine beauty that those four great religious books hold in common, and added to them a doctrine, a basis of reasoning, that may be termed mathematical'.[6] Even if Balzac's character here imaginatively distorts Swedenborg's sources, his novel presciently keys the later religious syncretism that would unfold across post Civil War America, and of which *Distant Voices* provides us with arresting glimpses.

The transnational vectors of these Swedenborgian readings and cross-references may, ultimately, aid in deterritorializing certain figures like Emerson out of a provincializing kind of nativism. 'Emerson . . . *is* American literature', the critic Richard Poirier had once stated,[7] somewhat bombastically, and more recent literary history has readily critiqued Emerson (and William James, and some of the other figures recounted in these sketches) for embodying and contributing to the aesthetic ideology of an American manifest destiny: a smug sense of self-assuredness at the given superiority and specialness of American culture, literature, laws and religion. Haller's *Distant Voices* unfolds wonderful cross-readings that belie this gross simplification, as we learn of Hindu writers such as Protap Chunder Mozoomdar and Swami Paramananda who were astonished to find that Emerson seemed 'more Hindu in his roots than Christian'.[8]

D T Suzuki, late in his life, also attested to his surprise upon first encountering the work of Emerson and Thoreau, and locating 'the awakening of an Oriental consciousness' within their Transcendentalist literary aesthetics.[9] From this perspective, the bridge that Swedenborg provided as a 'Buddha' between East and West leads not so much to the Orientalizing of American literature, as it does to new perspectives on Emerson, Trine, Harris and the others gathered in this volume, as 'threads in the fabric of world religions', as Wai Chee Dimock has put it, threads that cause 'American literature to burst out of the confines of the nation-state' into spaces of 'deep' time.[10] Emerson is as much an American author as he is yet another accretion of religious commentary on the *Bhagavadgita* that has been accumulating for well over two thousand years; the *Bhagavadgita* was, as Emerson appreciatively noted in his journal, in one of the first uses in English of this word, 'a trans-national classic'.[11]

Distant in time as these voices from the nineteenth and early twentieth centuries might be, the concerns which prompted their diverse explorations in Swedenborgian thought remain no less pressing for the twenty-first century; their words captured by Haller continue to reverberate very much with our present. The inequality of wealth and exploitive labour practices that galvanized the reform energy of Swedenborgian communitarian experiments in the 1840s seems, today, an intractable part of contemporary globalization. Just as Wilkinson giddily went to France to observe the 1848 revolution from behind the barricades with the people of Paris, and then wrote about the experience for Henry James, Sr's Fourierist newspaper, one wonders how Wilkinson, if he were alive today, would respond to Occupy Wall Street and other grass-roots forms of anti-globalization civil disobedience. In a so-called 'post-9/11' world that has been marked by, if anything, a 'return to religion', and the particular resurgence of violent fundamentalisms of all kinds, the critical interreligious dialogues undertaken by the World's Parliament of Religions in 1893, and by D T Suzuki and Thomas Merton later on in the 1950s, still hold valuable lessons about how we might listen and learn from religious others. As Haller notes, all the authors under discussion in this book were essentially reformists, possessing a 'social conscience' that made them stubbornly discontent with the status quo (be it social, medicinal or spiritual): they all respectively used Swedenborgian ideas as platforms for launching alternative prospects for what might be. To read them now, embedded as we are in their former future, is an unsettling encounter with the echo of an onus that asks us how we might answer the original clamour of their voices.

1   See, for example, Lars Bergquist, *Biblioteket i lusthuset: tio uppsatser om Swedenborg* (Stockholm: Nature och Kultur, 1996); Jonathan S Rose, 'Swedenborg's Garden of Theology', in *Emanuel Swedenborg: Essays for the New Century Edition on His Life, Work, and Impact*, ed. Jonathan S Rose, Stuart Shotwell and M L Bertucci (West Chester, PA: Swedenborg Foundation, 2005); Kristin King, *Gardens of Heaven and Earth* (London: Swedenborg Society, 2011).

2   Ralph Waldo Emerson, *Journals and Miscellaneous Notebooks of Ralph Waldo Emerson, Volume XIII: 1852-1855*, ed. Ralph H Orth and Alfred R Ferguson (Cambridge, MA: Harvard University Press, 1977), p. 335.

3   Debra A Klein, 'The Grape King from Shogunate Japan', in *The Daily Beast* (3 April 2014), at <http://www.thedailybeast.com/articles/2014/04/03/the-grape-king-from-shogun-japan.html>, accessed 1 June 2016.

4   Gilles Deleuze and Felix Guattari, *A Thousand Plateaus: Capitalism and Schizophrenia*, tr. Brian Massumi (Minneapolis: University of Minnesota Press, 1987), pp. 1-25.

5   Honoré de Balzac, 'Avant-Propos', in *Scènes de la vie privée* (Paris: Furne, 1842), vol. I, p. 24; and *Séraphita (and Louis Lambert & the Exiles)*, tr. Clara Bell (Sawtry, Cambs.: Dedalus, 1995), p. 237.

6   Balzac, *Séraphita (and Louis Lambert & the Exiles)*, p. 238.

7   Richard Poirier, *A World Elsewhere: The Place of Style in American Literature* (New York: Oxford University Press, 1966), p. 69.

8   See herein, p. 44.

9   D T Suzuki, *Zen and Japanese Culture* (New York: Bollingen, 1959), pp. 343-4.

10 Wai Chee Dimock, *Through Other Continents: American Literature Across Deep Time* (Princeton: Princeton University Press, 2006), p. 32.

11 Ralph Waldo Emerson, *Journals and Miscellaneous Notebooks of Ralph Waldo Emerson, Volume IX: 1843-1847*, ed. Ralph H Orth and Alfred R Ferguson (Cambridge, MA: Harvard University Press, 1971), p. 248.

INTRODUCTION

I n seeking to understand the Enlightenment which had its beginnings in late seventeenth-century Europe, historians have typically portrayed it in the context of a secular movement bringing together for the first time a coherent body of rational, liberal and classical ideas and attitudes. The truth arguably lies outside this paradigm in that many of its seekers of wisdom were also hoping to include elements of prophecy, millenarianism and mysticism in their fashioning of the social, economic and political landscape—a grab bag that included cabbalism, alchemy, Freemasonry, mesmerism and spiritualism. For this latter group, earthly paradise encompassed not only science's latest findings but spiritual and moral truths handed down through prophecies and ancient texts. Both spiritual and scientific wisdom were to accompany the regeneration of the individual and society, making for social and moral improvement, benevolence and greater service to humankind. Perhaps Yale historian Peter Gay explained it best by portraying the proponents of the Enlightenment as a 'family of intellectuals' whose interplay of ideas and strategies bumped noisily across the stage of history. United only in their love of freedom and criticism of authority, particularly Christianity, these intellectuals encountered the world from different angles and experiences. Emotional and quarrelsome, they ranged widely in their pursuit of modernity.[1]

One important contributor to this combined spiritual/material movement was

Emanuel Swedenborg who added measurably to both realms. The son of a pietistic Lutheran bishop and a mother whose family was connected to the nation's mining industry, Swedenborg immersed himself in mathematics and astronomy before casting his net into the fields of chemistry, geometry, metallurgy, anatomy, physiology and cosmology, which resulted in books and unpublished manuscripts of extraordinary significance both to his own age and the centuries that followed. Beginning in his mid-fifties, his life changed dramatically as he turned his attention from science and natural philosophy to a revelatory theology, a change evidenced by the publication of *The Worship and Love of God* (1745) in which he presented an allegorical retelling of biblical creation blending both science and visionary revelations.

Invigorated by this spiritual midlife crisis, Swedenborg assumed the mantra of theologian and mystic revelator whose writings encouraged many searchers to discover a more spiritualized setting for humanity's improvement. During the remainder of his life, his rationalist and scientific endeavours acquired a nuanced relationship with nature as he sought to plumb the essence of the human soul. In doing so, his opinions acquired a more mystical and revelatory meaning as he replaced or augmented his empirical research with teleological and ecstatic ideas gained through communications with the spiritual world.[2] In defending the introspective life of the Christian, Swedenborg was one of several eighteenth-century apologists of mystical theology, among whom were William Law, Thomas Hartley, John Fletcher, Francis Okely and Ezra Stiles. Each countered the Enlightenment's rationalism with mystic elements drawn from Anglican, Moravian, Methodist and Behmenist practices.[3]

The centrepiece of Swedenborg's world view was his denial of the Cartesian universe ruled by the mechanistic laws of physics where nothing existed that could not be confirmed by the senses. In Swedenborg's cosmology, everything in the material world had its corresponding cause in the spiritual world, linking the two in an inseparable bond. Drawn to the study of Neoplatonist, Hermetic and cabbalistic elements in Christian and Jewish traditions, he defined and elaborated on the doctrine of divine influx; the law of correspondences; the law of spiritual progression through series and degrees; the rejection of original sin; the evil of self-love or *proprium*; a universe organized around a triune realm of celestial, spiritual and natural existence; and human beings conceived as a triune of soul, mind and body. His law of correspondences served as a permanent fixture in nineteenth-century spirituality, providing a way of understanding and processing the new-found knowledge concerning the natural world without, at the same time, losing its spiritual meaning. The law became the century's principal tool for interpreting the wonders of the cosmos by seeing in nature, including the material body, a deeper meaning. Rooted in idealism, it recognized that empirical data provided an important pathway into spiritual insight. Although inert, nature offered a cornucopia of symbols that helped to fulfil a spiritual vision and raise human awareness to the work of the Creator and His purposes. Through the use of correspondences humankind was able to connect the natural world to the spiritual and celestial.

This new phase in Swedenborg's life was accompanied by visits to heaven and hell and conversations with spirit-beings, including Jesus and his disciples, concerning the true and underlining meaning of the Scriptures. One notable outcome of these other-worldly experiences was the prodigious production of some thirty volumes written in Latin—a corpus of theological work that included the multi-volume *Arcana Caelestia*, an exegesis of Genesis and Exodus; *Apocalypse Revealed*, an exegesis of Revelation; *Heaven and Hell*, a description of the afterlife; *Conjugial Love*, an explanation of marriage and love; and *The True Christian Religion*, a summary of beliefs that laid the basis for what later became the cornerstone of the New Church or Church of the New Jerusalem established by his devotees. For laymen and scientists alike, Swedenborg provided a cosmology that inspired a mystical understanding of creation. His was not a philosophy of orthodoxy but one that suggested a pattern in natural events greater than simply an expounding of cause and effect. Having concluded that human nature was always open to regeneration and still in the divine image, he viewed the progress of man as the realization of his divine nature over his material body. For Swedenborg, the will and the mind were free. Thus, through reason, spiritual regeneration, practical piety and hard work, he envisioned a world that found its angelic home as part of the *Maximus Homo* (a term largely unique to Swedenborg and variously translated into English as 'Universal Human', 'Grand Human and 'Grand Man' amongst others).

Because of the controversial nature of Swedenborg's esoteric beliefs and writings, his manuscripts were published anonymously in England and the Netherlands, countries whose approach to theological discourse was considerably more liberal than his native Sweden. After Swedenborg's death, the first New Church societies were founded in Manchester and London, and others followed, including some seventeen churches in the United States by the time of the first General Convention which met in Philadelphia in 1817. Although the number of churchmen was few, the influence of Swedenborg and of New Church members proved significant. According to religious historian Sydney Ahlstrom, the doctrines, laws and observations of Swedenborg and his followers filtered into all aspects of American life, including Transcendentalism, mesmerism, communitarianism, medicine, psychology, spiritualism, Theosophy, pragmatism and the movement popularly known as New Thought. Indeed, almost the entire metaphysical tradition in America came under the influence of Swedenborgianism in some form or another.[4]

Eventually, Swedenborg's conception of the universe, his contemplative insight, his imaginative foreshadowings and his warm-hearted picture of humankind found admirers in Oriental cultures who recognized concepts remarkably like their own— almost as if Swedenborg and the Gautama Buddha had spoken with a single voice. At roughly the same time that Swedenborgianism entered the lexicon of European and American intellectuals, New England's Transcendentalists were carrying the wisdom of the Orient into Boston's Back Bay neighbourhoods, gaining knowledge of the East from a small band of British, French and German travellers and civil servants who had laboured in their odd hours to translate Hindu and Buddhist writings. Thus Charles Wilkins's translation of *The Bhagvat-Geeta, or Dialogues of Kreeshna and Arjoon* (1785) and *Heetopades of Veeshnoo-Sarma* (1787); Sir William Jones's *Institutes of Hindi Law: or, the Ordinances of Menu* (1794), *Sacontala* (1789) and *Asiatick Researches* (1788-1839); Eugène Burnouf's *L'introduction à l'histoire du buddhisme indien* (1844); and Friedrich Schlegel's *Ueber die Sprache und Weisheit der Indier* (1808) all made an impression on New England's romantics. *The Dial* (1840-4), the principal publication of the Transcendentalists, included Thoreau's edited version of Sir William Jones's *The Laws of Menu* (1794), selections from Joshua Marshman's translation of the *Sayings of Confucius*, and an edited version of David Collie's translation of the *Chinese Four Books* (1828). Later, a second wave of interest occurred when William Henry Channing's son-in-law, Edwin Arnold, published *The Light of Asia* (1878) which was widely read and, as Channing explained to Bronson Alcott, served 'as mediator between Europe and Asia, to unite the East and West, the Ancient and Modern Ages, in unity'.[5]

After blossoming in the Romantic movement, both Hindu and Buddhist thought coursed a path to the St Louis Hegelians, the speculations of Helena Blavatsky's Theosophy, the World's Parliament of Religions and the subsequent publications of Paul Carus and his Open Court Publishing Company. It also emerged in the establishment of Oriental studies as an academic discipline in European and American universities, and surfaced again in the 1950s and 1960s as an expression of American society's counterculture, best represented in Alan Watts's *The Way of Zen* and Jack Kerouac's *The Dharma Bums*. Through these decades Orientalism became the object of intense examination as translations and interpretations of its literature served as a bridge between the East and West, sending images and meanings in both directions. Among the appealing elements of this wisdom was an elasticity of language which contrasted sharply from the stark literalism of Protestant tautology. In the East, doctrinal issues were much less consequential, avoiding the knotted tangles of Western sophistry. Open to many levels of apprehension and experience, Eastern philosophies offered an organically integrated mental and physical view of life's experiences. This was especially evident in the existential nature of Buddhism which sought a unitive awareness of the inner and outer man.[6]

Organized around nine chapters involving the life and times of several intellectuals, their friends and their colleagues, these sketches set out to explain how Swedenborg offered explanations for questions and issues long troubling them and their grounds for optimism as they looked to the future. The sketches also account for the migration of Hindu and Buddhist concepts into Swedenborgian thought, including their combined influence on Transcendentalism, medicine, communitarianism, New Thought and pragmatism; their critique of utilitarian ethics; their perspective in the areas of philosophy, epistemology, psychology and metaphysics; and the attention they gave to the discussion of values.

In these sketches of the individuals, friends and colleagues over the period of a century or more, their influence in three important ways will be examined: first, what they drew from their predecessors; second, their relation to contemporaries; and third, their legacy. Swedenborg influenced their ideas and, in some instances, that influence incorporated Oriental beliefs as well. Like pebbles dropped in water, their ideas rippled across oceans connecting peoples of diverse cultures, careers and interests. Despite the geographical distance between them and their intellectual points of origination, when offered the opportunity, they came together in surprisingly compatible ways. All were conscious of the great world movements of thought in which they played their parts, often side by side. While Swedenborg's writings made the first and most decisive exhibition of their potential in local pulpits (where they broke new ground by offering fresh simplicity to the ongoing war between intellect and affection), Hinduism and Buddhism captivated the imagination of cosmopolitan culture, filling peoples' needs with a taste of (if not a passport into) a world of new literature. Self-appointed in its social compassion to guide and humanize the world, this literature inspired the mind and character, captivating some of the nation's most distinguished intellectuals with a sense of the world that seldom if ever devolved into self-righteousness.

Chapter 1 ('Divine-Natural Humanity') examines one of the nation's premier intellectuals, Henry James, Sr, and the manner in which he and his coterie of friends, including Ralph Waldo Emerson, found Swedenborg's writings amenable to their intellectual needs. No one surpassed Swedenborg as the period's representative mystic. Both James and Emerson lived through a tumultuous period in America's history, sharing a mutual suspicion of tradition and authority. While they insisted that individuals belonged to something greater than themselves, neither could accept the fact that this greater thing could be found in the existing institutions of church and state. Though they were more similar than not in their goals for the individual and society, and while both were schooled in religion, James felt more at home in his Swedenborgian theology while Emerson, having vacated his pulpit at Boston's Second Church, roamed far and wide in his search for the mind's eye. For Emerson, the genius of Swedenborg had been wasted unnecessarily by his attachment to Christian symbols rather than a focus on the moral sentiment which encompassed 'innumerable Christianities, humanities, divinities, in its bosom'.[7] By contrast, James's vocabulary revealed an uncompromising logic of an equally undisguised theology. As a result, James seldom breached the boundaries set by Swedenborg while Emerson showed little restraint in his intellectual travels, many of which drew from Oriental philosophy and religion.

Chapter 2 ('Passional Attraction') recounts the life and times of Charles Fourier and the movement of phalansterian associations he inspired which found eager disciples in both Europe and the New World. Transformed into a compatible format for American audiences by Albert Brisbane, the movement entered into the lives of the Brook Farm experimenters near Boston, forming a mixture of Unitarianism, Transcendentalism, associationism and Swedenborgianism. At this moment in its history, Brook Farm sat at the crossroads of several religious groups—Congregationalists, Presbyterians, Episcopalians, Methodists, Baptists, Catholics, Unitarians and Transcendentalists—whose trappings cast a long shadow over the receding Calvinist consciousness and the community's aspirations to realize some form of Christian socialism. It was not surprising, therefore, that spirituality in some form or another would ultimately draw upon the emotions of the community's members. Inspirational lectures went only so far before there was a yearning for a more religious and emotional 'fix' to their newly chosen lifestyle. Having transformed the community to associationism, its believers wanted more from their new ideology than either Brisbane or Fourier was able to give. Out of this, a new consensus emerged among Brook Farm's members that wrapped Fourier's socialism in the warmth of a Swedenborgian mantle, evoking imagery of celestial planes intended to satisfy the communitarians' religious, aesthetic and emotional needs.

Chapter 3 ('Heavenly Fays') provides an intellectual portrait of Thomas Lake Harris whose revelatory visions drew disciples from Great Britain, the Continent, Japan and the United States, many of whom lived out their lives in Brotherhood communities organized in the Midwest and on the West coast. In both settings, Swedenborgianism provided the subtext for their spiritual, social and economic structure, while those Brotherhood members who were drawn to Theosophy and the revelations of Helena Blavatsky's Mahatmas served as a bridge between Harris's Swedenborgian beliefs and his application of Hindu ideas and concepts.

Chapter 4 ('Christian Homoeopathy') recounts the lives of James John Garth Wilkinson and James Tyler Kent, Swedenborgians and physicians who applied

Swedenborgianism to their method of therapeutics. While conventional American and European doctors chose to accept germ theory and moved assertively to incorporate more modern diagnostic procedures, as well as biochemistry, serology, endocrinology, vaccination and pharmacological agents, homoeopaths practised a metaphysical form of healing that repudiated reductionist science, choosing instead high-potency medicines based on principles as unchanging as Newton's law of gravitation. They envisioned health as a state of the body sustained through interaction between the material and spiritual dimensions of life. Forged from an alliance of physical heal- ing and Swedenborg's spiritual planes, homoeopathy emerged as a 'belief' system distinct from biomedical science with its reliance on the double-blind randomized clinical trial.

Chapter 5 ('The World in Miniature') examines the World's Parliament of Religions which met in Chicago concurrently with the Columbian Exposition in 1893. The brain- child of Charles C Bonney, a Chicago attorney and Swedenborgian, the Parliament invited eminent representatives of the world's major religions to share their beliefs— and the reasons for them—'with the greatest frankness, without, however, employing unfriendly criticisms of other Faiths'.[8] While the Parliament presented a public face of respectful and peaceable assembly, strong and unmistakable undercurrents of suspicion and acrimony coursed among the delegates. According to historian Richard Hughes Seager, the Parliament was 'a liberal, western, and American quest for world religious unity that failed [because] the god of the organizers . . . turned out not to be quite the same as the gods of the Asians'.[9] By contrast, for the many New Churchmen attend- ing the Parliament who volunteered their time and labour to support the delegates' needs, the outcome was an unmatched success as they saw a growing inner spiritual world arising among humanity and moving toward final perfection. For them, the great religions of the Orient were not objects of derision but sources of wisdom, if not the true birthplace of Christianity.

Chapter 6 ('Bridge-Builders') suggests that the World's Parliament of Religions served two very distinct and opposing purposes—one in which mainstream American Protestants celebrated the predominant role of the Judaeo-Christian tradition on the world scene, and the other, which encouraged a broader discourse between and among scholars of Eastern and Western religious traditions. It was this latter purpose that captured the energies of the German-American editor, author and philosopher Paul Carus and the Swedenborgian pastor and convert to Buddhism Herman Carl Vetterling. For Carus, the challenge was to bring a scholarly yet popular vision of Eastern religions and philosophies into the mindset of Eurocentric thinking. To accomplish this end, he encouraged a 'Religion of Science' that would connect the two cultures, shying away from the more esoteric and occult aspects of Swedenborgianism and Theosophy. By contrast, Vetterling's bridge consisted of both Swedenborgian and Theosophical components which together postulated the perfectibility of humanity, removed the idea of innate unregenerate wickedness in individuals, and offered a purpose for life consonant with the longings of the soul and its real nature. Man was a conscious spirit, the flower of evolution which, one day, would grow higher still.

Chapter 7 ('Making the Modern Self') addresses the Swedenborgian underpinnings in the writings of Ralph Waldo Trine, whose views were not only a reflection of the metaphysical movement known as New Thought which emerged in the 1880s and remains to this day a conspicuous force in American thought and culture, but also addressed problems and solutions that were integral to so-called Progressivism in American politics. Drawing from a combination of liberal Christianity, Transcendentalism, spiritualism, Theosophy and Swedenborgianism, Trine unfolded a practical creed that resonated through American culture, creating a Christian ethos that included westernized Asian concepts of mind energy.

Chapter 8 ('The Wood Chopper') investigates the intellectual world of Daisetsu Teitaro Suzuki of Japan and the close relationship he built between Zen Buddhism, Swedenborgianism and American thought. His influence covers a lengthy period from the time of the World's Parliament of Religions to the early years of postmodernism. Particular focus is given to Suzuki's time in Illinois where he worked for Paul Carus and the Open Court Publishing Company; his translations of Swedenborg's writings into Japanese; his years of seclusion during the Second World War; and his subsequent return to the United States where he lectured at Columbia University. The chapter concludes with an analysis of Zen and its relationship to American pragmatism, and an exchange between Suzuki and Trappist monk Thomas Merton on the subject of mysticism.

Chapter 9 ('Retrospective') brings the events in the sketches full circle, suggesting that the intellectual problems and challenges highlighted in this study led away from pathways of rationalist and empirical logic towards personal spiritual journeys that involved the confluence of both Occidental and Oriental modes of thought. They were journeys marked by an openness to change, including mystical encounters; the questioning of biblical inerrancy and drearily conventional worship empty of final meaning; and the erudite examination of unmediated awareness and ecstatic experiences that had for too long been pushed to the margins by contemporary culture. For those examined in this study, the transformative insight of Swedenborg on the subject of 'uses', self and the *Maximus Homo* fostered a lively encounter between East and West suggesting that much that was thought to be regional or national was actually transcultural in its extent.

The opportunity to become one with God (i.e., to contemplate the Infinite) brought energy and a sense of godlike exaltation to the individuals highlighted in this book. The experience brought a sense of antinomian sufficiency against all bonds, whether philosophical, political, economic or personal. Notwithstanding their many differences, all were genuinely troubled by the construction of a modern world view based solely on reason, science and material progress. At the same time, however, they deliberately chose to distance themselves from the rapturous paths taken by Christianity's acclaimed mystics and ascetics. Instead, they drew their strength from Swedenborg's revelatory visions which had a matter-of-factness about them that astonished believers and non-believers alike. From Henry James, Sr with his very personalized view of morality, to Zen Buddhist Daisetsu Teitaro Suzuki who called Swedenborg the 'Buddha of the North', to those who coupled the Swedenborgian doctrine of uses to communitarianism and the pragmatism of John Dewey, there is little question as to the impact of Swedenborg and his writings. In many ways, these sketches are representative of a world view that began with an admiration of Swedenborg and ended with the principle of humanity's capacity for limitless improvement.

DISTANT VOICES:
SKETCHES OF A SWEDENBORGIAN WORLD VIEW

HENRY JAMES, SR AND RALPH WALDO EMERSON
Divine-Natural Humanity

> *Man during his earthly life induces a form in the purest substances of his interiors, so that he may be said to form his own soul, or give it quality; and according to the form or quality of soul he thus gives himself will be his subsequent receptivity to the Lord's inflowing life: which is a life of love to the whole human race.*
>
> (Henry James, Sr, *Society: The Redeemed Form of Man*, 1879)

By the mid-nineteenth century, there existed in Western philosophy two competing world views. One gave its assent to a purposive and aesthetic interpretation of nature which gravitated to either idealism or an eclectic spiritualism, while its rival, inspired by recent discoveries in the physical sciences, inclined to either materialism or positivism. On one side were the positivistic systems of Auguste Comte's *Système de politique positive*, John Stuart Mill's *Principles of Political Economy*, Henry Thomas Buckle's *History of Civilization in England*, Herbert Spencer's formulation of his *First Principles* and Charles Darwin's *Origin of Species*. On the other could be found the romantic and intuitive literature of Samuel Taylor Coleridge's *Aids to Reflection* and Thomas Carlyle's *French Revolution*; the theism of Joseph Le Conte's *Evolution, Its Evidences and Its Relation to Religious Thought*; the theological thinking of Henry James, Sr's *Substance and Shadow: or Morality and Religion in Their Relation to Life*; and Ralph Waldo Emerson's post-Kantian *The Conduct of Life*. Although both world views were affected by theories of evolution, they nonetheless offered divergent views of the cosmos conceived by either the operation of blind forces or by laws impressed on matter by a benevolent Creator. Those aligned with the physical sciences believed that the sense perceptions were sufficient to fulfil the requirements of knowledge while the more intuitive drew their inspiration from the ideality of nature, with the mind imminent in nature. Despite their differences, both sides looked to the study of society as a way to realize their aspirations. Each in its own way, offered itself as a 'solvent' for a particular brand of materialistic, positivistic, or spiritualistic naturalism.

For Henry James, Sr, described by American literary critic and historian Van Wyck Brooks as the 'wandering New Yorker',[1] and Ralph Waldo Emerson, known lovingly as 'the Concord Sage', intuition took precedence over logic. Although science was not a force to be disputed, they nonetheless viewed it as one of the spirit's more expressive activities. The mind, more spiritual than substantive, was governed by forces that extended beyond mechanical laws. Thus, while the mind acknowledged an external natural order, this order shared a spiritual reality as well. God being the soul of the world, the soul of man was enveloped within the soul of God—an organic but also a spiritual unity of purpose. God, the ultimate substance of things, was accessed intuitively rather than by reason, and by the acknowledgment of beauty and goodness rather than by being known simply through sense perception. Intuition was the ultimate synthesis of the physical and mental worlds, the point of reconciliation for whatever spiritual reality resulted from the acts of reason and will. Intuition gave meaning to human enterprise.

Henry James, Sr (1811-82)

Reading the works of American theologian Henry James, Sr is almost as difficult as glimpsing the shadow of a branch in a windstorm. Born in Albany, New York, the son of wealthy Irish immigrants, James lived in an age marked by increasing religious diversity. Not burdened by having to work for a living, he gave himself wholly to the task of replacing what remained of Christianity's archaic dogmas with a new intellectually hardened and intensely positive conception of God and His relation to the human race. He spent much of his adult life in a spiritual quest to discover the meaning of self, God and eternity. Issues of free will, the splendour of God and Creation, self-righteousness, the act of salvation and the concept of Divine-Natural Humanity were obsessions that consumed him. In his hunger for holiness he became a perfectionist with millennial expectations, impelled by a vision of an ideal state for humankind. His theology was highly individualistic, formed from the meanderings

2

of a mind that never closed itself to older systems of belief as he forged new pathways of self-inquiry. James was a complex individual whose spiritual needs and beliefs in the moral equality of man and the fellowship of community outweighed all other demands on his life. The centrepiece of his thinking was his intense conception of God as Creator, which he announced as an a priori statement of fact. Since God simply *is*, the question then became, 'Who and what are *we?*' Given the loving nature of the Creator, James concluded that there was no other possibility than for the Creator to bring the human race into some ultimate harmony with Himself.[2]

Theological Schooling

In 1835, after enrolling at Union College in Schenectady, New York, which his father helped to establish and where he was a rebellious and inattentive student, an older and wiser James entered Princeton Theological Seminary to pursue a career in the ministry, relishing the opportunity for meditation and self-examination, and for constructing a moral code more to his own liking. A nonconformist on a spiritual path fast approaching unorthodox extremes, he was an original and vigorous thinker troubled by the disposition of fellow classmates who were all too anxious, in their zeal for personal holiness, to separate themselves from mankind and, at the same time, separate mankind from God. Two years into his studies, he left without graduating to travel through England and Ireland ostensibly to visit relatives but also to better understand the radical currents of Scotch-Irish Presbyterianism. In his travels, James came across the writings of the Scottish linen manufacturer turned preacher, Robert Sandeman, a primitivist and nonconformist who had set forth on a path democratic in organization, antinomian in spirit and indifferent to ritualism and ecclesiasticism. Breaking from his roots in Presbyterianism, Sandeman had organized independent congregations of 'Christians' in Scotland, England and New England whose beliefs centred on human depravity, divine providence and the sufficiency of Christ's atonement. For Sandeman and his followers, there was no need for a trained clergy since true Christendom stood apart from the contrived role of the professionally trained minister. These views resonated with James, whose quest for spiritual authenticity led him to reject organized religion and its representative clergy. Thus, the contours of

James's religiosity were tempered not only by the Presbyterianism of his forefathers but by his admiration for the works of Sandeman. Throughout his life, James remained a respectful admirer of the Sandemanian tradition, replacing the Calvinist cycle of sin and justification by faith with rich autobiographical excursions into the evils of selfhood (*proprium*) and of humanity's ultimate dignity through a commonly shared divine nature. As a way of honouring Sandeman's beliefs, James reprinted an edition of his *Letters on Theron and Aspasio*, first published in 1757.[3]

On his return to America, and before his marriage to Mary Robertson Walsh in 1840 (in a civil ceremony), James spent time in New York City and Albany, travelled to Washington, DC, and became an admirer of the Irish Calvinist John Walker whose followers, known as 'Walkerites', practised an uncompromising orthodoxy that looked remarkably similar to that of puritan theologian Jonathan Edwards. James was attracted to Walker's *Essays and Correspondence*, published posthumously in 1838, and Edwards's *Essay on the Nature of True Virtue* for their notions of disinterested benevolence, the sufficiency of God's grace and man's passivity in the act of salvation. From both these men, James discovered salvation by faith alone and not by individualized human endeavour or self-righteousness.[4]

Swedenborgianism

During the period of James's search for spiritual authenticity, others of his generation were being introduced to the mystical and revelatory world view of Emanuel Swedenborg whose writings, although principally in Latin, were now being translated into the English language. One of the early New England disciples of Swedenborg was Sampson Reed who, along with Harvard professor Theophilus Parsons and the Revd Thomas Worcester, is credited with introducing Swedenborg to New England's restless and awakening souls. Reed's *Observations on the Growth of the Mind* and the periodical *New Jerusalem Magazine* which he helped establish and edit, were all evidence of Swedenborg's influence upon the age and the emerging spirit of benevolence. Reed's 'Oration on Genius', delivered at Harvard as part of his master's degree in 1821, served as an indictment of formalism in religion and as a paean to Nature's creative force. So great was his interest in and fascination with

Swedenborg that his newly found views disqualified him for a Unitarian pulpit. Undaunted, he became a wealthy pharmacist who devoted his life to advocating on behalf of Swedenborgianism.[5]

James's own journey out of the stark and forbidding landscape of Calvinism came not from the efforts of Reed, Parsons, or Worcester, but from entirely different circumstances which took place in the spring of 1844 when he and his family were living near Windsor, England. Drawn to an introspective study of the Scriptures, he concluded from his endeavours that the inspired phrasing in the book of Genesis was best understood mystically and symbolically rather than through the different translations handed down by the Christian churches. As a consequence of this conviction, he experienced an explosive and highly charged spiritual crisis filled with doubt about himself and of humanity in general—a condition of spiritual desolation sometimes referred to as the 'dark night of the soul'.

> To all appearance it was a perfectly insane and abject terror, without ostensible cause, and only to be accounted for, to my perplexed imagination, by some damned shape squatting invisible to me within the precincts of the room, and raying out from his fetid personality influences fatal to life. The thing had not lasted ten seconds before I felt myself a wreck, that is, reduced from a state of firm, vigorous, joyful manhood to one of almost helpless infancy. The only self-control I was capable of exerting was to keep my seat. I felt the greatest desire to run incontinently to the foot of the stairs and shout for help to my wife,—to run to the roadside even, and appeal to the public to protect me; but by an immense effort I controlled these frenzied impulses, and determined not to budge from my chair till I had recovered my self-possession. This purpose I held to for a good long hour, as I reckoned time, beat upon meanwhile by an ever-growing tempest of doubt, anxiety, and despair, with absolutely no relief from any truth I had ever encountered save a most pale and distant glimmer of the Divine existence,—when I resolved to abandon the vain struggle, and communicate without more ado what seemed by sudden burden of inmost, implacable unrest to my wife.[6]

James's condition remained intermittent for more than two years, during which time physicians diagnosed him as suffering from an 'overworked brain' and recommended water-cure and open-air treatments. Heeding this advice, he travelled to Cheltenham, one of the more popular water-cure establishments frequented by England's wealthier families, where he met Sophia Chichester, an unconventional and spiritually minded woman who ventured to diagnose his problem as *vastation*, a sense of despondency identified in the writings of Swedenborg. Unfamiliar with the terminology, James proceeded to read several volumes of Swedenborg's works. As he did, he learned that Swedenborg had used the word to characterize an early stage in the regenerative process of spiritual growth, a condition that gave him a sense of relief.[7] After reading Swedenborg's *Divine Love and Wisdom* and *Divine Providence*, he felt himself immersed in the healing waters of an 'undiscovered sea' that restored his senses and reinvigorated his interest in religion, science and philosophy. 'With what relish my heart opened to the doctrine I found in these most remarkable books', recounted James. 'With what instant alacrity my intellect shook its canvas free to catch every breeze of that virgin unexplored sea of being, to which this doctrine, for the first time, furnished me the clue'.[8]

Braced with these newly discovered feelings, James became an unabashed admirer of Swedenborg who, like himself, had rejected the 'superficial judgments' and prejudices of ecclesiastical Christianity. Swedenborg provided a spiritual depth of explanation about the world that James failed to see from anyone else. Reading him, James learned that Swedenborg made no personal distinctions among individuals, denying 'the pretension of any creature of God to be spiritually any better . . . than any other creature, however comparatively degraded the latter may be in all moral or personal regards'. Petrified by his own former state of self-righteousness, James now questioned the possibility of moral righteousness of the individual before God.[9]

James discovered in Swedenborg a person of insatiable curiosity whose mind was attracted to processes that were both mechanical and spiritual. After reading *Arcana Caelestia*, the first of the Swede's major theological works, he reaffirmed his earlier belief that Genesis was a form of literature not to be taken literally but interpreted through varying degrees of cosmic subtlety. He took delight in the fact that someone of Swedenborg's intelligence would seek through induction (i.e., studying the intricacies of the human organism and its functions and relations to the various parts of the body) to understand the soul. From an interest in the fluids of the body to a general interest with the body's separate organs, Swedenborg had raised humanity from its physiological origins to philosophical and theological eminence.

With news in 1848 of the psychic wall 'rappings' which reportedly occurred at the home of the Fox family in Hydesville, New York, followed by a series of demonstrations conducted by sisters Catherine, Margaret and older sister Ann Leah Fish, communications with the dead became a common attraction in New York and later in New England and the Midwest, the United Kingdom and on the Continent. Before long, mystics and clairvoyants were spreading their mediumship abilities to enthusiastic audiences on both sides of the Atlantic. Notable figures such as Phineas P Quimby, Daniel Dunglas Home, Henry Slade and Joseph Rodes Buchanan became overnight sensations well known for their healing, slate-writing, table-rapping, mesmerizing, levitation and occult abilities.[10]

James rejected any hope that spiritual illumination might arise from such bizarre encounters. The extravagant hyperbole and public exhibitions that accompanied these earthy, sensual and devilish aspects of spiritism were of no consequence to him. The rappings of unseen spirits brought only uninvited publicity and Gnostic intrigue into his inspired world view. Swedenborg—not rappings—was his touchstone for understanding the spiritual path that led out of the natural and into a spiritual world. And it was Swedenborg's law of correspondences that provided the bridge connecting the material body to its higher and more spiritual purpose. In accepting Swedenborg's law, James found the link between empirical facts and spiritual insight, between the cause and effect activities of the material world and the purposes of divine creation.

James concluded that the intelligence garnered by the Fox sisters and their 'trans-sepulchral friends and cronies' was not especially helpful. He saw little benefit coming from their supposed communications, believing they would prove injurious in the end. 'I have never yet heard of any one's wits being improved by intercourse with departed spirits', he observed. Their 'busy-body' gossip of the other world reminded him of 'so many vermin revealing themselves in the tumble-down walls of our old theological hostelry'. Any attentive reader of Swedenborg would know that ghosts were roguish and full of 'spiritual deviltry'. Unless their communications resulted in a cure for smallpox, scarlet fever, gout, or even a toothache, it was best to reply: 'Be off—tramp—keep moving!'[11]

Immortal Life

In the mid-1860s, some twenty years after leaving Princeton Theological Seminary, James wrote *Immortal Life: Illustrated in a Brief Autobiographic Sketch of the Late Stephen Dewhurst*, an incomplete and fragmentary manuscript posthumously published in *The Literary Remains of the Late Henry James* by his son William. Intended as an autobiography, it consisted of a series of letters written to James from a fictional character, a former classmate at Princeton named Stephen Dewhurst. It has been suggested that James's preference for choosing a pseudonym was probably due to his abhorrence of human pride.[12]

As explained in the manuscript, Dewhurst (James's alter ego) had no anxiety about his own destiny for he was convinced that divine love was infinite, embracing all humanity and not restricted to the blessing of a particular people. In addition, he viewed himself as fundamentally different from others in his condemnation of religious zealots and the hypocrisy of those in religious vocations. These feelings led Dewhurst to question the moral righteousness of theology and the disparity it created between finite man and the Creator. In time, Dewhurst divested himself of his 'crude traditional faith' for one more spiritual. As the letters suggest, both Dewhurst and James came to entertain 'fatal doubts' concerning the purposes of the ecclesiastical church—both its ministry and its sacraments—to the point where both young men withdrew from the seminary. After returning to their respective homes in Maryland and New York, they continued to communicate by letter before marrying and drifting apart. Dewhurst took up government service in Washington, DC and, after suffering the loss of his wife and only son, threw himself into the writing of a manuscript that chronicled his most inward beliefs and which, when he contracted a deadly fever, became his dying legacy.[13]

Dewhurst made reference to his grandmother, a deeply religious individual who questioned whether the dogmatic logic of Calvin and other church fathers was a true reflection of divine truth. This trial of faith gave her little rest until, at the time of her death, she showed 'smiling confidence' in the resolution of her doubts. Dewhurst also wrote of his grandfather who had fought in the Revolutionary War, the generosity of his parents toward the needy poor, and his mother's protracted illness. As Dewhurst explained, his mother was a democratic woman who 'felt a tacit quarrel with the fortunes of her life in that they had sought to make her a flower or a shrub, when she herself would so willingly have remained mere lowly grass'. He described his father's prosperous career as a successful merchant, his ever-present emphasis on family prayers, and his incessant questioning of their studies at mealtime. Dewhurst also referred to a gun accident that had confined him to home for a length of time, an incident that provided James with a disguised method for introducing his own youthful accident when, at age thirteen, he severely burned his right leg in a turpentine fire and was forced to endure two painful amputations above the knee. [14]

Dewhurst also referenced his family's hospitality towards the clergy, noting there was nothing in his memory suggesting that such eminently respectable individuals, who exuded a self-proclaimed virtue and piety, were treated other than kindly when they visited the household. Having been instructed, however, by these moralizing ecclesiastics 'not to play, not to dance nor to sing, not to read story-books . . . nor, in short, to do anything which nature specially craved', he felt singularly pained by the loss of his youthful freedoms. As a consequence, he learned to arrive early at church to secure a certain corner pew where his view through the window could capture each passing pedestrian, including a certain shapely housemaid who regularly appeared on the steps of a house across the street where she would linger. Dewhurst often ruminated on the contrast between the maid's 'fresh, breezy, natural life' and his own 'lifeless, stagnant, [and] most unnatural Sunday mornings'. [15]

As he grew into manhood, Dewhurst came to rethink his feelings of the 'Divine wrath which he had incurred as the inheritor of a fallen nature' and the weight of human limitation, lifted only by the atoning blood of Christ. Such was the unquestioning tradition into which he had been born and for which he had suppressed much of his youthful enjoyments. 'I was habitually led by my teachers', he recalled, 'to conceive that at best a chronic apathy existed on God's part towards me'. Reduced to a feeling of self-abasement and indebtedness, he found himself unable to accept the quid pro quo form of clemency offered by church doctrine. Having taken on a 'free, inward, and spiritual evolution', he decided to acknowledge no ritual bonds. Instead, he imagined a 'universal family' and a spiritually divine end to which humanity was consecrated. In doing so, Dewhurst rejected the authoritatively interpreted Sunday-school theology that had been 'burnt into [him] as a red-hot iron' in place of a loving God. Along with this change, he came to view church doctrine as binding humankind to God by force and exercising its laws in a purely partisan manner. In its place, he saw human life as divine. [16]

Dewhurst regarded his hostility to the theology of his youth as due to the mental suffering it forced on his instinct for man's divine perfection. Every sermon he heard preached an 'inward remoteness from God' and an 'utter disproportion between Him and me'. In essence, he found no assurance of God's personal love. Recognizing that he had been seeking personal righteousness rather than the interests of humanity, he was left estranged and insensible to God's essential love of all humankind. Eventually, he saw the utter worthlessness of the ecclesiastical gospels which had turned God into a 'petty earthly despot' and came to understand that the moral experiences of the individual were incidental to the evolution of human destiny. 'An imperfect creature cannot come from a perfect creator', he reasoned, since 'the inference would be that the creative perfection had been to that extent inoperative, which would be tantamount to saying that the creature was not the work of a perfect creator'. He concluded from this that whenever one considered man's imperfect existence, there was a failure to discern the true creation of God. Since the word 'God' symbolized perfection, His perfection was incomplete unless it included the welfare of each and all creatures. In order for man to be perfect as God is perfect, it was necessary for man 'to find his life within himself, and not without. This is the life of God in man'. The divine end of creation, James discovered, was perfect unity of God with His creation. [17]

Using the imaginary Dewhurst as his foil, James arrived at several convictions that remained salient throughout his life: the priority of revelation over reason; Christ's redemptive purpose; and God's sovereignty. That Dewhurst represented James's most private thoughts helps to explain his alienation from the Calvinist God; his yearning to reconcile the problem of evil with his desire to share in God's goodness; his inordinate need to distinguish between the individual and the *Maximus Homo*; and the compelling effort to look beyond traditional morality to greater spiritual fulfilment. A twice-born Christian, Dewhurst (James) rejected stark Calvinism, pursuing instead a silent inward voice that brought him from spiritual angst to the sublime awareness of God's presence in his soul.[18]

The Ecclesiastical Church

A staunch anti-Catholic, James held dear those deep-seated beliefs within Protestantism that condemned the extravagancies of the papacy, the fanaticism of the Inquisition, and the obtuseness of the church in its ecclesiastical and sacerdotal ways. James considered the Roman church 'providentially doomed' by being 'hopelessly besotted' with its own selfish interests. Catholicism allowed the laity no nearness to God except through the intercession of its priests who, like kings, were 'swaddled' in their 'effete offices' and conducted themselves with shocking indifference to human equality and fellowship.[19] The ecclesiastical church was the 'devil's subtlest device' for keeping the soul in bondage. It was a 'masterpiece for ensnaring silly, selfish men' using ritualism and revivalism to control their appetites and passions.[20] Ecclesiasticism was an 'imposition' on Christianity that contrived to perpetrate sectarian divisiveness which weighed 'like a night-mare upon the soul of man, treading its sweetest blossoms in the dust, and turning its most poetic impulses into a reproach'. Ecclesiasticism was counter to the letter of Scripture and with the spirit of Christ himself in that it was conditioned upon a conflict between nature and society, between finite self-love and the Divine Humanity.[21] In essence, ecclesiastical Christianity was an insidious instrument used by clerics to emasculate and stultify the true intent of the Scriptures. Everywhere ecclesiasticism was employed it darkened the face of history. Under its influence, the Scriptures were emptied of their spiritual significance and replaced with the predicament of humanity's morally evil nature. Ecclesiastical Christianity separated humanity from God, leaving Christian theology and philosophy poorly equipped to solve the problems attendant on the nature and origin of evil. By offering shelter to traditions that demonstrated the 'intrinsic viciousness' of humankind, it provided a 'spiritual water-brush' to the question of evil.[22]

Reflecting the opinion of Swedenborg, James criticized the ecclesiastical churches as 'rigidly detergent' institutions whose self-proclaimed purpose was as a 'divine assessor in the earth, appointed to take stock of the existing inequalities in human character in order to build up an eternal heaven out of one kind of men, and an eternal hell out of another kind'. These churches conceptualized and dealt with God's creatures in a finite manner, regarding some as superfluously good, and others as naturally evil. In their grossest perversions, they functioned to exalt humanity spiritually only by humbling it naturally. Intending to rid the world of false gods, the churches had become mired in the literal or ritual side of self-hood at the expense of God's presence in every human life, or the Divine-Natural Humanity.[23] Trivialities such as public worship, sects, dogmas and priests had no place in James's world view. Nor was there any place in true Christendom for the pursuit of 'endless and desolating wars'. The historical church of Christ, he complained, 'resembled a huge Pandemonium, in which every giant lust stalked abroad uncontrolled [and where] every internal bond between it and heaven seemed snapped asunder'. Out of all this, the whole of Christendom had become 'one mass of festering corruption'. Having failed to perform their 'mediatorial function', the churches stood as formidable obstacles to human progress and 'accursed both of God and man'. For these reasons, James explained, Swedenborg had announced the end of the first Christian church and its sectarian struggles for power to which all nations had been party.[24]

Given Swedenborg's dismal picture of Christendom and his own confirmation from history, James had little doubt that humanity stood ready to be done with its nucleated churches and their myriads of priests and ministers. 'The people of this land earnestly seeking to secure the freest development of their human faculties, and the highest possible enjoyment of life, did not feel the established institutions of Christendom to be necessary to that end, and they made no provision for them in their polity', he wrote. This was a fact drawn from the country's history. 'As a nation we reject the name and the institutions of Christendom . . . we are out of

Christendom'. The Christian church as an outward entity had come to an end as it no longer connected humanity with heaven.[25]

James included Unitarianism in his criticism, believing that it lacked the warmth of a true religion of the heart. Besides, it engendered a level of pride that diverted the individual into a false sense of dignity and self-righteousness. Indifferent to the link between God as a distant creator and the loving God of creation, Unitarianism had made little effort to find the purely spiritual God within. James referred to Unitarianism as 'feeble sentimentality'. In their claim of 'strictly personal and individual worth in God's sight', Unitarians had chosen to deliberately differentiate one individual from another. This was precisely the attitude that caused James to show his greatest reproach. He had no quarrel with the spirit of Unitarianism but its literal and ritualistic character contained only the 'baleful exhalations' of the Divine. While not as culpable as other Christian denominations and sects, it nevertheless remained a foil for his animosity toward organized religion.[26]

James's disdain of Christendom also included the New Church (Church of the New Jerusalem) of the Swedenborgians, viewing its proponents as 'puppets of a remorseless spiritual jugglery'. Theirs, too, was a 'scaffolding' of ecclesiastical and political intentions designed to hide humanity's gaze from the 'majestic human house God has been silently building up from the beginning'.[27] In his *Letter to a Swedenborgian*, published in 1847, he explained that the New Church was yet another example of an ecclesiastical encumbrance unnecessarily placed on human freedom. He decried even the use of the term 'New Church' since there should be no new corporation to replace the old, only a spiritual or universal acknowledgement of the Divine-Natural Humanity. The New Church as conceived by Swedenborg had no social, political, or ecclesiastical attributes, only an inner spiritual and universal heaven representing the *Maximus Homo*. The New Church was a spiritual church dedicated to the end of individualism and the beginnings of a Divine-Natural Humanity pledged to the realization of creative love and wisdom. 'The new or mystic Jerusalem is neither a temple nor a place', James insisted. 'It is the regenerate earthly life of man, a life of complete subjection to the laws of the Divine Humanity operative in nature and full consequently of innocent and ennobling delights'.[28]

Despite his many antithetical feelings towards Christendom, James was quite agreeable to attending church on special holidays. But true worship had to be free, unforced and spontaneous. Nothing was more degrading to him than a life passed in ritual devotion and the exercise of formalized piety. 'It is an insult to God and man to dignify so sodden a routine with the sacred name of life; call it rather death and damnation to every soul of man *that finds it life*', he wrote in 1879. The visible church was nothing more than an 'abomination of desolation', a refuge of spiritual egotism and rank 'spiritual cupidity'.[29]

New and Old Theology

James used the term *Old Theology* to denote all the types of superficiality which derived from the Roman church and which continued in various forms into the Protestant Reformation. Together, their 'empty superstitions' served as barriers to the fulfilment of human fellowship and the equality of all human beings. No sooner had the Christian churches become prosperous than they 'attracted the coquetry of secular powers' and rapidly unlearned the spirit of Christ. Even worse, by joining with the secular state, they had unleashed religious wars that had branded Christendom with shame. As a curious archaeological artefact of human history, Old Theology continued into the present age without spiritual form.[30] Described variously as a 'bedizened courtesan and streetwalker', a 'brazen handmaid to worldliness' and an 'icy winter' blighting the summer, Old Theology's sole earthly errand had been 'to dog the footsteps of morality, to humble the pride of selfhood which man derives from nature, and so soften his interiors to the reception of divine truth, as that truth shall stand fulfilled in the organization of human equality and fellowship'.[31] For James, this was wrong thinking. How could evil have existence under a God of perfect goodness and infinite wisdom? If humanity derived its total being from God, its claim upon the Creator was that humanity 'should image that Creator's perfection, nothing more and nothing less'. How was it possible for God to punish and condemn His creatures for limitations of their nature which led them to sin? These were the fruits of blind adherence to ecclesiasticism's literal traditions.[32] James considered the Chicago evangelist Dwight Moody, whose clever conjuring and untidy zealotry had deflected fellow human beings from spiritual truth with the 'lusts' of a 'subterranean lair', symptomatic of the 'fashionable religious cant' of Old Theology that carried into contemporary life.[33]

New Theology, on the other hand, was not a creed or formulary but a spirit that showed how the birth, life, death and resurrection of Jesus symbolized the *Maximus Homo*. While Old Theology interpreted creation as a voluntary act on the part of God, leaving His creatures in a 'very insecure relation to Him', New Theology asserted a 'secure relation' between God and humanity, an outgrowth of His very selfhood. Humanity's welfare 'is as assured as God's own perfection', James argued. Essentially, New Theology viewed the *Maximus Homo* as the indwelling of God whose greatness was not defined by His distance from humanity but by His intimate nearness and 'by stooping as it were to our littleness and lifting us to the dimensions of His majesty'. New Theology had no sectarian scheme to promote, no immortal penalty to enact, no fable of self-abasement or degradation to believe, no ritual obedience, no mission of Christ to mediate between God and a vicious and debauched humanity, and no ecclesiastical view of Christ's atonement. Instead, it offered a view of Christ as proof of that 'perfect and unchanging love of God', of the Divine Humanity, a science of human unity, genius and inspiration. James's intent on making Christ fully incarnate in humanity presaged the movement known as New Thought which emerged in the latter decades of the nineteenth century.[34]

Substance and Shadow

James was burdened with the conundrum of explaining how, given God's perfection, evil could exist in His creatures. From both his philosophical and ecclesiastical mentors, he had been told that evil was a phenomenon of man's moral life, completely independent of the relationship between Creator and creature. But this failed to satisfy him. 'They were . . . unable to show me', James recalled, 'how this independence, which they made thus necessary to give me a capacity for sin, could come about, without at the same time . . . vitiating the very responsibility it was assumed to explain'.[35] He found the answer to this enigma in Swedenborg's explanation that sin was only 'a tough earthly rudiment', a crude 'unhandsome germ' of advancing spiritual growth. To do evil was the heritage of every person; on the other hand, to feel sin was something entirely different, belonging only to those spiritually born. The two were distinct as earth and heaven. The true confession of sin was never verbal such as the Roman church supplied with its private confessionals. Nor did it come in some public expiation; instead, it was the heart 'touched with God's overpowering love' that came to the 'interior ear'.[36]

In 1869, James published *The Secret of Swedenborg: Being an Elucidation of His Doctrine of the Divine Natural Humanity*, a portion of which appeared in the *North American Review*. In it, he rejoiced at what he saw as a 'brightening of the intellectual skies', believing that the time was not far distant when the 'idle, pampered, and mischievous' forces of ecclesiastical religion with its 'holiday God' would be disowned for a 'working God' who would cleanse humanity of its physical and moral failings. Although nature was essentially good, perhaps even divine, it had been repeatedly compromised by the selfishness of individuals. Blinded by pride, jealousy and self-seeking, humans lived a discordant life made worse by church and state. Once weaned of these illusions, the human race would form a kingdom of heaven on earth whose social order would be that of God fully incarnate in the Divine-Natural Humanity. 'I find myself incapable, for my own part', James wrote, 'of honoring the pretension of any deity to my allegiance, who insists upon standing eternally aloof from my own nature, and by that fact confesses himself personally incommensurate and unsympathetic with my basest, most sensuous, and controlling personal necessities'. Having moved beyond what he called a 'loutish conception of the deity', he chose a more humanized—albeit not Unitarian—glorification of humanity. God's presence was not to be at the expense of humanity's collective redemption.[37]

James explained the relationship between the Creator and His creation as analogous to the relationship between substance and shadow. The shadow of a thing was the measure of its finiteness but not its true being. Real substance was that which existed in itself, or what was vitalized from within. In short, real existence was spiritual in nature, possessing life within itself, while a shadow was phenomenal, existing only by virtue of its implication in something not itself. The infinite being was a faultless substance while the finite was a projection or image that attested to the substance's existence. Old philosophy had regarded humanity as a simple quantity, submerging its creative element and separating its selfish side from the face of the Deity. In rejecting this older philosophy, James restored humanity to intimate fellowship with the Divine.[38] Communion with the Deity was accomplished without reference to humanity's disobedience or betrayal of God's commands. Rather, it represented a celebratory reunion of God with His creation. This belief brought James closer to the metaphysics of Swedenborg with his inner and outer sense of divine influx and more distant from his Transcendentalist colleagues and their celebration of the individual. Like Swedenborg, James held that God's universal love meant salvation for the whole human race and not, as Christian theology avowed, to an elect few. God had an intimate and indissoluble bond with humanity.[39]

Swedenborg's contribution to James's philosophy was to furnish the key to understanding the Divine-Natural Humanity, namely, the growth of human consciousness from being a shadow of reality stamped upon the senses to a union with God through fellowship and brotherhood. True philosophy exalted not the *me* or subjective element in experience bound by the laws of space and time, but the creative act that brought the finite human mind together in complete harmony with God's perfection. Through Jesus, God became manifest in flesh and opened a pathway for humankind to the spiritual universe. The spiritual life forfeited by Adam and restored by Jesus, the second Adam, offered an absolute blessing to man conditioned only by his faith as a worshipper and not upon any specific activity or works. Due to Christ, the spirit of God was given freely to all humanity, with no possible obstacle—inward or outward—to interfere. Both good and evil were constitutional conditions of humanity and purely subordinate to the spiritual life which was the gift of God.[40]

Divine Incarnation was indwelling in every individual. Such was the righteous temper of mind that animated from the divinely begotten spirit. The divinity of humanity resided in no dead parchment but in the unselfish lives of those who looked inward for their spiritual faith. Human history was spiritual, not material, giving witness to a Divine-Natural Humanity with 'lordship both of nature and society . . . The secret of history from the beginning has been, not to make man healthy, wealthy, and happy, but . . . to develop in him an infinite genius or ability which shall ensure him the amplest obedience of nature, and turn society into his unlimited servant and friend'.[41]

17

Selfhood

Divine-Natural Humanity was James's name for perfection, realized through the replacement of 'finite selfhood' with 'infinite selfhood', meaning complete unity with God. None of this was possible, however, until church and state were cleansed of their viciousness. 'The vigorous life' which once gave them their justification had disappeared. Like Emerson, James viewed current institutions as effete, no longer blessing their subjects but leaving them 'naked and empty'. Society had been made for man, not man for society. Not until the spirit of God was truly evident in the Divine-Natural Humanity would society's tyranny end. 'What God is bound to hate', James explained, 'is the attempt of society to organize permanent division among His children'. For that reason, God's manifestations in nature bore hostility towards any institution that permitted one class to exercise superiority over another.[42]

Since, strictly speaking, each individual was dependent upon God for all that he or she was or would become, the question became whether, as a creature of God, the individual had selfhood, or a feeling of life in him or herself. Clearly, the moral sphere of the individual for absolute self-determination remained a stumbling block. What James learned from Swedenborg was that this selfhood or freedom was nothing more than an appearance 'contingent upon a certain strict equilibrium which the Divine Providence maintains in our nature between the opposing poles of good and evil'. The problem for philosophy was reconciling the freedom of the individual with his or her dependence upon the Divine. But as James explained, Swedenborg showed with commanding evidence that the selfhood of the individual was a reality *in* God. The seeming duality of Creator and creature was only 'philosophic child's play'. It was love, grand and perfect, that accounted for the majesty and mystery of life.[43]

James attributed to Swedenborg his first clear insight into the power to rise above those natural limitations which bound all human existence. Rather than selfhood becoming the true end of man's being, it was only the beginning of a social sentiment toward human society, brotherhood and equality. This social development constituted a new nature in man, a divinely renewed heart and mind that united creature and Creator. James realized that fellowship was the grand aim of God's providence on earth, to which moral sentiment was only incidental. Since moral and social sentiments were incompatible, the progress of human society could not occur while the self felt morally or personally superior. It was the destiny of humankind to attain a conscience of social unity and order over that of moral discord and disorder.[44]

James considered Swedenborg's writings utterly 'priceless' for their spiritual information, referring to them as 'Celestial Secrets'. They were the 'inmost, most innocent, and tender breath of our divine-NATURAL manhood'. Any serious reader found in them 'living truths' that dispensed with the 'rubbish [of] good-for-nothing ecclesiastical traditions'. Whether reading about heaven and its 'orderly peaceful vicissitudes', or hell with its 'insane delights', one felt alive from the inspiration. Over and over again, Swedenborg conveyed the truths of God's spiritual creation and of the fallacious emphasis given to the physical universe. His books were like a divinely constructed looking glass into the intrepid soul of humankind.[45] In them, James discovered the spirit of fellowship or equality among humankind—a concept alien to selfhood. He learned from Swedenborg the abject futility of selfhood which, in forcing every individual into utter dependence upon God's mercy, had constructed 'an everlasting heaven out of men's warring and divided personalities'.[46]

James returned over and over again to the question: How could one promote the divine kingdom on earth if serious-minded individuals are only conscious of sin? If the morally good man had no higher sentiment than duty or legal obedience, then natural selfhood would forever separate the individual from the Creator. Selfhood was representative of pride and arrogance, neither of which was spiritual. God, on the other hand, sought 'incessantly to build him up spiritually by allaying his natural pride of character and lust of dominion'. God was not distressed with the individual's evils any more than the movement of the tides. That was because the individual's natural evils were purely subjective and not at all given to divine sight. 'If he had it not', reasoned James, 'the creature would be undistinguishable from his creator; so that God's spiritual creation is absolutely conditioned upon it'.[47]

The State and Society

One of the principal characteristics of the Enlightenment was the coherent body of secular ideas that spilled forth from a vanguard of intellectuals seeking to provide rational, empirical and liberal explanations for humanity's present condition and potential improvement. A noteworthy number of these fellow seekers also held forth combinations of prophecy and millenarianism that, if realized, promised an earthly paradise of benevolence, peace, prosperity and human regeneration. These views excited a diverse group of nineteenth-century idealists attracted to the possibility of societal improvement through reason and human endeavour. Swedenborgianism took root in large patches of this thinking, touching a core of influential believers in England, Sweden, France, Germany and the United States whose writings and persuasiveness were sufficient to stir discussion and implementation of Swedenborg's ideas in a number of model societies.

James began reading the works of the French social and moral philosopher Charles Fourier in the mid-1840s and was encouraged by his social theories. Others were similarly impressed, including physician and translator of Swedenborg's writings, James John Garth Wilkinson, utopian socialist Albert Brisbane, Unitarian minister and social reformer George Ripley, newspaper editor Horace Greeley and journalist Parke Godwin. Implicit in Fourier's utopian millennialism were many of the latent aspirations of Transcendentalism, abolitionism, free-soilism and other spirited reforms that blossomed in the mid-century. Fourier's blueprint for society provided a close approximation to Swedenborg's angelic planes, including the transformative work of divine influx in the exercise of human fellowship. Fourier's outline of society was confirmation to James that God's plan did not end with original sin or the individual soul but in the broader construct of human nature, specifically, that which Swedenborg called the *Maximus Homo*.

From the start, James displayed considerable interest in Fourierism as evidenced by his 1846 lecture 'A True Education' and by the strong encouragement that he received from Godwin and Wilkinson.[48] Before long, James supported the Brook Farm magazine *The Harbinger*, provided an anonymous translation of Victor Hennequin's *Love in the Phalanstery*, and was singularly dismissive of critics who attempted to discredit Fourier because of his perceived openness to free love. In his *Moralism and Christianity*, James recommended Fourier's writings as an example of socialism's future: 'You will doubtlessly find in Fourier things of an apostolic hardness to the understanding; you will find many things to startle, many things perhaps to disgust you; but you will find vastly more both in the way of criticism and of constructive science to satisfy and invigorate your understanding . . . that your imagination will fairly ache with contentment, and plead to be left off'.[49]

In a lecture delivered before the Young Men's Association of the City of Albany, James affirmed the moral and social obligations of the individual to the state, insisting that the basis for such obligations was grounded in the distinctions that separated the human being from the brute. Nevertheless, there existed a spirit in humanity that had no reference to geography, political affiliation, or identity. He defined it as 'the tendency of man universally towards union with his brother, so that the perfection of society is felt to lie in its universality'. James did not refer directly to Swedenborg in his lecture, but he clearly drew from his writings to explain the universality of the divine love.

> First, the child is brought into obedience by outward methods, by motives addressed to his outward hopes and fears, in order to the formation within him of the inward man, the inner man of the heart; but when this inner man has thus become formed or pronounced in us, and is called forth into activity by the experience of our mature years, then this enforced subjection of the outer man gives place to a willing submission, and we refrain from evil and do good purely because we cordially hate the one and love the other. The divine kingdom is now established in us, and the heaven of the inner man stands reflected in the rejoicing and fruitful earth of the outer one.[50]

The history of the world had reached a point in time where Christianity was now poised to shift its emphasis from the outer to the inner sphere, 'from the natural to the spiritual world'. The sword of the warrior and the territorial gains of empire had been achieved. It was now time for the 'sword of immortal temper' and the empire of the human heart to merit attention. In this new era, such treasons as the divine right of kings and the 'gibbering incubus of Priestcraft' had lost their purpose as both operated against the moral life of the individual. Assisted by education and the spectacle of huge scientific achievements in the past half a century, James saw the 'voice of man's destiny making itself heard . . . above the roar of faction'. The age of the new moral man had arrived, one whose sympathies were 'pledged to no particular interests, but to universal goodness and truth', and whose true mission was in moving beyond the enemy of self-love to acknowledge the brotherhood of the *Maximus Homo.*[51]

James discovered in socialism the much needed remedy for the physical and moral problems inherent in civilization. His choice of term, however, did not carry the same meaning as found in the writings of Fourier, the Welsh social reformer Robert Owen, or the Christian socialist Henri de Saint-Simon. For James, the term was spiritual in nature, promising to 'lift man out of the harassing bondage' to which he had been placed in civilization and leave him to God's 'unimpeded inspiration'. It enabled individuals, by virtue of creation, to satisfy their natural appetites by possessing property commensurate with their 'inward and essential infinitude'. It offered fulfilment to the Christian hope of individual perfection by revealing a perfect harmony between God and humanity and eliminating that part of society which tended to cheat the soul of its rightful sustenance. Socialism, he explained, 'lifts us out of these frivolous and pottering responsibilities we are under to man, and leaves us under responsibility to God alone, or our inmost life'. It provided every individual with 'the orderly and ample satisfaction of their natural appetites and affections, the unlimited expansion of their intellect, and the complete education of their faculty of action, however infinitely various that faculty may be'.[52]

In looking at the works of contemporary reformers, James identified some who affirmed the natural depravity of humanity and its inability for self-governance, and others who believed in humanity's ability to organize an 'enduring harmony' that would eliminate crime, vice and suffering, all of which were incidental in human society. In affirming the 'inherent righteousness of humanity', this latter group of reformers was confident that socialism could repair human society utilizing the wisdom of its majority. As an unabashed believer in human destiny, James held that humanity's power was not limited by anything external to itself. Just as the Creator was perfect, so too was humanity since it was an image of the Divine. As a creature of God, humanity must reflect God by becoming 'the actual unity of internal and external, or of object and subject'. This divinely imposed destiny gave humanity 'universal dominion' over nature and society.[53]

In 1850-1, James delivered a series of lectures in New York City that were later published as *Lectures and Miscellanies*. In them, he celebrated democracy and the government's fiduciary obligation to carry out the will of the people. 'Democracy is not so much a new form of political life', he explained, 'as a dissolution or disorganization of the old forms'. It signalled the end of 'the period of puberty in the race' and the conversion of political institutions into social institutions intended for the welfare of the people. It marked an end to Old World polity with its 'burdensome yoke of kings and nobles', and the promise of a new more inclusive democratic rule. Reflecting the views of American historian George Bancroft who was influenced by Hegel's schematic philosophy of history and who served as the intellectual spokesman for Jacksonian democracy, James saw democracy transforming American culture, marking a transition from being viewed as a 'problem' to that of a 'faith'. Although still imperfect, it affirmed the sovereignty of the people over their institutions and the promise of the 'universal human heart'. From a moral and social point of view, its benefits derived from the increase of 'just, amicable, and humane relations' amongst its members. It heralded the 'moral perfection' of humanity and a time in the not too distant future 'when all coercion and restraint shall be disused in the conduct of human affairs'. The single purpose of government in the new age of democracy was 'to proclaim the unity of man, and guard the interests of that unity'. All other functions were to be in harmony with this objective. It represented the ultimate reconciliation of the public and private interests of humanity. As such, it was in accord with the inward or essential life that the individual had in God. Democracy was preparing the way for humanity's ultimate fellowship. It served to inaugurate 'the divine life on earth', a life which descended out of humanity's 'inward spirit', thus indicating 'the real presence of God in every soul'.[54]

'In no country in Europe has the citizen as yet consciously risen into the man', James observed. 'In no country of Europe does the government consciously represent . . . the unqualified manhood of the country'. When measured against American humanitarian ideas, all of Europe was muddled in selfishness and artificiality. The sentiment of human unity failed to inhabit its people, their political leaders, or their churchmen. They were nations deficient in human sentiment and the common rights of humanity. Neither their churches nor their governments were expansive enough to meet the aspirations of the people. By contrast, James observed, 'we [Americans] love our country . . . not because it is *ours* simply; on the contrary, we are proud to belong to it, because it is the country of all mankind, because she opens her teeming lap to the exile of every land, and bares her hospitable breast to whatsoever wears the human form'.[55]

In looking abroad, James saw the signs of human degradation in Europe's luxurious art, imposing edifices, elaborate pleasure palaces and wilful aggrandizement of selfish aims. There was nothing more tenacious in the world than the 'possession of useless wealth'. Valued too often for its own sake and seldom for enjoyment, it gave rise to naked power and institutional structures built for the sole purpose of prolonging it. Notwithstanding this impediment, the *possession* of property represented an outward reflection of humanity's essential perfection. It was the means by which the individual became rightly conscious of himself and therefore 'made aware of the exhaustless divinity he embosoms'. Sovereignty over property was the means by which individuals learned of their inner or spiritual being. Thus, to the extent that individuals subdued the earth, they acquired self-consciousness and self-knowledge. Through property, they came to know themselves and that which animated them. As an artefact of society, property was an expression of humankind's sovereignty over the natural world. 'It is the weapon by which man subdues nature to himself, to the service of his proper infinitude'. Thus the moral law affirmed the sacredness of private property and rightfully asserted man's superiority over nature. However, cautioned James, man's destined sovereignty over nature could not be realized except through society, i.e., the fellowship of humanity. In this sense, property was not an end in itself but a means for humanity to discover its inner spiritual attributes. No property was sacred in itself; rather, it was representatively sacred only when used with benevolence, honesty and candour. Property was a symbol not of any particular individual's power, but the sovereignty of the *Maximus Homo*. It was the 'prime monument and measure' of humanity's essential divinity. 'Hence when human fellowship or society is perfect, our natural or external *proprium* will be commensurate with our inward or divine one', he reasoned. When that occurred, 'all the resources of society will be the equal heritage of every man', meaning that property will become more equally distributed among the mass of society.[56]

Evolution and Creation

James was no scientist yet he knew enough of natural phenomena to accept the significance of Charles Darwin's theory of natural selection. While the propositions put forward by the English naturalist lacked any trace of an ontological divinity, James nevertheless assessed the theory as having established a living unity by which the mind had filled up 'all the crevices of nature, and account[ed] for all its changes'. Darwin's methods, which James considered irreproachable, made it 'scientifically very probable that natural and sexual selection account for all the varieties observable within our existing species'.[57] Although he did not welcome this naturalistic focus, he hailed the theory as a first step in building a more exact 'science' of belief. Scientific inquiry was an important, if not an essential component in the study of the natural world. Accordingly, James did not chafe at reductionist explanations of chemistry, anatomy and physiology; instead, he saw them as building blocks to a fuller understanding of physical reality and the ports of entry into the inner workings of the spiritual world. Physical data was no less important in fathoming the transcendent power of God. Knowing God came from recognizing His divine presence in the material world. Physical facts may be only shadows of God's power, but the reconciliation of the empirical sciences with religion helped the enquiring mind to appreciate divine providence. As explained by Paul Croce, James 'viewed science as a shadowland of clues for understanding the divine'.[58]

James had no objection to the new advances in science or, for that matter, the weight it bore 'upon the stagnant religious faiths of the world'. The strength of science was in its combination of reasoned observations and ideas planted firmly in 'a fixed physical or organic world existing objectively or outwardly to his senses'. At the same time, James was also a critic, believing that science was a 'craze' that would eventually lose its allure. In point of fact, he deemed science 'out of her wits when she identifies the mistress she professes to worship with the perishable mirror that reflects her'. Material facts were the 'ultimates' in the sphere of the senses in the same way that bricks and mortar were in architecture. However, science was far too conceited in its self-adulation, irreverently believing 'that it has got within its grasp the ineffable spiritual results of that order'. While James praised scientists for discovering no trace of the creative power in nature which had for so long inspired poets and the 'pretentious twittering' of churchmen with the display of God's super-natural power through miracles, he drew a distinction between science and spiritual truth. The former bound the individual to the finite world of the natural senses and therefore failed ultimately to provide entrée into the spiritual realm of God and the *Maximus Homo*. For all its strengths, the sensory world of the sciences remained secondary to philosophy and revelation.[59]

Understanding the creative power in nature came not from the Baconian world of observation, experience and reasoning, but from the realm of the soul. 'Scientific certainty is never a certainty of what is infinitely true, i.e. *true in itself*, but only of what is true to our intelligence, i.e. of what is merely phenomenally true . . . and may therefore be denied even all probability to-morrow'. Science was not the truth spiritually apprehended. Spiritual creation was of an order fundamentally different from that of the senses and could not possibly be understood using the tools of the senses. Spiritual creation was *subjective* creation; it was the means by which the Creator 'gives being to the creature only by giving Himself to him, or endowing him with his own infinite substance'.[60] As such, science held a middle ground between religion and philosophy. Less arrogant in its pretensions than religion, it had made nature a part of humanity. What science saw in nature was man, not God. That is to say, it decreed the universality of order in the universe. Science was the study of organized existence, shifting knowledge from the sensuous to the rational and purging mental induction of its impurities, thereby removing what James called the 'garbage of the gutters'. In short, the business of science was 'to convert sensible knowledge into rational belief, facts of sense into truths of reason, and so keep un-impaired that discrimination of high from low, of heaven from earth, of God from nature, upon which the reconciling mission of philosophy is absolutely contingent'.[61]

Like Swedenborg, James regarded human creation as a purely spiritual process and not a physical event in space and time 'else hounds and hares, cats and rats, spiders and flies were as authentic creatures of God as man himself'. It was impossible for God to create creatures devoid of spiritual consciousness—forms remote from His own image. For that reason, spiritual creation descended on the human race alone because only man was the true creature of God and alone competent to reveal Him. God created only the human race, 'a form of spontaneity or freedom exactly proportionate . . . to the Divine form'. Since to create was to give something 'inward or substantial being', he who created something actually constituted the substance of the thing being created. 'When I say that God creates me, I suppose myself already formed or existing; I take my existence for granted', wrote James. 'Accordingly in alleging my creation by God I do not refer to any mere fact of existence . . . but wholly to a spiritual and invisible operation; one which utterly transcends the realm of time and space'. By contrast, every other form of existence below the human species was a slave of its nature, unable to stand apart from its physical thralldom in a purely spiritual or subjective form. Its outward being was a natural existence destitute of any private individuality. It had no consciousness any more than water had of the sun and stars.[62]

Unlike the natural world, humanity's creation was no 'stupid' or 'brutal' event in space and time but a purely spiritual process, a communication by the Creator upon His creatures of a joyous marriage whereby the creature became spiritually united in the Creator. Spiritual creation was the philosophic name for natural redemption, best symbolized by the coming of the New Jerusalem and marked by the fellowship and equality of all humans. This concept of humanity was not a material fact but a spiritual truth discernible to the 'inward eye' which released the individual from his or her animal instincts by 'opening our interiors to spiritual Divine influx'.[63]

Assessing Unorthodoxy

There remains the task of defining who Henry James, Sr actually was. Both critics and admirers used terms such as pantheistic, idealistic, dualistic, antinomian and

Hegelian to describe James's account of the natural human and of humanity's super-natural redemption, but none were sufficient to account for his radical ideas.[64] Some have preferred to use the more generic 'theologian', while others have been more comfortable identifying him as a 'Swedenborgian', a 'modified Swedenborgian', 'supernaturalist' and even a 'socialist'. Unfortunately, these descriptions fail to capture the full measure of the man. Of principal import was James's acceptance of Divine-Natural Humanity which Swedenborg claimed for all humankind. It was this compelling aspect of the human organism that not only separated humanity from all other life forms, but contained an element of egalitarianism that defied all social and political distinctions. It introduced a spirit of optimism into the body politic that later social and economic reformers such as Edward Bellamy, Henry Demarest Lloyd and Henry George would find appealing.[65] The idea of God as creative love was a concept that ran through the centre of *Substance and Shadow* and resonated in the thought of the philosopher and mathematician Charles S Peirce whose evolutionary cosmology suggested an initial state of chance or chaos—a chance universe predicated upon a creative and idealistic power of reason which brought order and regularity out of nothingness. Similarly, James's concern with selfhood and the illusion of the individual's independence from God was something to which Peirce attached considerable import in his concept of community. For both men, individualism was subordinate to the importance of community.[66]

In his lengthy introduction to *The Literary Remains of the Late Henry James*, William James hoped that the posthumous publishing of his father's writings would awaken an appreciation for a man whose literary style 'united a sort of inward palpitating human quality, gracious and tender, precise, fierce, scornful, humor-ous by turns, recalling the rich vascular temperament of the old English masters, rather than that of an American to-day'. William knew, probably too well, however, that despite the filial love which he had for his father and for his intellectual odys-sey, few would grow attached to his views or his writing style which appeared as a 'monotonous elaboration of one single bundle of truths'. For someone whose unorthodox world was an intricate blend of naturalism and spiritual awareness, his style was unusually dry, obtuse and expressionless. Despite the originality of his insights, the passion and purposefulness of his rhetoric failed to connect with his generation because of its abstract and often convoluted style.

James's principal challenge was his inability to explain exactly what was on his mind, an impediment that caused him to restate his position over and over again, often in successive sentences and paragraphs using such phrases as 'Let me be perfectly understood', 'What I say is', 'That is to say', 'In short', 'Understand me', 'I only mean to say', 'Stated another way', 'Let me repeat once more' and 'I repeat then'. This became the burden of his life—once stated, a concept had to be restated again and again. The gap between the fervour of his ideas and the written word was often too much for him to bridge, explaining his failure to reach a wider audience for his writings. William described his father's burden of serial reformulations as a Sisyphean labour.[67]

While sons William and Henry rejected their father's idiosyncratic theology, they never strayed far from his spirituality and those elements of Swedenborgian philosophy that intersected it. The worlds of both sons were punctuated by layers of conscious and unconscious insight into the universe and the immaterial forces that seemed always to find a way into their writings. According to C Hartley Grattan in his *The Three Jameses: A Family of Minds*, that which the Jameses did 'individually and collectively, has long since become a part of the general stream of culture in the European and American world'.[68]

Like his father, William experienced a crisis of the 'sick soul' in his youth and used his *The Will to Believe* and *The Varieties of Religious Experience* to chronicle the experience in a manner that gave pragmatic utility to those values that led him through his struggles.[69] A positivist to the core, William still recognized the functional usefulness (i.e., the practical consequences) in harmonizing immaterial concepts with the material. His religiosity, such as it was, did not include a transcendent God; nevertheless, he allowed 'belief' to serve as a medium by which the individual could find functional meaning in the natural world. William's restlessness with the confining aspects of positivist science caused him to return again and again to issues on the borderlands of science and religion. His religion as well as his science embraced components that had long been a part of his father's spirituality. Schooled in a reductionist and positivist environment of medical school, he nevertheless retained an outlook on nature that openly accommodated otherworldly interpretations and meanings. He continually strayed into the world of his father if only to appreciate how such metaphysical belief systems 'worked' in making individuals more at home in the natural world and the complexities of human existence.

Like many in his age, Henry James, Sr's philosophy was a fusion of many elements. Unlike his peers, however, he was content to travel a path few followed. While he made little impact on his contemporaries, he left a huge imprint in American letters and a legacy of metaphysical thinking that filtered through his two sons. A devout believer in the spirit of Christianity and a staunch individualist, he chose to reject the egoism of selfhood for a more spiritualized community encompassing all of humanity. An amalgam of Sandemanian, Swedenborgian and Fourierist elements, James's imagination took him where few thinkers had gone before. As an eccentric philosopher of religion he was a genial but volatile critic of Calvinism whose vision of salvation came through knowledge of the Divine. It wasn't that Swedenborg and Fourier changed his thinking so much as they reinforced elements that were already nurturing within his post-Calvinist faith. At best, they gave him both a language and a structure within which he organized his thoughts.

That said, James's interpretation of Swedenborg puzzled and exasperated both critics and admirers alike, causing his friend Garth Wilkinson, for example, to urge James to desist from calling himself a Swedenborgian. No doubt a good part of James's exceptionalism was due to his struggle with the role and purpose of Christ, namely, whether the Christ was potential in all individuals or simply an expression of what human nature ought to be.[70] Another reason stemmed from the distinction James made between what he believed Swedenborg intended by the term 'New Church' and what his supporters had inferred by their use of the same term, something that James adamantly rejected. Though James considered himself a follower of Swedenborg and wrote *The Secret of Swedenborg* as proof, his was an interpretation that defied contemporary viewpoints. As Charles Eliot Norton explained to William Dean Howells, James was not only the author of *The Secret of Swedenborg*, but he also 'kept it'.[71] A formidable but delightful eccentric, James remained a professed Swedenborgian in spite of the fact that few Swedenborgians recognized any connection to his writings. Journalist Edwin Lawrence Godkin was fond of explaining that James belonged to a branch of Swedenborgianism of which he was the only representative, a factor that did little to deter him from fearlessly extrapolating what he found useful in the Swede's theological writings.[72] Perhaps William caught the essence of his father when he described him as one member of a 'band of saints and mystics' whose experiences and turn of mind had served to prevent religion from becoming a 'fossil' of convention.[73]

Ralph Waldo Emerson (1803-82)

While James struggled to define a spiritually divine end to which humanity was destined, Transcendentalism emerged as a full-blown movement, the collective achievement of Emerson, Henry David Thoreau, Nathaniel Hawthorne, Herman Melville and Walt Whitman. Its literature, separated from European moorings, expressed something genuine and authentic—a celebration of America's cultural independence, stretching in its hegemony to encompass ever broader regional identities. Adventuresome and exuding a spirit of self-confidence, it offered a perspective of humanity that was democratic, egalitarian, spiritual and fresh. No longer slave to tradition, it sought to undermine staid beliefs and abstract reasoning with intuitive insight. While the contributors to this new literature came with their own intellectual baggage, they nonetheless shared a common understanding of the problem of evil, the spiritual centredness of the universe, the symbolic construct of nature, and the importance of individual self and experience. Its three foremost spokesmen—Emerson, Thoreau and Whitman—found in their religious and philosophical idealism a response to the emotional sterility of Unitarianism and the 'sensationalism' of Locke.[74] For them, the answers to life's questions came by way of intuitive knowledge realized from a spiritual conjunction of the material and spiritual worlds achieved correspondentially using Emerson's figurative sense of *sight*, best understood with his 'transparent eyeball' in *Nature*;[75] Thoreau's medium of *hearing*, represented in his chapter on 'Sounds' in *Walden*;[76] and Whitman's medium of *touch*, expressed most notably in his 'Song of Myself'.[77]

In Transcendentalism, foreign ideas took root as if they had been part of the natural environment. Once planted, however, their fruit bore little resemblance to any Old World heritage. Thus, while the spiritual aspects of Transcendentalism betrayed foreign ancestry, its practical outcomes claimed for all what the Old World had promised to only a few. Its experiments in thought and life were done with the conviction that all ideas must not only be new in the New World, but demonstrate their applicability to the Old World as well. The test of truth was in its usefulness by improving the capacity to remake society and not for any indeterminate purposes. Nurtured in a liberal Christian environment, Transcendentalism provoked discussions in politics, art, literature, science, philosophy and religion that reflected a conscious break from the past. The genius of its representative thinkers was in the freshness of their contributions, not for private ends, but for broad democratic discussion. Despite the errors, delusions and superstitions they found in the world around them, they had no misgivings in bringing refreshment to minds dragged down by orthodoxy. They wanted the church and society to be rebuilt and renewed through intuition. It was not just the broadening of the views and content of liberal Christianity by placing emphasis on the practical aspects of doctrine, but a yearning for a more philosophical foundation reflective of man's more spiritual yearnings.

The Transcendentalists were as eager to draw from Confucian, Vedic and Buddhist philosophy as they were from Swedenborg, the German romantics and classical literature. Anything of the spirit they embraced. Poetic perspective, self-cultivation, introspection, reflection, visionary ideas and intuitive insight were food for the spirit. Seeing themselves a spiritual force more than an organized movement, they looked near and far for examples with which to rebuild society. Overall, the Transcendentalists were drawn to Eastern philosophy and religion, particularly its contemplative traditions, as proof of their own ecstatic eclecticism. Their use of orientalia was a confirmation of their passion to swallow the world and its contents whole without necessarily stopping to chew and savour its morsels. As a result, Hinduism, Buddhism, Taoism, Zoroastrianism and Confucianism were discussed without much effort to delineate their particulars. Nevertheless, the Orient's free spiritedness, its states of higher consciousness, social harmony and interfaith pluralism offered a welcome alternative to exclusivist Christian doctrines. While the Transcendentalists were not bashful when it came to borrowing Neoplatonic or even

Oriental forms of idealism, including tales and poems from the *Bhagavadgita*, there was a pragmatic nature to their use without a commensurate appropriation of their principal assumptions. In other words, they absorbed what they considered usable without construing some form of intellectual or spiritual obligation. Using the law of correspondences, they were content to make the connection without admitting to any paternity, real or otherwise.

Emerson, arguably America's most quoted writer through the first third of the twentieth century, has been depicted as the authentic representative of the nation's collective ideals. Though labels of one type or another have been used to capture his psyche, the simple fact is that he does not fit into any one definition for an extended length of time. As an eclectic thinker, he drew from a myriad of currents adrift in the canon of Western literature, as well as those he happened to discover from translations of Oriental philosophy and religion. An artistic dilettante in his choice of mediums, he conveyed to admirers the image of a polished, ambitious and highly literate thinker who had acquired the means to know, appreciate, cultivate and express the conscience, ambitions and dreams of a people. Above all else, he celebrated the individual whose voyage to self-discovery and self-reliance resulted in an optimistic and affirmative commitment to realization of the good society. He was an intellectual who begged acquaintance from anyone who aspired to be remembered beyond a simple notice in the registry of births and deaths.

While Emerson's interest in the religion of the churches declined precipitously after leaving the pulpit in 1832, his decision gave him the opportunity to borrow freely from ancient Greek and Indian philosophers, Neoplatonic mystics, French eclectics and German and French romantics in his formulation of non-empirical truths and moral principles. Like the French eclectic Victor Cousin, he grew fond of German romanticism, drawing directly from translations of Jacob Boehme, Johann Gottfried Herder, Georg Wilhelm Hegel, Johann Wolfgang von Goethe, Immanuel Kant, Johann Gottlieb Fichte and Friedrich Wilhelm Schelling, and indirectly through Samuel Taylor Coleridge, Thomas Carlyle, Henry Drummond and Herman Grimm. All shared his rejection of eighteenth-century British empiricism and shared as well his trust in an intuitive philosophy in which nature represented both the mind of man and the mind of God. Feeling no longer bound by Christianity's past, he approached life with a poet's insight. His advice was simple. 'To believe your own thought, to believe that what is true for you in your private heart, is true for all men,—that is genius. Speak your latent conviction, and it shall be the universal sense; for the inmost in due time becomes the outmost,—and our first thought is rendered back to us by the trumpets of the Last Judgment'.[78]

Emerson had shown some knowledge of Swedenborg when he was minister of the Second Church in Boston, but his interest peaked after reading Sampson Reed's *Observations on the Growth of the Mind*. As noted earlier, Reed had studied at Harvard's Divinity School but, having turned to Swedenborgianism, was deemed too radical at the time for a ministry and had to settle for a career in pharmacy. Emerson not only recommended his book to friends but referred to Reed as his 'Swedenborgian druggist'.[79] From this position, Reed contributed frequently to the *New Jerusalem Magazine*; served as editor of the *New-Church Magazine for Children*; published numerous pamphlets; and authored an important biography of the Revd Thomas Worcester, the Swedenborgian pastor of the Boston Society of the New Jerusalem, who Reed first met as a fellow freshman at Harvard in 1814.[80] Emerson also read Worcester's article in *New Jerusalem Magazine* which gave a Swedenborgian interpretation to the Apocalypse[81] and *The True Messiah* written by the French Catholic priest Guillaume Oegger who became a follower of Swedenborg around 1826, stressing the linking of the spiritual and natural worlds through direct illumination.[82]

So impressed was Emerson by Reed's book that he wrote to his aunt Mary Moody Emerson noting: 'Can anything be more greatly, more wisely writ?'[83] He also shared news of the author with his friend Thomas Carlyle who replied, 'He is a faithful thinker, that Swedenborgian druggist of yours, with really deep ideas, who makes me too pause and think, were it only to consider what manner of man he must be, and what manner of thing, after all, Swedenborgianism must be'.[84] In later correspondence with Carlyle, Emerson expressed his continued fascination with the Swedenborgians. 'They are to me . . . deeply interesting, as a sect which I think must contribute more than all other sects to the new faith which must arise out of all'. While they were philosophical and at variance with the popular theology of the day, Emerson qualified his curiosity with the observation that 'when they come to their descriptive theism . . . and then to their drollest heaven, and to some autocratic not moral decrees of God, that the mythus loses me. In general . . . they receive the fable instead of the moral of their Aesop'.[85]

In 1835 Emerson made his first visit to the Swedenborg Chapel at Phillips Place in Boston to hear Worcester preach. 'The sermon was in its style severely simple, and in method and manner had much the style of a problem of geometry, wholly uncoloured and unimpassioned', he wrote in his *Journal*. As he admitted later to Reed, with 'the exception of a single passage, [the sermon] might have been preached without exciting surprise in any church'.[86]

In his lecture on 'The American Scholar' before the Phi Beta Kappa Society at Harvard, Emerson seized the opportunity to break new paths for the nation's literary contributors. To every listener he evoked, cajoled, excited and energized to take hold of the future. 'All literature is yet to be written', he announced. 'Poetry has scarce chanted its first song. . . . Do not believe the past. I give you the universe a virgin to-day'.[87] Explaining that the terrors of past beliefs were now undone, he urged his listeners to embrace the unknown with the assurance that the human spirit was sufficient in its resourcefulness to answer the call to duty. In his oration, Emerson showed not only what his friend Oliver Wendell Holmes, Sr considered to be America's 'Intellectual Declaration of Independence',[88] but also his continued approval of Swedenborg.

> There is one man of genius, who has done much for this philosophy of
> life, whose literary value has never yet been rightly estimated; —— I mean
> Emanuel Swedenborg. The most imaginative of men, yet writing with
> the precision of a mathematician, he endeavored to engraft a purely
> philosophical Ethics on the popular Christianity of his time. Such an
> attempt, of course, must have difficulty, which no genius could surmount.
> But he saw and showed the connection between nature and the affections
> of the soul. He pierced the emblematic or spiritual character of the visible,
> audible, tangible world. Especially did his shade-loving muse hover over
> and interpret the lower parts of nature; he showed the mysterious bond that

allies moral evil to the foul material forms, and has given in epical parables a theory of insanity, of beasts, of unclean and fearful things.[89]

Considered the poet-priest and oracle of the Concord School, Emerson marked the turning point in the nation's literary independence from the Old World. An all-American romantic, his words played upon his audiences like a spring shower. But as James Russell Lowell wrote, 'We do not go to hear what Emerson says so much as to hear Emerson'.[90] People found comfort in his words, whether they understood them or not, for in them was an inner wholeness that left people satiated, if only for a time. Whether it was his essay on *Nature*, or his poem 'Ode to Beauty', his words were strung together in such a way that they gave expression to emotional needs long sought. His mind was eclectic in its pleasures, allowing his imagination to wander freely through histories, anthologies and translations without fear of succumbing to any particular faith or dogma. The same self-reliance he preached to others he kept himself. Using the Lyceum, the Boston Society for the Diffusion of Useful Knowledge and its London affiliate, as well as *The Dial*, *Atlantic Monthly* and other print mediums, he shared his insight with the world around him.

On 25 December 1845, Emerson lectured on 'Swedenborg; or, the Mystic' as part of his 'Representative Men' series of lectures under the auspices of the Boston Lyceum. Though he implied that Swedenborg may have been unbalanced and that his revelatory visions had been the object of numerous criticisms, he nonetheless considered him an exemplary type of prophet who broke through the ecclesiastical barriers constructed by religion. That Swedenborg could go directly to the Divine and so learn the meanings of the universe without stopping first to check a catechism or obtain a priest's approval put him in a much deserved category all his own. Emerson pointed to the introverted mind of Swedenborg who, being born into a world of great ideas, saw the Platonic doctrine of scale or degrees, the representations and correspondences of all things in nature with the spiritual world, and the source (influx) by which the soul is fed.[91]

From both Reed and Swedenborg, Emerson learned the law of correspondences for bridging the natural and spiritual worlds—a covenant so to speak that assured a role for both the inductive and deductive paths to wisdom. In this single law, Emerson brought together in harmony the ideal world of Plato and the empirical world of Bacon——a universe that was both organic and spiritual, and which adjusted effortlessly to his own metaphysical and psychological needs. For him, Swedenborg was an instrument of spiritual exploration——a method of discovering spiritual truths amidst the fragmentary world of nature——allowing him to transform his natural facts into spiritual ones. This conversion suited Emerson for it enabled him to visualize an idea without having to create literal or mechanical transpositions. With the law of correspondences he was able to express all the moments of perception in ways that revealed the inner and outer, the spiritual and material worlds.

It was the law of correspondences that warranted Emerson's placement of Swedenborg in his *Representative Men*. At a time when Christianity faced sobering new discoveries from positivist science, the law provided the prospect of a transcendent divinity to counter the mechanical thinking about nature. While empirical inquiries were a good first step in understanding natural phenomena, they were by no means the last word. For those facing a crisis of faith, the law underscored a conception of nature that included immaterial factors. Nature was the place to see and understand physical things and also to experience spiritual truths; nature was but a shadow of the life of the spirit but sufficient enough for man to grasp.[92]

The law of correspondences made an enormous impact on the sensitive souls of Emerson's generation, providing the tool to reinstitute an idealist and symbolic alternative to Locke's sensory world. The law had a quickening effect on individuals such as Sampson Reed, Garth Wilkinson and poets William Blake and Charles Baudelaire who took their earthbound spirituality to new heights. In their hands, the law became a science that allowed them to function in both the material and spiritual worlds——the connective link between means and ends, perception and its uses. Not through prayer or meditation but rather through 'uses' did the self join with God to become a creative force.

The sources for Emerson's lecture on Swedenborg included Nathaniel Hobart's *Life of Swedenborg* published in 1831 (with a second edition in 1845, five years prior to *Representative Men*), and printed serially in the *New Jerusalem Magazine* in 1828 and 1829. This was confirmed by Clarence Paul Hotson in a line-by-line comparison of passages written by Hobart and Emerson. Another source was Garth Wilkinson's article in the *Penny Cyclopaedia* in 1842 and reprinted in the *New Jerusalem Magazine* in 1843.[93] Thanking his friend Wilkinson for translating several of Swedenborg's books from Latin into English, Emerson explained the seer's ability to converse with spirits, understand the moral import of the sensible world, extricate the 'universal sense' from the literal words in Old and New Testaments, and recount how all things in the universe arranged themselves according to their ruling love. 'Man is man by virtue of willing, not by virtue of knowing and understanding', Emerson wrote. 'As he is, so he sees'.[94]

Unlike the vulgar exhibitionism that followed the eerie rapping sounds heard by the Fox sisters at their family home in Hydesville in 1848, Emerson was disposed like his friend Henry James to see Swedenborg as a legitimate seer and mystic who bore little resemblance to the claims of America's many mediums. Though keenly curious of the various forms of 'enthusiasm' evident among the Moravians, Quietists and Methodists, he attributed to Swedenborg a more measured spiritual experience which he likened to a form of mysticism. In his lecture 'Success' (1859) Emerson made his position eminently clear. 'I hate this shallow Americanism which hopes to . . . get knowledge by raps on midnight tables, to learn the economy of the mind by phrenology, or skill without study . . . They think they have got it, but they have got something else. . .'.[95] Similar to his criticisms of Popery, Mormonism and Mesmerism, he viewed the rappings as a 'black art' whose advocates were succumbing to 'the mummeries of the Dark Ages'.[96] Despite the sheer magnitude of these alleged manifestations, Emerson would have none of it. 'This is the Rat-revelation, the gospel that comes by taps in the wall, and thumps in the table-drawer', he wrote in his journal. 'The spirits make themselves of no reputation. They are the rats and mice of society. And one of the demure disciples of the rat-tat-too the other day, remarked that "this, like every other communication from the spiritual world, began very low." '[97]

Yet for all of Emerson's admiration of Swedenborg, it is puzzling why he included him among the world's seven representative men. Remarkable as Swedenborg was, Emerson found 'no melody, no emotion, no humor, no relief to the dead prosaic level' in the Swede's writings. 'In his profuse and accurate imagery is no pleasure, for there is no beauty. We wander forlorn in a lack-lustre landscape'.[98] Perhaps it was said best by Oliver Wendell Holmes, Sr who felt that Emerson admired Swedenborg at a distance, but the nearer he came to the seer, the more he preferred the German mystic Jacob Boehme.[99] Then again, perhaps, Emerson's decision to place Swedenborg among his representative men was due to the enthusiasm the Swede's ideas had generated among friends and acquaintances, not the least of which included Reed, the Revd Warren Burton, Artemas Stebbins, Benjamin Fiske Barrett and John Flaxman. Nevertheless, Emerson's feelings were not unlike Holmes, whose positivistic grounding caused him to lament how so many of his educated friends could lend their support to such revelatory musings. Holmes was a man with close connections to the intellectual currents of New England Unitarianism and Transcendentalism. As a member of the Saturday Club, a frequenter of the Old Corner Bookstore on Washington Street and as a writer for the *Atlantic Monthly*, he was a key architect of Boston's intellectual culture. That said, he kept at arm's length from those metaphysical breezes of mesmerism, phrenology, homeopathy, Fourierism and spiritualism that circulated in and out of the parlours of Boston's Back Bay. A man of medicine, he remained curious but aloof from those who had permitted themselves to be transported to such celestial visions.

Though less restrained than his friend Holmes, Emerson distanced himself from the Swedenborgians, thus allowing for the occasional ridicule. His comment, for example, that Swedenborgianism was all about 'patching the ecliptic of the universe with a small bit of tin' is a case in point.[100] Similarly, he wrote in his *Journal*, 'You must treat the men and women of one idea, the Abolitionist, the Phrenologist, the Swedenborgian, as insane persons with a continual tenderness and special reference in every remark and action to their known state, which reference presently becomes embarrassing and tedious'.[101]

Notwithstanding his reservations, Emerson could not deny his interest in 'a man who saw God and Nature for a fluid moment'. Nor could he ignore Swedenborg's laws of correspondences, influx, order and degrees—terms whose hegemony seemed to expand exponentially through the corroders of intellectual discourse.[102] While

Emerson appeared not too impressed with this new *living* religion, he had seen, heard and read enough to admit: 'This age is Swedenborg's'. [103]

Mysticism and the Orient

Mysticism, a form of religious experience addressed in William James's *The Varieties of Religious Experience*, Henri Brémond's *Histoire littéraire du sentiment religieux en France* and Cuthbert Butler's *Western Mysticism*, represents a special relationship which Spinoza described as a 'God intoxicated man' who acts on the conviction that God exists, that God is accessible to him and whose goal is union with God. For Quakers, Catholics and Hindus, mysticism was a religious activity that was ascetic, disciplined and progressive. Its impulse is the supreme love of God. [104] Emerson's understanding of mysticism, however, lay outside this tradition, showing little resemblance to the thinking of Meister Eckhart, the English Dissenter George Fox, Martin Luther, St Teresa of Avila, St Catherine of Siena, or even Swedenborg. When he wrote in *Nature*: 'I become a transparent eyeball; I am nothing; I see all; the currents of the Universal Being circulate through me; I am part or parcel of God', he inferred a mystical union with God. Yet, nothing in his writings suggests that he had such an experience. Indeed, his language implies he was speaking metaphorically in a manner that was suggestive of—but not actually—a mystical experience. Viewed from this perspective, Emerson was a poet-priest whose blend of insight, eloquence and moral force was carefully conveyed in proverbs which, although ambiguous and imprecise in their meaning, were expressed in memorable and unsurpassed eloquence. [105]

Protap Chunder Mozoomdar, the leader of the Hindu reform movement known as Brahmo Samaj and author of *The Oriental Christ*, considered Emerson more Hindu in his roots than Christian, viewing his perception of the occult relationship between man and the universe explained by the term 'transparent eyeball' as more in line with yoga and Hindu spirituality than Christianity. Emerson, he explained, laid the foundations of a true philosophy of the world 'by viewing matter, not as a soulless succession of appearances, nor yet a creation of the brain of man, but as a mysterious, marvelous putting forth in outward form of beauty that which he inwardly realizes in the spirit'.[106] He had the wisdom and spirituality of the Brahmans and, in that sense, 'Emerson was the best of Brahmans'.[107]

After Emerson relinquished his ministry and begun a career as writer and lecturer, he produced an essay on 'Religion' in 1837 which reflected some of his views on Hinduism, followed by his *Essays: First Series* which included 'Self-Reliance', 'Compensation', 'The Over-Soul', 'Intellect' and 'Spiritual Laws', many of whose themes were grounded in Indian philosophy. In his essay 'The Over-Soul', Emerson used the term 'soul' for 'mind', viewing the soul's advance as a form of ascension or inner metamorphosis that corresponded to man's physical evolution. In a cosmic sense, the universe, including human life, was neither incoherent nor hostile. Rather it was on a path that aligned just as easily to aspects of Swedenborgianism as to facets of karma in Hinduism. Emerson rejected any view of nature—including man—that was subjected to mechanical causality. While empirical science had its good points, it fell short of providing insight into the broader issues of the universe and human life. 'Here we stand, silent, unknown, dumb as mountains, inspiring curiosity in each other', he wrote, 'and what we wish to know is whether there be in you an interior organization as finished and excellent as the body. For if there be, then there is a rider to the horse; then has Nature a lord'. In this way did Emerson bridge Eastern and Western systems of thought.[108] Clearly, his essay on 'The Over-Soul' represented a key aspect of Hinduism and, according to Swami Paramananda, one of the early Indian teachers to spread Vedanta philosophy in the United States, was an 'almost literal translation of the Sanskrit word "ParamAtman (Supreme Self)" ' and the spirit of the *Upanishads*.[109]

In the pages of Emerson's *Journals*, in his *Essays: Second Series* and in his subsequent works such as *Representative Men* and *The Conduct of Life*, words such as 'Spirit', 'Experience', 'Nature', 'Individualism', 'Self-Reliance', 'Correspondence' and 'Compensation' took on new and imaginative forms. The words that graced his poetry and prose were lyrical to the ear and to the imagination, bringing into the mind a sharpened insight into nature and experience. In his essays on 'Character', 'Nature', 'New England Reformers' and his all important 'Experience', Emerson left little doubt how closely he regarded Hinduism (as well as Kantian idealism) and how closely his concept of the mind or self related to Hindu philosophy.[110]

A key element in Emerson's thought, explained philosopher Russell Goodman, lay in his connection to Hinduism. From college days onward, his thinking was founded on 'his knowledge of and interest in Hindu philosophical writing'.[111] Although the *Bhagavadgita*, a 700-verse scripture set in a dialogue between Pandava prince Arjuna and his guide Lord Krishna, had not been fully translated until his forties, the scholarship of William Jones, Henry Thomas Colebrooke in England, Eugène Burnouf in France, and Friedrich Schlegel in Germany were broadly cast during Emerson's lifetime. As with much that Emerson touched, Hinduism was quickly absorbed into his thought processes and transformed in a myriad of ways. Beginning in his college days at Harvard and continuing after graduation with Victor Cousin's *Cours de philosophie* which provided an insightful survey of Indian philosophy, to the works of Burnouf and Colebrooke, Emerson read a steady stream of translations and analyses of Hindu philosophy. No doubt Cousin's own *eclecticism* factored into Emerson's affirmation of a synthetic unity that depended upon finding and integrating the best in all systems of belief.[112]

Emerson's love of beauty also led him to Oriental poetry. His 'Brahma', published in the *Atlantic Monthly* in 1857, captured the wholeness of the *Bhagavadgita* whose subject was pure being.[113] Emerson considered it among the truly great syntheses of Hindu philosophy. Composed between the fifth and fourth century BC, it emphasized *dharma* as the instrument of goodness, *yoga* as the transcendence of action and *bhati* as loving devotion of God. Another source of reference for Emerson was the *Vishnu Purana*, a collection of legends, philosophy and rituals which dated from the seventh century AD and was translated by Horace Hayman Wilson in 1840.[114] In his essay on 'Plato; or, the Philosopher', published in *Representative Men*, Emerson drew heavily from the Vedas, the *Bhagavadgita* and the *Vishnu Purana* to carry his ideas on unity—an analysis that arguably spoke more of Emerson's own beliefs than it did of Plato.[115]

Although the doctrines of the Over-Soul, Correspondences, Degrees, Orders and Compensations have appeared to later critics as foreign importations, notions too distant from American thought to have much footing or taken too seriously, the truth is arguably somewhere in between. While it is correct to say that these ideas had intelligible origins in other cultures, they were also formulations grounded in

America's Puritan culture as well. To be sure, Emerson, Thoreau, Theodore Parker and George Ripley borrowed joyfully from the *Bhagavadgita*, the *Upanishads*, Swedenborg, Plotinus, Buddha, St Paul, the Stoic philosophers and Confucius, but they needed to look no further than their own New England forebears to realize the connection to mysticism and pantheism. Emerson's 'transparent eyeball' could be found with little trouble among the detritus of the Calvinist doctrine of regeneration and those seventeenth-century 'infidels' intent on opening the soul's access to God from within. As intellectual historian Perry Miller explained, 'the more one studies the history of Puritan New England, the more astonished he becomes at the amount of reeling and staggering there was in it'. For Anne Hutchinson and the Quakers, the marrow of Puritan divinity lay in feeling God's presence in the natural landscape. While most Puritans never lost sight of the distinction between God and the world, there were nevertheless some among them for whom nature was 'the garment of the Over-Soul, that man must be self reliant, and that when he goes into the woods the currents of Being will indeed circulate through him'. Though Emerson's generation chose to couch their mysticism and ingrained pantheism in the language of Swedenborg and the *Bhagavadgita*, there was only a thin line of demarcation between the language drawn from Eastern philosophy and the Edwardian vision of God in the soul and in nature. A continuity—both cultural and intellectual—existed between the seventeenth-century Puritan and the spiritually nourished intuitions of Emerson and his fellow Transcendentalists. The difference, as Miller explained, was that the mystics of the mid-nineteenth century 'were no longer inhibited by dogma. . . . They could give themselves over, unrestrainedly, to becoming transparent eyeballs and debauchees of dew'.[116] As René Wellek added, 'The Transcendentalists were merely looking for corroboration of their faith. They found it in Germany [and the East], but ultimately they did not need this confirmation. Their faith was deeply rooted in their minds and their own spiritual ancestry'.[117]

* * *

Emerson enjoyed a lifelong friendship with James, including thirty years of correspondence. James once commented that while he thought of himself as

43

'ridiculously undivine', he considered Emerson 'divinely begotten' and capable of coming 'face to face with the infinite in humanity' and accomplishing it with a natural innocence that could not be taught in books or in the examples preached by churchmen. Nevertheless, there were also elements in Emerson's 'divine presence' that detracted from James's admiration.

> In his books or public capacity he was constantly electrifying you by sayings full of divine inspiration. In his talk or private capacity he was one of the least remunerative men I ever encountered. No man could look at him speaking (or when he was silent either, for that matter) without having a vision of the divinest beauty. But when you went to him to hold discourse about the wondrous phenomenon, you found him absolutely destitute of reflective power. He had apparently no private personality; and if any visitor thought he discerned traces of such a thing, you may take for granted that the visitor himself was a man of large imaginative resources.[118]

While the friendship of the two men was genuine, it was a relationship fraught with issues. As explained by Giles Gunn, Emerson 'could not be brought to see the potential evil as well as good in the kind of self-consciousness he was always preaching, and, as a consequence . . . was inevitably disposed to promote as cure for the human situation what James took to be the disease itself'. Moreover, Emerson's indifference to criticism was evidence of the very egotism and selfhood that James so often disparaged.[119] Eventually James came to view his friend as having descended from 'a half-score of comatose New England clergymen, in whose behalf probably the religious instinct had been used up'. While James considered Emerson a superior genius, he had to admit that 'his intellect never kept the promise which his lovely face and manners held out to me'.[120] In an article posthumously published in 1904, James noted of Emerson: 'What he mainly held to be true I could not help regarding as false, and what he mainly held to be false I regarded as true'.[121] Perhaps, most significantly, James did not fit comfortably into the spontaneous world of Transcendentalists with their emphasis on the present and consequent lack of concern for the past, their egotism and their moral aloofness and indifference to the reality of evil.

Fascinated by Emerson's personal grace, warm sincerity and promise, James was nevertheless distracted by what some interpreted as Emerson's 'intuitive flights' and 'indifference to intellect', and what literary critic F O Matthiessen once described as Emerson's 'arrested state of innocence'.[122] 'It is painful to recollect now the silly hope that if I went on listening, something would be sure to drop from him that would show me an infallible way out of this perplexed world', recalled James, 'for nothing ever came but epigrams; sometimes clever, sometimes not'.[123] Except for James's public disagreement with Emerson over the significance of Fourier's social reformism, the two remained friends until their deaths in 1882.

CHARLES FOURIER AND ALBERT BRISBANE

Passional Attraction

The Error of Reformers is to condemn this or that abuse of Society,
whereas they should condemn the whole System of Society itself,
which is a circle of abuses and defects throughout. We must extricate
ourselves from this Social Abyss.

(Charles Fourier, *Universalist Quarterly*, 1845)

The New World's infatuation with communal experiments has been ongoing since the seventeenth century when the Protestant sect known as the Labadists settled in northern Maryland, and when Dunkers, Shakers and Moravians, along with foreign colonies of Brazilians and Venezuelans set out in the eighteenth century to reconstruct society on the basis of their particular religious and secular theories. These and subsequent communal groups were based in large measure on two main premises: first, a belief that society is defective in some manner, and second, a belief in the perfectibility of the individual. It followed, therefore, that the social environment of the individual needed to change in order to realize the individual's fullest capabilities.

In 1870, utopian reformer John Humphrey Noyes published *History of American Socialisms* tracing the previous forty years of socialistic experiments. Much of the research for the book had been carried out by A J Macdonald, a follower of Welsh social reformer Robert Owen. Before his death in 1854 from cholera, Macdonald had collected information through personal interviews and questionnaires on sixty-nine communities to provide future generations an accounting of their successes and failures. As Macdonald explained, he intended for his proposed book 'to waken dreamers, to guide lost wanderers, to convince skeptics, [and] to re-assure the hopeful'. Most importantly, he thought such information would 'increase the charity of all those who may please to examine it, when they see that it was for Humanity, in nearly all instances, that these things were done'.[1]

Noyes took ownership of the manuscript upon Macdonald's death, revising and updating the information to encompass several distinct types of movements: those communities having their origin in the Old World (Dunkers, Moravians and Zoarites); colonies of foreigners (Icarian, Brazilian and Venezuelan experiments); those strictly spiritualist in nature (Shaker, Mountain Cove and Brocton); and finally, the two principal groups of communities with Owenite and Fourierist roots. Owen, whose secular experimentation began in 1824, served as a catalyst to a national effort that resulted in the formation of twelve communities.[2] Fourierism, named after Charles Fourier and introduced into the United States by Albert Brisbane and Horace Greeley in 1842, produced yet another national effort that was far more extensive (largely because of its religious overtones), resulting in the formation of thirty-four different communities.[3] The average number of persons in all of these different communities was 192, with the numbers belonging to any single community varying between fifteen and nine hundred. The communities averaged in size about 1,000 acres, with the largest belonging to New Harmony and the McKean Co. associations with about 60,000 acres each. As for their duration, most communities collapsed within two years although one lasted twelve and another seventeen.[4]

The communitarian experiments discussed in this chapter and next include the seven-year history of the two-hundred acre Brook Farm experiment which began in 1840 as the brainchild of New England Unitarianism and Transcendentalism, and only afterwards became the propaganda organ of Fourierism and its marriage to Swedenborgianism; and the Wassaic, Amenia, Brocton and Fountain Grove communities founded by the mystic Thomas Lake Harris, who utilized a very idiosyncratic combination of spiritualism, Swedenborgianism, Theosophy and Orientalism to achieve his millennial expectations.

Charles Fourier (1772-1837)
Some reformers impact the world directly by connecting their ideas to events as they unfold. For others, years and even generations pass before their ideas are taken

whole or in part. While both are influential, it is the latter who demonstrate that the judgment of the day is not always the full measure of the true reformer, but that persons unknown in their time often cast the longest shadow over the destinies of humankind. Such was François Marie Charles Fourier whose writings failed to be appreciated by his own generation, but which were celebrated by later generations who laboured to incorporate them into their societal constructs. An incessant writer, he published *Théorie des Quatre Mouvements* (*Theory of the Four Movements*) in 1808, followed in 1822 by his most important work, *Traité de l'Association Domestique-Agricole* (*Treatise on Domestic and Agricultural Association*), then in 1829 with *Le Nouveau Monde Industriel et Sociétaire* (*The New Industrial and Societal World*) and finally in 1835 and 1836 with *La Fausse Industrie Morcelée, Répugnante, Mensongère, Et L'Antidote, L'Industrie Naturelle, Combinée, Attrayante, Véridique, donnant quadruple produit* (*The disgusting, false, fragmented and deceitful industry, and its antidote, the natural, truthful, attractive and harmonized industry, giving quadruple product*). Besides these works, amounting to eight volumes, he left numerous manuscripts, some of which were published in *Le Phalanstère*, *La Phalange* and *Démocratie Pacifique*, and others that were published posthumously. Dying largely unknown and unappreciated by his own generation, his ideas nevertheless took root, opening numerous innovative paths intended to bring universal happiness to humankind.

The youngest of four siblings, and only son, Fourier was born into a family of comfortable circumstances in the city of Besançon, in the north-east region of France, 215 miles from Paris. His father was a clothing merchant and consular judge to the Tribunal of Commerce and his mother's family ran successful business operations which contributed to the city's commercial success. Imbued with a sense of fair play and a penchant for investigation, Fourier was a diligent and precocious student, winning prizes for composition and poetry. His particular interests included geography, music and horticulture. At the completion of his classical studies, and several years following his father's death, Fourier accepted an apprenticeship in the clothing trade in Lyons, having recognized to his regret that admittance into the engineering school at Mézières was not possible due to his family's inability to purchase a commission in the army. His new career, however, was not without benefits. Acquiring a taste for travel, he took every opportunity to visit the major cities in France, Germany and the Low Countries where he absorbed the culture of the different regions. A keen observer, he studied the characteristics of their topography, learning their industry, principal buildings, materials, promenades and other vital statistics. He also observed the distribution of streets and, like the engineer he had hoped to become, looked for strengths and defects in their construction.[5]

In 1793, at the age of twenty-one, Fourier found himself caught in the storm of the French Revolution and returned home to distance himself from the horror. Sympathetic to the principle of equality, he was nonetheless distressed by passions and excesses that had spread like a contagion across the land. He openly reproved all forms of demagogical tyranny—from the apologists of the Terror to the patriotic fanaticism of the Old Regime. Still hoping to secure his fortune, Fourier converted his inheritance into cash to invest in products to sell in Lyons. His investment was foiled by the revolt of the town against the National Convention and the resulting appropriation of his goods by the city government. When Lyons surrendered to the troops of the Convention, Fourier failed to obtain indemnity for his losses and, thrown into prison, only narrowly escaped the scaffold. Faced with constant death threats, he fled to Besançon where he was obliged to enlist in the *chasseurs à cheval* until discharged as an invalid by the city's council of health. This military experience, while involuntary, was not wasted on Fourier whose mind focused immediately on the organizational and logistical challenges of maintaining an army in periods of peace and war. However, each time he presented to the government his innovative plans and studies, they were judged unrealistic. He even travelled to Paris in 1797 to seek a second opinion. There, too, his plans were dismissed as too extreme.[6]

In 1799, Fourier was working in a mercantile house in Marseilles where, in the course of his duties, he was directed to oversee the destruction of a rice cargo in order to stabilize the market. This troubling experience made him deeply critical of economists for their thoughtless praise of the free market, of philosophers for their disinterestedness in society's deceptive impulses, and of bankers, manufacturers and merchants for their intrigues for the sake of profit. As a result of the unregulated economy, products had been adulterated and sold at exorbitant rates or shamelessly destroyed to shield the market from falling prices. Fourier came to regard the principle of laissez faire as little more than a political scheme to protect the merchant class from the anger of the social body. He concluded that the nations of the world were in much need of a new system of government and that his principal calling and earthly destiny was to discover the exact laws of commerce which, if better understood and controlled, could be put to work for the improvement of society. If the laws of material harmony were found and put in place, they could bring happiness to the world, freeing its inhabitants of their social and pecuniary misdeeds.[7]

For the next nine years, Fourier devoted his energies to discovering the precise organizational unit or entity that would ensure equity, economy and productive industry. By studying the sciences he hoped to find an exact algebraic calculation that would combine all the orders of existence into a common unity. To accomplish this task, he began with the a priori or self-evident assumption that God had a plan or order that governed the material universe, including the social world of humankind. Both, he believed, conformed to God's will and, if properly understood, would result in a much improved world for humanity. The challenge was to identify those laws or principles on which the plan had been based. The first that he found was the *law of progressive distribution* which existed in the very order of creation. In other words, all matter formed a great *chain of being* rising from the most inanimate element to the spiritual. From this, he derived a second principle that since the Creator was one infinite harmonious being, everything in nature must be a reflection of His attributes, meaning that the different elements of creation were 'exactly in proportion to their respective functions and real destinies in the Universe'.[8]

Comparing himself with Newton, Fourier claimed discovery of a calculus of attraction and repulsion, believing that these forces applied to all aspects of creation and, when fully understood, could teach humans how to live in peace and harmony. He coined the term *attraction passionelle* (passional attraction) to explain the two forces—one active and the other passive—that impelled the human race toward its desired objects. The soul, or active principle, was represented in the passions, variously identified as sentiments, affections, feelings, faculties, impulses and instincts. The passive principle, on the other hand, consisted of the body or matter. Each had been created with mathematical precision. Here, then, was the secret of Fourier's philosophy, a divinely imposed and knowable unity applicable in all the sciences—from anatomy and natural history, to physics, chemistry and astronomy. This unity even carried into morality, philosophy, politics and the economy.

The compass of Fourier's research pointed in all directions. As a lover of truth and as someone who believed in overall harmony, he set out to capture and explain every new harmonic element and arrange them in series or groups. Almost everything he wrote included sketches of things—both spiritual and material. He had the instinct of a hunter searching the universe for the divine and mundane states of harmony, disassociation and discord that confirmed his principle of unity, theoretical consistency and universality. The nature of man, the providence of God, the harmonies of the universe, the action of human passions, the organization of society and the destiny of the species were all contained in his principles of series, universal analogy and attractions proportional to destinies.[9]

Like many of his predecessors in the Enlightenment, Fourier placed the human species under close observation, hoping to discover the full measure of human passions and then finding the right formula or calculation within which the passions, including those that were misdirected, could be channelled to produce harmony. The secret to his calculus of passionate attraction was acceptance of the human passions as given since it made no sense to change what God had decreed.[10] Rather than adapt the individual to the environment, it was better to modify the environment as the most likely mechanism for improving the individual. This task, Fourier believed, had been assisted by the school of mental philosophy founded by German anatomist and physiologist Franz Joseph Gall whose pioneering work in ascribing cerebral functions to specific areas (localization) of the brain was considered much more enlightening than older metaphysical theories. Nevertheless, Gall had not explained the functions of the passions to the satisfaction of Fourier. More needed to be done.[11]

Whereas prior philosophers had devoted their inquiries to explaining the functions of the soul through the use of abstract metaphysical concepts, Fourier chose to analyse those same desires, tendencies and attractions in mathematical formulae.

The passions corresponded to the five external senses connecting humankind to the material world. The affective passions, which comprised the moral feelings, united humankind and furnished the motivation for true organization, bringing humankind into unity with itself, nature and God. The desire for universal harmony, which Fourier called *unityism*, represented the noblest aspects of the soul.[12] 'Man being the mirror of the universe', he wrote, 'his anatomical details must exactly portray all the harmonies of the universe, and the osteological portion that shews [*sic*] itself externally, the only one that associates and harmonizes with light, must be a mirror of the harmony of the beacons of heavenly light and of the harmonic distribution of the passions'.[13]

Believing it his destiny to find the precise social code that would permit the perfection of the human race and the fulfilment of its destiny, Fourier changed his work commitments to become a courtier-marron or merchant-broker, allowing him time to complete *Theory of the Four Movements and of the General Destinies*, the first of his many works. In it, he set forth a plan to reform the four great world powers—France, Russia, Austria and Prussia—whose politicians, moralists and economists he accused of violating the principles of the fixed sciences to protect the economic interests of the business classes. He intended for the book to introduce what would later become a multi-volume treatise on his theories. Although he had not as yet elaborated the full dimension of his views, a fact exemplified by his lifelong effort to restate, refine and revise portions of his principles, this initial book was nonetheless written with an enthusiasm spurred by the horrors of French Revolution. Encouraged by the prospect of an unfolding discovery that would change everything, Fourier exuded all the confidence of youthful self-assurance that his theory would be welcomed by the world's great leaders.

In 1818, Fourier's *Theory of the Four Movements* came into the hands of M. Just Muiron, a gentleman of independent means who, struck by the book's originality, considered it the answer to the world's problems. Seeking out Fourier, he became his first disciple, encouraging him to explain the fullness of his grand plan in multiple volumes. It was also Just Muiron who, during his own spiritual crisis, had read Swedenborg and later, in letters to Fourier, urged him to seek verification of his theories in the Swede's works.[14] With Muiron's support, Fourier published his completed theory under the title of *Treatise on Domestic and Agricultural Association* in 1822. In it, he explained the order of distribution in the universe; the laws that governed the destiny of all created beings, including the passional nature of man; the organization of workers by groups and series; and the eventual elevation of humanity. Viewing the passional organization of the human species as the archetype of the universe, he applied the law of series to establish a connection between human destiny, social amelioration and the superiority of his agricultural and domestic plan for the parcelling of property and labour for all ages, sexes and classes. Despite numerous efforts to draw attention to the book, few took notice. Even the Welsh social reformer Robert Owen, to whom Fourier sent a copy, and who was about to establish a community at Motherwell, Scotland, failed to acknowledge it.[15]

In 1823, Fourier travelled to Paris hoping to attract support for his theory. As with his other efforts, he failed in his objective. Undaunted, he continued his quest, publishing in 1829 an abridgment of his grand scheme under the title *Le Nouveau Monde Industriel et Sociétaire (The New Industrial and Societal World)*. That same year, he attended a meeting of the Saint-Simonians after which he wrote painfully: 'Their rough-hewn dogmas are pitiful, yet they have an audience and subscribers'. Fourier's and Muiron's efforts notwithstanding, the Saint-Simonians refused to adopt his theory, causing Fourier to publish a pamphlet in 1831 protesting their pretended doctrines.[16]

For their part, the Saint-Simonians were not averse to appropriating elements of Fourier's theory, taking good care not to identify themselves with the author. Unlike Fourier, they adopted their economic theories to the prevailing needs of the day. Rather than advocating a total transformation of society, they saw the next logical step as adherence to the principles of liberalism, proclaiming an end to privileges that came by birthright. Eventually, however, their presumed threats to capitalism, their advocacy of women's rights and their pretension of creating a new religion lost them support.[17]

Dispirited and having exhausted his resources, Fourier became a cashier in a commercial house in Lyons earning a paltry 1200 francs annually. For a man with such breadth of knowledge and passion for reform, this was a heavy sentence carried out by a world that saw no need in applying his plan for a new economy. Indeed, his ideas hardly extended beyond a scattering of individuals, with Muiron at the centre. A few Saint-Simonians, including Jules Lechevalier and Abel Transon, rallied to the doctrines of Fourier, joining his disciples in the publication of the weekly journal *Le Phalanstère* to propagate the theory and seek a trial of his organizational model. By 1825, Fourier had a nucleus of Muiron, Jean-Baptiste André Godin, Victor Considérant and Mme Clarise Vigoureux; by 1832, five years before his death, Fourier's disciples also included Adrien Berbrugger, Philippe Hauger and the journal *La Phalange*.[18]

Ironically, much of Fourier's intellectual isolation was self-imposed. Obstinate to the core, he refused to modify those parts of his system that could have brought him before the public in a more positive manner. Nor did he show any desire to imitate the style of more popular writers, choosing instead a form of composition that was singularly his own. From his first work in 1808 until his last, his writings bore the stamp of his all-engrossing concern for the sufferings of humankind, contempt for chimerical changes to the existing system and an unwavering belief in the need for true social reform. Having lived a solitary life which began when he was young, he chose dignity and reserve over collegiality, and obstinate silence and evasiveness toward those who sought him out. Only with close family did he show any willingness to be communicative. To his listeners, his language had a simplicity and force of candour that was often misconstrued as disdainful. Fourier chose truth over hypocrisy, a characteristic that often led his listeners to grimace from its presumed offensiveness and straightforwardness. As a thinker and writer, he showed no temerity in expressing his views.[19]

Fourier never wearied of making his views known to government officials and policy makers; nor did he tire of hoping for someone to set his theory to work. Although he had everything in place, no one came forward to test its validity. He beseeched, flattered when necessary, and threatened—all to no avail. Nowhere did his views become so pressing as to force a trial of his discoveries. Instead, they remained useless in his hands, an empty gesture to be discovered only after his death. He remained unknown to the official world of the 1830s, a discoverer of a serial law intended to save humanity but which languished for want of a sponsor. The last years of his life were devoted to reading, reflecting, questioning and even talking to himself as he walked the streets of his town. When his health began to decline, he turned to homoeopathic physician Léon Simon for remedies that failed to bring back his strength. He died in 1837 poor, misunderstood and without having witnessed a test of his theory.

System-Builder

In some ways, it may be helpful to view Fourier as a curious self-educated lay philosopher who, much like Swedenborg, Locke, Montesquieu, Rousseau and other grand theorists of the Enlightenment, attempted to find the perfect 'system' for humanity. Both Swedenborg and Fourier embraced a broad swathe of disciplines—from cosmogony, psychology and political economy, to history, philosophy, commerce, politics and morals—all of which they sought to place into a single universal scheme or unity. Like Swedenborg, Fourier too had studied nature to better understand the causes and effects of life. In addressing the subject, he looked to the ascending and descending vibrations of movement which he divided into series or phases representative of every aspect of existence—from animals, vegetables and minerals to planets, suns and solar systems. His theory of series, his idea of the soul, and his concept of passions and attractions were all subject to scientific synthesis and ultimately to the purposes of what he called *associationism*, the basic unity or universal harmony.

Swedenborg's law of correspondences was not too different from Fourier's law of universal analogy; nor was the notion of divine influx distant from Fourier's law of passional attraction, although the latter seemed more influenced by Mesmer's animal magnetism as the connecting element in the universe. To religious liberals, however, Swedenborg offered sufficient reason to argue for a harmony between Fourier's series of harmonic society and Swedenborg's vision of the spirit world with its different planes of angelic existence. Fourier supposed that the soul descended from heaven into the world at birth and left it at death, returning into the world of spirits where it lived twice as long before returning again to the natural world. Both the invisible and visible abodes of spirits existed together on the same globe.

Like Swedenborg, too, Fourier explained that human progress consisted of a serial order of existence designed by and flowing from the divine life. Applying the names

Edenism, Savageism, Patriarchalism, Barbarism, Civilization (large industry), Guaranteeism (semi-association), Socialism (simple association) and Harmonism to history, Fourier identified eight initial stages of human development. Contrasted with God's plan, these stages were conflicted by false morality, cheating and lies. Once the eighth stage of harmonism had materialized, however, Fourier predicted that humanity would pass through several additional stages before realizing an earthly paradise. He chose not to dwell on those later periods as it was enough to explain the extent to which humankind had advanced into the present age.[20]

The pivotal role of women in all of these early stages of development had involved some degree of subjugation. In fact, Fourier blamed the decadence of prior social orders on the lack of liberty extended to women. Even marriage had been little more that 'pure brutality, chance coupling, induced by the domestic tie, devoid of any illusion of the mind or of the heart. . . . If this be love, it is a love most material and trivial'. By contrast, Fourier's principle of passional attraction included a stimulating sexual utopia once society had extended its privileges to women. Parke Godwin's *Popular View of the Doctrines of Fourier*, Victor Hennequin's *Love in the Phalanstery* and Marx Lazarus' *Love vs. Marriage* were popular interpretations of Fourier's more uninhibited visions.[21]

Fourier's concept of unity applied to communities, races and even federations of continents. Each involved stages of progression, beginning with the association and moving through successive bonds of fellowship. Each entity had its monarch or governor with sovereign authority vested in the people who elected them. The harmonies of human passions were reflective of the harmonies of divine passions. Even the planets formed societies in much the same way that individuals formed families and corporations. Their functions were similar with an order or ranking from inferior to superior. Much like Swedenborg, Fourier described the inhabitants of the various planets, some of whom were warlike and others living more or less in discord and each with its own type of associationism.[22]

Fourier identified the perversions of humankind as egoism, indifference to truth or lying, the mania for monopoly and exclusivism, measureless ambition, favouritism, irrationality and misanthropy. This applied as well to various forms of worship; their rites and doctrines; their local codes and constitutions; and the myriad of sects. All subverted the fundamental harmonic unity of the cosmos. Nevertheless, the whole of his analogical argument was arbitrary, if not fanciful, asserting proofs that begged justification. Fourier's writings are instructive, rich with facts and observations, but filled with imaginary notions and abstractions. This was never more apparent than in his attraction to flowers—a lifelong pastime—and his comparison of their aroma with the particular planets and the varieties of ethereal fluids that permeated the ether and affected the forms, colours and habits of animal and vegetable life.[23]

Given that labour was essential to the lifeblood of society and the fact that the human race was not naturally drawn to the purposes for which it was organized, Fourier set out to make labour an object of individual instinct, transforming what many judged repulsive into something attractive to the passions. By organizing labour into a personal choice that was both aesthetic and moral, he felt that it could engender attraction. Dividing production into labour, capital and talent, with each subdivided into series or groups, he set out to organize it in such a way that every individual spent time in at least two or three occupations most favourable to his or her instincts. It was this blending of personal interest and collective need that he felt would ultimately replace civilization's vices with harmony. All was to be achieved without force or appeal to authority. Even the word *state* did not exist in Fourier's lexicon as it was the attraction of the free individual that made the system work and the power that kept it in motion. Believing that society was made *for* man, and not vice versa, Fourier challenged governments to study associationism and its shareholding structure as a way to address the inequalities of property and of individuals. 'Association was a virgin field, a new scientific world', he wrote, but with its establishment came the promise of a world whose inhabitants lived in peace and harmony.[24]

The *phalanx*, the elementary associative unit in Fourier's system of associationism, was the social hive where individuals ate, lodged, worked and were educated. It was not the single family unit but a larger self-governing social body containing diverse groups of individuals that, demonstrating an economy of scale, was deemed capable of addressing society's conflicting interests and discords. Each phalanx, comprised of members representing youth, adolescence, maturity and old age, required between 1,500 and 1,600 persons participating in occupations that revolved around agriculture, manufacture, commerce and domestic economy. In addition there were the added components of art, science, education, self-government and social intercourse necessary to complete the full mission of the phalanx. Of this number, seven-eighths of the members were cultivators and manufacturers, with the remainder filling the roles of capitalists, scholars and artists.[25] Each individual had duties in occupations to which their instincts and desires were attracted. This ensured a sufficient combination of industry and labour to succeed. Unlike Owen's community at New Harmony where each member exercised a single calling, phalanx participants enjoyed multiple occupations, with no one calling prevailing over another. In each series or phalanx, the individual was a 'co-interested or associated proprietor', not a wage earner.[26] This meant that every labourer was a partner in the phalanx and remunerated with dividends—not wages—proportioned to the amount of capital, skill and labour contributed by each. At the end of each year, the profits of the phalanx were parcelled out: four-twelfths to the stock owners; three-twelfths to skilled employees; and five-twelfths to the manual labourers of the collective body.[27]

In the area of public instruction, Fourier complained that little had been done to bring children into harmony with society's needs. As a result, a child grew to adulthood with an aversion to useful industry, a hatred of superiors, and an overpowering instinct for deceit.[28] Within the phalanx, however, harmonic education functioned in graduated degrees designed to fit each child's abilities and instincts. Every phalanx contained a variety of occupations available for children, allowing them to pass from one to the other, attracted by the opportunities that satisfied their respective passions. Moreover, the association recognized the energy of the young and their exercise of patriotic virtues. Profiting from these inclinations, Fourier encouraged a combined religious and cooperative spirit. These 'little hordes', as he was fond of calling children, should be taught to direct their labours to the repairing of the roads, walks and flower gardens.[29]

With respect to the health of community members living in the phalanx, Fourier made physicians' earnings proportional not to the number of sick treated but to the reduction of sickness and death over the course of a year. In other words, remuneration to physicians was indexed to sanitary statistics that demonstrated their success at prevention over their actual treatment of disease. 'The interest of Harmonian doctors is the same as that of life-insurance men', Fourier explained. 'They are interested in preventing and not in treating disease; accordingly they keep active watch that nothing should endanger the health of any class, that the Phalanx should contain fine-looking specimens of old age, and hearty, robust children, and that mortality should be reduced to a minimum'.[30]

As for the competing domains of church and state, Fourier considered both use-less artefacts of civilization. Rather than attack them, he preferred instead to view them as decorative aspects of the new society. In like manner he chose not to speak of the different or competing socio-economic classes, promising instead to make each richer through their ownership of stock and participation in the profits of the phalanx. Thus, for Fourier, communism and capitalism were meaningless terms. In his pseudo-socialist system, all members of the phalanx were co-owners whose return on investment promised much better results for those who started out poor or who joined by purchasing stock. In general, the character of Fourier's system contained elements from all competing systems, drawing the best from each. From Christianity there was faith in a providential plan for humankind; from capitalism there was a return on individual investment; and from libertarianism there was antipathy to coercion. Above all, individual liberty was respected, with motivation drawn not from forceful intervention but through the free play of individual instincts or passions.

Agriculture was the pivotal component in Fourier's system and the natural vocation of its members. While all phalanxes would have some level of industry, he considered manufacturing an accessory to agriculture, not the principal oc-cupation. Accordingly, manufacturing was given no more than a quarter of the attention devoted to agriculture.[31] Notwithstanding this preference, Fourier lamented agriculture's condition, believing that mismanagement existed in all of its many components. From the destruction of forests and the primitive state of cultivation, irrigation and drainage, to ill-chosen crops such as rice in Asia, wheat in Europe, maize in Mexico and yucca root in the Antilles, agriculture lacked creative husbandry. In rectifying this situation, he advocated the increase of herds, fowls, pasturage, orchards and gardens to 'reduce the vast and gloomy fields of wheat which the country now presents to us under civilization'. In addition, he urged agriculture to move away from grains to the cultivation of fruits, nuts, fowls, bees, fish and vegetables—products that required less area to cultivate yet offered both nourishment and pleasure to the palate.[32]

Fourier's concept of a phalanx—whether located in cities or in the countryside—included stables, dining halls, libraries, workshops, telegraph, post office, assembly halls, ballrooms, cellars, observatory, classrooms and apartments for domestic privacy. The plan incorporated an avenue passing between the main edifice and the storehouses, granaries and other buildings; a public square; a garden enclosed within the central range of buildings; large portals or entrances; a church; and a large public hall for lectures and musical presentations.[33] Also included in each phalanx was a communal counting house whose purpose was to lend money at the lowest rate, ensure payment for services on fixed days and secure profitable employment for all.[34]

Altogether, Fourier claimed to have made eight distinct discoveries: Nature's laws of universal order and harmony; the theory of universal unity or general plan of creation; the natural order of human society; the theory of human passions; the science of passional attraction or laws that governed the moral universe; the immortality of the soul; universal analogy and comparative psychology; and cosmology, or the guide which the human mind was intended to follow in studying those aspects of the universe which were beyond the scope of observation.[35] One is forced to ask, however, how any of Fourier's discoveries found disciples since much of his writings read as a continuous digression from their intended purpose, lost amid examples, analogies, graphs, unnecessary details, choice words, lists, progressions and definitions. The charm, if there was one, vanished within the first twenty pages of almost any of his works. Chapter titles such as 'Of the Necessity of Foci Disposed in Gradation', 'Of the Omnigynes as Pivots of Infinitesimal Movement' and 'Of the Cabalist, the Tenth Radical Passion' were enough to discourage readers, even the most faithful.

Using symbols, graphs, inverted letters and an excess of tables to convey his principles, Fourier took his devotees on an intellectual journey that ran the gamut of expression—from narcissism to absurd fantasy, torturous digressions, serial analogies, strange naïveté and stern remonstration. He spoke often of the seventh degree of vision which gave the eye a 'transitive harmony' with the soul which must one day be united. He also referred to a somewhat somnambulist vision which allowed individuals to experience sensations without the aid of the senses. Some of this had been tested in his day by animal magnetizers (mesmerists) who, by giving 'fictitious sleep' to their subjects, supposedly brought subjects into contact with the spiritual world. Having read the works of French naturalist Joseph Phillipe François Deleuze, the librarian to the French Royal Botanical and Zoological Gardens, Fourier admitted having only a superficial knowledge of the subject. He made no judgment affirming the validity of Mesmer's theory of animal magnetism but he felt, at least in principle, that it acted in conformity with the laws of movement. Personally, Fourier was sceptical of Mesmer, mostly because his so-called science had masked a number of 'gallant liaisons' with young women drawn to his salons of magnetism for nefarious purposes. Even with the number of duped husbands, intrigues, exaggerations and abuses, he continued to hope that a germ of truth remained for others to develop.[36]

Within a decade of his death, Fourier's disciples grew to approximately 3,700, including Prince Louis Napoleon. Later publications by his followers included the *Revue du Mouvement social*, edited by Charles N Limousin; *Le Devoir* of Guise; and *La Rénovation* founded in 1888 by Hippolyte Destrem. Fourier never achieved the notoriety of Saint-Simon but his influence proved to be more pronounced and his disciples more faithful to his beliefs. Fourier's system was tested in several different countries, the first in 1832 when M. Baudet Dulaury attempted to start a phalanstery on 1,200 acres in Condé-sur-Vesgres near Rambouillet. The project failed for lack of subscribers and never became operational. The Familistère in Guise (1859) was founded by industrialist and political theorist Jean-Baptiste André Godin. Other efforts were begun in Algeria and in the United States.[37]

Albert Brisbane (1809-90)
With the decline of Calvinist orthodoxy in the late eighteenth century, Americans opened their doors to a generation or more of social ferment, transforming the

landscape into a potpourri of millennial sects, revivalists, perfectionists and all-round reformers hoping for universal salvation in an environment rich in opportunities. The sweep of ideas was enough to make any Burkean weep for the future of traditional philosophies and institutions. From Mother Ann Lee, George Rapp, Joseph Smith and John Humphrey Noyes, to William Ellery Channing, Henry James, Sr, Ralph Waldo Emerson and George Ripley, the creative juices had been unleashed on man's capacity for moral improvement and the coming together of a social order to create an ultimate *good* that would collectively bring an end to war, disease and poverty. As historian Carl J Guarneri expertly pointed out, Europeans 'invented' rather than 'discovered' the New World, using their encounters 'as repositories for the dreams, fantasies, visions, and hopes of a European culture teetering between enlightened self-confidence and chiliastic despair'.[38]

In this milieu, both secular and religious symbols were combined to give a new context, one that brought the natural and spiritual worlds together in a new Jerusalem or kingdom of humanity on earth. Angels and saints were sometimes part of the calculation but most of Christianity's otherworldly symbols gave way to a communion of the heart where political, sectarian and class differences were smoothed over by faith in the brotherhood of man. Gone were the concepts of original sin and belief in biblical literalness; in their place was a world of perfect harmony between God, nature and man. Robert Owen, for example, made clear his disavowal of the Bible and of ecclesiastical religion in general. Fourier's own beliefs were not so far removed from Owen's, having observed the worst aspects of the French Revolution and the dubious role of the Catholic Church in shoring up the monarchy.

Albert Brisbane, foremost among Fourier's American disciples, was born of a well-to-do family in upper New York State. Having the means to a broad education, he travelled through Europe and Asia, attended the lectures of philosopher Victor Cousin and historian François Pierre Guillaume Guizot in Paris, and philosopher Georg Wilhelm Friedrich Hegel in Berlin. During his time abroad, he also studied with Fourier, learning the details of his *Traité de l'Association Domestique-Agricole*. On his return home in 1834, he offered a series of lectures in Philadelphia and New York, explaining how Fourier's phalanxes could replace the highly volatile market economy of capitalism with joint-stock cooperatives free of the social and economic problems that beleaguered so many hard working people. In 1840, he published *Social Destiny of Man; Or, Association and Reorganization of Industry*, followed in 1843 with *Association; Or, a Concise Exposition of the Practical Part of Fourier's Social Science*. He helped establish *The Chronicle*, wrote columns for *The Dial* and co-edited *The Phalanx* which began a serialized translation of Fourier's *Quatre Mouvements*. After publisher Horace Greeley became one of Brisbane's avid supporters, he offered his *New York Tribune* as an outlet for associationist information. Drawing support from clergy, publicists, politicians and respected literary leaders, Brisbane transformed Fourier's secular society into a middle-class endeavour designed to capture the noblest aspirations of republicanism, democracy, nationalism, millennialism and Christianity.[39]

Brisbane's significance lay principally in his ability to translate Fourier's writings into a coherent format understandable to American society. Along with the elimination of poverty, ignorance, brutalizing toil, war, conflict of interests, slavery and disease, Brisbane promised that the new social order would bring wealth and prosperity, universal knowledge and intelligence, attractive industry, social concord, liberty in all relations, the social equality of the races, universal health and vigour, passional harmony and social unity. To realize these objectives, he explained the domestic arrangements of living in a phalanx; the securing of woman's right as 'an independent and rational being'; the care of children by 'collective mothers'; the organization of labour; the role of the industrial council; the beauty of gardens; the smell of orchards; and the aesthetic importance of parks and woodlands. Brisbane also recounted the choice of occupations and the guarantee of social pleasures and principles. Finally, he explained the passions that comprised personality and extrapolated from Fourier's writings a blueprint destined to harmonize the individual with the good of the whole—all without Fourier's maddening diversions and cryptic formulas.[40]

Across the American landscape, religious and secular communities such as the Shakers, Rappites and Owenites had expressed their concern with the existing manner of government. Some had found their solution in the control of property, others by formulating new views on religion, marriage, currency, etc. All of these so-called solutions, explained Brisbane, revealed a want of discrimination which a reflecting and impartial mind might exercise. Even universal suffrage and freedom of the press had failed to secure the peoples' happiness. Nor, for that matter, had the Democrat or Whig parties provided solutions, each advancing a different form of currency control. 'Political reforms operate merely on the surface of society', Brisbane reasoned. 'They cannot go to the root of social Evil and eradicate those deeply seated Miseries'. Individuals and groups had accomplished short-term reforms but they had not yet perceived the possibilities that could be realized through fundamental changes in social organization itself. The history of the United States had shown that the labours of twenty-six state legislatures, a national congress, an unshackled press and the Hamiltonian and Jeffersonian approaches to government had brought a modicum of peace and harmony to the nation. But were the people happier? Were they more elevated morally and socially? Were they moving onward toward some higher destiny? 'No, far from it', Brisbane insisted.[41]

Brisbane emphasized the benefits of the phalanx, explaining its joint-stock organization, the preservation of private property, the system of work shifts, collective responsibility, guaranteed income and health care for all, the protection of marriage and the family, and the dividend versus wage nature of its economic structure.[42] Associationism, the true and natural system of society predestined by the Creator, provided for the governance of the material, aromal, organic, instinctual and social spheres of creation. Here was the true and natural system of society destined for humankind, producing social order and harmony across the earth. This meant the unity of man with God in true religion; the unity of man with man in true society; and the unity of man with nature, the creative arts and industry.[43]

Brisbane reasoned that the proper number for a phalanx consisted of approximately sixteen to eighteen hundred members. The number was not arbitrary but based on calculations discovered earlier by Fourier. This meant that an association of sixteen hundred or more persons could accommodate a sufficient variety of talents and capacities to bring harmony to a group. 'Man is the OVERSEER of the Globe', explained Brisbane, 'charged by divine Wisdom with the cultivation and embellishment of its surface, with the improvement of its animal and vegetable creations, and with the realization upon it of material beauty, order, and harmony'. The objective of this grand scheme was harmony, realizing upon the earth the reign of 'universal art'——the perfect combination of man's five senses with the higher spiritual faculties. In time, he predicted, humankind would organize the 'administrative unity of the globe', creating a 'universal association' of the labours, operations and interests of all mankind. The result would be the social redemption of humanity from the evils which had long scourged the earth.[44]

As Fourier's ideas were making their way through American reform circles, exciting utopians to the prospect of model phalanxes that would demonstrate the ability to realize harmony and prosperity through the peaceful reorganization of society, his theories acquired an unmistakable Christian overtone in their transfer, a characteristic that became an indelible aspect of American associationism. Connecting elements of both reason and revelation into the currency of debate, the American brand of Fourierism proved different from its European counterparts by enlisting distinctly liberal Christian symbols. It was a form of Christianity whose members had graduated from the harsh dictums of Calvinist orthodoxy. The outcome was a combination of revivalism, free-will Arminianism, Transcendentalism, perfectionism, spiritualism, sectarianism and millennialism.[45] The kingdom of God was no longer relegated to a spiritual state attainable after death and final judgment, but realizable in earthly communities joined together in common cause for Christian social justice.[46]

American Fourierism was part of a utopian impulse whose roots lay in the nation's fledgling political and social conditions. It represented a desire to backfill the nation's spiritual needs at a time of receding Calvinist traditions; persistent beliefs in a redeemer nation for religious dissenters; and a native tendency to work in groups to achieve both individual (i.e., barn raisings) and community ends (i.e., cooperative associations). Like Owen's communal experiment in New Harmony, Fourierism was no marginal drama carried out in the backwaters of the American psyche but represented a recurrent pattern found in the very fabric of the culture, drawing inspiration from the public's intoxication with democracy, nationalism, capitalism and idealism.

In all, approximately thirty-five phalanxes formed across the American landscape dedicated to Fourier's principles and their communal identity with the phalanx.[47]

These included St Louis Swedenborgians who organized communistic colonies in Jasper and Lenox counties in Iowa; Cincinnati Swedenborgians who organized at Yellow Springs, Ohio; the North American Phalanx in New Jersey (1843-56); the Wisconsin Phalanx called Ceresco (1844); and the Brook Farm phalanx (1844-7) in West Roxbury near Boston. All were anchored in a combination of Fourierism and Swedenborgianism.[48]

Brook Farm

One of the more unconventional marriages in the early nineteenth-century reform movement was that of Brook Farm begun by Unitarians and Transcendentalists in the late 1830s. The pivotal concept of Revd William Henry Channing (nephew and successor of Dr William Ellery Channing) and George Ripley who initially suggested the experiment, and Emerson who gave it his imprimatur, the two-hundred-acre Farm became home to members and supporters who celebrated the non-conforming individual over all other allegiances. With a modest quarterly journal called *The Dial* edited by Margaret Fuller, Brook Farm organized in 1841 as a society whose members were expected to give of their labour or its equivalent in money to sustain its activities which included the 'leisure to live in all the faculties of the soul'.[49] Whether as members, boarders, or simply visitors, the Farm became home to a circle of ambitious writers such as Theodore Parker, Ralph Waldo Emerson, Nathaniel Hawthorne, George William Curtis, George Ripley and Elizabeth P Peabody, who took mutual pleasure in its friendly atmosphere, its literary production and its religious ambition of becoming the earthly home for the Second Coming of Christ.

According to its original constitution printed in *The Dial* in January, 1843, the ambition of the Brook Farmers was to create a 'glimpse' of Christ's idea of society.

> The plan of the Community, as an economy, is in brief this: for all who
> have property to take stock, and receive a fixed interest thereon: then to keep
> house or board in commons, as they shall severally desire, at the cost of
> provisions purchased at wholesale, or raised on the farm; and for all to labor
> in community, and be paid at a certain rate an hour, choosing their own

number of hours, and their own kind of work . . . After becoming members of this Community, none will be engaged merely in bodily labor. The hours of labor for the Association will be limited by a general law, and can be curtailed at the will of the individual still more; and means will be given to all for intellectual improvement and for social intercourse, calculated to refine and expand . . . This Community aims to be rich, not in the metallic representative of wealth; but in the wealth itself, which money should represent; namely, LEISURE TO LIVE IN ALL THE FACULTIES OF THE SOUL.[50]

Brook Farm amalgamated with Fourierism in late 1843 as the teachings of Brisbane took hold through Greeley's *New York Tribune* and as groups came together to reconstruct society based on Fourier's 'attractive industry', 'compound economies', 'equilibrium of the passions' and 'associationism'. The perceived incompatibility of Transcendentalism's celebration of the *individual* and Fourierism's centrality of the *community* caused many of the Farm's members to doubt a role for Fourierism in their community. Nevertheless, the two did combine as members like social reformer and Unitarian minister George Ripley, who was concerned with the fragmentation of the individual in modern society, justified reconciliation between the two competing parties as a way of fulfilling the complex needs of modern man. For Ripley and the members of his Purchase Street Church in Boston, associationism offered a blueprint for the fulfilment of individual self-development. The true social destiny of man's inner and outer nature was best realized in the migration of society to associationism.[51]

The changeover of Brook Farm from Transcendentalism to associationism was more than a simple change of heart. It represented recognition that the phalanx was at the forefront of human progress, a beacon of society's development into a phalansterian world view. It provided the world with a glimpse of the divine idea of society and an infallible indication of the divine order to come. Associationism was essentially a social science that rested upon Fourier's calculation of man's industry and natural tendencies or passional attractions. While past history was a record of strife, the future held the promise of ultimate unity or harmony. In Fourier's account of the historical process, human history had a supra-organic structure to it, with each series or time span represented by a successive change in the human mind as it evolved toward the future. Each step in the series reflected a different complexity of family, government, commerce, agriculture and industry. In other words, humanity proceeded on an inexorable course toward a heaven on earth. Rather than muddle through this change unthinkingly, the associationists were optimistically confident that Fourier had identified the guideposts of change and the route to be taken. The evolution of humankind could be tracked, with each series denoting an upwards movement of human consciousness towards Universal Unity.[52]

When Ripley took part in the formation of the community in 1841, he was already familiar with Brisbane's *The Social Destiny of Man* and thus aware of the social theories of Fourier. Nevertheless, this knowledge did little to sway him and others to veer from the community's choice of path which, as David A Zonderman explained, 'was a uniquely personal blend of Transcendentalism, Christian Socialism, and a pinch of hard-scrabble Yankee ingenuity'.[53] Once undertaken, however, Ripley and other community members looked for parallels between their own design and those which Fourier had conceptualized. As the community sought guidance from its friends and supporters, Ripley directed his energies to transforming the farm into a representation of Fourierist principles. In 1844, Brook Farm officially adopted Fourierism and Ripley's *The Harbinger* became the unofficial organ of association-ism in New England, if not the nation.

The index to both Ripley's *The Harbinger* and Brisbane's *The Phalanx* are revealing of the contributors and their professions which included historians, essayists, journalists, poets, artists and physicians. Among them were homoeopathic pharmacist and publisher Otis Clapp; writer and journalist Parke Godwin; Henry James, Sr; homoeopath Joseph Hippolyte Pulte, MD, founder of Pulte Medical College in Cincinnati; physician and translator James John Garth Wilkinson; poet John Greenleaf Whittier; Unitarian minister and Transcendentalist Frederic Henry Hedge; and publisher Horace Greeley. Others affiliated with associationism and its national conventions included journalist and author Charles A Dana, and author, translator and homoeopath Charles J Hempel. James wrote 32 articles for the magazines while Wilkinson wrote 12, Godwin 152 and Greeley 2.[54]

It is tempting to brush all of Transcendentalism with the attributes of Emersonian individualism and self-reliance, stemming in part, perhaps, from the unusual level of Brahmin aloofness which the movement's many adherents bore toward society in general. However, this would be an exaggeration since the participants in Brook Farm's communal living, including its Transcendental (1840-4) and Fourierist (1844-7) periods, challenge this assumption. Brook Farm became a stepping-off point for utopian advocates to reorganize society on a local and national scale, an undertaking that should have exposed a potential inner tension in their conflicting ideologies. If the Brook Farmers began as Transcendentalists and moved to Fourierism, how could this happen without their forfeiting the individual freedom celebrated by the Transcendentalists? How could Transcendentalism with its preference for self-discovery mix with Fourierism and its utilitarian pursuit of communal happiness? Or, were they closer than it might appear?

One answer is to look at the writings of the public historian George Bancroft, son of a Unitarian minister from Worcester, Massachusetts, who, having trained in the scientific school of Leopold von Ranke at the University of Göttingen and authored the ten-volume *History of the United States*, aligned himself with President Andrew Jackson and the advocates of democracy. His two sons were students at the Brook Farm school and Bancroft corresponded regularly with Ripley as well as contributed to the Transcendental movement by writing translations and reviews of German literature. His belief that God spoke through the democratic majority certainly challenged the community's elitist connotations, suggesting that the Farm was not only egalitarian, but served as an experiment in applied democracy.[55]

Charles A Dana's *Lecture on Association in its Relation to Religion* provided the official apologia linking Fourierism with Christianity's millennial mission. Speaking before the New England Fourier Society in Boston, Dana explained that the establishment of associationism was the equivalent of reaching heaven on earth—the 'realization of the visions and promises of the past, and of the hopes of the present'. Without war, pestilence, or revolution, the association had become the peacemaker in a world of material discord, offering universal wealth through the twin doctrines of universal unity and attraction. Dana did not hold with Fourier's speculations on cosmogony, universal government, or what presumably took place on other planets. Still, he stood by Fourier and his associationism, not as a blind follower, but as one who appreciated his effort to heal the public and private ills of humankind.[56]

Dana did not view associationism as an attack on religion. Instead, it provided a rational blueprint by which the social reorganization of society would lead to the actualization of Christian fellowship. 'It prescribes no special religious belief, but leaves every man to the enjoyment of his own faith and the practice of its rites, provided that he does not thereby infringe on what is justly due to others', he wrote. This meant that in regions where Catholics predominated, the phalanx would have a greater proportion of Catholics. Moreover, other sects would be admitted and sectarian quarrels minimized due to the fact that the principle holding them together was their worldly interests, thereby creating an attitude of tolerance and non-interference. The bond that brought them together was not their religious faith but their common material interests. 'It is no uncommon thing to see very bitter religious prejudices disappear before the potency of common interests and social contact', he explained. The promise of Christianity was to be fulfilled through the transfiguration of humanity in associationism. It was not the salvation of individuals but the whole race. Moreover, argued Dana, it was time for Christianity to divorce itself from the division it had created between the natural and spiritual worlds. 'We should know that even now we may breathe the celestial ether, and have our common life transformed and illumined by infinite spiritual glories'.[57] Ultimately, the aim of Christianity lay not in some spiritual world for individual souls but in an association where the past, present and future destiny of humankind formed a unity of purpose. This was the moral destiny of man, utilizing a combination of agriculture and industry to bring humanity together in material, moral and religious harmony. When the elements of socialist idealism and Christian teleology were conjoined, there would come to exist a Universal Church or Church of Unity. Then the separation of church and state would cease to exist.[58]

Though Brisbane found little redeeming value in the traditional symbols of Christianity, most American associationists retained core elements of Christian ritual hoping at some time in the future to arrive at a 'unitary' set of principles that could substitute for the competitive nature of the nation's denominationalism.[59]

This Christian component to associationism emerged full blown when Brisbane left for Europe in 1844. With his departure, Parke Godwin took over editorial duties for *The Phalanx* and, several months later, published *A Popular View of the Doctrines of Charles Fourier* which offered a distinctive Swedenborgian interpretation of associationism at the expense of Fourier's and Brisbane's more secular design. Before long, associationism and Swedenborgianism became synonymous terms for those who tended to see Swedenborg as the spiritual counterpart to the secular side of Fourier's socialism.[60] As Fourierism turned increasingly Swedenborgian in its tenor, supporters pointed to numerous similarities (i.e., 'correspondences') between the phalanx and the vision of the *Maximus Homo*.[61]

In 1845, Ripley gave a lecture that elaborated on Fourier's life, his power of intellect and the reasonableness of his ideas. As an aside, he noted that the same year Fourier had been born was the year that Swedenborg had died, implying the advent of a new great thinker to replace the former. Thus, Brook Farm became an experiment that combined Transcendentalism with the Divine-Natural Humanity as expressed by Henry James, Sr and embedded in Swedenborg's conception of the *Maximus Homo*. The farm's enthusiasts were taking on the prospect of a divinely prescribed communal society seeking to realize the fullness of human potential in Christian love. For Boston's Swedenborgians, Brook Farm became their 'New Church'—a society of like-minded individuals who traded self-expression for a mystical identity of collective solidarity. It was not self-reliance but collective destiny that reigned over the relations of community members. It was shared divinity, not individual identity that ultimately counted. The Brook Farm phalanx became a scientifically derived blueprint for a socialized version of the Divine-Natural Humanity and the reign of divine wisdom on earth—a redeemed society expressing Christ's Second Coming.[62]

Henry James, Sr, arguably the most influential Swedenborgian during the time of the Brook Farm experiment, viewed the phalanx as the *Maximus Homo* transported from the heavenly planes to earth. As noted earlier, James's concept of the New Church was not that of a sect or ecclesiastical organization with a distinctive group of worshipers, but a state of mind best expressed in the divine order that infused the *Maximus Homo* with the harmonic divisions of labour operating within the phalanx. It was the group identity or *Maximus Homo*—not the individual—who possessed divinity. Self-reliance had turned into God/Man-reliance, and then to a divine social order where no one individual was redeemed until all had reached their perfection. The phalanx had become the 'body' of Swedenborg's *Maximus Homo*.[63]

Emerson, unlike James, was less than infatuated with the prospect of Fourierism in the Brook Farm experiment. This was evident as early as July 1842 in his essay 'Fourierism and the Socialists', published in *The Dial*. Although Brisbane had pushed his doctrines 'with all the force of memory, talent, honest faith, and importunacy', Emerson thought there was little in the message beyond an elegantly contrived mixture of spiritualism and materialism—a strange combination of Fourier and Swedenborg with the latter offering a new heaven as well as a new earth.

> Our feeling was, that Fourier had skipped no fact but one, namely, Life. He treats man as a plastic thing, something that may be put up or down, ripened or retarded, moulded, polished, made into solid, or fluid, or gas, at the will of the leader; or, perhaps, as a vegetable, from which, though now a poor crab, a very good peach can by manure and exposure be in time produced, but skips the faculty of life, which spawns and scorns system and system-makers, which eludes all conditions, which makes or supplants a thousand phalanxes and New-Harmonies with each pulsation. There is an order in which in a sound mind the faculties always appear, and which, according to the strength of the individual, they seek to realize in the surrounding world. The value of Fourier's system is that it is a statement of such an order externalized, or carried outward into its correspondence in facts. The mistake is, that this particular order and series is to be imposed by force of preaching and votes on all men, and carried into rigid execution. But what is true and good must not only be begun by life, but must be conducted to its issues by life.[64]

In his lecture titled 'New England Reformers', Emerson noted that:

these new associations are composed of men and women of superior talents and sentiments: yet it may easily be questioned, whether such a community will draw, except in its beginnings, the able and the good; whether those who have energy, will not prefer their chance of superiority and power in the world, to the humble certainties of the association; whether such a retreat does not promise to become an asylum to those who have tried and failed, rather than a field to the strong.

Friendship and association were fine things but he reminded his listeners that 'no society can ever be so large as one man'. To the extent that associations multiplied, they would always be answerable to the needs of the individual.[65] According to Kenneth Walter Cameron in *Emerson, Thoreau and Concord in Early Newspapers*, Emerson opposed Fourierism and its phalansteries because of their diminution of individualism—a direct challenge to his self-reliant individual.[66] For his part, however, James was notably 'shocked and chagrined' by Emerson's dismissive attitude, attributing it to a 'monstrous misrepresentation' of Fourier.[67]

In consummating their union with Fourierism, the Brook Farmers published a new constitution (20 May 1845) which set out their beliefs in the divine order of human society and the initiatives that needed to be prosecuted in order to realize the universal unity so desired.

We announce to them the dawning of that day for which they have so hopefully and so bravely waited the up-springing of those seeds that they and their compeers have sown. To them it will seem no exaggeration to say that we, their younger brethren, invite their assistance in a movement which, however humble it may superficially appear, is the grandest both in its essential character and in its consequences, that can now be proposed to man; a movement whose purpose is the elevation of humanity to its integral rights, and whose results will be the establishment of happiness and peace among the nations of the earth.[68]

By 1846, the Brook Farm phalanx had become the poster child of associationism and the hub of its reach into American society. For this effort, Channing was clearly the guiding engineer. In his appeal to the convention of association friends meeting in Boston in May 1846, he laid out the makings of a broad new contract.

I. The name of this society shall be the American Union of Associationists
II. Its purpose shall be the establishment of an order of society based on a system of joint-stock property; cooperative labor; association of families; equitable distribution of profits; mutual guarantees; honors according to usefulness; integral education; unity of interests; which system we believe to be in accord with the laws of divine providence and the destiny of man.
III. Its method of operation shall be the appointment of agents, the sending out of lecturers, the issuing of publications, and the formation of a series of affiliated societies which shall be auxiliary to the parent society; in holding meetings, collecting funds, and in every way diffusing the principles of Association: and preparing for their practical application, etc.

We have a solemn and glorious work before us: (1) To indoctrinate the whole people of the United States with the principles of associative unity; (2) to prepare for the time with the nation, like one man, shall reorganize its townships upon the basis of perfect justice.

A nobler opportunity was certainly never opened to men, than that which here and now welcomes Associationists. To us has been given the very word which this people needs as a guide in its onward destiny. This is a Christian Nation; and Association shows how human societies may be so organized in devout obedience to the will of God, as to become true brotherhoods, where the command of universal love may be fulfilled.[69]

According to John Humphrey Noyes, Fourierism 'was too bald a materialism to suit the higher classes of its disciples, without religion corresponding'. For that reason, Swedenborgianism became a 'godsend' to the enthusiasts of Brook Farm who 'made it the complement of Fourierism'.[70] Characterizing their worldly community as heaven on earth, associationist members looked for space to house a chapel, a 'Church of Humanity', or church of 'Universal Unity' where they could meet. William Channing even encouraged a communion service. In addition, a Sunday school was organized to teach 'Attractive Christianity', and evening discussion topics examined many of the new secular and religious movements afoot in the land, including socialism, spiritualism, mesmerism and phrenology. Not to be outdone, some members even indulged in a form of public confession to expiate their souls of life's transgressions.[71]

The connection between Swedenborg and Fourier was made never more clear than in Parke Godwin's *Popular View*, published in 1844.

> Thus far, we have given Fourier's doctrine of Universal Analogy; but it is important to observe that he was not the first man of modern times who communicated this view. Emanuel Swedenborg, between whose revelations, in the sphere of spiritual knowledge, and Fourier's discoveries in the sphere of science, there has been remarked the most exact and wonderful coincidences, preceded him in the annunciation of the doctrine, in many of its aspects, in what is termed the law of correspondences. These two great mind,—the greatest beyond all comparisons in our later days,—were the instruments of Providence in bringing to light the mysteries of His Word and Works, as they are comprehended and followed, in the higher states of existence. It is no exaggeration, we think, to say that they are the two commissioned by the Great Leader of the Christian Israel, to spy out the Promised Land of Peace and Blessedness.[72]

A very similar comparison was made by the British Fourierist Hugh Doherty, who began as a follower of Robert Owen and later sought to spread the views of Fourier through England. As with many of the associationists, he insisted that Fourier had discovered the divine arrangement of society foreshadowed by Swedenborg. The doctrines of Series, Universal Analogy and Attractions were not unlike Swedenborg's expositions of the doctrines of forms; of order and degrees; of series; of influx; and of correspondences. The author of *Memoir of Charles Fourier* and *Charles Fourier's Theory of Attractive Industry*, Doherty wrote frequently for *The Phalanx* demonstrating the parallelism between Fourierism and Swedenborgianism.

> I am a believer in the truths of the New Church, and have read nearly all the writings of Swedenborg, and I have no hesitation in saying that without Fourier's explanation of the laws of order in Scriptural interpretation, I should probably have doubted the truth of Swedenborg's illumination, from want of a ground to understand the nature of spiritual sight in contradistinction from natural sight; or if I had been able to conceive the opening of the spiritual sight, and credit Swedenborg's doctrines and affirmations, I should probably have understood them only in the same degree as most of the members of the New Church whom I have met in England, and that would seem to me, in my present state, a partial calamity of cecity [*sic*]. I say this in all humility and sincerity of conscience, with a view to future reference to Swedenborg himself in the spiritual world, and as a means of inducing the members of the New Church generally not to be content with a superficial or limited knowledge of their own doctrines.[73]

The disastrous fire at the Brook Farm phalanx on 3 March 1846, placed a damper on the hopes and dreams of associationism. Although the organization remained intact, its strength and cheerfulness had vanished. On 30 October 1847, it was announced that future issues of *The Harbinger* would be published in New York, clear indication that the Fourier-Christian utopian experiment of Brook Farm had collapsed and that its members had begun to join other associationists in New York, Philadelphia and the Midwest where they dedicated themselves to carrying forward Christian millennialism. Though Fourierism began as a quasi-secular form of socialism, its American expression was quasi-Christian in form and substance, subscribing to a spiritual perfectionist community existing upon the earth. According to Noyes, had Fourierism survived, it would have had Swedenborgianism for its state religion.[74]

* * *

The full explanation for the merger of Swedenborgianism and Fourierism did not come until after the collapse of the Brook Farm experiment. Charles Julius Hempel, one of the country's earliest homoeopathic physicians, a member of the 'Associationists of the United States of America', a member of the executive committee of editors for *The Phalanx* and author of *True Organization of the New Church as indicated in the Writings of Emanuel Swedenborg and Demonstrated by Charles Fourier*, spelled out what James had urged, namely, the conjoining of Swedenborg's grand cosmographic scheme with Fourier's serial arrangement of the social order. Building on Swedenborg's law of correspondences, divine influx, and doctrine of degrees, Hempel explained that the time had come for the writings of Swedenborg to unite with those of Fourier to realize the kingdom of God upon earth, the collective life of humanity or the *Maximus Homo*. Fourier's science completed the mission of Christ. In his discovery of the science of association, Fourier had placed himself in a position to lead humanity toward its exalted destiny, namely 'the realization of Universal Peace and Happiness on Earth'. According to Hempel, Fourier and Swedenborg had expressed the destiny of man in different languages but they were nonetheless 'perfectly identical doctrines'.[75]

Hempel explained the similarity between the orderly arrangement which Fourier had laid out in his phalansterian association and that which the Swedenborgians knew as the New Church. Given the universality of providence as expressed by Swedenborg and the unity of design as expressed by Fourier, the conjunction of heaven with the world was not just a hope but something capable of realization through the law of correspondences. Furthermore, the combination of Swedenborg's love principle with Fourier's passional principle ensured the realization of the divine order of heaven on earth. With his watchword of 'Onward to Harmony', Hempel dedicated his book to Fourier and the application of his principles to the doctrines of Swedenborg. By combining the ideas of these two great men, Hempel believed it possible for the association to serve the needs of the *Maximus Homo*.[76]

In advocating this alliance, Hempel was mindful that the followers of Fourier had indulged too much in the pride of science while the members of the New Church had reduced Swedenborg's doctrines to 'mere formulas of individual moralization' rather than using them as the basis for a unitary organization of society. Moreover, both groups had overlooked the possibility that the human race could be regenerated from the internal to the external as well as from the external to the internal. Having contented themselves with purifying the interiors of their own minds, they had lost sight of reconstructing the external man through the collective use of science and religion. But the external form, explained Hempel, was potentially more holy than the internal, uniting all into the One, thus constituting the Lord, or Divine Human. The Internal Man existed in its fullness and in peace when the External Man was made celestial. Only when the External Man adapted to the Internal could the earth with its inhabitants become a true image of heaven. Thus, both Swedenborg and Fourier occupied critical roles in the regeneration of humanity, bringing together their philosophical and theological writings to construct a harmonious communing of humankind.[77]

THOMAS LAKE HARRIS

Heavenly Fays

There is a plethora of revelation:
Some play at adept as they game at ball.
They dream——the brain-sick, moon-wise generation,——
That Heaven but serves the wonder-seeker's call.

(Thomas Lake Harris, *Star-Flowers*, 1886)

Schooled in Calvinism, Universalism, spiritualism, Swedenborgianism and Fourierism, the Christian mystic Thomas Lake Harris had little difficulty combining his beliefs into a triptych of sagas whose panoramic view depicted scenes of multiple earths and heavens. From his first trance-poem *An Epic of the Starry Heaven* in 1854, to his *Song of Theos* in 1903, he wrote for half a century, expanding on an esoteric philosophy that included sexual mysticism and galactic battles with demon spirits. In the course of this odyssey, he organized several communitarian enterprises which operated on a hierarchical construct of authoritarianism with himself at the helm. Identified by William James as 'our best known American mystic', and by Irish poet William Butler Yeats as a 'half-charlatan American visionary', Harris succeeded in gathering around him hundreds of devotees enamoured not only of his charismatic charm but by his ability to provide a path from the natural world to the celestial heavens. Among his followers were many from the liberal wing of the New Church in search of a temporal theocratic community where both human and celestial beings could live in peace and harmony. As a preacher and prophet, Harris was second to none in his eloquent all-absorbing sincerity. Like the puritan theologian Jonathan Edwards, he could be stern, yet loving, as he preached his revelatory teachings. Unlike contemporary Mary Baker Eddy, the founder of Christian Science, he led a personality cult that, upon his death, lacked the ability to survive. Nevertheless, with language that was philosophical, architectural, statuesque, pictorial and lyrical, his words flowed with karmic charm, leaving a permanent mark on the esoteric tradition in American thought and culture.[1]

Thomas Lake Harris (1823-1906)

Born in 1823 in Buckinghamshire, England, Harris emigrated with his parents to Utica, New York, where his father found employment as a grocer and auctioneer. In his youth, Harris was a dutiful son in a pious Calvinist household. Soon after his mother died, and a failed relationship with his new step-mother, he left home to live with the family of a Universalist minister whose liberal religious leanings were far removed from those of his parents. Before long, Harris became infatuated with the possibility of entering the ministry and serving as a respected preacher. After testing his abilities in neighbouring pastorates, and publishing numerous poems—a form of communication he found especially appealing—he was called in 1845 to the pulpit of the Fourth Universalist Society in New York City where he remained for two years. That same year, he married Mary Van Arnum, who bore him two sons.

While serving his pastorate, Harris became an ardent admirer of Andrew Jackson Davis, the so-called 'Poughkeepsie Seer', who claimed not only special clairvoyant powers to diagnose and prescribe for various diseases, but was said to have conversed with the spirits of Galen of Pergamum and Emanuel Swedenborg.[2] Identified by the utopian socialist John Humphrey Noyes as the 'great American Swedenborg', Davis utilized his revelatory visions to explain the cosmological origins of the universe, including the androgynous relationship of Father-God with Mother-Nature, and proposed an organization of humanity that advanced his gospel of Harmonialism.[3]

Harris was thoroughly impressed with Davis's clairvoyant abilities and, dimly remembering visits of fairies that had woven spells around him in his youth, sought to learn more of Davis's exceptional powers of visioning. Soon, Harris claimed the ability to communicate with celestial spirits, attributing these otherworldly experiences to his mother's spirit. Armed with this new talent, he began preaching the benefits of interstellar communication, attesting to conversations with Moses, Galileo Galilei, Tycho Brahe, Nicolaus Copernicus, Swedenborg, Alexander Von Humboldt and Johannes Kepler, as well as the inhabitants of Mars, Mercury and Jupiter.[4]

By the mid 1850s, spiritualism had become a hotly discussed and widely popular phenomenon in both Europe and America as rosters of lay and professional mediums appeared before private and public gatherings in homes, churches and halls to demonstrate their ability to connect with the spirit world. Mediumship became the rage as seances produced rappings, shadows, brief words, flying candle sticks, slate writing, ringing bells, raucous trumpet noises, levitated books and chairs, and other 'proofs' that, around a table in a darkened parlour, an anxious man or woman could exchange greetings with a dearly departed relative. So significant were the numbers of testimonials, newspaper articles and books affirming the phenomenon that American clergyman Theodore Parker opined that 'it seems more likely that spiritualism would become the religion of America [in 1856] than in 156 that Christianity would be the religion of the Roman Empire, or in 756 that Mohammedanism would be that of the Arabian population'.[5]

Much of America's love affair with spiritualism came by way of two sources: Swedenborg's *Heaven and Hell* which proponents 'reworked' to provide an explanation for why spirits were interested in communicating with humans; and Franz Anton Mesmer's animal magnetism, a force thought to pervade the universe and provide the medium for celestial messaging. Other explanations for spiritualist phenomena came from the research of chemist and philosopher Baron Karl von Reichenbach who announced the existence of a natural Odic force or aura emanating from all objects and noticeable by sensitive persons who could not only feel its presence but see it as a form of electric fire. Later, the telegraph served as spiritualism's most notable analogy, followed by the invention of wireless transmission which furnished supporters with the best illustration of how spirit messages occurred. Here was no esoteric formula or mystic rite but an independent and empirically observable phenomenon.[6]

Most of those who practised spiritualism came from Christian churches opposed to the ecclesiastical side of old-line denominations and which stressed love and hope; embraced radical individualism; extended divinity to collective humanity; taught direct communication with the Divine; and opposed eternal punishment. As Catherine L Albanese noted in her *Republic of Mind and Spirit*, Universalist ministers and ex-ministers such as John Murray Spear, Adin Ballou, Charles Hammond, William Fishbough, Samuel Byron Brittan and Harris played key roles in facilitating the acceptance of the spiritualist movement. Some, like Harris, even offered a God-through-man 'open-breathing' method of communication. Despite clear demonstrations of fraud, the voices and apparitions of inhabitants of the spirit world continued to feed the needs of Americans and Europeans well into the late nineteenth and early twentieth centuries. Spiritualism remained a very real and respectable phenomenon drawing both partisans and critics to its myriad of claims and counterclaims.[7]

Harris's enthusiasm for Davis ended in 1847 after the seer began a scandalous affair with a married woman and justified his actions in a manner that offended Harris's moral sensibilities. Following this break, Harris returned to his pastorate at the First Universalist Society only to leave a few months later to join the Apostolic Circle in Auburn, New York, led by medium Ann Benedict, a trance-speaker and 'rapping' spiritist who claimed visits from 'Paul the Apostle' and other prophets. There, Harris connected with the Revd James L Scott from Brooklyn, partnering with him to publish the semi-monthly periodical *Disclosures from the Interior and Superior Care of Mortals* which they explained, was 'dictated by spirits out of the flesh, and by them edited, superintended and controlled'.[8] That same year, Harris joined Scott's Mountain Cove Community in Fayette County, Virginia (now West Virginia), which consisted of a mill, church, several stores and a school. A spiritualist community awaiting the Day of Judgment, its members believed that life continued after death and, more importantly, that among them were specially gifted individuals who could communicate through mediumship with the deceased. Both Harris and Scott claimed this ability and quickly became rivals in their efforts to lead the community. As the two men vied for the leadership role, Harris's overbearing nature became an object of derision. Fearing revolt, he fled the community to take up a new calling as a lecturer and poet explaining his visions and demonstrating his mediumship abilities. By 1853, the millennial Mountain Cove Community had collapsed, leaving behind a history that is now part of the region's folklore.[9]

Celestial Poetry
During his months on the lecture circuit, Harris wrote poetry, much of it reflective of material he found in Andrew Jackson Davis's two-volume *Principles of Nature, Her*

Divine Revelations, and a Voice to Mankind which poet Sarah Helen Whitman praised 'as the most astonishing prodigy the world has ever seen next to Swedenborg's oracles'.[10] With words and ideas borrowed from Davis as well as from a host of other sources, Harris learned how to filter his mysticism through the porous membranes of his poetry to bring about the emerging divinity of mankind. His poetry took readers and listeners on a spiritual journey. He claimed that three of his early poems—*An Epic of the Starry Heaven*, *A Lyric of the Morning Land* and *A Lyric of the Golden Age* were dictated when he was in a state of trance induced by the visitation of ministering angels.[11]

An Epic of the Starry Heaven, dedicated to the memory of his wife who died in 1850, was a lengthy 6,000 line poem allegedly dictated in little more than twenty-six hours. Introduced by publisher Samuel B Brittan as having emanated from the spirit world, it recounted the 'quickening' process whereby the 'divine Harmony' was communicated from the spiritual 'World of Causes' made gloriously manifest in the 'World of Effects', or natural world. The poem recounted Harris's travels through the 'electrical ocean' of the solar system and included descriptions of the different races that populated the solar system.

> This mighty ocean whose white effluence flows
> Around each star like daylight round a rose
> In some sweet garden, thrills on every side
> With Spirits, who, upon its radiant tide,
> Tread lightly as on pavements clear as amber.
> Not lonely, not alone, the bright ones wander;
> Divine Societies that seem to be
> Of kindred essence, beautiful and free,
> Yet varying as the colors in the prism,
> All holy, from the planet-worlds arisen
> With varied motion, everywhere appear.[12]

In *A Lyric of the Morning Land*, Harris introduced the concept of *conjugial* (not conjugal) marriage of counterpart with counterpart which constituted the only real and indissoluble marriage. The concept of counterparts, which Plato attributed to Aristophanes, and which Swedenborg and Harris popularized, implied that each person had one true counterpart, *not* necessarily the person chosen in natural life. This romantic conception of love was sometimes used to justify infidelity on the basis of a transcendental reality where true marriage depended on the spiritual bonding of two individuals. It was a concept that laid aside the moral order for a world of love celebrated in classical and romantic poetry. Harris used the poem to announce his own counterpart, 'Queen Lily of the Conjugial Angels', whom he introduced as his spiritual bride in the celestial world. After being borne by fairies to the magic isle of Pallas, an 'ocean-mantled paradise' that corresponded to the planet Earth, he was able to experience with his 'Queen Lily' the fullness of marital pleasures in the eternal sphere.

> How beautiful is Home in Heaven! For there
> Our thoughts become substantial, and assume
> Ten thousand glorious forms and visions fair;
> And loving eyes with light of love illume
> The loving soul; and love illumes the air
> Until it burns, exhaling incense rare;
> And love transforms to feeling all our thought,
> Till truth in conscious bliss through all the soul is wrought.[13]

Here again, Harris turned the mystical writings of Davis and Swedenborg into poetry of the inner soul.

> We change to Angels by degrees;
> We rise to Heaven, but not by dying;
> We cross no dark, tumultuous seas;
> We leave no form in grave-yard lying;
> We change, unfolding, through our love,

An inner form of purer essence,
Until we rise to Heaven above,
And Worship in the Father's presence.

We lay aside the earthly mold,
Breathing away our grosser nature,
Till we are glowing forms unfold,
Transformed at once in mind and feature.[14]

Over the years, Harris wrote reams of love poetry, some of it fairly explicit. It was understood by followers that Harris lived in the natural world during the daytime hours but, at night, consorted with his 'Queen Lily' with whom he supposedly fathered three baby angels. The secret to achieving this spiritual state was by forsaking physical sex in the natural world and consummating a counterpart union with a celestial soulmate.

She with lips like crimson buds unclosing,
Holy Issa, kissed me in the night;
O'er our Planet gliding yet reposing,
Then I saw the LADY OF DELIGHT
Loving Issa kissed me in the night.

Issa led through me, from lips to fingers,
Blisses exquisite, in pure divine;
And I weave the blessed sense that lingers,
For this song-cup, filled with holy wine——
Issa kissed me with her lips divine.

When ye meet in star-time, blithe and social,
Lady Issa, from her marriage Bed,
Wafts, to find your bosoms, the ambrosial

Sweets of Heaven wherewith my lips are fed—
Issa kissed me from her marriage bed.[15]

In *A Lyric of the Golden Age*, which publisher Brittan praised as a 'remarkable spiritual clairvoyance', Harris described having 'lift[ed] the vail [*sic*] from the inner sense, and thus reveal[ed] scenes of the immortal life'.[16] As a sequel to *A Lyric of the Morning Land*, the poem described the spiritual spheres and harmonic orbs connected to earth; the types of mankind harmonically existing in corresponding spiritual spheres; and the uses and employments of angelic spirits.

Earth is an atom floating in the light
Of summer sunshine with its kindred stars;
A dew-drop shaken from God's blossomed thought.
He suffers evil in it for an end;
This end is like himself, divinely good,
And pure and sweet and infinitely free
From pain. All men are parts of one great whole;
Let but a dust-grain burrow in the eye,
And consciousness is tortured till that eye
Is freed from it, and harmonized again.
Humanity is many minds in one,
And many hearts and many lives in one.
All men and Angels find their place within
The universal human race, that dwell
On every earth, in every spirit-sphere.[17]

First Independent Christian Society

Following his lecture tour through the seaboard states and his second marriage to Emily Isabella Waters, a dedicated spiritualist with whom he claimed to live in celibacy, Harris returned to New York where he was drawn to a group of Swedenborgians who at the time were divided over the meaning and purpose of the New Church.

One group, represented by Henry James, Sr, advocated a form of social and philo-sophical radicalism that opposed all forms of organized ecclesiasticism. James saw the New Church in spiritual garb, believing that Swedenborg had never intended a 'bricks and mortar' entity. In the other camp were those who proposed a formal church organization to channel Swedenborg's revelations.[18] Drawn to this latter group, Harris and a number of devotees, including Horace Greeley, organized the First Independent Christian Society in 1857. Using poetry as the principal medium of his preaching, Harris proceeded to weave Swedenborg's revelatory visions into his ministerial teachings. As a non-denominational minister, however, he also adopted elements of spiritualism which he found useful in explaining his notions of the cosmos and its multitudes of spiritual inhabitants. Staking his claim among the Swedenborgians, Harris changed the name of his ministry to the Church of the Good Shepherd. Although viewed by many traditional Swedenborgians as operating outside the boundaries of the New Church, Harris had little difficulty in drawing followers to his idiosyncratic interpretation of Swedenborg.[19]

Arcana of Christianity

Harris's most extensive application of Swedenborg came with the publication of his *Arcana of Christianity: An Unfolding of the Celestial Sense of the Divine Word* in 1858, with appendixes added in 1859 and 1867. Guided by the 'Apostle John', he described a universe filled with multiple suns and planets whose souls ascended from their respective earths to their celestial, spiritual and ultimate heavens. Over and above the entire Arcana with its divine chorus of angels reigned the enthroned Lord Jesus Christ.[20] Written in a format replicating Swedenborg's *Arcana Caelestia*, Harris indexed his principles for quick reference; spoke of series and degrees in the orders of spirits; and described heavenly expanses and streams of influx that flowed through their layered orbs. Like Swedenborg, he explored the analogies in the law of disease that affected the human constitution; examined the spiritual organs which formed the Divine Human; described the pandemonium of the different hells; and reiterated the promise of the Divine Spirit destined to cleanse and purify earth. He also recounted conversations with Swedenborg on such topics as internal respiration, conjugial love, the Church of the New Jerusalem, spiritualism, citizens from other planets, and man's love of self and the world which he referred to as *proprium*.[21]

One of the unique aspects of *Arcana of Christianity* was Harris's intense fascination with fairies, called 'fays' or 'little brothers'. Fairies were at the centre of belief among Victorians. A multitude of books and articles by eminent authors—including Scottish physician and writer Sir Arthur Conan Doyle; Welsh author and mystic Arthur Machen; Irish poet William Butler Yeats; geologist Hugh Miller; and English novelist and poet Charlotte Bronte—spoke of fairies living in the Anglo-Celtic enclaves of Cornwall, Wales and the Scottish Highlands.[22] Yeats even compared Swedenborg's angels to the fairies of Irish folklore, remarking on their sporting antics in the heavens and their preference to linger in the pastoral haunts of poets and other highly sensitive individuals. For Harris meanwhile, they floated in the ether in collections resembling doves and nightingales, visible only to those whose degree of sight called 'natural-aromal' had been restored.[23]

Fairies were infantile 'innocences' in human frame whose single most important task was battling the enemy of *scortation*, the debased sexual passion judged to be the 'world's greatest curse', which constituted the root of *proprium*. Those humans whose bodies were able to inhale the 'Divine Breath', were blessed with help from the 'fay' angels of 'Lilistan' to achieve the divine-natural sexual purity of celestial marriage. 'As the human body becomes demagnetized from the poisonous injections of infernal demons', wrote Arthur A Cuthbert, a long-time devotee of Harris, 'their melodious voices will be heard responding with a faint exquisite music to the high and holy inspirations of the Divine Love'.[24] Fairies became a preoccupation of Harris and his followers who gave special names to their favourites including 'Prince Wisdom', 'Sir Sunbeam Courage', 'Lady Precious Pearl' and 'Lady Pink-Ears'.

The universe is made of tiny men:
In holy infancy their endless lives
Round ever to an orb of perfect light:
And matter, in its varying forms and hues
And subtle harmonies of airy flame,

Is their pavilion, where, in choral dance,
They weave the flying tapestry of space.
These are the fays of Nature, brethren small
To Angels and the radiant human kind;
And love of good and truth, for their own sakes,
And the creative blessedness they bring,
And love of God, who is the Good and True,
Is the religion of the Fairy world;
Nor can they ever fall away from this,
But bloom and ripen with an infant's joy.[25]

Harris later politicized his *Arcana of Christianity* with appendixes suggesting that the American Commonwealth had been placed in the centre of the New Heaven where it served as 'the pivotal power of the earth' in search of divine harmony. Similarly, he noted the wickedness of Roger B Taney, Chief Justice of the United States, who delivered the majority opinion in *Dred Scott v. Sandford* (1857); the evils of debased and half-pauperized immigrants whose hordes 'vomit[ed] upon the shores of the Western Continent'; and the destruction of American institutions by the Roman Catholic Celt. Regarding Abraham Lincoln, Harris observed:

I heard in the night, an angel whispering in the ear of the President of the
United States, 'you must emancipate, you must emancipate'; but at the
same time the evil genius of this kind man, wove subtle spells to hold him
in a state of irresolution. I beheld the spirits of the lost inhabitants of the
Slave States, almost *en masse*, moving in advance of the rebel hordes; great
numbers of them being present in every battle. . . . The South was characterized by comparative unity of council and inflexible decision of purpose but
the North, spiritually, was a divided house.[26]

Identified by his disciples as the modern Swedenborg, Harris spoke frequently of his ventures into the spirit world, his meetings with heavenly spirits, his travels to the different planetary and heavenly orbs with their peculiar societies and races, and the requirements needed for entering conjugial habitation and ultimate beatitude. Combining cosmology and theology, he built upon Swedenborg's *Last Judgment* to explain the societies of men and angels, and the nuptial blending of men and women in celestial (and sexual) mysticism. Insisting that his mysticism extended beyond the revelatory writings of Swedenborg, he reasoned that the Swedish seer had revealed only a portion of the truth, leaving him to complete the Lord's work. Despite Harris's best intentions, however, his *Arcana of Christianity* and his New Church catechism titled *First Book of the Christian Religion* were repudiated by New Church leaders as a direct challenge to Swedenborg's *Arcana Caelestia* which they considered to be the only authentic Word.[27]

Herald of Light

As pastor of the Church of the Good Shepherd, Harris served as editor of *The Herald of Light*, a monthly magazine owned by the New Church Publishing Association, whose purpose was to extol the importance of spiritualism in the New Church.[28] The periodical's six volumes, published between May 1857 and August 1861, averaged four hundred pages each and were dictated mostly by Harris himself. Described as 'a journal of the Lord's New Church', it conveyed the principles of the New Church using a combination of Swedenborgianism, poetry and choice elements of spiritualism. The magazine also advertised Harris's books and pamphlets including *The Wisdom of Angels*; *First Book of the Christian Religion*; *The Song of Satan*; and *Hymns of Spiritual Devotion*. Several of these writings echoed the words of Andrew Jackson Davis's *The Philosophy of Spiritual Intercourse* and Robert Dale Owen's *Footfalls on the Boundary of Another World* in that they combined spiritualism with some form of theo-utopianism.[29]

Using the magazine as his voice, Harris laid out the divine plan of redemption, explaining the importance of internal breathing as a path to grace; the concept of the bisexual God; the turning points in history of the Flood and Incarnation; and his own role at the centre of the cosmic drama. In issue after issue, he called himself the 'pivotal man', defending humanity in the ongoing struggle between the forces of heaven and hell and recounting his personal battles with the 'infernal spirits' who sought to inject their influence into the world. 'Remaining sometimes for hours in prayer to the Lord for strength to combat, while the physical frame was subject to unheard-of tortures, I knew what it was to die daily', he wrote. 'Realizing full well, however, that it was needful for Divine ends that I should thus suffer, and that my agonies were continually mitigated by an interposing influence, I sought silently and in entire resignation to bear the heavy load'.[30] Reminiscent of the mesmerist and spiritual healer Phineas P Quimby of Portland, Maine, who, during the early years of his healing career, claimed to transfer the sufferings of his patients onto his own soul, Harris battled the world's evil forces in order to quicken the spiritual resurrection of his social circle. As he explained, not until the divine influx descended into his heart did he achieve victory over these infernals.[31]

Years later, in *The Intellectual Repository and New Jerusalem Magazine*, a publication of the General Conference of the New Church in London, Robert McCully accused Harris of plagiarism and of misrepresenting the views of Swedenborg. According to his investigations, Harris had used mediumistic communications with unseen beings not higher than the lowest plane of angelic life and, in the process, destroyed the very purpose and intended effect of the Incarnation. Profanity was at the very heart of Harris's writings, McCully charged, in distinct contradiction with the central facts of the revealed doctrines of the New Church. Moreover, he accused Harris of borrowing liberally from other writers, claiming that *The Great Republic: A Poem of the Sun* had been a plagiarization of Percy Shelley's *Queen Mab*; *A Lyric of Morning Land*, a watered down copy of Shelly's *Epipsychidion*; and *A Lyric of the Golden Age*, a close resemblance to the works of John Keats, George Gordon Byron, William Wordsworth, Samuel Coleridge and Thomas Hood. 'Alas! there is nothing *celestial* in [Harris's writings]', he concluded, 'except the beautiful truths taken from Swedenborg, and only too frequently placed upon the wrong poet's lips'. Remove from Harris's 'Apocalypse' (a series of lectures given in 1865) everything derived from Fourier and the doctrinal writings of Swedenborg and little remained. By the mid-1880s, most Swedenborgians had tired of Harris, recognizing that he had usurped Swedenborg's ideas only to sully them with nonsensical theories.[32]

Great Britain

Claiming to have received a spiritual directive to preach abroad, Harris resigned his ministry in 1859 and sailed to England with his wife where he was welcomed by members of the New Church and leading Swedenborgians, including James John Garth Wilkinson, a homoeopathic physician, translator, Fourierist and advocate of spiritualism. Wilkinson, a close friend of Henry James, Sr, and acquainted as well with Thomas Carlyle, Ralph Waldo Emerson, Robert Browning and Nathaniel Hawthorne, opened his home to Harris and his wife. Wilkinson's brother William, a solicitor who worked for the Swedenborg Society, was equally supportive of Harris's ministry and of spiritualism in general.[33]

Following his stay with the Wilkinson family, Harris retired to Bolton Abbey in Yorkshire where he spent twelve weeks composing *Regina: A Song of Many Days*, a lyrical poem published simultaneously in both London and New York. Drawing on scientific theory and theological lore, Harris recounted how atomic particles had evolved into human form. Without poetic understanding, he claimed, the true unfolding of the world could not be understood or appreciated for it was the poet who opened the inner layers of the mind, quickening perception of the planets and of the solar system. Embracing ninety-six pages, *Regina* began where *A Lyric of the Morning Land* ended, lifting its readers into the airy regions of Fairy Land.

> Where the rose-tree buds unbar,
> Where the purple pansies are,
> Where the crimson wildings play
> With the last-blown mountain May,
> Fairies all are glad and gay.[34]

At the end of the summer, Harris travelled to Manchester where he preached twice each Sunday for twelve weeks at the Mechanics' Institute. At first small, his numbers increased gradually until he reached audiences of four and five hundred. Topics included 'Love', 'The Divine Charity', 'The Philosophy of Decay', 'The Recognition of Friends in Heaven', 'The Last Words of Jesus', 'The Ideal and the Actual', 'The

Christian Pilgrim's Progress', 'Peril and Safety in the Path of Life', 'The Relation of Faith and Charity' and 'Our Future'. Published under the title *Truth and Life in Jesus*, the lectures explained that the New Church had, besides its spiritual mission, both a social and political obligation to bring salvation to the collective society of man; that no 'factitious value' attached to the rites and ceremonies of the New Church; that it was best for the advocates of the New Church to separate from their present ecclesiastical connections; and that the only objective of the New Church was to realize Christ's Kingdom on earth. Harris explained his ministry as a composite of an 'illumined' priest and an equally illumined lecturer, availing himself of influx from heaven. Accordingly, he announced Christ's descent (influx) into mental perception could be known by means of 'Divine Breath'. Here was the sustaining influx from the living God which flowed into the indestructible and immortal inner man, imparting the wisdom of the higher life.[35]

On his return to London, Harris gave a set of lectures at the Marylebone Literary and Scientific Institute, subsequently published as *The Millennial Age, Twelve Discourses on the Spiritual and Social Aspects of the Times*. He also published *Modern Spiritualism: Its Truths and Its Errors*, a pamphlet advertised as a manual on the facts and principles of Christian spiritualism in which he warned of the dangers of mesmerism and demoniacal possession. According to Margaret Oliphant, the cousin and biographer of Laurence Oliphant, one of Harris's followers, these were 'shabby little volumes of sermons and addresses delivered by him in various localities—chapels in provincial towns . . . which attracted sufficient interest to be taken down by a shorthand writer' and receive notice as some new religious doctrine.[36]

Overall, Harris's Swedenborgian audiences found not the spokesperson they were seeking but an American curiosity, namely, an evangelistic poet eager to take on the mantle of charismatic seer and 'pivotal man' in whom the cosmic forces of good and evil battled for predominance. This explains why Harris's visit failed to live up to expectations and why he spared few words in assessing the audiences who came to hear his message. 'Thought in America is electric', he observed, but in England it runs 'like a slow river through the marshes'.

Men walk in a half dream, oppressed with the nightmare of dead or dying institutions. The public conscience is deadened or corrupted by the impieties of the State religion. Ecclesiastical stipendaries, who for three centuries have sat in the place of confessors and Apostles, have biologized the land into the strangest of stupidities. England is now at the ebb of the tide in spiritual things. Her splendid universities represent the dead past, which returns no more, and produce, by their spiritual sphere, a profound torpor of all the nobler faculties.[37]

Harris concluded that England's dissenting sects were 'lost in the worship of wealth', having stripped themselves of the spiritual sciences and social truths. He lamented that the British had not risen above their official religion which served as a millstone around their necks. He also found the nation's preaching at fault, declaring it 'shallow, pedantic and empirical'. It was 'just what the Pharisees doled out to the perishing classes in Jerusalem, when Judea was in her darkest days'. Nevertheless, he found the preachers of the New Church to be men of 'hopeful and kindly spirit' who he trusted would unite in fashioning a 'more ardent and penetrative life' for the British people.[38] Noting that Swedenborgianism 'lingers rather than lives' in England, he predicted that Swedenborg's teachings would find a more hospitable home in America.[39]

At the end of his preaching tour, Harris and his wife relocated to Scotland where they stayed for much of 1861 gathering devotees, many of whom were seeking a less structured New Church, calling themselves the Brotherhood of the New Life. With the Brotherhood as his foundation, Harris decided the time had come to build a 'community' of believers rather than another church, and to announce the essentials of a new universal Brotherhood. Set apart from other church sects, this Brotherhood would share a celestial-natural environment with fellow brethren who would live in harmony with the pivotal man. Brotherhood members, none of whom were poor or uneducated, seemed more like middle-class bohemians open to a variety of beliefs including fairies, open breathing ('Divine Breath'), celestial counterparts, celibacy and asceticism.[40]

Returning to America with members of the Brotherhood, Harris found the country embroiled in Civil War which he interpreted as the beginning of a spiritual revolution that would eventually liberate, enfranchise, organize and protect the labouring classes from economic strife. Viewing the events as an opportunity, he proposed a theo-socialist community that was philosophical and mystical in nature, conceived as a return to a Golden Age which preceded the Fall and where all could live in divine harmony and participate in the 'Divine Breath'. Now with the imminent coming of the Golden Age, the work of the Apocalypse could commence. In this new perfected society, all would live in 'conjugial purity' (i.e., chastity) which meant the merger of earthly marriage with love of the Divine. This, he explained, would be the nature of the Brotherhood's New Jerusalem. As a New Church minister, Harris considered himself related to all believers in the Lord and welcomed newcomers to his invisible yet universal body of believers held together by 'Divine Breath'.[41] 'In the new respiration', Harris explained, 'God gives an atmosphere that is as sensitive to moral quality as the physical respiration is to natural quality; and this higher breath, whose essence is virtue, builds up the bodies of the virtuous, wars against disease, expels the virus of hereditary maladies, renews health from its fountains, and stands in the body as a sentinel against every plague'. The Divine Breath became the guiding power and primary doctrine which accompanied their pastoral life, their sense of chastity and their special theory of love and marriage. It was through this new respiration that mankind would become regenerate, that society would be reconstructed, that disease would banish and the doctrines set forth by Swedenborg would sweep over the earth which would come under a millennial reign.[42]

Wassaic and Amenia Communities

Harris's choice of site for his New Jerusalem was Wassaic, a small village in Dutchess County, New York, where members of the Brotherhood gathered in 1861 to anxiously await the dispensing of his revelatory visions. Within the Brotherhood, there was an overpowering belief that its members were witnessing a living religion whose leader communed regularly with the Divine. This experience was described in Mary S Emerson's *Among the Chosen*, a fictionalized account written in 1884 by one of the community's members, in which a follower, Rosalie, explained: 'Father John [Harris] had touched just the chord in her nature that was waiting to vibrate; he had shown her that she loved herself more than God, that she loved her children more than God's children'.[43]

In Wassaic, Harris led the Brotherhood in the exercise of the Divine Breath, considered to be Adam's original mode of respiration which he lost with original sin. Harris's wife was reputedly the second to experience the celestial breathing, followed by a succession of Brotherhood members. As explained by Harris, there were twelve different levels of respiration peculiar to the inhabitants of the universe:

> First, respiration from internals to externals through the Celestial Heaven: Second, through the Spiritual Heaven: Third, through the Ultimate Heaven: Fourth, through the Ultimate Earth of Spirits: Fifth, through the series of world-souls: Sixth, through the life-world of each Heaven: Seventh, through the love-world of each Heaven: Eighth, through the form-world of each Heaven: Ninth, through the essence-world of each Heaven: Tenth, through the harmony-world of each Heaven: Eleventh, through the most immediate access of the Divine Spirit through the inmost degree of the will: Twelfth, through the full and plenary possession of the man by the Divine Spirit.[44]

For Harris and the Brotherhood, the Divine Breath was a concrete reality, not a mystical or spiritual concept. It was the manner in which life (influx) had entered the body of Adam and later at the time of Christian redemption. Those who possessed it had true knowledge of Christ, uplifting their bodies to blessedness with clear consciousness of all the good there was in the world. Divine Breath prepared the individual and the community for the universal changes scheduled to occur over time. When the internal respiration opened and the Holy Spirit breathed into the individual, it vibrated through every part of the body—from internal to external—and from this ensued the ability of the individual to breathe 'against the breaths of the whole world, and against Hell itself'. The body became the 'theatre of a divine war' against the knowledge of evil in the natural world.[45] The 'higher breath', also protected the body from disease and hereditary maladies and 'stands in the body as a sentinel against every plague'. It fostered love of family, restrained the body from impetuosity, and overcame inertia. In essence, it was a 'great regulative power' uniting and inspiring humanity. Not until the twelfth and last mode did the Divine Spirit breathe directly through all the organs, suspending consciousness and making use of the individual as 'a direct medium and organ of communication'.[46]

Harris referred frequently to Swedenborg's writings on respiration and the nature of its application from ancient times into the present. This included the deep inhaling of the morning air; the varied respirations of the scholar and artisan compared to the glutton and drunkard; the breaths of a mob moved by violent passions; the respiration of a charmed audience or solitary thinker; and the breathing calm of the ecstasist in the reveries of prayer. Harris noted that as the mind left the world of natural things, the respirations grew feeble. 'The good man, possessing mere natural respiration, seeks God in prayer', he observed, 'but when he rises to heights of communion where language is drawn up to thought, then thought stilled in the quietude of love, there is hardly a breath in the body'.[47]

The Brotherhood remained at Wassaic from the autumn of 1861 to the end of 1863, when Harris decided to move the community to a better location at Amenia, four miles distant. There they followed a scheme of government that reflected a mixture of Platonism, Swedenborgianism and Fourierism. There, too, Harris built a gristmill and several small farm buildings, and established 'The First National Bank of Amenia' with himself as president.

Interestingly, the Brotherhood preferred to call themselves 'The Use', a Swedenborgian term, meaning 'all things useful in creation'. As one member of the Amenia community explained:

> With us everything must have a *use* and everyone his work. We have none set apart for the ministry, and we have no salaries to spare for any clergyman, minus a cure, who chanced to come our way. Our maxim is, that the more spiritual we become, the more practical we must become also. We must meet the world in its own way and on its own terms, and conquer all uses, arts, sciences, industries for the City of our God, until the time comes of which it is written 'that the kings of the earth do bring their glory and honour into her'.

Our community here we often call '*the Use*'. Everyone here must have his or her 'use' or 'uses', according to his or her special genius.[48]

Loved by his followers, Harris stood immune from criticism as the Brotherhood eagerly awaited his revelations from 'Queen Lily'. Even his occasional 'fits' or 'spasms', which were usually concealed from members, were interpreted as Harris's battle with demons in the struggle between good and evil. Like Jim Jones of the People's Temple and David Koresh of the Branch Davidians, Harris was a disciplinarian, meting out punishment and favours, and demanding total obedience. His authority included separation of families, changes in assignments, isolation, menial work and even banishment. Although he forbade the use of tobacco, both he and Jane Waring were smokers—Waring with a clay pipe and Harris with his imported cigars. Waring, a member of a highly respected New England family, had contributed nearly a quarter of a million dollars to Harris when she joined the Church of the Good Shepherd. She eventually married Harris in 1892 following the death of his second wife. Like Harris's former wives, she claimed that the marriage remained celibate, choosing not to usurp the role of 'Queen Lily' as her husband's spiritual counterpart. 'Father and his Lily stand *alone* the same as ever in their pivotal service and I am the same as ever their humble little handmaiden whom they have honored by a representative position before the world', she assured the Brotherhood.[49]

Even though Harris's community lived in chastity, rumours persisted of ritualistic intercourse among its members. As noted earlier, Harris opposed the natural affections and typically insisted on the separation of husbands and wives. All were to maintain celibacy by giving themselves wholly to God. Some marriages did take place, but chastity remained in force for all members of the community. This restriction, however, did not extend to celestial marriage where the topic of conjugal sex remained a preoccupation. Each individual had a counterpart of the other gender in the spiritual plane and communed with their celestial bride or bridegroom through an inner revelatory process that allegedly involved a non-physical experience of conjugial intercourse.[50] How this played out in practice became the subject of considerable debate since 'Miss X' in Ray Strachey's *Religious Fanaticism, Extracts from the Papers of Hannah Whitall Smith* was directed to get into bed with the 'Queen Lily' who, conveniently, was in Harris's body. Since Harris surrounded himself with a devoted circle of women, this, coupled with rumours of female followers sharing his bed in order to seek their celestial counterparts, made for interesting gossip.[51]

Along with a band which regularly played at community functions, music was used to evoke the powers of 'Queen Lily' and Harris's poetic revelations. In addition, individual members offered singing lessons, gave lectures on natural history and supplied other forms of entertainment intended to sustain their religious bent. Besides celestial marriage, the Brotherhood was fixated on the millennium which, over time, dominated much of Harris's revelatory preaching.

Harris was far less successful with the younger generation who, according to community rules, lived separate from their parents. Among them, Harris had little hold, and their years in the community were often described as unhappy. His refusal to send Brotherhood children to public school had a long-term negative effect on families, often leading to disloyalty. Most of the youth resented Harris's punishments, were suspicious of his claims, and objected to the attention he paid to the community's young girls.[52]

Laurence Oliphant

It is impossible to write about Harris without including his relationship with Lady Maria Campbell Oliphant and her son Laurence Oliphant, a prominent British aristocrat, author, traveller, diplomat and member of the House of Commons. A witty man with great personal charm, Laurence found himself drawn to social balls and other public events despite his desire to be God-fearing. Torn between the puritanical ideas of an evangelical childhood and the easy manner in which he succeeded in society, he lived a troubled life of contrasts. Seeking to satisfy his mother's concern for his soul, he practised self-examination, hoping through this process to resolve the emotional conflicts experienced between his reckless lifestyle and his more sobering moments. In one of his letters to Lady Oliphant he wrote, 'I can well understand any man giving up in despair the hope of finding a creed containing elements powerful enough to govern him absolutely. It is a long time before he . . . recognises again all that is good and beautiful in it. I do think that God satisfies every man's craving in this respect . . . if he keeps on fighting and groping'.[53]

When Laurence heard about Harris in 1860, his world changed irrevocably.[54] Although the two men were dissimilar in many respects, Laurence found in Harris someone who made no pretense of being anything other than a prophet who could heal his conflicted self. As explained by historians Herbert Schneider and George Lawton, 'There was no struggle of wills. Harris, a dominating personality to everyone at this time, was especially overwhelming to Oliphant, who was then in a most susceptible state of mind. He wanted to be dominated'.[55] Having searched for happiness by living a dissipated lifestyle which included fawning women, constant temptations and sexual license, Laurence found his life increasingly contemptuous and barren of meaning. For too long, he had submerged his yearnings through dissipation and travel. Reflective of this state of mind, he wrote an anonymous satirical novel titled *Piccadilly* whose characters lived hypocritical lives, acting out one in public, and another in the privacy of their homes.[56]

It seems clear in retrospect that Harris served as a catalyst for Oliphant who was anxious to make a momentous change in his life. In 1865, he and his mother asked for admission into the Brotherhood and, two years later, they joined the community at Amenia. For his part, Harris was a demanding taskmaster, who, after acquiring from the Oliphants much-needed capital to secure the purchase of land and buildings, demanded total humility from Laurence whom he ordered to begin a period of isolation, living apart from the rest of the community members and cleaning cattle sheds as part of his purifying process. Determined to sacrifice everything for the sake of salvation, Laurence accepted total obedience and a probationary period that lasted far longer than the community's other members. Nevertheless, he was prepared to leave the world he had known, including his seat in the House of Commons, for a voyage into self-discovery.[57]

Salem-on-Erie
With the addition of Laurence and his mother as Brotherhood members, Harris expanded his sights and, with the assistance of Lady Oliphant, whose money and

brains played a prominent role in the negotiations, purchased several farms (approximately 1,600 acres) near the village of Brocton, on the shore of Lake Erie, about fifty miles west of Buffalo. The new surroundings were such an improvement that membership in the Brotherhood expanded several fold. In time, the location, known as 'Salem-on-Erie', supported a railroad station, restaurant, general store and hotel. Although focused mainly on the dairy business, the community also invested in several varieties of grapes which sold well.

The members of the Brocton Brotherhood came principally from the northern and southern states, England, Scotland and Ireland. In addition, the group included four students from the samurai class in Japan who arrived by way of England and Scotland. The students were part of an original fifteen who, against the shogun's prohibition of travelling overseas, were smuggled out of Satsuma by the daimios with instructions to study Western ways and technology. One of the students, Kanaye Nagasawa, was thirteen at the time and lived with the family of Thomas Berry Glover in Aberdeen, Scotland. Glover, a successful merchant in Nagasaki, had made the travel arrangements for the fifteen students. When the funds supporting the students ended, all but six returned to Japan. At the request of Laurence Oliphant, Harris met those that remained and offered to continue their education in exchange for their labour. Four of the six agreed and travelled to the Brotherhood's colony in Brocton where their labour in the community's vineyards became their education in Western ways. Eventually three of the four returned to Japan, leaving Nagasawa alone to learn the art of viticulture.[58]

Initially the community practised communism but evolved into a form of modified socialism, advocating altruism, mutuality and the Christian ideal of social service. Salem-on-Erie claimed no written creed or form of government, no prescribed rituals, and no obligatory observance on the Sabbath. Instead, it adhered strictly to the revelatory dicta from Harris or his delegate, Jane Waring. In most years, the community, whose numbers averaged between eighty and a hundred members, operated at a deficit, which meant depending on new recruits and their possessions to support the enterprise. Once they had transferred their possessions into the common fund, they lived on the favours Harris chose to give them. According to Louis Le Grande in an article concerning the Brotherhood for *The Illustrated American* in 1892:

These people hold that the individual man has no real life in himself; that all life, and with it the virtues and energies of life, are the result of a divine inflowing; that our Lord is the one pure and living God, their sole ruler, actuator, and director. They are monarchists, who recognize the Divine Man for their sovereign; they are socialists who believe that the worship of God is the service of humanity. If they revere, in Christ, the Lord, they also accept in him the artisan. While they do not reject the sacred observance of accustomed religion, they believe in uplifting every avocation of life into a permanent religious ministration. They hold that it is the function of regenerate man to regenerate society; that this work must be initiated and carried out by the entrance of the cultured, the prosperous, the gifted, as well as those of humbler state, into those employments which have been counted menial; and that those labors should be done from the inspiration of the Divine love, which have heretofore been performed from selfish greed or at the mere spur of material necessity.[59]

With the exception of their long hair, community members were hardly distinguishable from their neighbours, and certainly no different from other religious communities in the day. All the members of the Brotherhood acquired special names. Laurence was 'Woodbine', while Lady Oliphant was 'Viola', Miss Waring, 'Dovie' and Harris, 'Father' or 'Papa Faithful'. Others carried names such as 'Steadfast', 'Harmonious', 'Dimple', 'Earnest' and 'Sweet Brier'. Living in a mansion called 'Vine Cliff' and in the company of several of the women 'elect' (including Waring), Harris led the faithful in dictatorial fashion, demanding total obedience. His wife, on the other hand, lived under strict supervision in another part of the estate as she was thought by many to be mentally unbalanced due to what critics attributed to the community's practice of celibacy.[60]

On occasion, the Brotherhood used the strength of its numbers to benefit the community at general elections—both locally and nationally. On the national scene, it voted as a block to support Horace Greeley's candidacy for President and, locally, to have a railroad station erected convenient to the hotel and restaurant built and operated by the community.[61]

Fountain Grove

In 1875, following several advance visits, Harris moved thirty-five to fifty of the Brotherhood's 'elite' to land several miles north of Santa Rosa where, surrounded by landscaped grounds, he established the 'California Use' to which he gave the name 'Fountain Grove'. Operating first as a dairy, and then as a winery, the community turned its six hundred acres into pasturage for cows, hay for grain, olive and fruit trees, and vineyards for the growing of commercial grapes which it processed into Cabernet, Pinot Noir and Zinfandel wines. The community also established the Fountain Grove Press which published Harris's ongoing revelations, including *Hymns of the Two-in-One*, *The Concept of the Word*, *Bridal Hours*, *Battle Bells*, *The Brotherhood of the New Life* and *Conversation in Heaven: A Wisdom Song*.

Like its sister community in Salem-on-Erie, Fountain Grove stood outside the mainstream denominations of the day, drawn to moral perfection and millennial expectations. By 1878, the faithful were living in anticipation of the divine drama that would soon bring forth the final victory over evil and the realization of the kingdom of heaven. In numerous letters, members expressed their anticipation of this culminating moment of truth and the beginning of the New Age. In this context, wine became central to the Brotherhood's communal activities, a sacramental substance used to enhance communication with the divine spirit.[62]

Harris invited only a select few from Brocton to join him at Fountain Grove. Among them was eighteen-year-old Kanaye Nagasawa, the Japanese Christian who Harris had first met in Scotland and who remained a lifelong follower; Alice Oliphant, Laurence's wife; and Jane Waring. Curiously neither Harris's wife Emily or Laurence were summoned to join the community.[63] By 1880, some sixty of Harris's followers were living at the theo-socialist community of Fountain Grove in structures built according to specifications that would allow them to be transported into the celestial spheres at the time of the millennium. Included among the buildings was 'The Manor House' where Harris lived with a small group of women; 'The Commandery', a three-storey structure that housed the men; 'The Cottage' which housed women; a massive stone winery with a capacity for 600,000 gallons; and numerous other smaller buildings. By 1890, Fountain Grove had become one of the largest wineries in California.[64]

Laurence Oliphant, among those members of the Brotherhood left behind at Salem-on-Erie, announced in 1880 that he was receiving revelations and began to challenge Harris's authority in the management of the community's property holdings. The outcome was a schism that resulted in the reimbursement to Oliphant of his initial investment in the community, a settlement that prompted other members to demand the same. The disruption led to the eventual liquidation of Salem-on-Erie in 1882. Still, Harris held firm control over Fountain Grove whose press continued to publish his revelations.[65]

After leaving Salem-on-Erie, Laurence and his wife Alice settled in Haifa, near Mount Carmel, in Syria (or what is today Israel), where they founded a community with themselves as prophets of a new religion. There, too, Oliphant authored *Sympneumata: Or, Evolutionary Forces Now Active in Man* and *Scientific Religion; Or, Higher Possibilities of Life and Practice Through the Operation of Natural Forces* in which he laid out his own revelatory visions before dying of cancer in 1888.[66]

Theosophy and the Adepts

Given that Harris's beliefs were the outgrowth of esoteric elements within Christianity, and particularly Swedenborgianism, his interest in Eastern religion and philosophy did not mature until the late 1870s when several Scottish members of the Brotherhood were drawn to Madame Helena Blavatsky and Henry Steel Olcott and their occult movement known as Theosophy. Unlike the spiritualist Andrew Jackson Davis who claimed conversations with Swedenborg, and the Fox sisters whose communication with the other world consisted of tapping or rapping sounds on walls, Theosophy encouraged religious and philosophical thinkers to look to India for their enlightenment. Preceded in their efforts by the Transcendentalists who had found solace in the poetic, inspirational and meditative literature of Vedantic teachings, Blavatsky and Olcott linked their fascination with the occult to the cosmological theories of the Hindu and Buddhist religious traditions, including the law of karma.

Being critics of American spiritualism, Blavatsky and Olcott offered the swelling ranks of spiritualists in the United States and abroad with a more focused approach through the auspices of the Theosophical Society which they organized in 1875.

Soon thereafter, Blavatsky revealed the existence of the Great White Brotherhood (i.e., Indian and Tibetan Adepts or Mahatmas) who conveyed through occult messages the secrets of the universe—all of which were intended to awaken the spiritual nature of man by pointing East to the cradle of the occult. Blavatsky's principal publications were *Isis Unveiled*; *The Secret Doctrine*; and *The Key to Theosophy*, while Olcott's publications included *People from the Other World*; *A Buddhist Catechism*; *Theosophy, Religion, and Occult Science*; and *The Life of Buddha and Its Lessons*. Together, they published the Bombay periodical *The Theosophist* which served as the official voice of the movement.

Born into an aristocratic family in the Ukraine, Blavatsky left an early and unsuccessful marriage to begin a twenty-year sojourn through Europe, Egypt, Tibet and the Indian subcontinent, learning the techniques of mediumship before moving to New York in 1873. Her cosmology sought to meet the challenges of modern science by embracing a universe where each particle carried a spark of the divine and where the orders of life became increasingly spiritual until they were absorbed into the eternal One. In this manner, she bypassed the issues raised by geology and evolution, replacing the Christian idea of creation with an eminent God who was constantly creating the world through natural processes. The supreme deity of Brahmanism was not the personal God of Christianity but rather an impersonal principle that worked through evolution. As such, everything contained a spark of the divine. By making India the source of ancient wisdom, Blavatsky was able to offer convincing arguments that Buddhist missionaries had provided the foundation blocks for all of the great religions of the world. Buddhism, which later merged into Brahmanism was the 'mother-trunk' of all religions.[67]

Blavatsky portrayed Hinduism in nuanced ways that were new to the Indians themselves. Her romantic and even idyllic view of its primitiveness and simplicity became easy elements to accept and reinforce. Thus she not only had an impact on the popularity of Orientalism in the West, but introduced ideas that became fashionable in India as well. In both, she helped to reconcile religion with the modern world. In *Isis Unveiled*, Blavatsky transformed occultism into a unified whole, demonstrating to the world that the master key to life could be found in Eastern philosophy. In joining religion with science, she constructed a vision of the spiritual evolution of humanity and the cause and effect laws of the universe.

Blavatsky described Swedenborg as 'the greatest among the modern seers'. Notwithstanding this compliment, she was also critical of his legacy, claiming that he never rose above his Christian world view which was coloured by Scripture; that he was untrained in clairvoyance and seership and therefore unable to distinguish between genuine spiritual insight and imagination; and that his clairvoyance had been limited to a single 'astral plane which is only one level above the physical and which to a large extent is merely the psychic atmosphere of our Earth'.[68]

Operating in close association with Blavatsky was Henry Steel Olcott who was raised a Presbyterian and began his career as an agricultural expert and highly regarded military officer, lawyer and correspondent. While on assignment for the *New York Sun* and *New York Graphic* to cover the psychic phenomena at the farm of William and Horatio Eddy in Chittenden, Vermont, he met Blavatsky and was immediately charmed by her person and the remarkable accounts of her adventures.

Like Blavatsky, Olcott treated Buddhism as a scientific rather than a revealed religion, grounded not in miracles or inspiration, but in the indestructibility of force, evolutionary theory, equality among individuals, an emphasis on consciousness and reason, and social virtue of personal responsibility. Similar to the German-American author, editor and student of comparative religions, Paul Carus, he chose to offset the disparaging characterizations of Buddhism with a view popularized by Arnold's *The Light of Asia* which swathed the character of Prince Siddhartha (and later of Buddha) in enlightenment, teachings and poetic expressions intended to improve mutual understanding between East and West. He portrayed the Buddha as a 'modern' freethinker who, besides serving the masses in Asia, was relevant as well to the most modern societies by promoting the brotherhood of all men.[69]

Known as the 'White Buddhist', Olcott helped build unity among the different sects, brokering a form of Protestant Buddhism that resonated as much among Western thinkers as it appealed to millions of Buddhists in the East seeking to modernize. He fashioned his Theosophic beliefs from an adaptation of evolutionary science; modern Western philosophy; the academic Orientalism of philologist Max Müller and

Pali scholar Rhys Davids; and American Protestantism, including its more radical Transcendental elements involving Swedenborg and Emerson's self-reliance. Olcott's popular *Buddhist Catechism*, which went through forty editions before his death, fuelled a redefinition of Buddhism that served both Eastern and Western audiences. Standing between the two cultures, he was able to construct a combination that was decidedly his own but which resonated with both.[70]

Constructed in a format common to Christian catechisms, the *Buddhist Catechism* disentangled much of Buddhism's ritual baggage for a leaner more modern world view.

1. *Q. Of what religion are you?*
   A. The Buddhist
2. *Q. What is a Buddhist?*
   A. One who professes to be a follower of our Lord Buddha, and accepts his doctrine.
3. *Q. Was Buddha a God?*
   A. No.
4. *Q. Was he a man?*
   A. In form a man, but internally not like other men; that is to say, in moral and mental qualities he excelled all other men of his own or subsequent times.
5. *Q. Was Buddha his name?*
   A. No, Buddha is the name of a condition or state of mind.
6. *Q. What is its meaning?*
   A. Enlightened; as one is who has the perfect wisdom.[71]

Employing the law of evolution and the indestructibility of force to counter Christianity's claim of God's creation of the universe out of nothing, Olcott explained how Buddhist doctrine was as relevant to the present age as it had been in the past. Recommended for teachers in Buddhist schools, it offered an easy-to-learn approach to the principles of Buddhist doctrine, and was an alternative to what he claimed were the 'idolatrous ceremonies and customs, some derived from Hinduism, some from primitive nature-worship [and commonly practiced] without protest from the monks of Buddha but with their connivance, and often encouragement'. Thus removed of its devil worship, idolatry, astrology, omens and other corruptions, Olcott offered the *Catechism* as a true representation of Buddhist doctrine. Translated into multiple languages, it was adopted by almost all Buddhist countries as representative of their common elements of faith.[72]

In 1878, Olcott and Blavatsky moved the headquarters of their Theosophical Society from New York City to Adyar in India. Dedicated to the furtherance of Buddhism and Hinduism, and even a revival of Zoroastrian teachings, Olcott worked hard to unite the Buddhist sects of Ceylon, Burma and Siam under a uniform set of *Fourteen Propositions of Buddhism*; organized the twelve sects of Japanese Buddhists; and, in 1886, invited representatives from all the great religions to India to celebrate the founding of the Adyar Library. All but Christians accepted. Nevertheless, the meeting marked the first meeting of representatives from many of the world's great religions.

Harris and the Adepts

With Theosophy gaining in popularity in the 1880s, Harris deliberately chose not to ridicule its claims of communication with enlightened Adepts; instead, he found the opportunity to account for their ancient wisdom within the constructs of his own Brotherhood by publishing *The Wisdom of the Adepts. Esoteric Science in Human History*, a five-hundred-page study of Buddhist literature. Harris had no desire to start a new religion, superseding the teachings of any of the sacred texts or leading to the formation of another priesthood or ecclesiastical system. Rather, he intended to reveal 'that sacred Brotherhood whose office throughout the ages [had] been to lift the load and alleviate the sorrows of this long-suffering and afflicted race'. Much of the book consisted of conversations between himself and 'Adonai', an ancient leader among the Brotherhood, who offered Harris a more complete understanding of the universe with its orbs and purposes.[73]

With Adonai as his guide, Harris identified the cardinal planets in the solar system whose earthly races, after a long succession of eras, stood in a state of degradation, much like 'desiccated plants of autumn, as the dried perennials, as the scant remains of withering foliage'.

> We class the existing mankind of the earth into three divisions: the Survivalists, the Unfitnesses and the Inversives. The great portion of the race is of this middle type; unfit. Their internal spirituality is but little more than a living germ; their soul-form is but a small embryo; their spiritual self-life is but as the resemblance of an inferior orb; their memory form is but a sketch or an unfilled outline: their natural soul is but as cogener to the ape: their natural self-desire, unless disturbed, is easy and acquiescent; satisfied with the solace of a few inferior appetites: their life-body is filled up mainly by absorbed magnetisms, and the outer physical form imperfectly generated and made up of substances that are but partially cohesive . . . their seeming evil is largely from the drift of a general current of depravity and disease.[74]

Harris intended for his book to open access to the occult powers of the ancient Brotherhood and pave the way to a new order of 'Divine-Natural Humanity'.[75] Claiming that certain Adepts were seeking to overthrow faith in Christ in America and Europe using occult methods to invade the mind and infuse it with magical elements and self-worship, he intended the book as a prophetic warning against such nefarious efforts. Using words and terms such as 'proprium' and 'Divine-Natural-Humanity', 'self-ego', 'inmost' and 'outermost'—all of which seemed to fall off his pages in recurring numbers—one might have thought he was reading some lost occult manuscript from Henry James, Sr. However, as Harris greeted readers with additional terms such as 'Lady of God', 'Devachan', 'karma', 'Father-Mother Land', 'astral light', 'metempsychosis' and 'aspiration toward God', any such comparison with James failed to materialize. Each of these words and phrases introduced images that evoked a fundamentally new and esoteric world that breathed the beneficence of Eastern religion and philosophy—all accessed by means of a sixth organism that formed the spiritual personality of each individual.[76]

With the help of Adonai, Harris explained the nature of the spiritual body, the world soul of the globe, the etheric atmospheres that populated the universe, the winged boys and girls ('sportive innocences') who filled the atmosphere, and the vortices of holiness that moved through the universe. Although vast societies of Adepts had lived in remote antiquity preserving the secrets of science, religion and philosophy, and retaining them for future minds, most had disappeared leaving only a few destined to become the conveyers of the lost secrets, sacred rites and divine sciences to future generations. In large measure, Adonai reaffirmed the world view earlier explained in Harris's *Arcana of Christianity* but in a manner that appealed to those members of his community and outsiders enamoured by the recent popularity of Theosophy. More occult in his discussion of the 'inter-space' between the twelve cardinal planets and their peoples, Harris spun the mysteries of long lost tribes, orders of sages, of sacred choral dances and songs, the majesty of 'Goddesshood', the history of the 'Silver People', and the epochal cataclysms that disturbed the universe from time to time.

Harris included an attack on the Mormon Church which he identified as carrying the same evil magnetism as the Jews with their personal attributes of 'self-lust', 'foul interiors' and 'evil spirituality'.[77] He also reaffirmed the significance of 'Queen Lily' whose presence was made visible during periods of divine visitation;[78] the paralysis of the pontiff and the Holy See;[79] the subtle qualities of English poet Bulwer-Lytton who served as Viceroy of India in 1876; Emerson, whom he considered the 'Brahmin of the Brahmins';[80] and Swedenborg who 'glimpsed at heaven with but half a sight, heard of heaven with but half an ear, tasted of heaven with but half a taste, and when he inhaled of heaven it was but by a chilled and unpotential fragrance'. He predicted Swedenborg would be accepted more broadly on account of the clarifications made by Adonai concerning the seer's *Arcana Caelestia*.[81]

Harris's critique of Swedenborg laid the groundwork for placing himself as the true inheritor of the ancient wisdom. With this as his presumed intent, he used Adonai to explain the Swede's faults.

[Swedenborg's] doctrine of the Lord is a misstatement, couched in such vague phraseology that already there are several schools of interpretation among the most strict and learned of his followers. His doctrine of heaven, as exclusive of space or dimension, is illogical and purely impossible. His doctrine of a spiritual sense in sacred scripture is as old as scripture. His theory of correspondences is true, so far as it is true that every form implies its own idea; but not true in the manner of his special application. . . . [H]e stood where rays of light streamed through him and that, while he held pictures from the rays in his mental sight-mirrors, he failed to apprehend the system of their sciences. He would tread all round a truth, whilst yet the truth, as to its divine-natural form and order, would remain invisible. . . . [H]e lived with his back turned to Nature: hence the occult laws and processes of the nature-world were to him unknown and incomprehensible.[82]

Expounding on a theory that was confusing, disjointed, accusative, narcissistic and complex to the point of disbelief, Harris wove a story much like Blavatsky had achieved with her *Isis Unveiled*. William Quan Judge, a fellow mystic, esotericist and occultist who assisted in the spreading of Theosophy, disclaimed any similarity between Harris's Brotherhood and the Mahatmas, but the discerning reader knew better. Reminiscent of storied histories such as J R R Tolkien's epic *The Lord of the Rings* or, more recently, J K Rowling's *Harry Potter* fantasy series and George R R Martin's *Game of Thrones*, the book paralleled Swedenborg's *Arcana Caelestia*, Davis's *Great Harmonia* and Joseph Smith's *The Book of Mormon*. Each, in their own distinctive way, constructed a universe filled with concentric layers of life; good and evil kingdoms; processions of psychic souls passing from form to form; special rites and festivals; joyous repose interspersed with existential threats; configurations of World-Mother and -Father; and glimpses of karma. In each, the reader was introduced to a rich new vocabulary of names, ancient traditions, primeval secrets and animating powers of the universe. Out of their imaginations were born kings and potentates of the earth; ennobled Adepts; esoteric science; inter-spacial realms; mediumistic phenomena; ancient tribes and arcane mysteries; peaceful and learned civilizations; ancient books; spirit forces of evil intent; chambers of priests and pontiffs; black magnetism that flowed during the night; phenomenal occurrences; and vortices connecting outwardly visible and outwardly invisible aspects of the universe.[83]

Turning Point

Beginning in the mid-1880s, Harris secluded himself in a cottage south of Fountain Grove where he turned his visioning to politics and what he saw as a coming crisis in American society. From there he wrote occasional letters reflective of his concerns which were printed in *The Open Court* magazine, published by Paul Carus in LaSalle, Illinois.[84] His first major publication in this new period in his life, however, was a pamphlet published as a letter to the Hon. Thomas L Thompson, a Sonoma Democrat, titled *Brotherhood of the New Life: Its Fact, Law, Method and Purpose*. In it, Harris recounted his dream of a 'New Harmonic Civilization' that marked the end to all feuds and the elimination of all disease in a 'fulfilled Christian era; a new golden age of universal peace'. As he explained to the legislator, he was prepared to demonstrate to the world the secret of 'Divine Breath' and the promise it held for humankind. 'I hold in quickened mind and flesh the final secret and method and law and power for the resuscitation, the re-habiliment, the organic restoration of the nobler multitudes of Earth's aged and almost exhausted race', he wrote. 'This American People, whom I love, and to whose best interests my life is pledged and consecrated, will now hear from me . . . as an annunciator and demonstrator of supreme vital laws, and of verified facts, of largest value when applied either to the individual or the public good'. Claiming the key to the harmonic law of Pythagoras, a law which, according to Harris, encompassed both the natural and supernatural, he assured Thompson that he could open the race of man to a whole new life. The key or secret lay in the rhythms of divine respiration which unified and rededicated the body to its 'inward and indestructible humanity'. This, he wrote, was all there was of the mystery in the Brotherhood of the New Life. It allowed one to live and grow in organic and social Christianity.[85]

Harris distinguished his beliefs from the socialistic thought that was emerging from Germany and the bourgeois associationism of Fourier and Brisbane. Neither system had learned from evolutionary science; or, for that matter, had they understood the true nature of reform. Instead, he referred to Laurence Gronlund's *The Co-operative Commonwealth* and Edward Bellamy's *Looking Backward* as the model for society's advancement.[86] Here was the nexus of creative and redemptive evolution, namely, the emergence of nucleated groups such as the Brotherhood who would transition society into a national cooperative without experiencing the pain of revolution or class conflict.[87]

Harris believed there was an additional missing piece which, if discovered, had the potential of bringing the nation's most powerful capitalists together with the working classes in a unity of purpose, reconciliation and cleansing. Provided there were individuals with the financial means and purpose to support him, he offered to reorganize the state of California on 'social-national' lines to demonstrate to the world its potential destiny. True government began from a small centre of activity and expanded outward with purpose, courage and unity. Admiring men like Collis P Huntington, Mark Hopkins, Charles Crocker and Leland Stanford for their organizational skills in building the Central and Southern Pacific Railroads, he saw them as models of power that befitted the needs of the American people on the 'chess-board of Destiny'. Their combination of intelligence, persistence and trust was a lesson to be learned by those drawn to the needs of humanity. 'The wisdom of the disorganised masses, if it ever is a wisdom, is a wisdom after the event', he observed. Each age had brought forth new leaders. In 1776 it had been Thomas Jefferson, John Adams and Benjamin Franklin. In 1845 it had been William Lloyd Garrison, Theodore Parker and Wendell Phillips. In 1861 it was Abraham Lincoln, Charles Sumner and Edwin Stanton. 'Where shall '91 find her sages of the council?' he asked. The transition from capitalized egotism to humanized collectivity required the same level of leadership that served the previous generations of humankind. The hour was at hand to show that 'God is with us and within us'. Before civilization could progress, however, it needed to move beyond the 'competitive system' with its 'plutocratic passions'.[88]

Harris explained that 'national socialism' was the only route to the divinely socialized humanity of the future which, if nurtured properly, would arise not from the practices of political parties but from individual and collective dignity, honour and self-sacrifice. With help from the 'elite' of men and the 'divine flowerage' of women, national socialism would lead humanity forth 'full armed, full illumined, into beatific and energised association'. Paraphrasing Henry George's *Progress and Poverty*, he noted that a plutocracy of powerful interests was 'armed, fortressed and massed, by means of such modicum of the unearned increment as is held as an investment in the mechanism of production and transit—a force equivalent at least to ten times the daily working power of the entire proletariat'. But 'the People' were stirring and out of their numbers a new set of leaders would emerge. 'Let the occasion last, let it ripen, and the fated leaders are sure to arrive'. Harris lamented the savageness that attended recent strikes and boycotts; the power of Pinkerton's police and state militia; the mortgaged farms with their ruined and failing crops; onerous rates of rail transportation; high interest rates; and miscreant legislatures and courts. He warned that 'the People' were patient, conservative and, by nature, non-aggressive. However, the fire when aroused was not small but 'the fierce heat of enduring anthracite'. Once awakened to find the franchises of their existence lost to the plutocracy, they 'will emerge gaunt, ghastly, but terrible and inexorable'.[89]

For a brief period leading up to the 1896 national election, Harris supported William Jennings Bryan, believing that he would be the great solvent for the nation's economic woes. In 1899, however, he turned to Theodore Roosevelt and what Harris hoped would be a Christian-Imperial-National Collectivism.[90]

* * *

In his cottage at Linn Lilla, Harris lived in quiet expectancy of events to come. Together with Jane Waring and 'Queen Lily' with whom he shared immortality, he awaited the Last Days. When his revelations failed to materialize and, following an exposé by Alzire Chevaillier, a Christian Scientist, suffragette and journalist who accused Harris of sexual misconduct involving several of the women at Fountain Grove, he sold his interest in the community, deeding the property over to several members of the 'elect', one of whom, Kanaye Nagasawa, managed the property through Prohibition.[91] Until his death in 1906, Harris and his wife divided their time between homes in New York City, New Brunswick and a thousand-acre estate in Florida known as Royal Oak. All his life, he aspired to establish a pure theo-socialist society guided by his revelatory visions. How he reconciled his unique perspective on the world with actual events must surely remain a puzzle. Here was a man of extraordinary talents whose personal force built a mythology that won him the admiration of many. For better or worse, he played a signal role in identifying the weaknesses of the age and showing how, in a society of accomplished competitors, one could utilize a bundle of half-truths to become a trusting and imaginative advocate for unconvincing ideas.

J J G WILKINSON AND JAMES TYLER KENT
Christian Homoeopathy

There is, in the present day, a constantly increasing enquiry among
intelligent persons, respecting the life and labors of Swedenborg,
whose name begins to be whispered, with more or less respect, and
with undefined feelings, throughout Christendom.

(J J G Wilkinson, *Emanuel Swedenborg: A Biography*, 1849)

T rue to the Enlightenment, Emanuel Swedenborg was one of several philosophers in his day who sought to discover the underpinnings of physics, biology, chemistry and mineralogy. By 1744, however, his interests turned inward as he sought a more mystical, intuitive basis of knowledge. As Ralph Waldo Emerson explained in 'The American Scholar', an oration he delivered before the Phi Beta Kappa Society at Cambridge in 1837, Swedenborg chose to focus his efforts on piercing 'the emblematic or spiritual character of the visible, audible, tangible world'.[1] Thus, long before the explosion of alternative and complementary systems of healing, those enamoured with Swedenborg's writings concerning influx, correspondence, degrees and the *Maximus Homo*, recognized a complex but orderly arrangement of philosophy and theology which they believed captured the totality of human experience, including the order, harmony and consequent health of the physical body. There was no sickness that did not originate in the falseness of understanding acted out through the will.

This metaphysical approach to healing carried into the nineteenth-century reform movement known as homoeopathy, whose members included large numbers of Swedenborgians. Among them was James John Garth Wilkinson, whose reputation was first made by his translations of Swedenborg, but who later helped to transform homoeopathy into a distinct form of Christian therapeutics. Eventually, *Wilkinsonism* transitioned into *Kentianism*, named after the Swedenborgian homoeopath, James Tyler Kent, who contributed almost as much to homoeopathy as its founder Samuel Hahnemann. Kentianism represented what historian Joseph Kett has referred to as a 'synthesis of matter and spirit [and] since homeopathy was traveling in the same direction [as Swedenborgianism], it too basked in the sun of approval'.[2]

With its adoption of Swedenborgianism, homoeopathy held to a vitalist philosophy that explained health as the result of various internal (psychological) and external (physical) causes that affected the individual's spiritual state. As a belief system, it relied heavily on the law of correspondences to explain health and disease, offer insight into the living organism, and explain the actions of different remedies on the individual. In effect, it proved inherently sympathetic to concepts such as potency, energy, spirit, hierarchies and archetypes within the organic and inorganic worlds. Health and disease were attributes of the spirit clearly distinct from reductionist science, the senses and the physical world.

Homoeopathy

Homoeopathy, from the Greek *homoios* meaning 'similar', and *patheia* meaning 'suffering', is a holistic system of medicine involving body, mind and spirit. Founded by German physician Samuel Hahnemann, it is based on the a priori concept of *vitalism*, the belief in an intelligent energy force that controls the body's ability to heal itself (*vis medicatrix naturae*), and on the principle of 'like cures like' (*similia similibus curantur*), or the use of medicines which, when given to a healthy person, create a symptom-complex (i.e., the physical and emotional characteristics of the disease) similar to that of the patient. The only true manifestations of a perverted vital economy are to be found in symptoms that are considered collectively, not separately. Rather than suppress or control disease with harsh medicines, homoeopaths prefer to treat the symptom-complex with a single dose of a *similium* that has been first tested on healthy provers. In doing so, the homoeopath intends for the drug (whose profile emulates the patient's physical and emotional characteristics) to stimulate the body's energy force and thereby spur its natural defence mechanisms to begin the healing process. Every simple substance contains a healing principle with its own formative energy or vitalistic force. Silica, for example, has a degree of simple substance within it that, when *potentized*, becomes a curative agency for symptoms such as mood treatment, colds, sore throat and headaches.[3]

The mother tincture, a homoeopathic remedy derived from plant, mineral or animal substance, is serially diluted in distilled water, ethyl alcohol, or triturated with milk sugar (lactose), in multiples usually of ten (X) or one hundred (C). Only when the dilution or trituration is energized through a shaking or rubbing process does the medicine become an energy source capable of affecting the body, mind and spirit. The more diluted the similium, the greater its healing potential and the fewer doses needed for cure. Most homoeopathic medicines are manufactured at the 6C level of potency but some are so attenuated they virtually lack even a single molecule of the original menstrum. Although Avogadro's law indicates that virtually no molecules remain when a substance is diluted beyond 24X or 12C, this appears to be no impediment to the homoeopath who insists that *something* must remain since homoeopathy 'works'.[4]

The law of *similia* is built on the premise that the body is the organ through which the vital force is expressed, that sickness in the body is evidence of the disorder of the vital force within, and that the effects of any medicine are more manifest in the will and understanding than in tissue changes. This represents no purely mechanistic phi losophy but a spiritualistic conception of disease. Treatment is similar to 'chi' or 'ki' in Chinese and Japanese cultures in that the outcome depends on an energy or life force that exists in every living organism and enables an inherent, self-healing process. This spiritualist conception of disease embraces a psychology and metaphysics distinctively individualistic. Disease originates in a derangement of the *dynamis* and this, in turn, is reflected in the organs or parts. Drugs, when properly potentized, are endowed with inherent virtues that can be liberated for use in healing. When Hahnemann referred to the spirit-like power resulting from potentization, he meant that as the inherent healing power was liberated, the coarser, more materialistic aspects of the drug were removed. That which remained was an invisible, unweighable, vibrating essence of life itself that, applied according to the law of *similia*, became the source of power to the living organism. As Hahnemann explained, 'During the healthy condition of man this spirit-like force (autocracy), animating the material body (organism), rules supreme as *dynamis*. By it all parts are maintained wonderfully in harmonious vital process, both in feeling and functions, in order that our intelligent mind may be free to make the living, healthy, bodily medium subservient to the larger purpose of our being'.[5]

Accordingly, homoeopathic potencies act on human psychology as well as on physical pathology. Psychologically, they expose the patient's innermost obsessions, emotions, dreams and idiosyncrasies; and on the material level they expose the body's physical aberrations or abnormalities that result in the organism's weakness. In this sense there is a clear affinity between homoeopathy and psychotherapeutics, on patient individuation (within the archetype), and on the importance of dreams and symbols to achieve physical and spiritual purification. Believing that the subtlest influences often have the most powerful effects, the infinitesimal attenuation of material remedies serve to restore the archetype to a non-material level and thereby influence the individual's governing or vitalistic centre, passing it on to the physical organs. The art of the homoeopathic cure lies in the use of non-material archetype remedies which connect to the physical body by way of the mind. In other words, the homoeopathic cure carries certain idealistic attributes through the mind's non-material sphere to form, correct and influence the physical body. The objective of treatment is to rid the body of its constitutional disease or miasma.

Medical Jeremiads

Many of the earliest homoeopaths in the United States were Swedenborgians, including Dr Hans Burch Gram of New York; publisher and pharmacist Otis Clapp of Boston; pharmacist John Ellis of Michigan; pharmacists and publishers Francis E Boericke and Adolph J Tafel of Philadelphia; Constantine Hering of Philadelphia; William Henry Holcombe of New Orleans; and Charles J Hempel of Michigan. As Marguerite Block perceptively noted in *The New Church in the New World*, 'Homeopathy went like wild-fire through the New Church. Its periodicals are full of discussions of its relation to the teachings of Swedenborg, and a large proportion of its membership embraced it. . . . There was soon a large number of

Homeopathic physicians also on the rolls of the New Church, several of whom later became ordained ministers'.[6]

One early American proponent of homoeopathy was author, translator and compiler Charles Hempel who, as noted in Chapter 2, had been an ardent supporter of Brook Farm's marriage of Fourierism and Swedenborgianism. A graduate of New York University Medical College, his Swedenborgianism was never far from his therapeutics. His translations included Hahnemann's *The Chronic Diseases*, and *Materia Medica*; G H G Jahr's *New Manual*; and Jean Paul Tessier's *Clinical Researches Concerning the Homeopathic Treatment of Asiatic Cholera*. He also authored *Organon of Specific Homeopathy* and *System of Materia Medica and Therapeutics* clarifying what he perceived to be inconsistencies in Hahnemann's system. An active member of the New Church, Hempel believed there was much in Swedenborg's writings to assist homoeopaths. 'The day is fast approaching', he predicted, 'when the homeopathic profession will bow to Swedenborg as the great expounder of the philosophy of homeopathy'.[7] Borrowing from Swedenborg's principle that a correspondence existed between all things spiritual and physical, he concluded that the principle of *similia*, the foundation block of homoeopathic dogma, really implied 'a perfect correspondence between the drug disease and the natural pathological disturbance'. For Hempel, the law provided a much more accurate explanation of this outward resemblance of drug symptoms to the symptoms of disease. Accordingly, he suggested the substitution of the phrase *correspondentia correspondentibus curantur* for Hahnemann's *similia similibus curantur*.[8]

Another early leader was German-born Constantine Hering, known as the 'Father of American homeopathy', who emigrated to the United States in 1833 and founded the North American Academy of the Homeopathic Healing Art in Allentown, Pennsylvania. A devout Swedenborgian and member of the New Church in Philadelphia, Hering introduced the so-called 'second law of cure' (following Hahnemann's first law of *similia*), which addressed the direction in which the symptoms of the patient appeared as a disease and disappeared during homoeopathic treatment. Each cure proceeded from the centre to the circumference, from above downward, and from within outwards. In other words, the cure proceeded from more important to less important organs, i.e., from the head to the hands and feet. As the mental and psychological characteristics of the disease dissipated and the symptoms improved, the physical aspects of the disease were the last to heal. Conversely, when an individual's symptom-complex worsened, showing signs of disease, the characteristics moved in reverse order.[9]

Not all homoeopaths accepted the relationship between Hering's law and Swedenborgianism. This second law of cure, insisted André Saine, Dean of the Canadian Academy of Homeopathy, came from observation and not from Hering's Swedenborgian beliefs.[10] Even if true, homoeopathy and Swedenborgianism nevertheless maintained an intimate relationship over the decades and, while it may be argued that Hering kept his medicine and religion separate, the facts are muddied and conclusions accordingly mixed. 'It's no accident that so many of the early homeopaths were either Swedenborgians or students of his writings', observed Cincinnati homoeopath Shirley Reischman, 'Even today, it's almost impossible to go to a Swedenborgian church or a Swedenborgian study group without being introduced to several homeopaths'.[11]

James John Garth Wilkinson (1812-99)
The eldest of eight children, James John Garth Wilkinson was born in 1812 to James John Wilkinson, a writer on mercantile law and judge in Durham, England, and Harriet (Robinson) Wilkinson. In a memoir begun in 1872, Wilkinson remembered his childhood as one of 'dark shadows' in which, because of a devoutly religious mother and ghost tales told by servants at the family home on Acton Street, off Gray's Inn Lane, in London, he lived in dreadful fear of death. Nevertheless, as the births of brothers and sisters added to the family, he concealed his fears in order to assume the responsibilities of the oldest child and his duty to teach by example. Sent to private school following his mother's death, young Wilkinson learned Latin, along with an appreciation for poetry, especially Milton and Byron. Still, the sense of his own mortality weighed heavy during childhood where, amid multiplication tables, dance lessons and holidays at his grandmother's cottage in Sunderland, he learned to cope with his fears.[12]

Though desirous of following his father's footsteps into law, Garth was apprenticed in 1829, the day after his sixteenth birthday, to serve Thomas Leighton, senior surgeon at the Infirmary of Newcastle-upon-Tyne. In his role as a 'master's dresser', Wilkinson acquired the basics of surgery in the pre-antiseptic and pre-anaesthetic days of medicine and learned to compound drugs, bleed and perform other duties as assigned. Given his childhood terrors, his experiences in the operating room caused him frequent misgivings. Nevertheless, by 1832, he was walking the wards of Guy's Hospital in preparation for qualifying as a Member of the Royal College of Surgeons and Licentiate of the Society of Apothecaries.

In 1835, with the help of loans from family members, Wilkinson opened a private medical practice at 13 Store Street, Bedford Square, whose 'front shop', an over-the-counter apothecary, produced most of his income. Idled by the paltry nature of his practice, he spent hours attending lectures on mesmerism and hypnotism, visiting the occasional seance, and prowling the reading room of the British Museum where he discovered the works of Swedenborg. Persuaded by his uncle, a wealthy Swedenborgian and secretary to the London Printing Society (now the Swedenborg Society) to consider translating the Swede's scientific writings into English, Wilkinson established his own Swedenborg Association to undertake the task.

While working at his translations, Wilkinson received a copy of William Blake's *Songs of Innocence and of Experience* which the poet had published privately in 1789. Wilkinson was so impressed by the work that he honoured Blake with his own cloth-bound octavo which, with financial assistance from his brother William, he published in 1839. The book consisted of a twenty-one-page preface detailing the life of Blake and of Swedenborg's influence on the poet's work. Wilkinson modestly chose to leave his preface unsigned. Nevertheless, he explained Blake's dark imaginings as the product of *vastation*—a term first introduced by Swedenborg—which Wilkinson described as 'the gradual destruction of men as spiritual organisms, down to the level which the evil has successfully evaded, and to which the freewill has been voluntarily, by acts of life, extinguished. . . . The man that is left is still a free will; he freely chooses to be what he is, and calls round him the divine necessity of his state, to stay where he is. He cannot change because he will not, because with constant will he kills the faculty of change'.[13]

That same year, Wilkinson published the first two of his Swedenborg translations, *The Doctrine Concerning Charity* and *The Last Judgment* (originally printed in 1758), with both translations being reissued in the following years by the London Printing Society. He also became acquainted at this time with Scottish essayist and historian Thomas Carlyle to whom he sent a copy of his work as a gift. Carlyle thanked him, adding that he had been apprised of Swedenborg through the writings of Sampson Reed of Boston.[14] A year later, Carlyle wrote that he had found Swedenborg to be 'one of the most wondrous men; whom I cannot altogether undertake to interpret for myself! I can love and honour such a man, and leave the mystery of him mysterious'.[15]

Wilkinson next set himself to translating Swedenborg's *Angelic Wisdom Concerning the Divine Love and the Divine Wisdom*, followed by *The Animal Kingdom, Considered Anatomically, Physically, and Philosophically*, which was published in two volumes in 1843-4, laying out the principles and doctrines constituting the natural sciences. While he considered Swedenborg's anatomy and physiology limited in their scientific validity, he found his principles nonetheless rooted in universal law and therefore true. In the book's introduction, Wilkinson directed readers to Swedenborg's doctrine of series and degrees which, he explained, was the path to a more intimate knowledge of nature. He also pointed to Swedenborg's views on forms and forces, and the universal analogy and correspondence that existed throughout nature and human society.[16]

Next, Wilkinson published Augustus Clissold's two-volume translation of Swedenborg's *The Economy of the Animal Kingdom, Considered Anatomically, Physically, and Philosophically*, with a lengthy introduction designed to place the work in the context of the seer's other writings and consisting of observations as well as answers to potential objections that stood in the way of a full understanding. The introduction was also printed separately as an eighty-six-page work entitled *Remarks on Swedenborg's Economy of the Animal Kingdom*. Wilkinson explained that Swedenborg's writings were best understood in two categories— scientific and theological—and that the focus for the present work, as with *The Animal Kingdom*, was on the scientific, which contained both practical and theoretical components. Although the sciences were premised on that which was known through the senses, they were also philosophical since 'they rise through the particular sciences, to that universal science which alone is philosophy'. In other words, Swedenborg's intent was to show the potential reconciliation of philosophical ideas with science by way of induction. By this he did not mean that the senses governed the mind, but only to demonstrate that every faculty, when used properly and for its specific ends, imparted important principles relevant to the analysis of being. As Wilkinson remarked, 'Swedenborg's instruments leave to man the whole play of his faculties, and indeed require their utmost exercise; and merely feed them, through an appropriate channel, and in proper quality and quantity, with matter derived from the various degrees of the created universe'. In short, nature was multi-dimensional in scope, discernible at both the physical and spiritual level. [17]

In this regard, Swedenborg represented a synthesis of Aristotle and Bacon, using the ascending method of Bacon and the descending method of Aristotle, each connected to the other to form 'a legitimate and widening spiral, revolving from the senses to the mind, and from the mind to the senses'. To this end, Wilkinson explained, Swedenborg had pursued the sciences, finding in their study a treasure trove of spiritual truths, including knowledge of the human soul. The challenge was in learning how to elevate induction from a common fact to a science of laws or rational facts. Here, Swedenborg applied the doctrines of forms, of order and degrees, of series (i.e., unities) and society, of communication and influx, of correspondence and representation, and of modification to achieve his end. These were the tools that led to universal truths. [18]

In 1847, Wilkinson translated *Outlines of a Philosophical Argument on the Infinite, and the Final Cause of Creation; and on the Intercourse Between the Soul and the Body*, originally printed in 1734. The work represented an attempt by Swedenborg to establish through rational means those facts visibly discovered in nature respecting God, the soul and eternal life. The work applied the principles of mechanics and geometry to the discovery of the single primitive cause and the genealogical descent from this active first cause or *ens* to subsequent elementary particles differing in degrees and dimension but progressing by means of a contiguous series and intermediates. From these finites and their subsequent mutations, Swedenborg explained the formation of the sun, earth and planets. Wilkinson was unapologetic of Swedenborg's focus on mechanics 'as an exponent of the inward sphere' rather than on metaphysics which seemed to be 'hanging in middle air . . . bewailing a suppositious past [and] dreaming of an unlikely future'. As with Swedenborg's later works, *The Infinite and the Final Cause of Creation* was connected with the spiritual world. Its proper study involved no 'umbilical contemplations' or contrivances, but rather positive knowledge using facts acquired by the senses. Philosophy had much to learn from the sciences in dealing with scepticism, disputation and 'those insurrections of the mind' which were constant 'pests' in the churches.[19] Eventually, however, Swedenborg abandoned his endeavour of studying the soul through nature and chose instead to have the spiritual world reveal itself more directly through revelation, a source of knowledge that required no proof of its authority. 'And whatever is confirmed by Holy Scripture', Swedenborg wrote, 'is in no need of confirmation from reason, from rational philosophy, or from geometry; this being already sufficiently implied in the fact of confirmation by the Infinite Himself'.[20]

Wilkinson's faith played a central role in his life as he relied on the writings of Swedenborg to assuage his deep psychological longings. In undertaking the exhaustive task of translating Swedenborg's writings, Wilkinson sought to absorb and understand the intent of the author's Latin meanings before finding the words to make them meaningful in English. In doing so, he acquired an intimacy into the mind of Swedenborg that only a few before him had known. With his translations and introductory comments, he was able to convey an intense spiritual understanding of Swedenborg to a reading audience that may have lacked the benefits of his classical education. Through a succession of translations, which included *Posthumous Tracts* and *The Generative Organs*, Wilkinson provided the basis for a fresh new covenant and a distinctly new understanding of the Incarnation, including confirmation of the Divine Humanity. In making Swedenborg available to a wider audience, he opened the English-speaking world to the presence of the Divine-Natural Humanity. In doing so, he dispensed of any claim of infallibility for Swedenborg such as the Roman church formally declared in 1870 as a way of enforcing its beliefs and believers.

> Swedenborg never said he was infallible. What he implied was that he was over-ruled by the Lord——his own will evidently capable of the obedience necessary to write the internal sense of the Word, as it could be received by Mankind. No angel helped him; on the contrary, the Angels often told him what poor matter he was writing from their standpoint; and he, guided by the Lord, replied, that it was up to the level of the intelligence of the receptive world in his day.[21]

Wilkinson's admiration of Swedenborg was without caveat. 'You ask me, who, in my opinion, is the greatest Philosopher of the present time?' he once wrote. 'My answer is, Emanuel Swedenborg. His writings recognize and adequately demonstrate all the faculties of man, and see them in their connexion from the highest to the lowest as the creations of a Divine love and wisdom'.[22] Wilkinson considered himself a Swedenborgian but not in the sense of membership in the sect calling itself the New Church. He believed, as did his friend Henry James, Sr, that Swedenborg had no intention of creating yet another sect waiting for the unfolding of the Final Days. In his staunch individualism, which grew stronger by the decade, he insisted that membership in such groups violated the very heart and substance of what Swedenborg had intended. By their very existence, the different denominations and sects, including the New Church, were visible examples of the barriers created by their competing and tyrannical creeds, all of which were diversions from the Word. 'It is not that there is not all the Truth in Swedenborg that we ever contended for', Wilkinson opined, 'but in his followers it is unprogressive and destitute of hope and charity, and therefore their state is liable to be superseded by any real manifestation, however low, which goes to the Tables and hearts of the people'.[23]

According to one of his biographers, Frederick Evans, Wilkinson was able to set forth the genius of Swedenborg in a way that made him more tangible, compelling readers not to shirk or avoid the conscious peril of their soul. Wilkinson conveyed the significance of revelation and the fact that it had been too long obscured by the 'cunning of the natural man' and the 'mean judgments of creeds'. With Swedenborg, 'the cloud is lifted, and the divine light shines down again, this time with rational force, and with the sevenfoldness of the Divine Humanity, upon human character as its special mission'. Evans found in Wilkinson's explanation of Swedenborg 'A very workaday gospel to fill the real need of all men, and more especially the average, the common man, who makes up the great bulk of humanity'. He provided a commonsense approach that allowed the average man to gain philosophical understanding of difficult concepts. No longer was it the bravado of an angry God, of arbitrary eternal punishments, determinate sin and poisoned heredity. Instead, there was the compelling explanation that men and women were responsible for their actions and the loves which brought them after death to those celestial societies to which their choices in life had most closely corresponded.[24]

Today, Wilkinson's translations and introductory comments remain classics in the Swedenborgian canon, carrying forward not only Swedenborg's far-reaching doctrines of forms, of series and degrees, of influx, and of correspondences, but expositions on what Emerson liked to identify as 'Whence? What? And Whither?'

Friends in High Places

While busy with his translations, Wilkinson wrote occasional articles for the *Monthly Magazine*, edited by his friend John A Herraud. One which appeared in 1841 concerning Coleridge's comments on Swedenborg's *Oeconomia Regni Animalis*, was read by Henry James, Sr. This chance reading led to a lifelong correspondence between the two men, some of which became the basis for James's *The Church of Christ Not an Ecclesiasticism* and *Christianity the Logic of Creation*. Not only did James help finance Wilkinson's translations through Otis Clapp, a Swedenborgian publisher and homoeopathic pharmacist in Boston, but, as evidence of the closeness of the two families, the Jameses named their third son Garth Wilkinson ('Wilky') in Wilkinson's honour, and the Wilkinsons reciprocated by naming their daughter Mary James after James's wife.[25]

The friendship proved not only satisfying for both men and their families, but also opened to Wilkinson a much larger world of writers and intellectuals, including Ralph Waldo Emerson who, in 1848, visited Wilkinson, bringing with him an introduction from James. Emerson proved to be a valuable friend, recognizing Wilkinson as a literary and professional colleague and introducing him to the sponsors of the Society for the Diffusion of Useful Knowledge and the Mechanics' Institutes which flourished in many of England's larger towns to stimulate education, information and understanding among the working classes. These organizations, similar to the Lyceum and Chautauqua movements in America, served Carlyle, novelists William Thackeray and Charles Dickens, and a host of other prominent writers. With Emerson's endorsement, Wilkinson joined the circuit, offering a series of lectures on the 'Physics of Human Nature' before the Whittington Club in London, and at venues in Liverpool, Manchester, Birmingham, Derby and Leeds. His talks on elementary anatomy and physiology utilized Swedenborg's doctrine of correspondences to explain the import of the animal spirit; the function of the cortex in the brain; and the distribution of influx into the body consonant with the intervals of lung respiration. His lectures, a vintage presentation of Swedenborgianism, proved useful later when he published *The Human Body and Its Connexion with Man*, drawing on both his Swedenborgian and Hahnemannian views of the body in health and disease.[26]

Emerson's admiration of Wilkinson was best expressed in his 'Swedenborg; or, the Mystic', a lecture given during his visit to England in 1847-8, later published in *Representative Men*, and which served to accelerate Swedenborg's popularity and the message he brought to the Christian world. As Emerson explained, Swedenborg's scientific books were neglected until Wilkinson, 'a philosophic critic . . . restored his master's buried books . . . and transferred them, with every advantage, from their forgotten Latin into English, to go round the world in our commercial and conquering tongue. . . . The admirable preliminary discourses with which Mr. Wilkinson has enriched these volumes, throw all contemporary philosophy of England into shade'.[27]

Wilkinson discovered that his translations had given him 'a passport to recognition and hospitality wherever he laid his foot'. With James and Emerson providing entrée, Wilkinson entered into to the literary world of Henry Wadsworth Longfellow, Thomas Henry Huxley, Josephine Butler, Hugh Doherty, Laurence and Lady Oliphant, William

Boericke, James Dwight Dana, Horace Greeley and George Ripley, to name a few. Besides James, his extensive correspondence included Thomas Carlyle, Alfred Tennyson, Charles Dickens, James Anthony Froude, Dante Gabriel Rossetti, Edward Augustus Freeman, Harriet Martineau, Sampson Reed, Robert Browning and Coventry Patmore.[28]

Swedenborgian Homoeopathy

Due to Wilkinson's dissatisfaction with traditional medicine and, at the urging of his wife and Henry James, Sr, he explored the similarities between Swedenborgianism and homoeopathy, particularly with regard to the law of correspondences and the strong relationship between disease and drug effects. Learning for himself the striking similarity between the two belief systems, he turned to homoeopathy and, for the first time in his career, enjoyed practising medicine.[29] '*You*, more than any other man, led me into Homoeopathy', he wrote to James. Having long been repulsed by the drenchings common to orthodox medicine, he found homoeopathic treatment much more satisfying for his patients and for his own peace of mind. Like Hahnemann, he tended over time to prescribe smaller and smaller doses, believing that the higher (and more spiritual) attenuations would prove more effective in the treatment of disease.[30] With a homoeopathic practice overlaid with Swedenborgian metaphysics, best illustrated by the publication of *The Human Body and Its Connexion with Man* which he dedicated to James, he thought it possible to connect 'the technical facts of anatomy and physiology with the truths of Revelation'.[31]

In 1850, the family moved to Sussex Lodge in St John's Wood where Wilkinson remained until his death. The residence served him during some of his most productive years, a symbol of his successful medical practice and his greatly broadened literary connections. Among his more notable patients were John Winston Spencer Churchill, Margarete Conway, Edward Maitland, Mrs Josephine Butler, Thomas Lake Harris, Daniel Dunglas Home, Nathaniel Hawthorne and F W Newman, the cardinal's brother.[32] When first starting out in his career, Wilkinson considered himself a writer who specialized in theology and practised physic on the side; after his conversion to homoeopathy in 1850, he considered himself a physician first and foremost, whose pastime was translating Swedenborg's writings.

My life now is for the most part a routine. Practice increases month by month; and the prospects of income are good. The pleasures of skill also attend me, whenever God gives any of the skill. What is best, I take a leading interest in my dear Medicine, and especially in Homoeopathy: and I reckon myself truly fortunate to be able at length to connect my mind to my daily work; and to see in the latter a most ample field for the exercise of my thoughts.[33]

Reformer

As a medical reformer, Wilkinson was opinionated on laws that curtailed the right of the individual to make his or her own choices. His 'Wilkinsonianism' placed him in a camp that one of his friends described as 'radically liberal conservatism', or what today might be called 'libertarian'.[34] He was an individual with an eclectic and independent mind who often threw himself at unpopular causes including opposition to vaccination and vivisection; advocating repeal of the Contagious Diseases Act requiring compulsory examination of prostitutes in garrison towns; and generally opposing any interference with the rights of the individual. Over and over again, he chastised the medical profession for its narrow-mindedness. Only by allowing a more laissez-faire approach to the delivery of health care could reform systems such as homoeopathy be free to practise without the heavy hand of government interference.[35]

In *War, Cholera, and the Ministry of Health, An Appeal to Sir Benjamin Hall and the British People*, published in 1855, Wilkinson attacked the 'social fortresses' of the medical, clerical and legal professions which he accused of pursuing their own mercenary interests at the expense of those they vowed to protect and defend. Among the worst offenders was the medical profession whose 'black, innumerable dungeons, is at present brought, by the benignant pestilence, into clear opposition with the interests of man'. Powerless against cholera, it had turned to protecting its monopoly against the growing number of dissidents, including homoeopaths who, because of their success, were capturing the patients of allopathic doctors. Citing hospital mortality statistics across Europe, Wilkinson pointed out that, on average, mortality rates at allopathic hospitals were thirty per cent higher than those at homoeopathic hospitals. [36]

> My assertion is borne out by hundreds of practitioners in all parts of these is-
> lands, of the British possessions, and of the civilized world; from the Himalayas
> to New Orleans, cholera and yellow fever and other kindred fiends, cower,
> crouch, and run away before the Homoeopathic rifles: the experience of these
> practitioners is duly registered, and may be easily read; they use no other drugs
> but the Homoeopathic means, with of course an abundant realm of hygienic
> resources also, fine dieting, skilful cold water, cheery words, real hopeful faces
> not stereotyped smiles, mesmerism and the rest: and these practitioners have
> an abundant clientry, who are not used to run away from them to the violent
> inefficacious people, whenever disease is sharp and sudden.[37]

Disgusted with the unbridled power of allopathic medicine, Wilkinson appealed to the General Board of Health to take cognizance of the mortality tables; study care-fully the system of homoeopathy, including its law of *similia*; test homoeopathy's pharmacopoeia and its winning new medicines (i.e., lachesis, cobra, arnica, rhus toxicodendron, cuprum, veratrum, camphor and podophyllum) against the drastic purges and narcotic extracts of old physic; and consider that the dangers to the health and longevity of the British people lay not in so-called irregular practice but in the legal protections summarily employed to protect medical orthodoxy. 'There is no more reason, Sir, why Government should directly patronize one kind of medical education, and destroy the practice of those medical practitioners who have not received it, than why they should grant privileges to one set of bakers, landlords, or butchers, and declare all others irregular'. Without the 'props' of diplomas, licensing and governmental patronage, he predicted a wholesale migration of the populace to homoeopathy. He called upon Parliament to protect the liberties of the public by modifying the laws employed to defend the 'despotism' of the medical colleges. [38]

An example of Wilkinson's unconventional approach was *Epidemic Man and His Visitations* in which he expressed his disbelief in microbes and all manner of disease causation unless understood as 'wrong-doings' which he categorized as sins, evils and vices which became hereditary over time. 'The origin of disease is in man's evil will, present and past', he insisted, causing the body to rot 'in various ways called diseases'. What was needed were 'theological pathologists' gifted with the ability to perceive how the law of correspondences connected the spiritual and natural man. Drawing from Swedenborg's writings to shore up his argument, he attacked the 'fabrications' of Jennerian vaccination, quarantines and fumigation as useless practices, placing the blame for disease, epidemics, plagues and pestilences on the spiritual state of individuals and the respective histories of the races from which they arose. Disease demanded the application of homoeopathic infinitesimals which he considered 'harmless as doves yet wise as serpents' in that they artfully and effectively countered the spiritual causation for disease.[39]

The reason for Wilkinson's strong commitment to homoeopathy was not just his success with patients but the close similarity he drew between the principles of homoeopathic medicine and Swedenborg's doctrine of correspondences, creating an alignment between God and human conduct. Homoeopathy opened to him a whole new understanding of disease and an inseparable bond between his spiritual and medical beliefs. In an open letter to Dr Robert T Cooper and the members of the Cooper Club, a group of renowned British homoeopaths, Wilkinson spoke of the 'anarchy and disorder of scientism', the lack of belief in a vital principle or 'Ruling Soul' to explain the living organism, and the need to introduce the law of *similia* which offered a true road map to the treatment of disease. Homoeopathy, he insisted, was best understood from a spiritual point of view. Ranking Swedenborg with Plato, Aristotle, Kant and Leibniz, Wilkinson chose to view him not as a scientist who limited his concerns to the mortal body but as someone in search of the soul. 'The fact is', he wrote, 'every new function which Swedenborg has assigned to organ after organ is a dawning spiritual truth, and thus a path to theology'. He invited his medical colleagues to study Swedenborg as a theologian whose scientific endeavours in anatomy and physiology were not on behalf of any materialistic objective but, instead, served as a 'medium' for revelation. For both Swedenborg and Wilkinson, every word in the Bible contained an internal meaning and every meaning, however slight, became a path to the Divine.[40]

Wilkinson compared Hahnemann's infinitesimal medicines to Swedenborg's doctrine of degrees, with high attenuations reaching 'different phases of spiritual effort' in the brain while the lower attenuations touched on the inferior parts of the body. The doctrine of degrees was as applicable to medicine as it was to an understanding of the spiritual world where angels dwelt and where all mortals upon death became part of an organically defined but spiritual *Maximus Homo*, whose placement in the body reflected their choices of good or evil. The homoeopath's attenuated medicines were 'heavenly manna' conjoining heaven and earth, the natural and the spiritual man. Just as Swedenborg had provided intimate knowledge of the spiritual world, Hahnemann had shown how infinitesimals supplied spiritual power through the blood to cure disease 'by the rank and dignity of special penetration to . . . the very *penetralia* of organ after organ'. Both raised man higher than the quantities and qualities of the material cells, atoms, waters and gases that constituted his natural body. For the New Church physician, the material body became a spiritual organism whose treatment required correspondence between material science and revelation.[41]

Looking to the future, Wilkinson predicted revolutionary changes in medicine—changes that would demonstrate to the world the importance of both Hahnemann's and Swedenborg's contributions to medicine.

> This time will belong to the ages of inspiration transcending genius. Evil methods will pass away. Medicine will have new insights and capacities because it will have new honesty, bravery, tenderness and virtue from the Lord. These commonplaces will then be the miracles of its life. Surgical homicide will cease, and hospitals will not be the educational laboratories in which the poor are the clay which the doctor moulds into the costly and mortal chalice of orthodox practice for the rich. Operations will be private for whoever demands it, and will never be performed in wards where sick persons lie. A non-medical board will decide upon those chirurgical meddlings that are unlawful. Vivisection will be penal through the length and breadth of the land. The places of its laboratories will be ploughed over,

and sown with salt. Huge fees for surgery will be forbidden, as being rank baits to cutting and mutilating. The contamination of men by inoculation of diseases from man or beast will be scouted as heinous. Deaths by any surgical interference, great or small, in hospitals or elsewhere, will be submitted to inquest under non-medical coroners for justice and judgment. The doses of poison will be infinitesimal by decree. Medicine will be disestablished, shorn of power borrowed from the State, so that cases of death and injury may have fairplay before juries. All men and women will be free to practise with this justice over them.[42]

Spiritualism

Wilkinson's interests led him from mesmerism to spiritualism, Swedenborgianism, Fourierism and Harrisism (followers of Thomas Lake Harris). Throughout his life, he retained a fascination for the esoteric side of life, a subject on which he wrote extensively for *The Monthly Magazine*. Both he and his brother William frequented the lectures of John Elliotson, founder of the London Mesmeric Infirmary, whose patients included Elizabeth Barrett Browning, Wilkie Collins, Harriet Martineau and William Thackeray. The Wilkinson brothers were also avid supporters of spiritualism, a movement that Henry James, Sr kept at arm's length. Indicative of this interest was Wilkinson's *Homoeopathic Principle Applied to Insanity: A Proposal to Treat Lunacy by Spiritualism*; the brothers' joint editorship of *Spiritual Health* and *The Spiritual Magazine*; and their promotion of Thomas Lake Harris and his Brotherhood of the New Life. Clearly, too, Wilkinson's poetry, which he published under the title *Improvisations from the Spirit* in 1857, reflected his strong fascination with spiritualism. Dedicated to his wife and printed by the New Church Publishing Association in New York and by William White in London, the poems ranged across numerous subjects—from medicine ('Chloroform: What of It?' and 'The Birth of Aconite') which reflected his homoeopathic proclivities; to fairies ('The Fairies' Welcome' and 'The Fairy Veils') which showed his continued interest in spiritism; to reform communities in Europe and America ('Charles Fourier'); and the mysticism of Blake and Swedenborg ('The Birthday of the Human Soul').[43]

Wilkinson eventually grew tired of spiritism, repulsed by the multitude of frauds. He did not deny the 'spontaneous motions of the spiritual world upon and in the natural world' but insisted that it was wrong to solicit communication through seances and other means.[44] 'Spiritist informations tell us nothing', he concluded. 'They are only *continua* of the earthly senses, which are nowhere continuous with the spiritual or heavenly. They are brainless for the upper realm'. Here, he and James were finally speaking the same language.[45] Despite Wilkinson's repudiation of spiritualism, he remained friends with the Oliphants and with Thomas Lake Harris whose poem *Regina* included references to Wilkinson's eldest daughter, Emma Marsh Pertz. In later years, however, their friendships waned. 'I cannot see that T. L. Harris has continued the Revelation of the Divine Sense of the Word, though he has broken ground in social and practical life: perhaps deep ground'.[46] Interestingly, when Laurence Oliphant requested an introduction to Harris, Wilkinson declined, believing that it was not in Oliphant's interest to make himself known to the mystic and prophet.[47]

Wilkinson was also an enthusiastic supporter of Fourierism and the Brook Farm experiment in Boston, believing that the spirituality of Swedenborg, when combined with Fourier's societal planning, could realize humanity's heavenly hopes in the natural world. Swedenborg's law of correspondence and Fourier's social planning provided the keys to humanity's future. They connected Swedenborg's analogical construction of subjects, beginning with particulars, and brought them together into single and general ideas as a prelude to what Fourier had advanced in his construction of society. Just as Swedenborg's animal kingdom began with the examination of different visible phenomena, Fourier started with the social mechanics of society, mapping out its attributes to give practical truth to speculation and hypothesis.[48]

In a period when the ideas of Fourier, Saint-Simon and Robert Owen were interpreted as possible answers to the eclipse of the aristocracy, increased signs of class conflict, and the destructive effects of unregulated capitalism, Wilkinson was encouraged by the ideas of Fourier and understood the close similarity between Fourier's writings and Swedenborg's. By 1847, he found it a *'jolly human'* reform movement that brought the spiritual and natural worlds together in a highly respected manner. 'All you say of the Association movement', he wrote to his friend John Morell,

'I echo from my heart. It is *the* morning brightness of the world's day'. His visit to Paris during the 1848 insurrection helped to solidify his support when he saw at first hand the cannonading and musketry that took the lives of thousands. Wilkinson came away from the experience scarred by 'the bayonets of the upper Classes'.[49]

According to his nephew and biographer, Wilkinson was best understood in terms of his mysticism, Transcendentalism and impatience. As a mystic, he had a sense of God's immanence in nature, viewing life as a continual reference to Christ and the promise of godliness for humankind. In his books and letters, Wilkinson had emphasized the Word of God as a means of providing an appreciation for the 'inner life' during periods of doubt, and his understanding of Swedenborg helped him to appreciate the essential elements of faith in God and the manhood of Christ. As a Transcendentalist, Wilkinson enjoyed a sense of freedom from traditional ties—freedom that relied on individual conscience and, through the medium of correspondences, an understanding of the relationship between the natural and spiritual worlds. Wilkinson's 'Plodding work, patient reiteration, a brilliant versatility, indomitable perseverance' were qualities that consumed his years and included an occasional tendency 'to fling off red-hot fragments from the periphery at unexpected angles'. Feeling the presence of the unseen spiritual world, he trudged a path with the impatience of one who felt that the appointed hour of discovery lay just around the corner.[50]

A man of letters and personal friend of James, Emerson and Carlyle, Wilkinson won the praise of a coterie of admirers. As explained by biographer Evans, Wilkinson's style was 'spontaneous', 'unaffectedly honest' and 'heart-searching', indulging in no clichés or affectations. Wilkinson published a compendium of books, pamphlets and articles over his lifetime, most of which, according to Evans, were 'completely neglected by the ordinary reading world, and known to but a few among the super-intelligent'.[51] In an age preoccupied with the writings of Karl Marx, John Stuart Mill, Georg Wilhelm Friedrich Hegel, Søren Kierkegaard, Friedrich Nietzsche, Auguste Comte, Charles Darwin, Herbert Spencer and Thomas Carlyle, the contributions of Wilkinson were largely ignored except for a small and appreciative reading audience. For those to whom he appealed, however, his message pulsated with hope that the twin pillars of Swedenborg and Hahnemann would replace the crumbling edifices of religious and medical orthodoxy.

A time-honoured pioneer of homoeopathy and Swedenborgianism, Wilkinson was overlooked in an age whose literary currents found little in his books of lasting or discerning value. Nevertheless, as explained by Ralph Waldo Emerson, he 'brought to metaphysics and to psychology a native vigor . . . equal to the highest attempts, and a rhetoric like the armory of the invincible knights of old'.[52] Swedenborg had 'found a pupil in Dr. Wilkinson, a philosophic critic, with a coequal vigor of understanding and imagination comparable only to Lord Bacon's, who has produced his master's buried books to the day, and transferred them, with every advantage, from their forgotten Latin into English to go round the world in our commercial and conquering tongue'.[53] Born forty years after the death of Swedenborg, Wilkinson had proudly served as his translator, as an annotator of Fourier's writings and as an advocate of Hahnemann, bringing metaphysics and physiology into a new and invigorated relationship. He died at his home in Finchley Road at the age of eighty-seven and was commemorated by a bust and portrait in the Swedenborg Society on Bloomsbury Street in London.

James Tyler Kent (1849-1916)

While Wilkinson served in England as an advocate for a combination of Swedenborgian and Hahnemannian medicine, America had James Tyler Kent. Born in 1849 in Woodhull, New York, Kent was raised as a Baptist and attended Franklin Academy in Prattsburgh, New York, before enrolling at Madison University (Colgate) in Hamilton, New York, where he graduated with a bachelor's degree in 1868. Two years later, at the age of twenty-two, he matriculated at the Eclectic Medical Institute (EMI) in Cincinnati, writing his thesis on 'True Eclecticism' and graduating in 1871.[54] Although it remains unclear how Kent learned about EMI and why it became his school of choice, EMI was one of the early reform medicine colleges that organized in the first half of the nineteenth century. The word *eclectic* in the school's title was meant to imply an approach to medical therapeutics that was cumulative, drawing from all theories and practices that proved beneficial and using only those therapies that best served the needs of the patient.[55] Reflective of the Paris Clinical School of the 1830s and 1840s which eschewed theories and dogmas, EMI's faculty countenanced scepticism and the twin principles of observation and experimentation. By the time Kent matriculated, the school had settled on a more narrow approach consisting of herbal medicines as substitutes for traditional animal- and mineral-based drugs, a distrust of foreign influences, and a distinctly democratic bias in its educational philosophy.[56]

As a student, Kent enrolled in the classes of John Milton Scudder, Benjamin L Hill and Eli Jones, all three of whom were devout Swedenborgians. Scudder was not only dean and owner of the college, but held the chair of pathology and philosophy of medicine. Because of the school's close relationship with the Lloyd Brothers Pharmacists, Inc. of Cincinnati, the curriculum emphasized simplicity in prescriptions, meaning the use of small single doses with comparatively few combinations. Single remedies were, of course, a principal factor in homoeopathic practice and, while eclectics accepted the concept of specific medication and specific diagnosis, including the fact that physicians should not be treating according to disease names but to a symptom-complex, they gave little credence to Hering's second law of cure. Nevertheless, it is clear from Scudder's *Specific Medication* and *Specific Diagnosis*, and from Jones's *Definite Medication* that EMI chose to incorporate those components of homoeopathy that best suited its purposes, a factor that arguably made an imprint on Kent's medical education and his subsequent practice.[57]

After graduating, Kent opened a practice in Woodhull, New York. In 1874, two years after the death of his first wife, he married again and moved to St Louis where he joined the Eclectic National Medical Association and supplemented his practice by teaching at the American Medical College (eclectic) of St Louis. When his wife Lucia became ill with 'nervous weakness, insomnia, and anemia' and requested a homoeopathic physician, Kent consented albeit reluctantly. Impressed, however, by her quick recovery, he became less sceptical of the system and eventually completed a second medical degree at the Homoeopathic Medical College of Missouri where he graduated in 1879. Given his now formidable education, he joined the school's faculty and, in 1883, was appointed chair of materia medica. He remained affiliated with the school until 1888.[58]

In his early years as a practising homoeopath, Kent relied on low-potency medicines as his preferred choice for drug delivery. Eventually, he was drawn to the position taken by the classical homoeopaths in St Louis who insisted upon adherence to strict Hahnemannianism, meaning the use of single doses of high-potency medicines. After testing the 30th potency which he found more effective than the lower dilutions, particularly in chronic diseases, he introduced what he called 'Series in Degrees', treating chronic diseases with ever higher potencies, starting at the 200th level and moving upward. In doing so, he believed he was treating not only the physical body, but the patient's mental, emotional and spiritual states as well. Before long he was advocating 1M, 50M, CM, DM and even MM potencies made on the centesimal scale. Given the labour-intensive challenge this created, he joined with Urban Joseph Ehrhart and Louis Karl, homoeopathic pharmacists in Chicago, to design and build a machine to manufacture his high serial dilutions known as 'Kent Potencies', which remained in production into the 1940s.[59]

Beginning in the 1880s, major changes occurred across the medical landscape. The germ theory of disease and the impact of bacteriology forced the medical community, including homoeopaths, to refocus their energies in a number of new directions. Universities and medical colleges established chairs of bacteriology, and regimens long considered mainstays against disease fell before new serum therapies that were soon integrated into everyday practice. In addition, the rise of laboratory science threatened the very bedside authority that had given homoeopathy its distinctive reputation and professional identity. Other changes included a more in-depth understanding of infectious diseases, the promotion of disinfectants and their power to neutralize disease, and the establishment of scientific societies and groups of specialists, including the American Surgical Association, the Association of American Physicians, the American Physiological Society, the American Association of Anatomists, the Pediatric Society and the American Association of Pathologists and Bacteriologists. The members of these organizations, many of whom were educated abroad, became strong advocates of curricular reform, higher admission standards and advanced university-based medical training.

In their recognition of the importance of laboratory-based medicine, low-potency homoeopaths were drawn closer to conventional medicine. In doing so, they became increasingly eclectic in their practices by showing greater openness to novel therapies; a willingness to collaborate with regulars, including specialists; and less opposition to the formation of integrated examining boards for the licensing of physicians. When, in 1903, the American Medical Association revised its Code of Ethics, giving members greater freedom in matters of consultation and admitting into its ranks eclectics and homoeopaths willing to relinquish their sectarian titles and use only the MD after their name, many of homoeopathy's rank and file switched allegiances. The familiar features that once defined homoeopathy remained alive, but just barely, as homoeopaths crossed over into conventional medicine and as their remaining medical schools chose to pay lip service to Hahnemann's teachings in order to retain relevance in the new biomedical world. Tensions became so fractious between the low- and high-potency groups within homoeopathy that schism became an ongoing issue among its members.[60]

Exemplary of Kent's rising status within the profession was his founding of the Organon and Materia Medica Society and his election as president of the International Hahnemannian Association in 1887. Having changed his allegiance not only from eclecticism to homoeopathy, but to becoming a champion of pure Hahnemannianism, Kent was not at all hesitant to turn against his former colleagues for 'living a lie'. In his presidential address before the association, he explained: 'Eclectics, building upon the uncertain sands of *theory*, need to be continually rebuilding, as each new theory causes a shifting of their foundation'. By contrast, his new-found system was built upon an 'unchangeable rock of *law*'.[61]

In 1888, Kent moved to Philadelphia where, as the emerging spokesman for Hahnemannianism, he organized the Post-Graduate School of Homeopathics, the funding of which came from John Pitcairn, founder of Pittsburgh Plate Glass and a prominent Swedenborgian. As dean and professor of materia medica, Kent intended for the school to follow the design of the North American Academy of the Homeopathic Healing Art in Allentown, Pennsylvania, by providing postgraduate study for those who had already earned the MD. Many of the school's graduates became leaders in homoeopathy through the first half of the twentieth century and one of the school's graduates called it 'a Swedenborgian School', a sure indication of its educational philosophy.[62]

Following the death of his second wife in 1895, Kent married Clara Louise Toby, a homoeopathic physician and well-known Swedenborgian who assisted in the editing of his many writings. In 1900, the couple moved to Chicago where Kent relocated his Post-Graduate School of Homeopathics at Dunham Medical College, serving as its dean. Although the college had broken away from Hering Medical College, the two schools merged again in 1903. Reflective of its status in the city, the college enjoyed connections with numerous local hospitals including Chicago Baptist, National Temperance, Woman's Christian Temperance Union and Cook County. It also acquired laboratory privileges at the University of Chicago. Kent remained affiliated with the college until it closed in 1913.[63]

In 1910, Kent was instrumental in organizing the Society of Homeopathicians, consisting mainly of his students, as a way of disseminating the principles of Hahnemann. The group published its own journal, *The Homeopathician* for which Kent served as senior editor. Known for his astute observations and his ability to link Hahnemannian principles with Swedenborgian concepts, he earned the reputation of being a brilliant, albeit dogmatic teacher, particularly in linking the materia medica with specific archetypes or profiles.

Kentianism

As with Wilkinsonism, Kentianism was built on the Swedenborgian belief that a fundamental correspondence existed between the material and spiritual worlds. Everything that happened in one was reflected in the other. 'Through familiarity with Swedenborg', Kent wrote, 'I have found the correspondences wrought out from the Word of God harmonious with all I have learned in the past thirty years'.[64] Thus, the study of the individual human organism was also a study of the soul with its will, its reasoning or intellect, and its imagination, memory and desire. All human acts began in the spiritual world and moved outward from the soul through the mental world of desires, intentions and sensations, to the physical world of actualities. To understand the causes of a particular pathological condition it was thus necessary to know that the body's spiritual condition would eventually affect its physical functions. Any remedy that cured had to be guided by symptoms that reflected the innermost causes. The centre for each individual was his or her loves, and when those loves were drawn to inappropriate ends, the individual became sick in the will, the very centre of his or her being. Disease, manifested through subjective and objective symptoms, began as a distortion of the will and understanding before affecting the body through various physical derangements, all of which affected the vital force.

Kentianism began with the Swedenborgian proposition that all existence had a degree of vital substance. Nothing could exist without a cause or force that held it in 'continuance'. This implied a God whose influx held together the animal, vegetable and mineral kingdoms of the world. In man, the vital force was the *vice-regent* of the soul which existed within every part of the body. The vital force kept the body animated and adapted to its uses and purposes. When the vital principle was disturbed to the point of demonstrating signs of a disease character, the physician needed to 'read' the disorderly condition as action from the interior individual and find a substance whose symptoms in a healthy individual were similar. Unless the symptoms demonstrating the signs of the disease were matched by the totality of symptoms in the substance, disease would remain. This required the homoeopath to thoroughly 'prove' each of the substances used to treat the characteristic signs of disease. The phenomena of cure depended entirely upon the fixed law of *similia* which applied to both the substance and its attenuation.[65]

When the vital force became deranged, it inclined the body to irregular symptom-complexes, an indication of early signs of disease and subsequent changes in the cellular structure. Such changes occurred over a series of intermediate degrees until they were observable in the outermost surface. Since disease could only be detected from its effects on the natural senses, medicines would work only if they were turned into something similar in kind. Drugs in their coarser levels created changes to the exterior of the body but had no effect upon the disease itself. In their physical form, coarse drugs failed to correspond with the sickness and therefore failed to cure beyond the outermost effects of the disease. The ultimate causes (miasms) of disease were reached only through potentized medicines and, the higher the potency, the more effective it operated on the interior causation. 'Medicines will not act curatively', explained Kent, 'unless potentized to correspond to the degrees in which the man is sick'.[66]

> Nutritive substances are material; curative substances are immaterial simple substances. There is always a tendency to influx where simple substance is active. When there is a disturbance in the inner planes of man's economy there is an influx, from the atmosphere, of some deleterious simple substance. If there were a curative immaterial substance, it would be drawn in by influx and act as an antidote. If remedies are given on the plane of disturbance they will cure.[67]

According to Swedenborg, the worlds of nature and spirit were distinct, but intimately related by analogous substances, laws and forces. Disease originated in the soul, which included individual conscience and the freedom of choice or will. Bad decisions led to the body's estrangement from nature, leaving a corrosive effect on the organs and parts which, in turn, led to disease. All diseases, even those whose origins were in the distant past, had at one time been caused by a lack of conscience or bad choice. While the true nature of man was reflected in a sound mind and body, sin with all its elements of selfishness, was the primal cause of disease. Like other falsities of life, it sprang from placing the senses above the spirit.[68] As Swedenborg explained, 'if it were the case that the person was leading a good life his interiors would lie open into heaven, and through heaven towards the Lord, and so too would his tiniest invisible *vascula*...If this were so man would not know any sickness...And when his body was no longer able to serve his internal man, which is his spirit, he would pass, without knowing any sickness, from his earthly body into a body such as angels possess, and so would pass from the world directly into heaven'.[69]

The centrepiece of Kentianism was Swedenborg's concept of *love* which descended through degrees from divine influx. Love produced affections and intentions which, when assimilated, became part of the thinking human being. True spiritual and celestial love was love toward one's neighbour and love of the Lord while natural and sensual love was love of the world and of self. When purified by wisdom, love became spiritual and celestial. When defiled, it became natural, sensual and corporeal, making the natural man less spiritual and sincere.[70]

As an organized spiritual being, each individual possessed a material body whose thoughts constituted the reigning principles of the soul. Thus, the quality of life and health evident in the body was determined by the influx of the soul's life into the heart and lungs which represented the will and understanding respectively, and corresponded to the loves and thoughts of the soul which passed into the body. All aspects of the natural body—both internal and external—were correspondences of forms found in the spiritual world. This included the organic parts of the body which, by themselves, could not live, feel or move except by influx of the corresponding form from the spiritual world. Together, they acted in unity. Human anatomy and psychology were interdependent fields. At the top was the soul with the will as its incentive; in the middle was reason, with intellect and intention; and the lower level involved imagination, memory and desire. The will and understanding moved the body and its members. Without influx from heaven, however, no person could stir even a step. As explained by Swedenborg, 'For whatever the man thinks, the mouth and tongue speak, and whatever he wills the body does [but not] without influx from heaven'.[71]

In formulating his Swedenborgian-based homoeopathy, Kent transformed Hahnemann's vital force or life principle into 'God' which, as a consequence, limited his therapeutic message to a highly esoteric audience. Some even called Kent's supporters a religious cult. By confusing God (i.e., a reasoning spirit) with the indwelling *power* or *force* that animated the organism, Kent went beyond the intent of Hahnemann and his basic laws of *similia*, single remedies, minimum doses and individualization. As noted by French homoeopath Denis Demarque, 'the enlightenment of Kent has given homeopathy in the Anglo Saxon world the allure of a religious sect'.[72] This also explains why Kent was less dependent on the emerging biomedical model of his day, including the lessons learned from German pathological science. For him, symbolism, revelations, intuition, imagination,

147

analogy, the theory of signatures, medicinal personalities, polycrests, generals and mentals were of much greater significance.

For Kent and his disciples, orthodox medicine's failure lay in the fact that modern physiology lacked a vitalistic doctrine on which to base its teachings. Without the doctrine of vital force, there could be no cause and therefore no relationship between cause and effect. Without the doctrine of vital force, there was no way of understanding what it meant to be sick. Since tissues of an individual did not become deranged unless something prior acted on them as a cause, the physician had to have a conception of the living 'internal man' who wills and understands. Only the living individual exercising his or her will and understanding caused the body's expressions of health and disease. Implied in this observation was the realization that there was no such thing as a disease, only sick persons, which meant that the role of the physician was to restore order (Kent preferred the term *government*) to the body, meaning 'to put in order the interior of the economy, i.e., the will and understanding'.[73]

The manner in which an individual lived was the outward expression of a person's thinking, willing and understanding. Since disease was the result of that which the body knew and willed, it was the knowing and willing that needed to change before there could be permanent cure. Willing and understanding constituted the individual—the 'house' in which the body resided. Although Kent expected doctors to learn the structure of the physical body—muscles, nerves, organs, etc.—it was not these parts but the 'life' of the body that gave disease its human form. This meant that the duty of the physician was to bring 'order' to the interior of the body (i.e., will and understanding) before the effects could be addressed. 'The man who considers disease results to be the disease itself', Kent opined, 'and expects to do away with these as disease, is insane'.[74]

Kent refused to countenance the emerging role of the specialist whose interest lay in the study and treatment of specific organs and functions. The true physician treated the *whole* body, not a specific organ or function. 'The smallest part of the body', he insisted, 'should never be treated except by a remedy that fits the symptoms of the entire constitution, organs, and parts'.

There should be no fashion in medicine; what was good fifty years ago in the hands of the masters should be just as good today, and the deviation comes out of departing from the methods of the early physician who had not the labor-saving and brain-saving machines. If the masters could cure such cases with simply great labor, how much better ought we to do. The high degree of perfection will never come to our specialties so long as the specialists are content with the palliatives now in vogue.[75]

Condemning the experiments of German microbiologist Robert Koch and French chemist and microbiologist Louis Pasteur as 'useless', Kent insisted that not only did bacteria come *after* disease, but they were 'perfectly harmless in every respect'. Bacteria were the outcome, not the cause of disease; they were simply harmless 'scavengers accompanying the disease'. Destroying the bacilli did not destroy the disease. Similarly, no organ made the body sick as the causation was prior to the organ's dysfunction. Proper cure, then, lay in the very vital force which lived in each individual; it was the living-force of the patient that required correction. Disease began before any germ announced its existence and ended when the living force was strong enough to restore the power and functions to all parts of the body.[76]

True and permanent healing required the physician to perceive that which was perverted in the living being, not from observations made on dead bodies or abstract science. The laboratory, Kent insisted, was no place to discover causes or remedies since it focused not on life but on the effects of disease. Nothing ever discovered by studying the dead led to a remedy for sickness. Only if the laboratory could discern what the individual loved and hated and the extent to which his or her rational mind deviated from the normal could this 'dead science' be of any help. The true beginnings of disease were not found in looking through the microscope; they were discoverable only in the 'manifestations of the perverted vital economy'. In the symptoms one could know the disease. The law of cure was the law of *similia*, and when physicians understood this law they would perceive 'the relation of sick images in sick people and in our pathogeneses'. Until the laboratory could yield information on the inherited tendencies that resulted in tuberculosis, cancer and other diseases, research was a useless squandering of dollars. When the physician perceived sickness in the symptoms that represented the personality of the sick patient there could be a true diagnosis. 'What is common', he explained, 'will never lead the physician to perceive what is peculiar in any individual'.[77]

Aphorisms

Kent's numerous aphorisms and precepts are testimony to the inflexibility that pervaded his lectures and writings. His medicine, rigidly dogmatic in its defense of Hahnemann's laws and principles, treated laboratory science and biomedical reductionism as little more than opinion. His matter-of-fact statements and deductive logic concerning the spiritual origins of disease, bacteria and pathological science were simplistic for a medical doctor. Nevertheless, they served him well among those disciples who thought his ideas and concepts expounded a coherent and fundamentally complete bridge connecting homoeopathy with Swedenborgianism. Examples of his dogmatic world include:

> *You cannot divorce Medicine and Theology. Man exists all the way down from his innermost Spiritual to his outermost Natural.*
>
> *The external man is but an outward expression of the internal; so the results of disease (symptoms) are but the outward expression of the internal sickness.*
>
> *The Vital Force is of the Soul, and cannot be destroyed or weakened. It can be disordered, but it is all there.*
>
> *Man cannot be made sick or be cured except by some substance as ethereal in quality as the Vital Force.*
>
> *The Vital Force dominates, rules and co-ordinates the human body.*
>
> *We potentize so as to render the remedy simple enough to be drawn in by influx by the Vital Force.*
>
> *That changes in the body correspond to wrong thinking is true. The fault of the world today, is reasoning from externals. Man elected in the early part of his history to think from lasts to firsts, and thereby lost his ability to know.*

Thinking, willing, and doing, are the three things in life from which finally proceed the chronic miasms.

He who sees not in Bright's disease the deep miasm back of it, sees not the whole disease, but only the finishing of a long course of symptoms which have been developing for years.

It would seem as if the Old School would have asked long ago 'What are the effects of drugs upon healthy people?' Their experiments on animals do not answer this.

The mind symptoms, if you can know them, are the most important. If the pathological symptoms seem to contra-indicate a remedy, and the mental symptoms to indicate it, these are to be taken.

There are degrees of fineness of the Vital Force. We may think of internal man as possessing infinite degrees and of external man as possessing finite degrees.

The greatest comfort on earth to man in incurable diseases is Homeopathy.

Unless the inner nature of the remedy corresponds with the inner nature of the disease the remedy will not cure the disease but simply remove the symptoms which it covers; that is, suppress them.

Pathology has no place in an effort to select a medicine for the sick.

The body became corrupt because man's interior will was corrupt.

Every sensation has its correspondence to something that is within.

Two sick people are more unlike than two well ones.

We do not have to go into a plane called the other world to find a place where spirits dwell. Spirits are no longer unthinkable.[78]

Kent's Repertory

While Old School physicians were content to remove the symptoms of a disease with whatever medicine would bring a prompt 'cure', the homoeopath argued that most medicines in their armamentarium were 'insidiously violent' and unnecessarily dangerous. They damaged the patient's interior while the disease remained unaffected or grew worse. Only mild and gentle medicine that 'flows with the stream, scarcely producing a ripple', was effective in adjusting the internal disorder which then affected the outermost, and returned the patient to normal. All true and permanent cures proceeded, as Hering had explained, from centre to circumference, from above, down, and from within, out. In other words, the interiors of the patient must cease to be affected before the exteriors showed signs of health.[79]

When Kent began teaching materia medica in 1883, he had already immersed himself in George Heinrich Gottlieb Jahr's *Symptom-Codex*, Clemens Maria Franz von Boenninghausen's *Therapeutic Pocket Book*, Constantine Lippe's *Repertory of the More Characteristic Symptoms of the Materia Medica*, Henry Minton's *A Practical Homeopathic Treatise on the Diseases of Women* and Timothy Field Allen's *A Handbook of Materia Medica, and Homoeopathic Therapeutics*, most of which he found useful, but limited. All were deficient in some manner due to their organization, arrangement of symptoms, condensed form, or incompleteness. As he explained, pathogenesis had increased so much in the intervening years that none of these works could fill the requirements of modern practice. Believing that it was important first to understand the mental symptoms of the patient before looking at the physical symptoms, he adopted the plan used by Lippe, carefully recording mental characteristics before looking at physical symptoms.[80]

In 1897, Kent published *Repertory of the Homeopathic Materia Medica*, a compendium of mental, psychological and physical symptoms categorized by body part or system. Each entry contained an alphabetical listing of the substance known to have caused or cured that symptom. The substances were arranged by intensity, or how strongly they were associated with each symptom. The *Repertory* proved exceptionally useful, representing a compilation of previously determined symptoms that, for many, seemed like a maze which, when penetrated, caused one to become 'hopelessly lost'. For those who mastered the *Repertory*, symptomatology became 'simplicity itself', beginning with *mentals*, then *generals*, then *particulars*. True symptomatology meant looking at the mental symptoms first to see if the patient was jealous, suspicious, tearful, indifferent or reserved. With this as a guide, the physician could work rapidly until a remedy was found that fitted the whole patient. The mentals of greatest importance were those related to the will (jealousy), followed by those that affected the understanding (delusions of grandeur), and then memory. After this came symptoms considered strange, rare or peculiar, followed by the physical (i.e., appetite), physical generals (i.e., reaction to environment), character of discharges, and particulars.[81] As Matthew Wood noted in *The Magical Staff*, Kent was an Aristotelian who, besides having an intense interest in cause and effect, essence and existence, conceived of a world of descending levels of being—all emanating from the Divine. Kent found in Swedenborg's theology a universe organized by degrees in an orderly descent from the Divine, whose human beings lived two lives—one interior and spiritual and the other exterior and material.[82]

In his president's address before the Society of Homeopathicians in Chicago in October of 1913, Kent identified this innermost/outermost phenomenon as the *vertex presentation*, meaning that perversions of the desires, of the intelligence, and of memory were sufficient to disturb the body's functions and organs and bring about consequential perversions to tissues and pathological conditions. Properly understanding *how* sickness arose allowed the homoeopathic physician 'to secure evidence that [would] enable him to adjust the materia medica so that order will certainly be re-established'.[83]

Kent admitted the difficulty of explaining disease as something that began as perversions of the will and understanding. Nevertheless, he considered disease, including the miasms, as moral in their origin, originating from Adam's Fall or from subsequent wickedness on the part of mankind. Accordingly, he reminded his disciples that the true homoeopathic physician was a philosopher first and foremost who conceived sickness in its perversions:

Of the Loves,
Of Intelligence,
Of Memory,
Of Bodily Sensations,
Of Causes and
Of Circumstance;
In Greater and in Lesser;

In General and in Particular;

And these as they extend into Ultimates.[84]

Like Hahnemann before him, Kent insisted that *psora* was the oldest and original cause of most diseases, a spiritual invasion of the vital or life force, followed close behind by *syphilis* and *sycosis*. At some point in the early history of the human species, a particular thinking and willing made man susceptible to the disease manifestations of psora, making it the equivalent of original sin and the Fall of the *Maximus Homo*. The more disordered the individual, the more susceptible he was to the external world in which he lived. As the primitive or primary disorder of humanity, psora embraced most of the designated groupings which were called diseases; it was the basis for their different manifestations. When man thought, he willed, and what he willed, he acted upon. Diseases corresponded to man's affections; they did not derive from what the eyes observed with a microscope but what was the immaterial operating upon the interior of the individual.[85]

In its deeper aspects, homoeopathy resembled a religion which rested on a series of principles, including:

1. The universe was the creation of a spiritual being;
2. The living organism contained an invisible *dynamis* or vital force which came from a spiritual being or entity that maintained its functions and structures;
3. The vital force was non-physical and its ancestry stretched back to the origins of life;
4. Man was not only a living physical entity but a not-physical and immortal being;
5. Disease symptoms arose from invisible sources within the organism and represented impediments to vitalism's control over the mind and body;
6. Remedies stimulated the vital force; and
7. Death represented the separation of body and spirit.

These points, singularly and together, illustrated the consanguinity between homoeopathy and religious and philosophical systems of thought. In both homoeopathy and religion were found spiritual, emotional and philosophical elements as well as emphasis on trust and belief, the paranormal, and some form of personal or collective salvation. Best understood in the writings of Kent, Timothy Field Allen, James Compton Burnett, Otis Clapp, the Boerickes and Tafels—all of whom were Swedenborgians—homoeopathy was not too removed from some of the more abstruse forms of religious mysticism.[86]

Kent was known for his 'pictures' of patient types or constitutions and for condensing his remedies into similar personality profiles.[87] The true homoeopath was an artistic and intuitive diagnostician whose study of the materia medica made it possible for him to retain an image of the sick personality and match it to the totality of symptoms experienced by provers. 'I have often known the intuitive prescriber to explain a so-called marvelous cure saying: "I cannot quite say how I came to give that remedy but it resembled him" '.[88] Every remedy represented a specific picture of a symptom-complex, including the patient's state of mind; when used on a patient with a similar physical and psychological state, the medicine was capable of affecting a cure. This required every well-chosen remedy to be based on exacting data drawn from the repertory. Kent's 'drug pictures' became a factor in George Vithoulkas's 'essence pictures' and the foundation of most homoeopathic practice in the US and elsewhere today.[89]

This element in Kent's methodology looked strikingly like phenomenology in that he dismissed theories and preconceptions as abstract intellectualism and replaced them with the desire to observe the patient as a whole directly and intuitively. 'Throw aside all theories, and matters of belief and opinion, and dwell in simple facts', Kent advised. 'You must see and feel the internal nature of your patient as the artist sees and feels the picture he is painting. He feels it. Study to feel the economy, the life, the soul'. Rooted in the neutral and essentially 'as-is' aspect of the experience, he decried theories, causes or mechanisms. 'Here are people essences and here are drug pictures—your task is to match them by neutrally viewing the patient and intimately coming to know the drug pictures', he wrote.[90] In this regard, Kent's holistic approach was not much different than Edmund Husserl's phenomenological method, the experiential admonitions of John Dewey, Charles Sanders Peirce and William James, or the Zen way of direct enlightenment. The *truth* of something lay not in endless reasoning or idle speculation but in perceiving the world as a blank sheet without judgments or explanations.

In amplifying Hahnemann's *Organon*, Kent built a spiritual bridge between homoeopathy and theology, making Kentianism look more like a 'creed' than a 'practice'. Pushing further and further away from conventional medicine and its marriage with biomedical reductionism, he formulated a vision of homoeopathy that was philosophical, anti-materialistic and contemptuous of modern science. There existed a mystical correspondence between the spiritual and natural worlds with man's form and function modelled on a spiritual, higher reality. Everything that existed in this higher world was reflected by its counterpart in the natural world. Kent's metaphysical approach, along with his blend of miasmic theory, spiritual forces and psychology, tested the intellectual rigour of his colleagues, many of whom found it difficult to fathom his approach, particularly as he chose to mix medicine and theology. Nevertheless, Kent valued philosophy above experience and observation.[91] Much like Swedenborg who, in his mystic period, sought to amplify and reinterpret every word of the Bible, Kent seemed intent on revising Hahnemann's *Organon*. His fundamentalism and his doctrinaire arrogance were difficult for some of his followers to accept, especially his insistence that 'a man who cannot believe in God cannot become a homeopath'.[92]

Much like the early Christian theologian and apologist Thomas Aquinas in his defence of the Bible, Kent treated Hahnemann's *Organon* with reverence, helping to solidify what became known as *classical* homoeopathy. Rather than drawing homoeopathy into the medical mainstream by reducing its friction with conventional therapeutics, he pushed it into the esoteric side of healing. With his monumental repertory, materia medica and philosophy, his high potencies, his emphasis on psora and his alliance with Swedenborgian metaphysics, Kent took his devotees on a journey far removed from the material and practical side of therapeutic theory and practice. According to Matthew Wood, Kentianism 'encouraged the development of a narrow, tiresome approach which restrict[ed] creativity . . . creating a cultish atmosphere' that affected both aspects of homoeopathic theory and practice.[93]

While allopathy looked at disease as an entirely human phenomenon, Kent's view was that of a religious fundamentalist who gave disease a moral dimension packed with aphoristic certitudes regarding the pathways of life and signs of imbalance that derived from slackness within the human race. As an Aristotelian devoted to deductive logic drawn from a few basic principles, he had an enormous impact on twentieth-century homoeopathy, arguably accelerating academic homoeopathy's decline and the rise of lay homoeopathy that dominates homoeopathy today.[94] At a time when homoeopathy's remaining medical schools were seeking to close ranks with conventional medicine, Kentianism offered a response that, in the words of homoeopath Francis Treuherz, was 'metaphysical, dogmatic, puritanical and millennial'. Those homoeopaths who failed in their diagnosis and treatment 'lacked intellectual skill and rigor, as well as the moral fiber for the arduous task of identifying the similimum'.[95] Kentianism became the mainstay of lay homoeopathy around the world and was exemplified by its rejection of biomedicine. As research associate Peter Morrell observed, it also 'probably alienated more people than it converted and in many respects hastened [academic homoeopathy's] decline rather than serving to revitalize a flagging movement, as had been hoped'.[96]

* * *

The question, 'What is homoeopathy and how does it work?' has never been answered with any level of confidence due in large part to the fact that it is considered by some to be a belief system attuned more to religion than a system of healing. While Hahnemann's *Organon of the Healing Art* identified the effects of various material remedies, their symptomatology in health and disease included mental attributes or qualities reminiscent of those found in religion. As in Buddhist meditation, healing resulted from a process directed at the mind, and the non-material mental formations, perceptions and sensations that accompanied its actions brought equipoise to the body's governing centre. Alchemistic in its mixture of matter and spirit, it aimed to accompany any physical effects with a spiritual purification of sorts. Thus, homoeopathic remedies were constitutional in nature, assigned as an archetype inherent of some primal form or psyche that passed through the inner world of the individual to the outer physical world. Each archetype represented an ideal form that manifests itself in certain thinking, behaviour and physical attributes.

The art of Kentian homoeopathy differed in no significant way from Zen meditation with its goal of enlightenment. Nor did it differ significantly from the phenomenology of Edmund Husserl and Martin Heidegger or, for that matter, from the gestalt psychology of Max Wertheimer. As Morrell explained:

> Homeopathy is not about classifying or compartmentalizing or theories, but about perceiving the patient. It is rooted in perception, direct viewing in an undogmatic fashion without prejudices. It is not about explaining—the patient must be viewed, not judged or classified. Thus homeopaths reject the teleological approach as unhelpful. They do not wish to find the causes of the patient's problems, they merely want to describe them accurately. This description can then be matched against the images of sickness found in the proving of the materia medica.[97]

Implied in this process is the challenge to observe the patient 'as-is', meaning that the homoeopathic healer has the obligation to observe and describe without theorizing, and then intuiting or perceiving the patient's 'innate essence'—a practice used in phenomenology, pragmatism and Zen. Rather than compartmentalizing or classifying isolated symptoms or aspects of the body's functioning organs and ascribing various types of causation, the phenomenological method looks behind the reductionist data and its quantitative evaluation or logic by taking a more introspective approach to perceive (i.e., intuit) the nature or essence of the object. Although many homoeopathic healers consider the idea perverse and unacceptable, homoeopathy should be viewed as a religion or form of psychotherapy where vital force, the vice-regent of the soul, stands between mind and matter, where miasms represent sin, and where potentized remedies act as a form of saving grace or placebo therapy on the patient.

The history of homoeopathy has been the history of a metaphysical system of healing seeking coequal status with reductionist medicine without reference to the double-blind randomized clinical trial and the obligation of demonstrating replicability. Its individualized medicines used to stimulate the body's defence system (i.e., its self-regulating, self-organizing and self-healing capacity) rely on a 'picture' of the patient from all aspects. To borrow from Jack Canfield's *Chicken Soup for the Soul*, homoeopathy is a form of soul therapy whose remedies are selected on the basis of a patient's emotional and physical characteristics, i.e., diet, environment, personality, perceptions and physical disabilities. The objective of the homoeopathic healer is to narrow the selection of remedies to one that centres on the patient's individual picture or portrait.

CHARLES BONNEY AND THE
WORLD'S PARLIAMENT OF RELIGIONS
The World in Miniature

What men deemed impossible, God has finally wrought. The Religions
of the world have actually met in a great and imposing assembly;
they have conferred together on the vital questions of life and
immortality in a frank and friendly spirit, and now they part in
peace with many warm expressions of mutual affection and respect.

('Address', Charles Bonney, *The New Jerusalem*, 1894)

For one hundred and eighty-four days in 1893, twenty-eight million people, or nearly a third of the American population, visited the World's Fair in Chicago to celebrate the quatercentenary of Christopher Columbus's discovery of the New World. Designed by Daniel Burnham and Frederick Law Olmsted and constructed on six hundred acres in Jackson Park on the shores of Lake Michigan, the Fair resembled a neoclassical, Romanesque and Beaux-Arts utopia. Known as the 'White City' because of its nearly two hundred painted stucco buildings and extensive use of street lights, it became home to approximately 65,000 exhibits from forty-seven nations. Financed largely by Chicago's business and financial titans, the Fair provided a snapshot view of America's coming-of-age, with products ranging from Quaker Oats and Aunt Jemima pancake mix to phosphorescent lamps, moving walkways, alternating-current generators and Edison's moving-picture Kinetograph. The nation's material and industrial accomplishments, displayed in specially designed buildings housing transportation, machinery, electricity, mining, agriculture and manufacturing, offered a sharp contrast to the mock African villages, Middle Eastern bazaars and artefacts of the world's 'exotic' peoples and 'primitive' cultures.[1]

Charles C Bonney (1831-1903)
Charles C Bonney, a lay member of the Swedenborgian Church and one of the more

active members of the Exposition's planning committee, is credited with introducing the idea of an 'Intellectual and Moral Exposition' that would accompany the Fair and extol the achievements of mankind in the areas such as religion, art and philosophy. A lawyer, judge and orator, Bonney shared his concept with Walter Thomas Mills, editor of *The Statesman* magazine, and was encouraged to put his idea on paper. His article concluded by suggesting that: 'The crowning glory of the World's Fair of 1893 should not be the exhibit then to be made of the material triumphs, industrial achievements, and mechanical victories of man, however magnificent that display may be. Something higher and nobler is demanded by the enlightened and progressive spirit of the present age'.[2]

When Bonney's suggestions appeared to resonate with the public, the Fair's planners appointed him chair of a committee to bring the concept to fruition. By 1891, the committee had been transformed into the World's Congress Auxiliary of the World's Columbian Exposition with Bonney as president. As a result of his efforts, and those of the Auxiliary, twenty separate congresses were planned to address the topics of: Women's Progress; Public Press; Medicine and Surgery; Temperance; Moral and Social Reform; Commerce and Finance; Social and Economic Science; Music; Literature; Education; Engineering; Art; Government; Science; Philosophy; Labour; Religion; Sunday Rest; Public Health; and Agriculture. Bonney first estimated that the congresses would assemble over the course of a few weeks, but because of the size and numbers of interested parties, he found it necessary to extend the congresses through the entire six months (1 May through 30 October) of the Exposition. The congresses met in more than two hundred venues, sharing their contributions for an enlightened humanity. Approximately 700,000 visitors ultimately attended this panoply of auxiliary events.

Bonney was particularly interested in planning a World's Parliament of Religions. As a Swedenborgian, he had always enjoyed cordial associations with the different Protestant denominations. Serving as a Bible teacher in the Baptist Church in Peoria and later at St John's Episcopal Church in Chicago, he learned to respect their differing views. 'Thus I came into a state of charity, not only toward the various religious denominations of Christendom, but also in regard to the different religions of the world'.[3] Bonney later reflected that the ecumenical idea of a World Parliament had grown not just from his experiences in the different churches, but from his understanding of Swedenborg's revelatory visions of the New Jerusalem that included the following:

> There is a universal influx from God into the souls of men, teaching them that there is a God, and that He is one. (T.C.R. 8.)
>
> It is of the Lord's Divine Providence that every nation has some Religion, and the foundation of all religion is an acknowledgment that there is a God . . . (D.P. 322.)
>
> It is of the Divine Providence that every man is capable of being saved, and that those are saved who acknowledge God, and lead a good life. (D.P. 325.)
>
> These are the common essentials of all religions, by which every one may be saved; to acknowledge a God, and not to do evil because it is against God. . . . (D.P. 326.) . . .
>
> The Mahometan Religion was permitted by the Divine Providence of the Lord for the extirpation of idolatries in countries where Christianity would not be received. . . . (D.P. 255.) . . .
>
> Every infant, wheresoever born, whether within the Church or out of it, whether of pious parents or impious, when it dies is received by the Lord . . . (H.H. 329.)[4]

In his charge to the Parliament's sixteen-member planning committee, all of whom were of the Judaeo-Christian faith, Bonney directed it to formalize his dream by bringing together 'in frank and friendly conference, the most eminent men of different faiths . . . who will strive to see and to show what are the supreme truths, and what light religion has to throw upon the great problems of our age'. He intended for the Parliament to be the crowning event of the Exposition by showing that, despite differences among the world's religious traditions, there was 'something underlying them all, which constitutes an incorruptible and indestructible bond of brotherhood, which, like a golden cord, binds all the races of men in one grand fraternity of love and service'. His purpose was not to form or recommend a new religion, nor place any delegates in any 'false position', nor set a trap for any faith, nor demand the surrender of any conviction. Instead, he envisioned a 'royal feast' in which representatives from every faith would 'bring the richest fruits and the fairest flowers of their religion'.[5]

To fulfil his objectives, Bonney appointed the Revd John Henry Barrows, pastor of the First Presbyterian Church of Chicago to chair the committee. A clergyman and author, Barrows was a graduate of Yale Divinity School, Union Theological Seminary, and Andover Theological Seminary. He would later become the fifth president of Oberlin College. Barrows, however, had his own agenda which did not always comport with Bonney's goals.

When Barrows and his committee members began their planning, believing the Parliament represented a unique event in the history of the world, they learned that they were not the first to organize a religious convention. The Buddhist Emperor Ashoka had presided over the Pataliputra Council in the third century BC; another conference met in Delhi under orders from the Mogul emperor Akbar the Great in the sixteenth century; the Free Religious Association of Boston had suggested such a convention in the early 1870s; and Henry Steel Olcott had sent invitations to religious leaders to celebrate the opening of Theosophy's Adyar Library near Madras, India, in 1886.[6] Thus, while the plan for the Parliament proved not especially new, Barrows was comforted by the fact that theirs would be the first all-religion parliament sponsored by Christendom. Indeed, Max Müller, a German scholar of comparative language, religion and mythology, thought that it stood not only 'unique' but 'unprecedented in the whole history of the world'.[7]

The committee's first duty was to formulate its objectives around ten distinctive points:

1. To bring together in conference, for the first time in history, the leading representatives of the great historic religions of the world.
2. To show to man, in the most impressive way, what and how many important truths the various religions hold and teach in common.
3. To promote and deepen the spirit of human brotherhood among religious men of diverse faiths, through friendly converse and mutual good

understanding, while not seeking to foster the temper of indifferentism, and not striving to achieve any formal and outward unity.

4. To set forth, by those most competent to speak, what are deemed the important distinctive truths held and taught by each religion, and by the various chief branches of Christendom.

5. To indicate the impregnable foundations of theism, and the reasons for man's faith in immortality, and thus to unite and strengthen the forces which are adverse to a materialistic philosophy of the universe.

6. To secure from leading scholars, representing the Brahman, Buddhist, Confucian, Parsee, Mohammedan, Jewish, and other faiths, and from representatives of the various churches of Christendom, full and accurate statements of the spiritual and other effects of the religions which they hold upon the literature, art, commerce, government, domestic and social life of the peoples among whom these faiths have prevailed.

7. To inquire what light each religion has afforded, or may afford, to the other religions of the world.

8. To set forth, for permanent record to be published to the world, an accurate and authoritative account of the present condition and outlook of religion among the leading nations of the earth.

9. To discover, from competent men, what light religion has to thrown on the great problems of the present age, especially the important questions connected with temperance, labor, education, wealth, and poverty.

10. To bring the nations of the earth into a more friendly fellowship, in the hope of securing permanent international peace.[8]

In a circular sent in June 1891 to approximately ten thousand recipients, the committee invited the world's religious leaders to send representatives to enter into a close and friendly relationship with each other and show 'the moral and spiritual agencies which are at the root of human progress'. The circular also stipulated that all of its proceedings would to be conducted in English.[9] The response, however, was mixed. While some saw it as an opportunity to demonstrate their legitimacy, others their superiority, and still others to clarify misconceptions commonly held by outsiders, several eminent Christians replied that holding such a Parliament would belittle Christianity by implying that it was simply one among many rather than the *only* true religion. Prominent among the naysayers was the Revd E W Benson, Archbishop of Canterbury, who replied that he could not understand how Christianity could be a part of a Parliament of Religions 'without assuming the equality of the other intended members'. Such a position was untenable since the Christian religion 'is the *one* religion'. Beyond that, he objected to having the Christian religion 'produce its evidences before any assembly'. As far as he was concerned his religion was 'too sacred for such treatment'.[10]

The Archbishop was not alone in his opposition. William Ashmore, appointed by the American Baptist Missionary Union to work among the Chinese in Siam, accused the members of the Planning Committee of flirting with the 'daughters of Moab'.[11] In yet another vitriolic response, the Revd E J Eitel of Hong Kong objected on the grounds that, despite the best intentions, the Parliament represented an unconscious treason against Christ and warned Barrows that he was endangering 'the precious life of [his] soul by playing fast and loose with the truth and coquetting with false religions'.[12] Similar objections came from Bishop McQuaid of Rochester and Bishop A Cleveland Coxe of the Diocese of Western New York. The Parliament, Bishop Coxe claimed, 'seems to have brought together the elements which were parted at Babel, for a babble in our own land about the respective unbeliefs which they represent'. Allowing such an assembly gave license to the 'clever heathen' to claim superiority over divine revelation. In declining the invitation he stated that as 'a Catholic Christian and successor of the Apostles, I could not have forgotten my commission, nor could I have compromised it by ambiguous words'.[13]

Despite opposition from the Presbyterian Church in the United States (Barrows's own church) as well as from the European Catholic hierarchy, the Archbishop of Canterbury, numerous Evangelical churches in North America and the Sultan of Turkey, Barrows was inundated with letters of support from around the world, including not only liberal Christian leaders but the vast majority of Christian missionaries and their associations. Because of the response, Barrows was able to secure support from the leading Anglo-American Protestants as well as from Cardinal James Gibbons, Archbishop Patrick Feehan of Chicago, Bishop and Rector John Joseph Keane of Catholic University and the Catholic Archbishop John Ireland of St Paul, Minnesota—support he very much appreciated despite his personal dislike of the papacy and its priests.[14]

Planning Continues

In March, 1893, the committee sent out a second circular containing a draft of its proposed seventeen-day programme of events. Besides providing time for initial welcoming addresses from the delegates, the programme included presentations on the topics of revelation; immortality; the incarnation of God; universal elements in religion; the ethical unity of religions; the role of missionary work; and the relationship of religion to morals. It even included a congress on evolution which, although initially intended for inclusion in a separate Parliament of Science, was given to the Parliament of Religions 'by the courtesy of the committee of organization'. To accomplish the full intent of the programme, the committee scheduled forty-five individual congresses to be held under the auspices of the Auxiliary.[15]

In his update to the World's Congress Auxiliary, Barrows announced that he had secured the financial backing of the city's business elite to underwrite the publication of the Parliament's proceedings. He also reported that he had spoken before church groups, attended Chautauqua rallies, met with newspaper and periodical editors, and written numerous articles highlighting the Parliament's anticipated agenda and raising money on its behalf. Exemplary was his address at Carnegie Hall in New York where he remarked: 'I have no doubt that this phenomenal meeting will make apparent the fact that there is a certain unity in religion,—that is, that men not only have common desires and needs, but also have perceived more or less clearly, certain common truths'. The report ended with the announcement that fifteen hundred religious leaders from around the world had accepted the Parliament's invitation.[16]

In the final months leading up to the event, the prospect of opening on schedule was temporarily clouded by differences over whether the Exposition should remain open on Sunday or respect the nation's traditional adherence to its blue laws. When the Exposition's management decided to remain open to accommodate working families, the Baptists denounced the action and removed themselves from the Parliament. The Christian Endeavor Society made a similar decision, objecting to any violation of the Sabbath. [17]

In anticipation of bringing together so many religious leaders and in light of the Parliament's naysayers, Barrows sought to temper the anxieties of fellow Christians using carefully scripted remarks. He explained to any who would listen that that the Parliament provided 'a matchless opportunity' for Christians to set forth the 'distinctive truths' of the Gospel and its unique message to the world. He assured his home audience that Christianity could claim to be the true religion, 'fitted to all and demanding the submission of all'. Accordingly, he urged his Christian listeners to pity the poor heathen and to use the upcoming Parliament to display the 'grander facts of our Christian civilization' rather than its more dubious accomplishments. By this he meant the Chinese Exclusion Act, the whiskey and gunpowder trafficking of Christian commerce and Europe's enforcement of the opium trade on China. By no means, however, did he disparage the work of Christian missionaries. 'The heart that is aglow with a wise Christian patriotism must plead earnestly for foreign missions', he insisted. 'Let no one fear that the solar orb of Christianity is to be eclipsed by the lanterns and rush-lights of other faiths'. Indeed, he assured his audiences that 'the kingdoms of this world shall become the kingdoms of our Lord and of his Christ'. [18] Similarly, in a speech delivered before the Christian Endeavor Convocation in New York in 1892 Barrows remarked: 'We believe that Christianity is to supplant all other religions, because it contains all the truth there is in them and much besides . . . God has not left himself without witness, and those who have the full light of the Cross should bear brotherly hearts toward all who grope in a dimmer illumination'. This comment, even without its condescending tone, revealed the true intent of the Planning Committee. With comments such as these, Barrows exposed a not too subtle subtext which filtered into the Parliament's seventeen days of presentations and dimming the initial hubris of Bonney's goals. [19]

Actually, the context underlying the Parliament was not unlike the intent behind the Columbian Exposition itself in that the Parliament's organizers accepted not only the Eurocentric values of Anglo-Protestant Christianity but recognized as well the rhetoric of science as its validation. American society at the time of the Exposition was confident in its future and untroubled by the possibility of any reversal of its fortunes. Under the guise of social Darwinism, the Parliament's universalizing religious discourse became an expression of enlightened Protestantism reaching out to the superstitious and uncivilized religions of the world. Beneath this placid display of benevolence was a nation with hegemonic intentions reflective of Henry Adams's observation a decade or two later that American society 'offered the profile of a long, straggling caravan, stretching loosely toward the prairies, its few score of leaders far in advance and its millions of immigrants, negroes [sic], and Indians far in the rear, somewhere in archaic time'. [20]

This view of Anglo-Protestant civilization and its fusion with the Judaeo-Christian tradition provided the American delegates with a solipsistic version of religious unity. For Barrows, Christianity stood at the apex of the world's religions, the culmination of human progress to which all other religions aspired. Although the non-Christian world 'may give us valuable criticism and confirm scriptural truths and make excellent suggestions as to Christian improvement . . . it has nothing to add to the Christian creed'. [21] Barrows supported a Christian interpretation of social Darwinism believing that 'the best religion must come to the front, and the best religion will ultimately survive, because it will contain all that is true in all the faiths'. [22] Though he viewed the Parliament as a welcoming convention to the world's religions, he was disinclined to believe that they had anything to add to the finality that Christianity represented to the world.

Barrows was not alone in his assessment. 'The glory of Christianity', explained Oxford theologian Benjamin Jowett, 'is not to be as unlike other religions as possible, but to be their perfection and fulfillment'. [23] 'Christianity is the Final and absolute religion', added Robert Elliott Speer, 'because it contains all the good and truth that can be found in any other religion, and presents it to men in its divine fullness, while other religions have none but partial good; because it is free from the evils which are found in all other religions, and because it alone can satisfy all the needs of the human heart and of the human race'. [24] Notwithstanding these lofty ideals, explained historian James Ketelaar, the assembly's planners touted 'an irrefutably oppressive ideology thinly disguised with a veneer of evolutionary theory, comparative religious studies, and assumptions of universal brotherhood transcendent of all difference'.[25]

The Parliament did not materialize without its share of impediments. Days before its opening, Barrows learned that the Japanese delegation of Buddhists had been warned to expect unfair treatment. This, combined with the temporary loss by the Parliament's secretary of their prepared remarks, caused the delegates to pack their bags. To his credit, Barrows was able to find the lost documents and disabuse the Japanese guests of any unjust treatment.[26]

Opening Session

On 11 September, the world's religious leaders gathered in Columbus Hall (now the Art Institute of Chicago) with four thousand spectators in attendance as the 'peace-bell' tolled ten times to recognize the ten historical religions and also to announce 'the death-knell to intolerance'.[27] So great was the demand for tickets to the plenary session (scalpers were asking three and four dollars for tickets) that the overflow was directed to the adjoining Washington Hall which seated another three thousand and where the event was later repeated.[28]

Amidst the august body of cardinals, bishops, priests and scholars sat the Parliament's president and organizer, Charles C Bonney, and his Swedenborgian pastor, the Revd Lewis Pyle Mercer. As the Revd Frank Sewall observed proudly, 'we see the tribes of the earth all assembled by their representatives into this Religious Parliament, called together and presided over by a New-Churchman'. Absent were representatives of the Sikhs, the Native American tribes and other indigenous peoples who would wait another hundred years for representation at an international interreligious gathering. Neither the Mormons nor African Americans were formally recognized although Bishops Benjamin W Arnett and Daniel A Payne of the African Methodist Episcopal Church were present at some events, and the Mormon Tabernacle Choir performed at the Grand Choral competition organized by the Exposition.[29]

Declared secularists were not among the American delegations attending the Parliament, but there were individuals like Paul Carus who was appointed to the Advisory Council on Religious Congresses and whose speeches before the Parliament advocated a new synoptic religion based on empirical and evolutionary science. Also present at the Parliament and its Congresses were Unitarians, Universalists, Christian Scientists, Theosophists and Swedenborgians who advocated for a non-creedal, liberal and more humanistic idealism. Their religious sensibilities were tuned to the world's literature rather than any single set of dogmas, symbols or creeds. Significant is the fact that of the 216 presentations given at the Parliament, 109 were delivered by delegates whose beliefs operated on the fringes of the Protestant mainstream.[30]

The ceremony began with the doxology: 'Praise God, from whom all blessings flow/ Praise him, all creatures here below/ Praise him above, ye heavenly host/ Praise Father, Son and Holy Ghost'. Cardinal Gibbons then delivered the 'Lord's Prayer'. Following his invocation, Bonney opened the Parliament by asking all to rejoice that they had 'lived to see this glorious day', noting that the views represented among the delegations should not be 'causes of discord and strife, but rather incentives to deeper interest and examination'. Barrows followed Bonney to the podium where he, too, welcomed the delegates where, in the shadow of the adjoining Columbian Exposition celebrating the 'jubilee of civilization', they had come together to better understand the moral and spiritual roots of human progress. 'This Parliament is likely to prove a blessing to many Christians', he promised, 'by marking the time when they shall cease thinking that the verities and virtues of other religions discredit the claims of Christianity or bar its progress'. It was his hope that the temper of love would prevail instead of the 'sharp hostilities' that divided the world's religions. 'We are not here as Baptists and Buddhists, Catholics and Confucians, Parsees and Presbyterians, Methodists and Moslems; we are here as members of a Parliament of Religions, over which flies no sectarian flag . . . but where for the first time in a large council is lifted up the banner of love, fellowship, brotherhood'.[31]

In his welcoming remarks, Cardinal Gibbons, like others representing the West's principal religions, could not help but insert a less than subtle remark. 'I should be wanting in my duty as a minister of the Catholic Church', he announced, 'if I did not say that it is our desire to present the claims of the Catholic Church to the observation and, if possible, to the acceptance of every right-minded man that will listen to us'. Not to be outdone by the Roman Catholics, the German Count A Bernstorff, speaking on behalf of Evangelical Protestantism, observed: 'I should never have set my foot in this Parliament if I thought that it signified anything like a consent that all religions are equal and that it is only necessary to be sincere and upright. . . . I believe only the Bible to be true and Protestant Christianity the only true Religion. I wish no compromise of any kind'. To his credit, Archbishop Francis William Redwood of New Zealand was less combative, admitting that as a representative of the Catholic Church, he did not 'pretend as a Catholic to have the whole truth or to be able to solve all the problems of the human mind'.[32]

Noticeable among the papers read by Christians was that the starkness of Calvinism 'shrank out of sight' while the 'great banner of the God-Messiah and of his redemption was brought more and more to the front'. Similarly, the 'fissures and rents in the Christian body were everywhere covered up as far as possible'.[33] There was also an understanding made clear during the opening remarks that the Christian delegates held fast to a hierarchical ranking of the world's religions. Beginning with the Protestant denominations at home and abroad, the list descended to Jews, Catholics, representatives of the Syrian, Armenian, Russian and Greek Orthodox churches, prominent scholars in the scientific study of religion, followed by representatives from the ten Eastern religious traditions, a number arbitrarily identified through contemporary books on comparative religions. With broad evolutionary strokes, the organizers had placed Christianity at the apex of human progress whose influence extended outward to the non-Christian world while recognizing little in the way of their contributions.[34] Supporting this hierarchy was a belief that each culture underwent successive stages of development characterized by increasingly detailed and refined growth during which it moved inexorably toward a goal foreordained by the Creator.

The word 'evolution' was repeated over and over again by delegates—both from the West and the East—applying it to the political, economic, social and religious changes affecting all nations, tribes, races and classes. For the Judaeo-Christian delegates, however, the language of evolution was intended to disabuse the Oriental delegates of any interpretation that suggested the irrelevance of Western science. By making use of scientific vocabulary they staked their claim to Christianity's growing significance from ancient times into the present. Evolution explained how multiple beliefs would somehow vanish and how one religion would rise to worldly eminence and ultimately disseminate across the globe, countering opposition by leveraging the economic, political and military muscle of their secular states. This teleology, which in no way conformed to Darwin's theory of natural selection, was marvelously adapted by the Protestant delegates to explain a process that moved steadily from primitive belief systems to that which placed Protestant America at the apex. 'Up to this time', explained Scottish evangelist and author Henry Drummond, 'no word has been spoken to reconcile Christianity with evolution, or Evolution with Christianity. And why? Because the two are one. . . . Evolution and Christianity have the same Author, the same end, the same spirit. . . . Christianity is the Further Evolution'.[35]

This corrosive subtext, which lay tucked away beneath the Parliament's joyful harmony, ecumenical discourse and common purpose, incited the Eastern delegates to respond in kind. Exemplary of this was the combative statement by the Pure Land Buddhist priest Yatsubuchi Banryu: 'Our age is the age of collision between European and Asian cultures. It is the age of competition between the white and yellow races. It is the age of conflict between the powers of the Orient and of the Occident'. Even more truculent was the Buddhist delegate who accused the Parliament's Judaeo-Christian delegates of portraying all non-Christian religions 'as perverse and ravenous jackals . . . for the sole purpose of expanding the glory of Christianity'.[36] Others, more subtle, questioned why Christianity had so many different spokesmen and so many different beliefs. As one Japanese scholar remarked: 'I was baptized by a Congregationalist missionary, but I never meant in so doing to be baptized a Congregationalist, but a Christian. What we want in Japan is not Methodism, nor Presbyterianism, nor Protestantism, nor Catholicism, but the pure Religion of Jesus Christ and of His Word! Where shall we find it?'[37]

Further complicating the agenda was the fact that many of the Oriental delegates had to rely on translations and stand-in speakers whose lack of appropriate words and gestures failed to convey the delegates' true intent. Some translations borrowed the language of Theosophy, a choice that produced images reminiscent of 'table rappings' and 'spirit talk' rather than what the delegates had truly intended. Thus comprehension became an issue for speaker and listener alike as both struggled to understand concepts that either lacked the proper translation or used 'borrowed' terms to connect with the centrality of the author's intent and meaning.[38]

Swami Vivekananda

Scarcely disguised by the ecumenical speeches, receptions, papers and presentations was an emerging East/West duel between Barrows and Swami Vivekananda (1863-1902), a Hindu monk and native of Calcutta who later became India's spiritual ambassador to the West, and Anagarika Dharmapala (1864-1933), otherwise known as David Hewavitarne, who came from a Sri Lankan family of ardent Buddhists. Educated in Christian missionary schools, both men acquired an expert command of the English language which they used to master the art of persuasion.

Swami Vivekananda gave several speeches before the Parliament and its congresses, all of which drew attentive audiences. Knowledgeable of Western religion and philosophy and, in an accent that sounded remarkably Irish, he proved to be a masterful communicator, advocating a hybrid version of Hinduism and Theosophy that resonated with his audience's sensitivities. A virtual lobbyist, he became both an evangelist and an apologist, interpreting Hinduism in a form acceptable to the Western mind.[39] So great was the American response to his comments that the Honourable Mr Merwin-Marie Snell, President of the Scientific Section of the Parliament, reluctantly admitted that 'he was received with greater enthusiasm than any other speaker, Christian or pagan'.[40]

In his inaugural address before the Parliament, Vivekananda opened with the words 'Sisters and Brothers of America, it fills my heart with joy unspeakable to rise in response to the warm and cordial welcome which you have given us'—a remark that brought accolades from the audience. But it was what he said afterwards in a quiet manner that set the tone for a subtle war of intent between himself and Barrows. 'I am proud to belong to a religion which has taught the world both tolerance and universal acceptance', he announced. 'We believe not only in universal toleration, but we accept all religions as true'. He then quoted from a hymn he remembered from boyhood: 'As the different streams have their sources in different places all mingle their water in the sea, so, O Lord, the different paths which men take through different tendencies, various though they appear, crooked or straight, all lead to Thee'. In recounting this hymn, Vivekananda affirmed his belief that all religions existed because of their distinctive appeal to the people and culture they represented. All religions shared with Christianity a path to God.[41]

Vivekananda chose not only to place Hinduism on equal footing with the Western religious traditions of Catholicism, Protestantism and Judaism, he also affirmed Hinduism as one of the most ancient of religions serving all classes of people. It was the 'mother of religions' which had survived the evolutionary criteria of 'survival of the fittest', thereby linking its past to centuries yet to unfold. With a combination of charm and command of the language, he legitimized Hinduism—both its antiquity and modernity—for Western audiences.[42] With the words 'that the bell that tolled this morning in honour of this convention may be the death-knell of all fanaticism, of all persecutions with the sword or with the pen, and of all uncharitable feelings between persons wending their way to the same goal', he predicted a new era of universal peace among the religions of the world.[43]

Vivekananda made frequent use of the terms 'God', 'soul', 'salvation', 'spirit', 'mercy', 'sin', 'ethics' and 'cosmic energy' to make himself understandable to his Western audience. Similarly, he avoided the words such as 'karma', 'atman' and 'Brahman', fearing they might appear too obscure or remote from Western thought. His choice of language, explained Kay Koppedrayer, 'reflect[ed] Vivekananda's earlier interactions with Christian thinkers and missionaries in India, and [was] also a response to popular notions of Hinduism'.

> [Vivekananda reminded] his audience that even before Newtonian thought
> 'discovered' the law of gravity, it existed, implying through this juxtaposi-
> tion of words, that Vedic thought had much earlier captured what Western
> science only later recognized. The Western post-Enlightenment endeavor,
> that seeks to understand through verifiable observation the laws of the
> natural world, [had] already been anticipated by Vedic thought. . . . Here,
> Vivekananda [was] also implying that the fundamental configuration

of Hindu thought is empirical, even if that has gone unrecognized, and that there is no difference between Hindu religious thought and scientific thought, except, perhaps, that Hindu science developed first.[44]

On 15 September, the Swami delivered a talk titled 'Why We Disagree' which began with a story of a frog born in a well where it lived out its life and, when another frog visited from the sea, spurned him for explaining that the world was much bigger than the well.

> I am a Hindu. I am sitting in my own little well and thinking that the whole world is my little well. The Christian sits in his little well and thinks the whole world is his well. The Mohammedan sits in his little well and thinks that is the whole world. I have to thank you of America for the great attempt you are making to break down the barriers of this little world of ours, and hope that, in the future, the Lord will help you to accomplish your purpose.[45]

Four days later, he again addressed the Parliament, explaining that Hinduism provided the common basis upon which beliefs could converge without contradiction. It was a religion without a beginning or end, a continuous accumulation of spiritual laws discovered by different people in different times. The whole object of life was 'to become perfect, to become divine, to reach God and see God, and this reaching God, seeing God, becoming perfect even as the Father in Heaven is perfect'. This, he affirmed, constituted the religion of Hinduism.[46] In a subsequent presentation he counselled Christian missionaries to consider spending more time saving their own souls instead of erecting churches. The people of India had religion enough, he observed, 'It is an insult to a starving people to offer them religion' when it is bread that they need to sustain them.[47]

In his final remarks before the Parliament on 27 September, Vivekananda reiterated his belief that the differences between and among the world's religions came from their presentation of truth, which was simply their particular adaptation to the circumstances around them. All of the great religions were equally true and justifiable. Beneath their outward expressions of ritual, a universal sameness prevailed which precluded the necessity of one religion to assimilate another or to claim superiority over another. All were justified in expressing their individuality and right to existence. 'Do I wish that the Christian would become Hindu? God forbid', explained Vivekananda. 'Do I wish that the Hindu or Buddhist would become Christian? God forbid'.[48]

Anagarika Dharmapala

Anagarika Dharmapala held a position halfway between priest and layperson and became a popular promoter of modern Buddhism with its emphasis on rationality, science and meditation. When he announced that Buddhism rejected the notion of a Creator and substituted in its stead the law of cause and effect, he did this not by quoting from Buddhist texts but from British writer Grant Allen who, in his *Life of Darwin* (1891), explained that 'The teachings of the Buddha on evolution are clear and expansive. . . . We see in it all not a yawning chaos restrained by the constant interference from without of a wise and beneficent external power, but a vast aggregate of original elements perpetually working out their own fresh redistribution in accordance with their own inherent energies'. Like Vivekananda before him, Dharmapala chose his words with clear understanding of how they would resonate with his Western audience since the terms 'evolution' and 'cause and effect' were at the centre of intellectual discussion in the West. His purpose was to make Buddhism consistent with Western science and in step with the most recent theories of evolution. Buddhism might be 2,400 years old but it remained relevant to the most modern views of Western science.[49]

Educated in British-run schools, Dharmapala experienced at first hand the West's negative characterizations of Eastern religions and philosophies. He knew only too well that the Judaeo-Christian tradition viewed the religions of the East as pessimistic, nihilistic and filled with superstition and empty ritualism. Intending to revitalize Buddhism and re-establish its prestige, he promoted it as an optimistic alternative to Christianity and a solution as well to the Victorian crisis of faith. His version of Buddhism was scientific, rational and living—an ethical improvement to Victorian utilitarian morals. Critical of Christianity and its doctrines, he was able to turn liberal middle-class Protestantism to his own uses by exploiting and then capitalizing on the fissures in Christianity's façade.

In his comments to the delegates, Dharmapala made a clear distinction between Barrows's remarks and his own. For him, Buddhism, and not Christianity, was at the pinnacle of the great religions. He reminded the assembly that the Parliament was a 're-echo' of the work of the great Emperor Ashoka who had convened a similar congress twenty-four centuries earlier in the city of Patna (Pataliputra) where a thousand scholars remained in session for seven months. At its conclusion, the emperor dispersed Buddhist missionaries to instruct the world. Dharmapala ended with the comment that he hoped that 'the noble lessons of tolerance learned in this majestic assembly will result in the dawning of universal peace which will last for twenty centuries more'.[50]

In recounting Buddha's contributions to the world, Dharmapala pointed out that most Western scholars had erroneously concluded that Buddhism was little more than the detritus of abstract metaphysics and fanciful mysticism. On the contrary, Buddhism was a 'comprehensive system of ethics, and a transcendental metaphysic embracing a sublime psychology'. For the 'simple-minded', it provided a code of morality while, for the 'earnest student', it offered a system of pure thought. For both, it provided a path to self-purification. 'Spiritual progress is impossible for him who does not lead a life of purity and compassion'.[51]

In starting one's pilgrimage to truth, Dharmapala stressed the importance of having an unprejudiced mind and a willingness to relinquish all that was no longer true. This meant giving up all prejudices, ignorance, passions and the fear of expressing one's convictions. It meant reasoning and thinking in an environment of calm thought without 'extraneous interventions'. This formula for truth could 'be attained by the humblest, and this consummation raises him above wealth and royalty'. At the centre of the Buddha's teaching was human brotherhood, a 'universal love and sympathy with all mankind and with animal life'. Salvation was attained through charity, purity, self-sacrifice, self-knowledge, 'dauntless energy', patience, truth, resolution, love and equanimity—all characteristics that resonated with virtues espoused in the West.[52]

Following the close of the Parliament, Dharmapala spent the next forty years lecturing, establishing schools and building temples and hospitals in Ceylon and

India. His form of Buddhism, sometimes called 'Protestant Buddhism', a term coined by Princeton University anthropologist Gananath Obeyesekere, was as much a reflection of Protestant characteristics such as freedom of conscience as it was a protest against British colonization and the racism expressed by Christian missionaries. Inspired by Edwin Arnold's *The Light of Asia*, Dharmapala travelled widely through the United States, joining with Henry Steel Olcott and the Theosophists in pursuing an ambitious plan to offset the influence of Christian missionary schools with a rejuvenated Sinhalese Buddhism and an accompanying nationalist movement. Dharmapala and Olcott visited Japan in 1888 where they were warmly received and where Olcott gave a series of lectures intended to build a bridge between the northern and southern branches of Buddhism. For Dharmapala, Japanese Buddhism had found a way, albeit troubling, to offset the cultural and political imperialism of the West with its own mixture of Buddhism and militarism.

For Barrows, of course, the concept of a universal sameness encouraged by both Vivekananda and Dharmapala was unacceptable. Christianity, not Buddhism or Hinduism, was at the apex of religion, the product of the nineteenth century's version of 'struggle of the fittest'. Christianity contained 'all that is true in all the faiths', leaving it standing alone in its cosmic greatness. For him, only Christianity had the capacity to embrace all.[53]

The Japanese Buddhists

Prior to the journey of the Japanese Buddhists to Chicago in 1893, earlier visits had been made to Europe (England, France, Germany, Switzerland and Italy) by priests of the Higashi and Nishi Honganji sects in 1872. Omenoue Takeyu of the Nishi sect continued on to America before returning to Japan in 1873. Others had visited Greece, Turkey and India. These initial journeys were soon followed by priests from other sects. In part, the trips were intended to better understand Christianity's strengths and weaknesses, how Christianity was viewed in its own lands, and how it justified its missionary, political and military presence in Japan and elsewhere. Attempts also were made to learn of Christianity's own internal dialogue with science and to study its response to issues such as monogamy, suffrage, women's roles, temperance and individual rights. Much of the information gained during these early visits was later used by the Buddhist delegates to the Parliament to structure their own comments, some of which were purposely designed to offset the hegemonic predilections of the Parliament's organizing committee.[54]

Also prior to the Japanese delegation to the Parliament there had been visits by Unitarians to Japan and scholarly and artistic exchanges such as those of art historian Ernest Fenollosa, physician and collector William Sturgis Bigelow, and author and educator Lafcadio Hearn. In addition, several admirers of Theosophy, spiritualism and psychic phenomena had exchanged visits, including Olcott, Albert J Edmunds and Herman Carl Vetterling.

The Japanese Buddhists who presented papers at the World Parliament included Yatsubuchi Banryu, Toki Horyu, Ashitsu Jitsunen, Hirai Kinza and Shaku Soyen. Of the five, only the first two held priestly rank, a factor that reflected the divisive sectarian politics present within Japan's Buddhist communities since many of their most prominent members refused participation. Only the lay Buddhist Hirai spoke and read English, and it was his intended address before the assembled Parliament that was barred by Barrows, who considered the paper unnecessarily inflammatory and counter to the purposes of the assembly.

Even so, Hirai's revised paper titled 'The Real Position of Japan Towards Christianity', revealed the nakedness of his hostility to those 'false Christians' (i.e., Christian missionaries) who had brought racial and cultural stereotypes along with their Bibles.[55] In his remarks, Hirai, who had high regard for Swedenborg, expressed hope for 'religious affinity' over the world but admitted that the greatest hindrance to progress was Christianity's perception of Japan as a heathen nation and, by implication, its view of other nations as well.[56] He insisted there were few countries in the world with as open a mind to religious beliefs as Japan. Over the centuries, outside faiths had comingled with native religions with utmost harmony, a fact admirably demonstrated by the close affinity among the teachers of Buddhism, Shintoism, Confucianism and Taoism. This, however, had not been the case with Christian missionaries. Given that so many Christian nations were 'encroaching upon the Orient', it was little wonder that the Oriental mind viewed Christianity as an 'instrument of depredation'. Since the convention at Yedo in 1858, the Japanese government had been placed in a 'very disadvantageous situation'. The 'ex-territoriality' forced on Japan, along with restrictions on any use of the tariff, ranked high among the list of wrongs imposed by foreigners. 'Would not the people of America and Europe think that they were trampled upon and their rights ignored, if they were denied the application of their judicial power over those cases which occur at home? Would not the western nations be indignant and consider that they were deprived of independence, if they were compelled to renounce their rightful custom duty?' Hirai asked.[57]

Admitting that he had been among the first in his country to organize against Christianity, Hirai justified his action on the basis of the injustices committed by Christian missionaries against his people. He insisted that he was not against Christian beliefs but only their application. '[U]nless the inconsistency which we observe is removed', he warned, 'our people will never cast away their prejudice about Christianity in spite of the eloquent orator who speaks its truth from the pulpit'.[58] The Japanese people were judged to be idolaters and heathens by the Christian nations, Hirai complained, and this bias extended to California where Japanese children were prohibited access to public schooling, where unions opposed the use of Japanese labourers, and where Japanese in the Hawaiian Islands were denied suffrage. He went on to rebuke America's un-Christian treatment of Japanese migrants who endured racial slurs and a barrage of legal restrictions. 'If such be the Christian ethics', he concluded, 'well, we are perfectly satisfied to be heathen'.[59]

Hirai's comments were followed by Yatsubuchi Banryu who explained that while Western civilizations were marching to all corners of the earth, their achievements were thus far limited to 'the mere material world', not the more 'truthful spiritual world' of which Buddhism was an example. He identified numerous similarities between Buddha the man, Buddha 'the Saviour', Buddha 'the spirit incarnate of absolute self-sacrifice' and the Buddha of 'divine compassion'. These attributes sounded remarkably like the Christ of Christianity except for the fact that innumerable Buddhas had attained that final grade of perfection of virtue and wisdom. He noted that the multitude of sects preaching Buddhism was due to the differences in human character. Just as doctors cured patients by giving them medicines according to the severity of their cases, so the schools of Buddhism differed due to the character of the individual (i.e., cravings, anger, stupidity) and the general condition of people in various parts of the world. This explained the divisions of Mahayana and Hinayana in India, the thirteen sects in China, and the twelve sects and thirty different schools in Japan.[60]

Shaku Soyen, the Rinzai Zen master of Engakuji, brought with him thousands of copies of Buddhist literature which he distributed among the delegates. As he did not speak English, his paper, 'The Law of Cause and Effect, as Taught by Buddha' was delivered by Barrows. In it, Soyen challenged the necessity of a Creator God, arguing that human morality could rely on self-discipline rather than the authority of a wrathful external authority. Like Dharmapala, he rejected the notion of a Creator, insisting that Buddhism was in perfect alignment with modern science.

Shintoism, Confucianism, Brahmanism, Christianity, and Mohammedanism, when considered from the standpoint of our Buddhist religion, are, in my opinion, but larger or smaller planets revolving around this brilliant sun of the Truth, though each of them claims to constitute a solar system of its own, quite different from others. For who is Confucius but another Bodhisattva that appeared in China; and Jesus and Mohammed are Arhats in the West. Some religious doctrines are inferior to and less deep than others, and they were all preached according to the needs of the time in which their founders were born; but as far as they are consistent with the Truth, they may freely find their place within our Buddhist doctrines.

If Brahmanism had not arisen in India, Buddhism would never have come into existence; if Confucianism had not taken a strong hold on the minds of the Chinese people, it would never have found its way into that empire; if Shintoism had not had its worshippers in our country, it would never have risen in the land of the 'Rising Sun'; lastly, if Christ had not appeared, nor Mohammed, there would have been no Buddhism in the countries where those religious teachers are worshipped! For all these religions, I make bold to say, are nothing but so many conductors through which the 'White Light' of Buddha is passing into the whole universe.

The advanced state of modern science has contributed a great deal to make truth more and more clear, and there are many signs in the Western civilization that it will welcome Buddhism. Originating from the indefatigable researches of some Sanskrit scholars, a new interest has been excited in the West to investigate the Eastern literature, history, and fine arts. Since, in addition, a new and powerful interest in comparative religion has become more and more general, the time is at hand in which Western scholars begin to see how brilliantly our Buddhism shines in all its glory. This is partly shown by the results of that great event the late Parliament of Religions in America.

Many Buddhist scriptures have been translated, both from Sanskrit and Chinese, by Western scholars, and a dozen of books relating to Buddhism have also made their appearance, but only a few of them are read in our country. They are Max Müller's *Nirvana*, Olcott's *A Buddhist Catechism*, Arnold's *The Light of Asia*, Swedenborg's *Buddhism*. Swedenborg entered the realm of Buddhism from his deep mysticism, Arnold from his beautiful poetical thoughts, Olcott from his mighty intellectual power, and Max Müller from his extensive knowledge of the elegant Sanskrit literature. Every one of them shines in his special department, according to the peculiar excellence of his genius. But as for the first and ultimate truth of Buddhism, I am not sure whether or not they have thoroughly understood it.[61]

Soyen and his colleagues presented themselves as modern defenders of their religious traditions, working in parallel with Japanese nationalism which was beginning to reshape the country's self-image. With the exception of Hirai Kinza's remarks, the Japanese Buddhists stayed on point in their speeches, complying with the organizing committee's request that speakers focus on only six topics: God, man, the relation of man to God, the role of women, education and morality.

The Swedenborgians

Included in the Parliament's planned events was a New Jerusalem Church Congress, whose chair, the Revd Lewis P Mercer, sought to 'procure . . . such a hearing before the whole religious world as was never before attained or even hoped for by its apostles'.[62] Determined to discuss the historical importance of Swedenborg, the significance of the Second Advent of Christ, including the light it threw 'upon the unities and diversities of the Historic Faiths', and the present conflicts of opinion in Christendom, Mercer urged his fellow Swedenborgians to observe the catholic nature of the assembly rather than focus on the explicit or distinctive character of New Church doctrines.[63]

Not surprisingly, the Swedenborgians played a significant role in the Parliament's success as thousands of visitors received souvenir copies of Chauncey Giles's *Nature of Spirit and of Man as a Spiritual Being* and Mercer's *The African and the True Christian Religion* (a review of J J G Wilkinson's book of the same name) and *Emanuel Swedenborg and the New Christian Church*. Altogether the Swedenborgians presented six papers before the Parliament's main assembly and gave additional addresses in their Congress on: the origin and nature of the New Church; its doctrines; the planting of the New Church; the future of the New Church; and women in the New Church. For the New Churchmen attending the Parliament, the outcome was an unmatched success as they saw a growing inner spiritual world moving toward final perfection.[64]

Disturbed by the dialogue that exposed a growing divide between the delegates from Eastern religions and those from Western Christendom, Bonney opened the New Jerusalem Church Congress by calling on his fellow Swedenborgians to become the 'Church of Reconciliation' on the issues of reason and faith, science and religion, miracle and law, and revelation and philosophy. The New Church, he argued, should seek to reconcile 'the contending sects of Christendom, and the multiform religious systems of the other parts of the world'. Because of this, the responsibilities of New Churchmen were 'greater and more serious than [the] disciples of any other Faith'. The New Church was the 'Religion of Common Sense' to which the world's religions had reason to abide. To this end, he urged all New Churchmen to assist rather than undermine the work of the historical religions around the globe.[65]

For both Mercer and Bonney, the New Church represented 'the true Catholicism and the true Protestantism; the true orthodoxy and the true liberalism; the science of revelation and the logic of faith'. Mercer explained that while the New Church was certainly the youngest of the historical faiths, it had the ability to reach out to the oldest to 'complete and crown them all with the final revelation which restore[d] their pristine wisdom and Divine sanctions'. With the instrumentality of the law of correspondences, the course of Providence had been revealed. With communication from the heavens now open, a path had been made for every religion to enter the spiritual world and for a 'Universal Church' to emerge.[66]

In a series of papers, the first of which was 'The Soul and Its Future Life', the Revd Samuel M Warren explained that the body was the earthly form and instrument of the soul—an assemblage of organs that corresponded to and embodied the faculties of the soul that constituted the 'real man'. When individuals entered into the spiritual world they were subject to the law of association whereby their souls were mutually drawn together by spiritual affinity and their real character emerged whereby the good and bad were separated and 'thus prepared for their final and permanent association and abode'. Those societies and communities of the good constituted heaven while those of the evil constituted hell. None of this was done through the arbitrary judgment of an angry God but by each person's voluntary choice, which led them 'to prefer and seek the companionship of those most congenial to themselves'.[67]

The Revd Julian K Smyth's paper on 'The Incarnation of God in Christ' explained the nature of Christ whose life had been 'creative of spiritual hope and purpose'. Christianity, in its deepest sense, implied the presence of God in humanity. As a result of man's sinfulness which caused his spiritual perceptions to be dimmed, the mind of the Divine chose to manifest itself through the Incarnation. Christ was the Word revealing itself to man. 'And so we think of this Humanity of Jesus Christ as so formed and born as to be able to serve as a perfect instrument whereby the eternal Logos might come and dwell among us; might so express and pour forth His love . . . and so become literally, actually God-with-us'. Aside from Christianity's denominationalism and dogmatism, its prejudices and differences, the Incarnation remained the centrepiece. It was the heart of the New Testament and Christianity's message to the world.[68]

Other papers addressed the doctrine of Divine Humanity; the mystery of the Trinity; the meaning and purpose of redemption; the world of spirits intermediate between heaven and hell; the spiritual and metaphorical nature of the Scriptures;

185

the difference between redemption and salvation; and the future eternal home of humanity.[69] The Revd John Worcester gave particular attention to the 'higher criticism' which had unsettled many of the preconceived opinions regarding the character and authority of the Scriptures. He found the effort wholesome in that it freed the world from 'servile adherence to particular instruments of revelation', laying the groundwork for a more informed understanding of the truths in scriptural stories, prophecies, laws and psalms. While science had rooted out the myths, fables and magic from Scripture, it was clear to Worcester that its conclusions did not speak the whole truth. The key to the Scriptures' full meaning, he insisted, was in the law of correspondences which revealed the truths of the divine wisdom.[70]

In addressing 'The Future of the New Church', the Revd Willard Hinkley distanced himself from his Anglo-Christian colleagues who considered all pagans and gentiles consigned to hell. As a Swedenborgian, he believed that all souls were received into the spiritual world after death where they were instructed in the genuine truths of the heavenly world.[71] Like other New Churchmen, Hinkley did not adhere to a separate church organization but, instead, believed that the seeds of Swedenborg's truths could be fully understood and admired within all faiths and denominations.[72] Reinforcing Hinkley's views was the Revd Albinus F Frost of Detroit who noted that nearly 800 million inhabitants of the earth were gentiles or heathens having no knowledge of Christ. He referred to Swedenborg's *Arcana Caelestia* which explained that, having lived outside the church and through no fault of their own, individuals were nonetheless 'accepted in another life, and are there instructed by the angels with the utmost care in the goods and truths of faith'. Recognizing that the ancient gentile nations were among the most highly educated in philosophy, art, literature, oratory and drama, he found it impossible to believe they were lost to hell. Neither were the gentiles of more modern times, including 'the naked and partially civilized people of Africa, of the islands of the Pacific Ocean, and the Indians of North and South America'.[73]

At the close of the congress, Mercer returned to the podium to speak on 'Swedenborg and the Harmony of Religions'. Taking note of a new age of inquiry, expectation and experiment demonstrated by the Exposition, he expressed his belief that not only had new inventions and new ideals inspired man to seek one mastery after another, he also noted a new freedom in 'willing and thinking' that had entered the realm of religion. Central to this freedom was Swedenborg, whose personal character and revelatory visions awaited the thoughtful study for those seeking to understand the course of events. There was a catholicity in Swedenborg's teachings that demanded the world's attention. The law of correspondences revealed that the Scriptures contained 'an internal spiritual sense' for addressing the regeneration and spiritual life of the soul. Now was the time to convey this message to the ancient church whose remnants had been scattered to the far ends of the earth, and remove the errors and superstitions in non-Christian religions as well as those within the current Christian faiths. The Parliament of Religions was testimony, he insisted, 'for a universal Church in the faith of one visible God in whom is the Invisible, imparting eternal life and enlightenment to all from every nation who believe in him and work righteousness'.[74]

Ending Ceremonies

In all, nearly 150,000 attended the seventeen days of meetings, many of which ended with evening receptions hosted by notable Chicago families, including numerous Swedenborgians. On average, the Chicago press gave fifty columns a day to the proceedings as did numerous magazines which devoted pages to the delegates, their colourful robes and their discussions. In addition to the thousands of books and pamphlets distributed, several notable histories were written of the gathering. Barrows assembled a two-volume collection of papers as the official record titled *The World's Parliament of Religions: An Illustrated and Popular Story of the World's First Parliament of Religions, Held in Chicago in Connection with the Columbian Exposition of 1893*. Other more abbreviated histories included Walter R Houghton's *Neely's History of the Parliament of Religions and Religious Congresses at the World's Columbian Exposition*, J W Hanson's *The World's Congress of Religions: The Addresses and Papers Delivered Before the Parliament* and Lewis P Mercer's *The New Jerusalem in the World's Religious Congresses of 1893*.

The Parliament was an event that was never far removed from the domestic and global forces affecting the world in the waning years of the nineteenth century. That alone was enough to produce a sense of euphoria among its participants. On the surface, it represented a meeting of religious minds from across the world in an environment of mutual respect and understanding. Beneath the surface were any number of issues that, while probably not directly intended by the Parliament's organizing committee, were nevertheless the outcome of beliefs and values commonly shared by its organizers. In his concluding address before the delegates, for example, Barrows declared that the Parliament had been a 'blessing to many Christians'. Reflecting a Christo-centric view, he explained 'there is no teacher to be compared with Christ' and that human progress 'would objectively reach its culmination through Christianity. As the apex of all religions, Christianity can influence other relations meaningfully, but not vice versa'.[75] His comment, intended to counter Vivekananda's opening remarks, did little to pacify the feelings of the Parliament's non-Christian delegations.

The Parliament and Fair were not without grief as the Mayor of Chicago was assassinated two days before the close of events and the site of the Fair was destroyed by fire three months later.

* * *

It is arguable that, given the problems of translation, the outcome of the Parliament was a wholesale misreading by the delegates. It appears that the delegates were selective in what they heard or read and subsequently how they portrayed their own and other religions to the Parliament and to their native land. While outwardly an ethnographic display of the world's religions, many delegates viewed it as America's assertion of being the new Rome of Western civilization and, more broadly, a Judaeo-Christian expression of imperialism and outright racism. From another perspective, it reinforced the dangers of engagement as evident in Pope Leo XIII's subsequent censure of the Catholic speakers at the Parliament and his prohibition of participation by the Roman Church in any 'future promiscuous conventions'.[76]

Religious historian Donald Bishop has pointed out that the attitudes among the delegates included exclusionists[77] who believed that only one true religion was destined to become universal, and inclusionists[78] who held out hope that one true religion would evolve in the future—a synthesis of the best elements of existing religions into one that would unite all humankind. Seen in this light, the Parliament was no isolated or singularly conceived event; nor was its agenda separate from the world stage, a factor clearly evident in the venue of the Exposition which, while marking the four-hundred-year anniversary of Columbus's discovery of the New World, represented the symbolic staging of American achievements and the nation's rising status in the world. The focus of the Exposition was clearly on America's material achievements and its imprimatur of Protestantism. For many delegates from the East, the Parliament had been conceived as an effort to present a set of contrasts demonstrating not only the military and industrial strength of the West, but its moral and spiritual superiority as well. This was a conclusion drawn easily from the addresses of American and Eurocentric delegates who juxtaposed depictions of the East as 'culture-bound' and 'traditional' with the terms 'rational' and 'scientific' to portray the West.

Despite the negative connotations implicit in much of the Parliament, three clear outcomes served to justify Oriental participation: first, their vocal denunciation of the West's missionary activity which they almost uniformly condemned as racist; second, their ability to enlighten the West to the religious traditions of the East and rectify its many misunderstandings; and third, the establishment of their own missionary presence on Western soil. Unexpected outcomes of the Parliament were the enthusiasm with which Hinduism, Buddhism and the Baha'i faith were received by affluent urbanites and the popularity of subsequent nationwide tours made by Vivekananda, Dharmapala and others; the founding of the Vedanta Society; and the connection of the Baha'i faith with the Greenacre retreat in Maine. Ultimately, the Parliament resulted in what historian Sydney Ahlstrom identified as 'wells of truth outside Christianity'.[79]

The strains between traditionalism and modernism were evident in the complex relations not only among the different world faiths but within the faiths themselves, and never more so than among the denominations and sects constituting the Protestant establishment. The Parliament reflected in embryo the degree to which pluralism would eventually take hold but, for that moment in time, inter- and intra-pluralism was considered to be more of a threat than an objective. Though the small liberal wing within Protestantism represented a more apologetic response to the ethnocentric and condescending nature of Christian missionary work, the preponderance of delegates reinforced the more conservative political and social perceptions of traditional Protestantism.[80] There was a tacit presumption that mainstream Protestantism remained the source of the nation's greatness—politically, economically and morally. The idea of the United States as home to religious diversity rather than the moral capital of mainstream Protestantism was a mid-twentieth-century phenomena and by no means an objective of the Parliament's organizers.[81]

Before the close of the Parliament, the delegates called for the creation of 'The World's Religious Parliament Extension' with the motto 'Come now, and let us reason together, saith the Lord' (Isaiah 1:18). Dr Frank M Bristol of Evanston, Illinois, was appointed chairman of the local planning committee and Paul Carus, its secretary. Operating alongside the local committee was an 'associate committee of women' with Elizabeth Boynton Harbert as chair and Mrs Frederick Hawkins, secretary. In this manner, it was hoped, the Parliament would continue into the future.[82] Within a decade, the International Association for Religious Freedom held its first meeting, followed by the first meeting of the International Congress for the History of Religions which gathered at the Paris Universal Exposition in 1900, and the World Fellowship of Faiths which met in Chicago in 1929. Not until the first East-West Philosophers' Conference in Hawaii in 1939, however, did scholars come together to explore once again their differences and similarities.

PAUL CARUS AND HERMAN CARL VETTERLING

Bridge-Builders

The Parliament of Religions is undoubtedly the most noteworthy
event of modern times

(Paul Carus, *The Dawn of a New Religious*
Era and Other Essays, 1916)

Buddhism migrated in the sixth century BC from its home in India to Tibet, and then into China along the Southern Silk Road. From China, it moved into Korea and Vietnam, reaching Japan around AD 550. As its different sutras were translated into native languages, two principal schools of thought emerged: the older Buddhism of the Hinayana school which had a tendency to preserve traditions more faithfully; and the Mahayana school, especially prominent in Tibet, China and Japan, which was more religious than philosophical. The Hinayana was the religion of thinkers, not a gospel for 'those who are poor in spirit, who are ignorant, who are weak'. By contrast the Mahayana school was intended for the multitudes and proved to be much more adaptable in those regions or cultures where it spread. In large measure, Buddhism's success as a cross-cultural and transnational religion was due to its welcoming catholicity to all races and socio-economic levels, adjusting to native cultures rather than forcing a transformation of the host culture to its own self-image.[1]

The spread of Buddhism to the United States was similarly dramatic in scope, opening a discussion not only into the nature of geographical and cultural diffusion but affording an opportunity to observe how both sides of this transnational diffusion contributed to and benefited from the exchange. In essence, Buddhism underwent numerous adaptations in its diaspora suggesting that its transference to America was similar to its diffusion elsewhere. The exchange raises the question of what it means to be 'Buddhist' since the Japanese acquired some of their understanding of Buddhist literature by reading European translations of its ancient documents.[2] When, for example, Otani Koei and Ishikawa Shundai learned of a copy of a Buddhist sutra written in Sanskrit while visiting France, they relied on a Western translation since they were unable to read the canonical work in the original.[3]

Until midway through the twentieth century, the American conception of Eastern religions had been largely negative, caught up in the hagiography of militant Christian missionaries who viewed the peoples of the East as heathens and their religions as atavistic holdovers from an ancient world. Motivation for the study of Buddhism was for purposes of subversion, not understanding, let alone appreciation. Except for a few—such as Ralph Waldo Emerson and Henry David Thoreau, who had been drawn to the great books of the East; psychologist William James, who found justification in scholarly study of Eastern religions; the scholarly inquiries of James George Frazer, Edward Westermarck and Edward Burnett Tylor on primitive societies and religions; and the comparative studies of Albert J Edmunds and Dwight Goddard—there was little interest by the general populace in Eastern cultures, philosophies and religions.[4] This Eurocentric approach to Judaeo-Christian history with its linear and progressive interpretation of human destiny only reinforced the West's solipsistic view of its own importance once theologians and social scientists adjusted their teleology to evolutionary theory. All this, of course, would change in the 1950s and 1960s as American scholars and artists showed increasing interest in Asian civilizations, religions and cultures for reasons entirely different.

To what extent Buddhism influenced Western thought remains an ongoing question, fed by political, cultural, philosophic and religious biases that heavily punctuate the West's characterizations and scholarly conjecture of Eastern civilizations. As noted in the previous chapter, American and European religious leaders at the World's Parliament found few Buddhist contributions to the Western world. Most, in fact, found it hard to imagine that any of the religions that had shaped the 'lost' or 'lesser' civilizations had much to offer the European mind. Rather than explore the migration of ideas linking Buddhism with ancient Greece and Rome, including the

Neoplatonists and Essene communities in the Near East, they chose to focus on those centuries marked by waves of European explorers, traders, soldiers and missionaries who breeched the boundaries of China, Ceylon, Japan, India, Indochina and Tibet. Accounts such as Charles G Leland's *Fusang, or the Discovery of America by Chinese Buddhist Priests in the Fifth Century* (1875) and Edward Payson Vining's *An Inglorious Columbus; Or, Evidence that Hwui Shan and a Party of Buddhist Monks from Afghanistan Discovered America in the Fifth Century A.D.* (1885) were assigned to the backwaters of scholarship.

Even if these early trans-Pacific contacts were judged more fanciful than real, or at least failed the test of objectively identifiable historical evidence, there were still individuals from the West who had undertaken the study of Oriental art, philosophy, religion, languages and mythology, and whose writings and early translations of Persian and Sanskrit literature had introduced the West to the greatness of Asia, including being the mother of an earlier Indo-European language. These early works not only piqued interest in the West but, more importantly, affected the East's understanding of its own religious and philosophical traditions which, up to then, had been comfortable with its many competing schools. The West's insistence on a synoptic view had an unintended effect on Eastern belief systems by encouraging a more prescribed than open-ended self-image.

In the immediate aftermath of the World's Parliament of Religions, three individuals stood out as bridge-builders connecting the religions and philosophies of the Occident and Orient. The first, Paul Carus, a German-American author, editor and student of comparative religions, awoke to the significance of the Parliament of Religions and its transcultural impact on Western religions and philosophies. The second, Herman Vetterling, a Swedenborgian philosopher and convert to Buddhism, focused heavily on Swedenborg's theory of correspondences, using it as a bridge between Swedenborgianism and Buddhism. For Vetterling, Swedenborg remained the essential link demonstrating the relevancy of Buddhism to the Western world, suggesting that Buddhism and Swedenborgianism were practically one and the same. After taking this position, Vetterling gradually transitioned into a form of Buddhism infused with the Theosophical concepts of Helena Blavatsky and Henry

Steel Olcott. The third, Zen Buddhist Daisetsu Teitaro Suzuki, will be examined separately in Chapter 8.

Paul Carus (1852-1919)

Born into a devout Christian family in the town of Ilsenburg in Saxony-Anhalt, Germany, in 1852, Paul Carus was expected to follow his father's footsteps into the ministry. A gifted student whose interests spanned philosophy, classical philology and the natural sciences, he suffered an early crisis of faith which put him on an intellectual journey to the universities of Greifswald, Strasburg and finally Tübingen, where he earned a doctorate in mathematics and philosophy in 1876.[5] In 1880, while teaching at the military academy of the Royal Corps of Cadets of Saxony, in Dresden, Carus authored a pamphlet denying the literal truth of the Scriptures, comparing them instead to literary works such as the Homer's *Odyssey*. Because of his challenge to accepted orthodoxy, the Royal Corps gave Carus the option of rescinding his beliefs or resigning. He chose the latter and left Germany for England where he taught for a brief time before emigrating to the United States where he published his first philosophical work, *Monism and Meliorism* (1885). Monism, a term popular among a growing number of European intellectuals, offered a path between knowledge and belief without resorting to agnosticism. Aligning himself with the progressive thinking of French philosopher and founder of positivism Auguste Comte; political economist John Stuart Mill; and French philosopher and educational reformer Victor Cousin, Carus concluded that all religions contained elements of truth which, when cleansed by science, could attain a new spiritual identity worthy of humanity. A proponent of the scientific method, Carus thought it possible to investigate religion scientifically, separating its truths from its often hazy myths and symbols. Along the way, Carus also placed ethics on an objective and scientific basis.[6]

Convinced that the path of progress was foreordained by the law of evolution and that science was slowly but surely transforming the world through its methods of exact inquiry, Carus considered it his duty to treat science not as a secular alternative to religion, but as a divine gift revealing God's purposes. Observation and exactness in measuring and experimentation afforded opportunities never before considered possible. Though society had not yet reached the ideal of the scientific method, progress in all the domains of practical life had set the age apart from the past. 'Mankind has learned through a millennial experience that investigation is possible and, if conducted with proper circumspection, must lead to the discovery of important truths. . . . Nature is not dumb to an intelligent inquirer'. As the great destroyer of error and superstition, science had become a reform agent whose spirit was carried into all domains with the building of railroads, lighting of darkness, discovering cures for disease and unveiling the wonders of nature. Still missing was a philosophy of science and a religion of science. Carus believed that religion, philosophy and art were inseparable; constituting a trinity that ensured 'an all-round manhood of Goodness, Truth and Beauty'.[7]

Carus's book caught the eye of Edward C Hegeler, a zinc industrialist from LaSalle, Illinois who, finding Carus's monist views to his liking, hired him to tutor his children. Hegeler had founded the Open Court Publishing Company whose magazine *The Open Court* was dedicated to addressing the vexing philosophical and religious issues of the day. After a falling out with his editor, Benjamin Franklin Underwood, over the underlying philosophy of the magazine and its editorial management, Hegeler appointed Carus to succeed Underwood as the paper's editor. Hegeler's daughter Mary, a graduate of the University of Michigan who helped with the publishing company and who also played an important role in managing the family's zinc works, married Carus in 1888.[8]

In working for Hegeler, Carus found his vocation: utilizing the scientific study of religion and the religious study of science to formulate a 'Religion of Science', a series of books and also the title of his own book in the series. As Carus explained in his preface, 'it is by no means necessary to abolish the old religions, but only to purify them and develop their higher possibilities, so that their mythologies shall be changed into strictly scientific conceptions. It is intended to preserve of the old religions all that is true and good, but to purify their faith by rejecting superstitions and irrational elements, and to discard, unrelentingly, their errors'.[9] Carus rejected any religion that postulated a personal God, believing it little more than an atavism of ancient times. He was equally adamant in rejecting atheism, agnosticism and pantheism. In their place he proposed an evolutionary process and a moral world order as real as mathematics.[10] With monism, he intended to establish no new sect, nor to have a visible church with its own members, rituals, by-laws and creeds. His was an invisible church, much as Swedenborg had intended.[11]

Carus considered scientists as seekers of truth, the 'prophets' of the religion of science. While individuals were subject to error, 'no amount of error [could] overthrow science and the authority of science'. Science taught, step by step, that all individual laws formed a harmonious *system* of laws; each law became a corollary in an 'all-pervading regularity'. The religion of science did not speak of God in an atheistic, anthropomorphic, polytheistic, pantheistic, deistic or monotheistic sense; nor did it teach asceticism or hedonism. All were erroneous. Instead, Carus urged an ethic that required one to know the laws of being, the duties which the laws implied, and unfaltering attendance to their fulfilment. 'The eternal of nature only is God. . . . we must not look up with reverence to forces of nature which we utilise', but only to that power 'which moulds worlds, which fashions all beings, . . . and which moves onward in the progress of evolution'.[12]

In numerous essays, books and communications, Carus showed little reticence in calling dogma the 'wreck of religion' which slowed the advance of true religious thinking. Thankfully, the old doctrines had become increasingly 'unpreachable' and were now under scrutiny by scientifically schooled Bible-researchers in the movement called the higher criticism. 'Let us not be afraid to analyze religion', he advised. This included the doctrine of eternal punishment and stern damnation meted out to the heathen and the infant, as well as the doctrine of election. The Bible was only a part of God's revelation as He had also revealed Himself in the works of Shakespeare, Goethe, Lamarck, Darwin and Edison.[13] Religion, for Carus, had to be in perfect accord with science or it would fail. Science was divine and the truths of science were actually revelations from God. 'Through science God speaks to us', he insisted, 'by science he shows us the glory of his works; and in science he teaches us his will'.[14]

As for immortality, Carus accepted the concept of the soul, which neither began with birth nor ended with death. 'Our life is only a phase in the evolution of a greater whole, and the spiritual existence of ourselves, our soul . . . will evolve in future generations to higher and ever higher planes of being and to nobler and ever nobler destinies'. The soul's life after death was a scientific truth embedded in the very law and purpose of evolution. Notwithstanding the soul's existence after death, Carus did not conceive of the soul's life as a continuation of the ego. Immortality did not mean posthumous human existence. 'We have to give up the idea that our real self belongs to ourselves', he wrote. 'Our soul is not our own, but mankind's; and mankind in its turn is not its own; the soul of mankind is from God, it develops in God, and all its aspirations and yearnings are to God'.

> The souls of the dead form an ever-living presence in the souls of the living. Progress and evolution to higher stages is only possible because the souls of former generations continue to live. If the souls of our ancestors were not with us and in us, what a wretched, and, indeed, merely amoeboid existence would we lead. . . . Nothing is lost in this world, least of all a human soul. To be gathered to our fathers does not mean to be buried in the ground, but to be embodied as a living element into the evergrowing organism of mankind. There we are preserved as a living presence with all our peculiarities and with the entire personality of our being. Death is a dissolution of our body; it is the end of our career; it is the discontinuance of our activity in this individuality of ours. Yet it is no annihilation of our thoughts, of our soul, of our spiritual existence, of ourselves.[15]

Carus did not find mysticism dangerous since, under the proper circumstances, it could be as 'beautiful as art and sometimes even wholesome'. Still, mysticism was opposed to science and did not, as its proponents claimed, provide an equally valid method for understanding the spiritual world. Carus was convinced science was un-limited and, whether the object studied was material or spiritual, all problems could be solved. His criticism of mysticism was its lack of 'critical acumen'. At its best, it served as the conscience of a 'simple-minded but well-intentioned' individual who relied on an inner voice that spoke to him with divine authority on matters he could not understand. This was no proper criterion of truth.[16]

Not surprisingly, Carus considered Swedenborg to be 'one of the most representative mystics', adding that 'The appreciation which he has found among a number of adherents proves too well how deeply his way of presenting metaphysical problems in the shape of allegorical dreams is founded in the peculiar constitution of man's spiritual system'. It was characteristic of mystical minds, explained Carus, to live in a world of symbolism in such a way that they believe their own dreams and make statements 'so convincing that they easily find followers among those who are kin to them in their mental constitution'. This explained Kant's indignation with Swedenborg's *Arcana*. As a mystic, Swedenborg's imagination was so vivid that the space he invented to represent the spiritual world became an actual space to him; his spirits become materialized shapes, and thus it happens that he can speak 'with departed souls whenever he pleases'. Like other mystics, however, Carus felt that Swedenborg's imagination had outrun his sobriety.[17]

Prior to the World's Parliament, there was little indication that Carus had anything good to say concerning Buddhism.[18] In an unsigned article titled 'The Religion of Resignation' published in *The Open Court* in 1890, he doubted its usefulness in the modern world. Though a precursor to Christianity, and arguably superior, Buddhism had not succeeded in shedding its superstitions. Much like Christianity, it had ossified to where its mythology had transformed into theological dogmas.[19]

This early judgment changed dramatically as a result of the Parliament which Carus helped organize and where he presented a paper on science and religion.[20] In his address, Carus noted that religion, helped by scientific inquiry, had gained in depth and importance. 'Religion is indestructible', he insisted, 'because it is that innermost conviction of man which regulates his conduct'. But belief *was* different as a consequence of science. 'God is to me not what he is according to the old dogmatic view, a supernatural person'. He was neither a father, nor mother, or both; instead, God was the 'authority of the moral ought'. There was no discrepancy between scientific truth and moral truth; there was but one truth and one science, especially since Darwin had succeeded in explaining the process of evolution. Moreover, science, not Scripture, was God's true revelation. Through science, God communicated with humanity. Those who refused to accept the discoveries of science became slaves of tradition. Only through science could religion find the path to progress.[21]

As a delegate to the World's Parliament of Religions, Carus met Anagarika Dharmapala and Shaku Soyen and learned of Buddhism's modernized and westernized approach to religion. After these meetings, he felt he had at last discovered the closest resemblance to his religion of science among the historical religions. Using his position at Open Court Publishing, he authenticated his new-found discovery by disseminating books and articles about Buddhism to his readers. According to historian David McMahan:

> [Carus] presented the broad outlines of Buddhism as a religion containing many essentials of Enlightenment rationalism and late-nineteenth-century science; karma was natural law translated into the ethical realm; rebirth anticipated the Darwinian understanding of species transforming themselves into other species; the detailed analyses of mind in Buddhist texts were in fundamental agreement with modern psychology; the exhortations of the Buddha to be 'lamps unto yourselves', not blindly believing but to verifying his statements experimentally, contained the quintessence of the scientific spirit.[22]

In 1894, Carus published the article 'Buddhism and Christianity' in which he explained that forty per cent of the world's inhabitants were Buddhists who had much in common with Christians—so much in fact that scholars Arthur Lillie[23] and Rudolf Seydel[24] suggested the Buddhist origin of Christianity. Carus set out to identify their most obvious similarities and dissimilarities, concluding that both religions addressed many of the same problems of life, solving them in a similar spirit (although using different modes of expression).[25]

In years following the Parliament, Carus continued to present Monism as the bridge linking the science of religion to the religion of science, but he also sought to build a bridge between Western and Eastern religion, philosophy and culture. After listening to the Buddhist speakers at the Parliament and from his own subsequent investigations, he concluded that Buddhism offered a religion that was scientific in a very modern sense of the word and that his prior beliefs had been in error, most notably the denial of the existence of a higher self and his understanding of nirvana.[26] A flurry of articles and book reviews subsequently emerged from the pages of *The Open Court* and *The Monist* addressing the origins and doctrines of Buddhism and Christianity, the issues affecting Christian missionary work, and several notable translations of Eastern religious classics. Convinced of the future role of Buddhism in the West, he announced that Buddha was 'the first positivist, the first humanitarian, the first radical freethinker, the first iconoclast, and the first prophet of the Religion of Science'.[27]

Before long, *The Open Court* and *The Monist* magazines became outlets for a broad investigation and popularization of East/West philosophy, including studies demonstrating similarities between the two. At the same time, the publishing company enacted a robust plan to translate Eastern philosophic and religious texts into English. In all of these undertakings, Carus sought to reject any view of Buddhism as a religion of negativism, insisting that it alone among the great religions of the world, had adjusted to the modern world. More so than Christianity, it came closest to his ideal religion of science. Carus's more important books included: *The Dharma or the Religion of Enlightenment: An Exposition of Buddhism* (1896) which explained key Buddhist doctrines; *Buddhism and Its Christian Critics* (1897) which served as a rebuttal to Western critics; and *Chinese Philosophy* (1906) which laid out the principal elements of Chinese thought. Other works included *Lao-Tze's Tao-Teh-King* (1898); *Karma: A Story of Buddhist Ethics* (1905); *Buddhism and Its Christian Critics* (new and revised edition, 1905); *Amitabha: A Story of Buddhist Theology* (1906); *Portfolio of Buddhist Art: Historical and Modern* (1906); *The Buddha: A Drama in Three Acts and Four Interludes* (1908); and *Nirvana: A Story of Buddhist Psychology* (1913). Besides these volumes, Carus wrote seven articles on Hinduism and thirty-nine on Buddhism in the period between 1887 and 1909. Under Carus's direction, the Open Court Company published thirty-eight books on Oriental thought between 1893 and 1915, fifteen of which he authored. Carus was so committed to bridging the East/West divide that in 1897 he even revised the masthead of *The Open Court* from 'Devoted to the Work of Conciliating Religion with Science', to 'A Monthly Magazine Devoted to the Science of Religion, the Religion of Science, and the Extension of the Religious Parliament Idea'.

Carus observed that many of his contemporaries were fearful of recognizing Buddhism's priority as it would imply that Christianity was 'a deteriorisation of Buddhism', negating Christianity's originality and truth. Notwithstanding this reticence on the part of Christians, he thought it silly not to accept the fact that Christianity embodied numerous concepts from prior philosophies and religions including the Logos idea which derived from Neoplatonism; the God idea common to Jewish tradition; baptism, which was an Essenian rite; communion, which was part of Dionysianism; and the idea of a world saviour, which was Buddhist in origin. None of these elements had originated with Christianity.[28]

For his part, Carus chose not to take sides in the debate over whether Christianity and Buddhism had a common origin. In his opinion, this was much less important than the fact that Buddha lived in the fifth century before Christ which meant that the Buddhist canon was well established by 250 BC. 'This excludes at once', he insisted, 'the supposition that Buddhism is indebted to Christianity for its lofty morality and the purity of its ideals'. Besides, there were numerous channels by which Buddhist doctrines could have reached Palestine, like the connections made by Alexander in his military conquests and the missionary legations of Buddhist monks into western Asia in the third century before the Christian era. Carus suggested that given the missionary zeal of Buddhists and the fact that they tended not to attack the religions they found in their travels but sought to adapt as much as possible to the ideas of native cultures, they may well have influenced the Christians they met.[29]

Carus's most popular work was *The Gospel of Buddha*, an abbreviated and idiosyncratically chosen selection of Buddhist writings drawn from two thousand years of canon. In explaining his methodology, Carus admitted that many of his selections were literal translations of the original texts while others were rendered in a manner that would make them more understandable to modern readers. Given that Buddhism had split into numerous sects, he chose only those portions of the canon that could stand as 'common ground'. Of all the representative schools, Carus believed that southern Buddhism (i.e., Mahayana) accurately preserved the traditions of Buddhism in its most pristine manner.[30]

Soon after the first edition was published, Shaku Soyen had a Japanese version

(*Budda no fukuin*) translated by his assistant Daisetsu Teitaro Suzuki, and a Chinese version translated by Ohara of Otzu. Other editions followed in German, French, Spanish, Russian, Czech, Italian, Siamese and other Eastern languages. When Soyen wrote the preface to the Japanese edition, he listed three objectives: '(1), To make our readers know how much our Buddhism is understood by Western scholars; (2) to point out to beginners a short road of studying Buddhism; (3) to teach the masses the life of Sakyamuni and give them an outline of the general doctrines of Buddhism'.[31] *The Gospel of Buddha* was testimony not only of the West's interest in Buddhism and its compatibility with Western science, but also its success in meeting the spiritual needs of Japan's younger generations. The Japanese did not need Christianity to find compatibility with the modern, scientific world; they had only to look to their own native religion.[32]

Another of Carus's more popular books was *The Dharma or the Religion of Enlightenment* in which he explained the tenets of Buddhism including 'The Four Noble Truths'; 'The Seven Jewels of the Law'; 'Karma'; 'The Anatman'; 'The Soul'; 'Selfhood and Enlightenment'; and 'Nirvana'. Dharma, meaning truth, especially religious truth, was formulated in statements known as 'the four noble truths': (1) the existence of suffering; (2) the origin of suffering being desire; (3) the emancipation from suffering; and (4) the eightfold path that led to the emancipation from suffering. This eightfold path, as Carus explained, consisted of: right comprehension, right aspirations, right speech, right conduct, right living, right endeavour, right self-discipline and the attainment of right bliss. Salvation came to 'him whose self disappears before Truth, whose will is bent upon what he ought to do, whose sole desire is the performance of his duty'.[33]

The seven jewels of the law which, when united, formed nirvana, included purity, calmness, comprehension, bliss, wisdom, perfection and enlightenment. These, in turn, manifested themselves in meditation, struggle against sin, aspiration for saintship, moral power, and the production of organs of spiritual sense, wisdom and righteousness. Meditation was practised to teach the concept of emptiness of existence, meaning that the body is a transient thing and cannot be the purpose and aim of life. The struggle against sin involved the effort to prevent sin from arising, putting it away when it did arise, producing goodness in its place, and increasing that goodness over time. The road to sainthood involved the concept of *use*, meaning the will to acquire it, the exertion itself, the preparation of the heart and self-discipline. Without these components, sainthood was impossible.[34]

Karma was the object of the soul (atman) and while the journey was transient, it was nonetheless permanent. Karma was the sum total of a person's character and identity; it was the moral and intellectual essence of man that passed from one 'fleshy tabernacle' to another, and from one generation to another. Karma linked them together in a chain of transmigrations which became an inheritance. 'It is the "last inheritor and the last result" of all the conditions that have affected a line of ancestry which goes back for many millions of years to the time when life first appeared on the earth', explained Carus. Though reincarnations appeared as new individuals, they were identical to those from whom they sprang. Evolution supplied the path, as 'Nothing springs into being without a gradual becoming . . . There is a continuity of deeds and reincarnations, as milk turns to curds, and curds to butter'. Every being was the product of its deeds—past, present and future.[35]

As Carus explained, Buddhism did not deny the existence of the soul, only the theory of a 'soul-in-itself', meaning its independent existence. There was no such thing as an absolute separate individuality. There was no separate atman and karma. Atman *was* karma, meaning that all that was now is all that has ever been and or ever can be. 'As there is no âtman, there is no âtman that dies; or in other words, life, death and rebirth are simultaneous and continuous. Every event that happens passes forever away while it happens; it dies yet it continues for all eternity in the effect it produces'.[36]

The state of nirvana was attained when the illusion of selfhood was dispelled from the body (i.e., when the 'I', 'me' and 'mine' disappeared). With enlightenment the personality was not annihilated; existence continued as usual but there was nothing that one possessed as his or her own. What constituted one's character no longer served the self, only others. Nirvana was the surrender of self to wisdom, virtue and all-comprehensive love, all of which dominated one's thoughts and regulated one's sentiments and conduct.[37]

Carus presented Buddhism in a way that was rational, scientific, practical and understandable to the West. Unlike the Theosophists Blavatsky and Olcott, Carus was not drawn to the occult but to explanations that fitted within the mainstream of liberal Protestantism. Believing that the Christianity of his youth demanded a more thorough purification, he stressed that the religion of the future 'must be in perfect accord with science'. Through science, God spoke to man. True religion could never be in error and, when attained, would replace all the older beliefs of the world with their dogmas, rituals and mythical beliefs.[38]

For all Carus's efforts, American academics were critical of his scholarship, his idiosyncratic choice of material and his ignorance of key pieces of Oriental literature. Donald Meyer, for example, thought he had 'oversimplified human nature, overestimated human reason and relied upon an inflexible methodology which rendered it inadequate to the complexities of human life'.[39] Perhaps the most critical was Michel Foucault whose paper 'Zen and the Author Function' dismissed *The Gospel of Buddha* as a flawed effort to convey Carus's religion of science. Even Swedenborgian Martin Verhoeven, who wrote the introduction to the 2004 edition, considered it a 'regrettable conflation' of hybrid Christianity, science and monism. In effect, Carus had 'Americanized the Buddha', creating an attractive set of religious, philosophical and social values that resonated with American values. Verhoeven concluded that the value of the book now is to remind us 'how easy it is to notice and embrace only those elements of Buddhism that seem consonant with our way of life and disregard the rest'.[40]

Notwithstanding criticism from academics, Carus used the resources of the Open Court Company to fulfil his dream of building a bridge between religion and science. *The Gospel of Buddha* seemed to capture those elements of Buddhist literature most appealing to both East and West.[41] Believing that Christianity had been changed irrevocably by Darwin's theory of natural selection, Carus looked to the future with optimism believing it possible to move forward with a new scientific world view.[42] Over the course of his editorial career, he cultivated a stable of highly educated and competent contributors including John Dewey, Charles Sanders Peirce, Lester Ward, Joseph LeConte, Arthur O Lovejoy, Alfred Binet, Hugo de Vries, Bertrand Russell, Ernst Haeckel, George John Romanes, Francis Ellingwood Abbot, William Salter, Edward Drinker Cope, Ernst Mach and Wilhelm Wundt. Also included among the contributors were Max Müller, Hermann Oldenberg, H G Creel and D T Suzuki, whose interests focused on Eastern thought and culture.[43]

Herman Carl Vetterling (1849-1931)

Like Carus, the physician, philosopher and publicist Herman Carl Vetterling had been a member of the Advisory Committee of the World's Parliament of Religions and was as much an admirer of Swedenborg as he was a disillusioned believer in Protestantism. Born in Sweden, he emigrated with his parents and three siblings to Holmes City, Minnesota in 1871. Raised in the Swedish Lutheran State Church, he briefly attended St Paul University and worked for a time on a local newspaper. As he matured, his quest for true spirituality led him away from Lutheranism and into the fold of Swedenborgianism which his family regarded as heretical. In 1873, he matriculated at Urbana University in Ohio, a Swedenborgian school founded in 1850, where he remained for two years on scholarship. In 1875, he moved to Pittsburgh, Pennsylvania, where he pursued ministerial studies and was ordained a minister of the New Church in 1877. From 1877 until 1881, he served as a New Church pastor in Pittsburgh, Detroit, and Salem, Ohio. After being accused by the *Detroit Post and Tribune* of molesting two women while drunk, he resigned his post and moved to Philadelphia where he matriculated at Hahnemann Homeopathic Medical College before transferring to Hahnemann Medical College of Chicago from which he graduated in 1883.[44] In 1884, Vetterling was living in St Paul where he joined the Theosophical Society of Blavatsky and Olcott and where he also showed an interest in the psychic claims of Emma Hardinge Britten and Andrew Jackson Davis, along with legends concerning an ancient church in Central Asia whose brotherhood served as protectors of the world's esoteric wisdom.

Between October 1884 and December 1885, Vetterling wrote a series of articles titled 'Studies in Swedenborg' in volumes six and seven of *The Theosophist*. In them, he noted the similarities between Swedenborg's philosophy and that of Buddhism and Theosophy. Placing Jesus on a par with Buddha Gautama, he explained the internal and external mind, the will and understanding, affections and thoughts, memory and recollection. He compared Swedenborg's writings to Olcott's *Buddhist*

Catechism, Thomas Taylor's *Eleusinian and Bacchic Mysteries* and Huc's *Souvenirs d'un voyage dans la Tartarie, le Thibet, et la Chine pendant les années 1844, 1845 et 1846*; the manner in which the 'science of correspondences' became the vehicle connecting the spiritual and natural things worlds; and similarities between Swedenborg's writings and Buddhism on the powers of abstraction, quietism and introspection.[45]

After reading Britten's *Ghost Land; or Researches into the Mysteries of Occultism* (1876), Vetterling immersed himself in Blavatsky's *Isis Unveiled*, Alfred Percy Sinnett's *The Occult World* (1888) and *Esoteric Buddhism* (1883), and *The Theosophist* magazine, all of which led him to read Anna Bonus Kingsford and Edward Maitland's *The Perfect Way; Or, The Finding of Christ* (1882). In it the authors claimed to have recovered the basic doctrines of all the great religions of antiquity, including Christianity, discovering in the process that the dogmas of Christianity were substantially identical with those of the great historical religions and that true religious belief was best practised on the subjective and spiritual plane. Vetterling's quest for a true spiritual religion led him first to Swedenborg where he found hidden meanings behind the words of the Bible. From there, he was attracted to Theosophy where he learned that Buddha and Jesus were the head and heart of the same religion. The more he examined Theosophy, the more he came to believe it was a system of truths discovered and preserved by remnants of an ancient Great Brotherhood who revealed them as advances in human evolution permitted. Theosophy represented the underlying truths of all the world's scriptures, religions and philosophies, a repository of ancient wisdom whose Mahatmas watched over the world and stimulated human evolution to ever higher levels of spiritual awareness. Vetterling declared himself a Buddhist in 1887—a form of Buddhism that assimilated both Swedenborgian theology and Tibetan Buddhism as interpreted by Theosophy.[46]

In 1886, Vetterling was living on a farm in the mountains near Santa Cruz, California, with Margaret Curry Pitcairn, a Swedenborgian whom he met while serving as pastor of a New Church in Pittsburgh. Between 1887 and 1894, he edited and published the first English language Buddhist magazine, *The Buddhist Ray*, which recounted throughout its many articles that Swedenborg was actually a Buddhist and that Buddhism was a religion and philosophy morally superior to Christianity. Many of its articles were translated and disseminated in India, Ceylon, Siam and Japan.[47]

In 1887, using the pseudonym Philangi Dasa, Vetterling authored an occult novel titled *Swedenborg the Buddhist; Or, the Higher Swedenborgianism: Its Secrets and Thibetan Origin*. The contents were presented in the form of a conversation between a Swedenborgian, a Buddhist monk, a Brahmin, a Zoroastrian, a Norse Icelander, an Aztec, a Confucian and a Theosophist. The dialogue consisted of questions and answers regarding the similarities between and among their respective religious beliefs, with special emphasis given to Buddhism, Theosophy and Swedenborgianism. The narrative, like Plato's *Phaedrus*, drew the reader through topics such as conjugial love, divine providence, the numerous planets in the universe and the Last Judgment, with Swedenborg answering most of the questions and moving the dialogue toward a synthesis of sorts. Throughout the book were references to the dangers of selfhood and mediumship; the importance of seeking the God within; the relative role of women in Buddhism and Christianity; the issues of earthly and celestial chastity; the intellectuality of science versus intuition; and the secret doctrines taught by the 'Guardians' of the ancient world. The book also referenced German physician Franz Mesmer, French mystic Madame Guyon, philologist Max Müller, Victor Cousin, Thomas Lake Harris and Cardinal John Henry Newman.[48]

Borrowing material from Alfred Sinnett's *Esoteric Buddhism*, Vetterling argued that much of the ancient wisdom of the East had migrated from Hinduism to Buddhism where it was kept by the same monks who contacted Swedenborg in his revelatory visions. In demonstrating this connection, Vetterling referred to Abbé Huc, a French missionary priest who, in the company of fellow missionary Joseph Gabet, travelled through the northern and western provinces of the Chinese empire, taking up temporary residence in the Buddhist monastery of Kounboun, and eventually reaching the sacred city of Lhasa, the capital of Tibet. Huc's travels, recounted in *Souvenirs d'un Voyage, dans la Tartarie, le Thibet, et la Chine, pendant les années 1844, 1845, et 1846*, gave credence to Swedenborg's claim of having conversed with inhabitants from Lesser Tartary near China,[49] drawing parallels between Buddhist and Catholic ceremonies, and suggesting that Christianity was a symbolic synthesis of ancient beliefs. Vetterling's effort to tie Swedenborg with Buddhism was not only encouraged by Theosophists but also by Japanese Buddhists who translated the book in 1893.[50]

Vetterling provided his readers with a list of parallels in the lives of Buddha and Jesus, including:[51]

1. Of royal lineage
2. Born of a virgin mother
3. A heavenly messenger announced their royal lineage
4. Angelic messengers announced their birth
5. Princes and wise men appeared with gifts
6. Extermination of children born around the time of their birth as a preventive to a powerful competitor
7. Presentation to the temple
8. Called the 'Word', the 'All-wise', the 'Messiah', the 'Way', the 'Saviour', the 'Prince of Peace', the 'Good Shepherd', and the 'Light of the World'
9. Parents who marvelled at their understanding
10. Retired in solitude to fast and pray
11. Were purified in the river
12. Tempted with promises of wealth and glory
13. Anointed a number of apostles
14. Began a mission and public speaking
15. Remained homeless and poor
16. Befriended a despised woman
17. Walked on water
18. Taught self-denial and meekness
19. Deserted by closest friends during a time of danger
20. Following their deaths, the earth trembled

Vetterling's appendix to the book outlined the full extent of Swedenborg's philosophy. Although the book's literary style was often confusing due to its mixture of theology, mysticism and folklore, it nonetheless provided an overview of Swedenborg's ideas, with each concept tied by reference to his writings.[52]

Vetterling's last work, *The Illuminate of Görlitz; or Jakob Böhme's Life and Philosophy: A Comparative Study*, a fifteen-hundred-page tome published privately in 1923, concerned the life and times of the Christian mystic Jacob Boehme who joined a mystical study group known as the 'Conventicle of God's Real Servants'. Claiming an inner vision into the structure of the universe, Boehme authored *Die Morgenröte im Aufgang* (*The Rising of Dawn*) in 1612 (later given the name *Aurora*), followed by *The Three Principles of the Divine Essence* (1618-19); *Answers to Forty Questions Concerning the Soul* (1620); *The Great Six Points* (1620); *The Signature of All Things* (1621); *Of Regeneration* (1622); *The Mysterium Magnum* (1623); and *Of Illumination* (1624). Consistent throughout his writings were elements of Mariology; the Fall as a necessary part of the divine will in bringing forth good; the significance of free will in seeking divine grace; and the suggestion that without Creation, God would have been incomplete. Popular among the Cambridge Platonists and millenarians, Boehme became a source of inspiration for English poets John Milton, William Blake and Samuel Taylor Coleridge, as well as the German Romantics. What attracted Vetterling to Boehme was his deep spirituality which pre-dated both Swedenborgianism and Theosophy. He was especially enamoured with the mystic's belief that there was only one universal religion for mankind which, for Vetterling, was Buddhism.

Vetterling maintained a medical practice until 1907. Except for a brief mention of it in his *Illuminate of Görlitz*, there is no indication that he concerned himself with the feud ongoing between the low- and high-potency homoeopaths. He considered much of the phenomena in the healing process the result of the paranormal which explained his interest in Boehme's writings and suggested that he was much taken with the manner in which patients were affected by his cures. 'In former days', Vetterling explained, '[I] cured instantly many persons merely by stroking them with [my] hands; or by giving them tinctured water or sugar-pills. They thought [I] gave them powerful medicine; and [I] let them think so'.[53] For much of the Santa Cruz community, he was known as 'Dr Vetterling', a homoeopathic specialist on diseases of the eye and ear. From 1901 until 1927, Vetterling lived in east San Jose and, according to the census, reported himself as a physician from 1901 to 1907 and a farmer from 1910 until his death in 1931 at the age of seventy-three.

* * *

In the decades following the close of the World's Parliament of Religions, the United States became the garden spot for swamis and yogis eager to carry their messages to curious and attentive audiences. Emissaries such as Swami Vivekananda, Anagarika Dharmapala, Virchand Gandhi, Protap Chunder Mozoomdar, Shaku Soyen and Daisetsu Teitaro Suzuki went on lecture circuits to promote their Hindu, Zen Buddhist, Zoroastrian and Baha'i beliefs, tendered in a manner designed to accommodate the Western mind. Those Americans drawn to their siren appeals were not only the descendants of New England's romantic generation, but those inclined by gender, class, religion and region to the esoteric and occult.

Continuing a tradition begun by the Transcendentalists, Unitarians, visiting scholars and artists, and Buddhist migrants, both Carus and Vetterling served as bridge-builders between East and West in the late Victorian and early modernist periods. Most importantly, they lent credence to the validity of mysticism on both sides of the Pacific while distinguishing it from modern science on the one hand, and the eccentricities, visions and ecstasies claimed by mesmerists, spiritualists and other occult traditions on the other.[54] The connecting links in their bridge were both Swedenborg and a blend of Theosophy and Buddhism that travelled back and forth across the Pacific. Swedenborg had not only devoted his theological acumen to verse-by-verse exegeses of Genesis, Exodus and Revelation, but shared his visionary contacts with Buddhist ascetics from the Great Tartary. Building upon this foundation, Vetterling's *Swedenborg the Buddhist*, the subtitle of which is *The Higher Swedenborgianism: Its Secrets and Thibetan Origin*, not only noted similarities between Swedenborg's references to Jesus and the legendry saint Padmasambhava who was said to have brought Buddhism to Tibet, but asserted that Swedenborg received instruction in Buddhism from Tibetan, Chinese and Mongolian spirits.[55] Others would find similar parallels between the Greek New Testament and the Pali Buddhist Canon as well as historical similarities in the lives of Swedenborg, Buddha and Jesus. It seemed for many advocates of Buddhism and Swedenborgianism, their 'holy grail' was to identify and validate the historical connections, however obscure, between Christianity and Buddhism. Thus, while Swedenborg did not actually advocate Buddhism to the West, he remained a person of interest among those anxious to popularize Buddhism in the West. His rejection of original sin and his emphasis on free will, the evils of self-love and the importance of good works (i.e., 'use') for the benefit of humankind were elements that seemed common to Buddhism and most relevant in making this connection.

Interestingly, those who brought attention to Swedenborg's Buddhist elements were also advocates of Theosophy who, for many years, became the principal interpreters of Buddhism in the West. Thus, before Swedenborgianism fell into relative obscurity, numerous individuals had explained Swedenborg's mention of the Great Tartary as a reference to the Buddhist and Hindu teachings of the Brotherhood which had become the basis of Theosophical teachings. Vetterling's *Swedenborg the Buddhist* and his magazine *The Buddhist Ray*, along with Olcott and Blavatsky's *The Theosophist*, asserted the Buddhist origin of Swedenborgian thought, including breath control, sexual powers, meditation and visualization. What this suggests is that Swedenborgianism, Buddhism and Theosophy were intricately connected in the way Western and Eastern esotericism influenced religion, culture and intellectual history on both sides of the Pacific.

Not only has there been considerable diversity in the Buddhism practised in the United States but, as Peter Gregory explains, it defies explanation since 'there is no single belief or practice that is common to all Buddhists'. Divided by socio-economic differences, sects, beliefs, rituals and many who self-identify as Buddhists but have no membership in any specific group, efforts at both the quantification of Buddhists and the delineation of their types tends to defy explanation as to its numbers and character. This impediment has been reinforced by the dauntingly complex fact that American Buddhism——in general and in particular——is punctured by a multitude of organizations, temples and fellowship centres that defy easy characterization. Thus, the challenge of explaining Buddhism remains at best, a cautionary tale for those stalwarts who choose to attempt it. Gregory said it best in noting that Buddhism was 'akin to intermarriage, in which a new set of genes is introduced into the pool as Buddhism becomes assimilated into a new culture, the pool thereby being more diluted and enriched at the same time'.[58] Estimates of the number of Buddhists in the United States run from one million to as high as five million, with the actual number probably somewhere in between.[59]

RALPH WALDO TRINE
Making the Modern Self

Nothing in this world can be truer than that the education of one's head, without the training of the heart, simply increases his power for evil, while the education of his heart, along with the head, increases his power for good, and this, indeed, is the true education. The mind is everything; what you think you become.

(Ralph Waldo Trine, *Every Living Creature*, 1899)

Among the many legacies of the World's Parliament of Religions was renewed interest in the comparative study of religions and, along with it, a gradual change from bias to a more open approach to religious pluralism. With this came the emergence of interfaith organizations that followed in the footsteps of Swami Vivekananda and the celebration of what he identified as a 'universal religion'. There was also impetus given to the movement known as New Thought which lured millions to its pragmatically oriented ministries of spirituality whose ethic was most frequently manifested in the virtues of health, happiness and economic success. With roots in mesmerism, Gnosticism, Swedenborgianism, Theosophy, Transcendentalism, Christianity and Freemasonry, New Thought sought to realize the presence of God (aka 'Force', 'Spirit', 'Energy') through constructive thinking, optimism and highly personalized forms of meditation. In following this eclectic form of spirituality, New Thought's advocates—both churched and unchurched—sought to realize what William James called the 'religion of healthy-mindedness'. James identified the movement's theme as 'an intuitive belief in the all-saving power of healthy-minded attitudes as such, in the conquering efficacy of courage, hope, and trust, and a correlative contempt for doubt, fear, worry, and all nervously precautionary states of mind'.[1] New Thought's earliest teachers, writers and healers included Warren Felt Evans (*The Divine Law of Cure*), Emma Curtis Hopkins (*Spiritual Law in the Natural World*), Ursula Gestefeld (*The Breath of Life*), Annie Rix Militz (*The Renewal of the Body*), William Walker Atkinson (*Thought Vibration or the Law of Attraction in the Thought World*), H Emilie Cady (*Lessons in Truth*), Horatio W Dresser (*The Power of Silence*) and Ernest Holmes (*The Science of Mind*), all of whom promoted Buddhist and Hindu meditation practices involving breathing and 'entering the silence'. Several were founders of the denominations Unity, Religious Science, Home of Truth, Divine Science, and Seicho-No-Ie, the Japanese hybrid society which combined Oriental spirituality with New Thought.

On the secular side were motivational writers and lecturers such as James Allen (*As a Man Thinketh*), Orison Swett Marden (*How to Get What You Want*), Florence Scovel Shinn (*The Game of Life and How to Play It*), Napoleon Hill (*Think and Grow Rich*), Bruce Barton (*The Man Nobody Knows*), Norman Vincent Peale (*The Power of Positive Thinking*), Catherine Ponder (*The Dynamic Laws of Prosperity*), Wayne Dyer (*Your Sacred Self*), Deepak Chopra (*The Seven Spiritual Laws of Success*) and Rhonda Byrne (*The Secret*), who celebrated the principle of self-sufficiency, or the ability to go within to soothe discord by turning thought into energy. Both churched and unchurched writers and lecturers expressed a cosmic optimism that individuals could produce almost any desired outcome.[2]

From the late nineteenth century to the present day, large sectors of America's urban culture have participated at one time or another in New Thought's efforts to correct the sense of fragmentation and loss of self-direction stemming from the rise of modernity. By the early twentieth century, the movement encompassed approximately four hundred churches and centres. By the Second World War, its adherents numbered between fifteen and twenty million. Today, its church and non-church membership is global, having multiplied several-fold with its 'thought-as-power' message. With guides like Gayle Delaney's *Living Your Dreams*, Michael Beckwith's *Life Visioning*, Caroline Myss's *Three Levels of Power and How to Use Them* and Lissa Rankin's *Mind Over Medicine*, this uniquely American ethic of cheerfulness has come to dominate the shaping of postmodernist society and the transnational reconceptualization of religion. Believing that all matter is subject to the power of concentrated thought and that all thought can be transposed into matter ('thoughts are things'), the movement has gathered around it a myriad of church-based and secular spokespersons whose appealing concepts of 'mind', 'spirit', 'law', 'nature', 'life', 'universal principle' and 'the absolute', have become watchwords holding almost magical properties for the realization of health, wealth and happiness. For those who choose the metaphysical side of this call to virtue, New Thought provides a spiritual explanation of life's complexities. For those seeking a more secular explanation, New Thought fits handily into the idea that virtue transforms into material success. Today, the formula for American individualism encourages the concepts of selfhood, self-mastery and a core belief in 'thought-as-power' to alter material reality.[3]

Despite being Western in its origins, the early proponents of New Thought sought to build a bridge between Eastern and Western religions and philosophies. Examples include Sarah J Farmer who founded the Greenacre Conferences and the Greenacre Baha'i School in Eliot, Maine; Warren Felt Evans's 'Christian Pantheism' which sought to link East and West by identifying Emerson's Over-Soul with the atman of the Vedanta; Annie Rix Militz's Home of Truth which disseminated the teachings of Hindu teacher Swami Vivekananda; Horatio W Dresser who wrote extensively on Vedanta philosophy and the importance of Swedenborg's concept of 'uses'; and Emma Curtis Hopkins who likened Buddhism's nirvana with Christ's words 'I and my Father are one'. There was also William Walker Atkinson who wrote under the pseudonyms Swami Panchadasi, Theodore Sheldon, Theron Q Dumont, Yogi Ramacharaka, Swami Bhakta Vishita, Three Initiates and Magus Incognito, authoring books such as *A Course of Lessons in Practical Yoga*, *The Development of Seership* and *Reincarnation and the Law of Karma*. Encouraged by the World's Parliament of Religions, both the Swedenborgians who helped organize the Parliament, and the mind-cure advocates of New Thought, reached out in all directions to capture the parallels and possibilities of conjoining Western and Eastern spiritual traditions.[4]

Ralph Waldo Trine (1866-1958)
Ralph Waldo Trine, one of the leading spokesmen for the New Thought movement, began his writing career in his thirties and continued for more than forty years, authoring more than twenty books, some selling a million or more copies. According

to Alfred Whitney Griswold in 1934, Trine was 'one of the rare purists whose books were guileless optimism'.[5] Although this description was certainly true of his early works, it became less so in later years as his writings took on a more urgent political tone. A public philosopher, spiritual spokesman and social critic, Trine drew millions of admirers who found in his writings a Rorschach exercise in self-discovery. There was only one religion, the religion of the living God, and the obligation to live in the conscious realization that God dwelt in each individual. Trine urged all religions to centre on personal spirituality, not the furtherance of their respective institutions. His theme, that humanity possessed a divine inner nature, was based on the premise that all humans had the potential strength of character to transform their own lives. This spiritual message, at a time of growing fear of life's deterministic forces, enabled his readers to gain a new appreciation of the teachings of Jesus.[6] As Trine explained, 'We are dropping our interest in those phases of a Christianity that [Jesus] probably never taught, and that we have many reasons now to believe he never even thought—things that were added long years after his time'.[7]

A native of Mount Morris, Illinois, Trine attended Carthage Academy before enrolling at Knox College where he earned a baccalaureate degree in 1891. He continued his education at the University of Wisconsin and Johns Hopkins University, studying history and political science, and showing a strong interest in social and economic issues. After leaving Johns Hopkins, he became a special correspondent for the *Boston Daily Evening Transcript*. Directed to report on interesting conferences and symposia, he spent hours listening to and writing about a host of fascinating thinkers—from physician and geologist Joseph LeConte, philosopher and historian John Fiske and Indian Hindu monk Swami Vivekananda, to author and Unitarian clergyman Edward Everett Hale, actor Joseph Jefferson and Frank B Sanborn, a member of John Brown's 'Secret Six' and one of the oldest surviving members of the Concord School of Philosophy. As a special correspondent, Trine was encouraged by the paper's editor, Edward H Clement, to find a way to introduce the great thinkers of the age to the general public.

Early in his career as a correspondent, Trine lived a Thoreau-like existence in a rustic cabin outside Boston where, in the quiet of the evening, he enjoyed uninterrupted periods of reflection, reading again and again the works of his favourite authors, especially Emerson, his namesake and archangel of American optimism. Trine was a long-time friend of Dr Edward Emerson of Concord, Emerson's son, who, when asked about his father's methods of work, responded: 'It was my father's custom to go daily to the woods—*to listen*. He would remain there an hour or more in order to get whatever there might be for him that day. He would then come home and write into a little book—his 'day-book'—what he had gotten. Later on when it came time to write a book, he would transcribe from this, in their proper sequence and with their proper connections, these entrances of the preceding weeks or months. The completed book became virtually a ledger formed or posted from his day-books'.[8] In his reading of Emerson, Trine learned to understand how this self-directed and self-reliant scholar had undergone a crisis of identity in the years leading up to the Civil War. 'As long as our civilization is one of property, of fences, of exclusiveness, it will be mocked by delusions', wrote Emerson. 'Our riches will leave us sick, there will be bitterness in our laughter, and our wine will burn our mouth. Only that good profits which we can taste with all doors open and which serves all men'. From these words Trine concluded that a growing number of Americans had lost standing in the new social and economic order and, while some relocated their purposefulness in the comforting environment of social groups and reform movements, others sought equally rewarding answers in mystical experiences where the topology of the self came face-to-face with the Absolute and where the individual mind and the Divine became one.[9]

Throughout his writing career, Trine was fond of quoting William Shakespeare, Charles Darwin, Walt Whitman, Episcopal clergyman and co-founder of the Emmanuel Movement Elwood Worcester, English physicist and parapsychologist Sir William Barrett, Scottish physician and writer Arthur Conan Doyle and British physicist Sir Oliver Joseph Lodge. He also admired the Scottish evangelist, writer and lecturer Henry Drummond, author of *The Greatest Thing in the World*, a meditation on Corinthians 1:13 which sold over twelve million copies. In Drummond, Trine saw someone whose uplifting words engaged large sectors of the reading public, demonstrating the connection between mind and body, the origins of perverted mental states and emotions, and the understanding that all life was from within, out. Trine was similarly impressed with William James, whose practical metaphysics and simplified psychology reflected the directing, moulding and sustaining forces that belonged to the kingdom of mind and spirit. James viewed the individual as a great reservoir of energy provided he or she was able to realize the laws that underlay them and was equally wise and diligent enough to flow with them. Life was not so complex that it belied any understanding of its creative powers. The new psychology of the day, which James pioneered, focused on the subconscious mind, its nature, powers and practical uses.[10]

Trine's other major source of inspiration came from Swedenborg whom he considered 'one of the most remarkable and valuable men who ever lived in the world'. He found in Swedenborg's writings the pulsating force of divine love and the assurance that there would be a union of the Creator with His creation.[11] In order for this to occur, however, Trine realized that creatures had to receive divine love and wisdom by a power which seemed to be their own, thereby lifting themselves up to the Creator and uniting with Him. If spirit was the real nature of man, then the history of human life would be the gradual coming into consciousness of this oneness with the infinite. As Swedenborg explained, there was 'only one Fountain of Life, and the life of man is a stream therefrom, which if it were not continually replenished from its source would instantly cease to flow'. Those capable of thinking in the light of the interior reason 'can see that all things are connected by intermediate links with the First Cause, and that whatever is not maintained in that connection must cease to exist'.[12]

Trine also referenced German philosopher Johann Gottlieb Fichte for whom truth for its own sake had been life's objective. Standing free of all institutions, organizations and systems of philosophy, Fichte identified with Life and Being. 'God alone is, and nothing besides him,——a principle which, it seems to me, may be easily comprehended, and which is the indispensable condition of all religious insight', he once wrote. Drawing from Fichte's explanation of how the Divine Being incarnated Himself in human life, Trine discovered that the latent possibilities and powers once demonstrated by Jesus could be activated in man to become a cooperator with the Divine.[13]

The Laws

As he matured as a writer, Trine chose to explain life by way of several select laws common among New Thought proponents——the laws of vibration, attraction, indirection, compensation, correspondences and cause and effect. Each individual had the capacity to understand these laws and whose challenge lay in appreciating their purpose, and then obeying them. The *law of vibration*, for example, represented life itself, or rather the means by which life manifested itself in both the material and spiritual world. It was an energy force (vitalism) that scientists and philosophers struggled to apprehend. According to the *law of cause and effect*, things never occurred by chance or coincidence but always through the operation of an originating force. 'We invite whatever comes', Trine insisted. 'There is never an effect without a cause'.[14] The *law of indirectness* held that it was easier to put something out of mind, not by dwelling upon it, but by directing the mind to other lines of thought.[15] With the *law of attraction*, all individuals were drawn to those forces and influences most similar to their own life. Each created an 'aura' or 'atmosphere' determined in large measure by the thoughts that entertained the mind and could be detected by other people and influenced by them. The aura set into operation a subtle, silent and irresistible force to actualize that which began as a mere idea.[16] 'But ideas have occult power', Trine liked to remind his readers, 'and ideas, when rightly planted and rightly tended, are the seeds that actualize material conditions'.[17]

Not surprisingly, Trine referenced two especially important laws, the first being Emerson's *law of compensation*, which explained that each person was compensated in life to the degree that he or she contributed to it. 'It is one of the beautiful compensations of this life', Emerson wrote, 'that no man can sincerely try to help another without helping himself . . . . Serve and thou shall be served'.[18] The second was Swedenborg's *law of correspondences* which proposed that one's inner or spiritual self was a reflection of the greater spiritual world which, in its entirety, was in human form. According to Swedenborg:

> although the heavens mentioned above do certainly correspond to the
> organic forms themselves of the human body—on account of which these
> communities or those angels have been spoken of as belonging to the province
> of the brain, or to the province of the heart, or to the province of the lungs,
> or to the province of the eye, and so on—they correspond primarily to the

functions belonging to those viscera or organs. The position really is that, like the organs or viscera themselves, their functions make one with their organic forms. For it is impossible to gather any idea of sight, for example, except from the eye, or of breathing except from the lungs. . . It is the functions therefore to which heavenly communities correspond primarily, and then because they correspond to the functions they correspond to the organic forms too. . . The same also applies in every single thing a person does. When he wishes to do this or that, and to do so in this or some other way, and is thinking of it, the organs move in response, and so in accordance with the aim of the function or use; for it is the use they serve that governs the forms.[19]

Each of these various laws provided Trine and his generation of New Thought proponents with resourceful and simplistic answers to the complex issues of the day. Having a 'law' to fall back on gave cover as well as meaning to life's many challenges.

Jesus of Nazareth

Trine admired the prophets and seers from all the great religions but felt most comfortable writing about Jesus of Nazareth, thereby giving validity to the Judaeo-Christian tradition and Reformed Christianity's sequence of faith, action and results. The truth of Jesus came not through dogmas, intolerance or man-made institutions, but through the 'living truth'.[20] Over and over again, he returned to what Jesus said or did, looking upon him as a great teacher who understood the inner spirit, its relation to the mind and the power to transform both into action. By virtue of his unique powers, Jesus 'was able to anticipate . . . the facts pertaining to certain laws and forces that the most advanced psychology, metaphysics and philosophy, and some by actual experimentation, are finding only today'. Possessed of the highest attributes of humanity within the Godhead, Jesus had explained that living the God-life gave humanity its power. He taught, as no one before or since, how man should come to know God and live his life in God. It was from Jesus, too, that Trine learned the two great fundamentals of love and service to humanity.[21] The greatest principle of practical ethics, he was fond of saying, was in finding our lives by 'losing them in the service of others'. To the extent that one placed life in harmony with this principle, life would be full of meaning and purpose. This was the sum and substance of all truly great religions in that it explained the conscious union of the human with the Divine.[22] Living these two commandments brought essential oneness with the Divine Life.

Jesus revealed in his teachings and in his life a spiritual philosophy not chained to restrictive laws, functions and mechanisms, or to a belief in man as a duality of mind and body. Instead, man was a trinity of soul, mind and body, each contributing to individual expression. The body functioned in the physical universe and used its resources to sustain life. The soul, made in the image of the Divine Life, was spirit——one and indivisible——which manifested itself in individual forms of existence. Essentially one with the Divine Being, its essence was the same in quality, different only in degree. It was through the mind that the body and soul functioned in harmony.[23]

In *The Greatest Thing Ever Known* (1898), Trine borrowed from Swedenborg to explain that *being* (a term meaning the self-existent principle of life) was prompted by love, projected into existence by will, and assumed form as a consequence of its existence. What made this concept so important was the realization that humanity could not exist separate from the Divine, the source of all existence. As a part of the Infinite Being, each life was one with the life of God. 'It is utterly impossible that there be any real life that is not one with the life of God . . . the life of man and the life of God are essentially and necessarily one and the same'. The difference was not one of essence, but of degree. Only by reason of thought was the life of man separate from the life of God. Although man had the ability to direct and rightly use his mind as a redeeming power to become one with the Divine Mind in the natural world, most were 'not awake' to this conscious realization of heavenly possibility and therefore unable to actualize the kingdom of heaven while living on earth. Thus, in the 'Adam-man', the ability lay latent in the natural life. However, by living the Christ-life, individuals removed themselves from the bondage of sin and realized oneness with the Divine. 'But only as man becomes conscious of the Lord Christ within, only as he becomes conscious,——realises in thought that he is one with the Infinite Life and Power,——does this great fact become a moving and mighty force in the affairs of his daily life'.[24]

Trine used the term *philosophy* to connote the science of cause and effect and, just as philosophy traced effects from their cause, religion dealt with man's relations to the Divine by finding the consciousness of God in man's soul. Similarly, he viewed *intuition* as the power of getting to the very heart of things. This he learned from the world's great mystic philosophers who had demonstrated a wonderful grasp of life's fundamentals. They were the master teachers who, in the debates with scientists, explained intuition as a function of man's spiritual nature, an illumination conveying to the mind knowledge from the Divine. This ability connected the thinking mind with the inner life—a spiritual channel through which the divine wisdom communicated giving it life, purpose and power. The power of intuition varied among individuals, but it remained latent in all, a spiritual organ open to the inner faculties of the soul, providing knowledge of the forces at work in the material world. In its fullest realization, intuition raised the natural man to a spiritual plane, bringing a new understanding of the sciences.[25] To the degree that individuals opened themselves to the power of intuition, they were able to see into the heart of things. Thus, true wisdom came by intuition which far transcended empirical knowledge. When in doubt as to which course to take, Trine urged readers to 'let the inward eye see, let the inward ear hear'. Intuition was to the spiritual nature what observation was to understanding. This 'inner spiritual sense' connected the individual to the secrets of life through which he was brought into conscious unity with the spirit. Only in this manner was spiritual illumination realized. A spiritual sense opened inwardly just as the physical senses opened outwardly.[26] The inner life into which man was partly born required the greatest attention—the place where he could find refuge in the eternal God. There man discovered life beyond the mere sense world—what Bergson identified as the *élan vital*, or life force found in every living thing and which grew to the degree that each willed it so.[27]

The common thread which ran through the world's great prophets and entered into the lives of those who sought their teachings was belief in a 'Spirit', 'Infinite Life', 'Over Soul', 'Providence' or 'Power' manifest in all being. When energized, these thought forces brought forth the secrets to success and happiness. To the extent that each individual partook of this influx, the essence of both man and spirit became one. To the degree that individuals opened themselves to this divine inflow they took on 'God-powers'. Those who acquired these powers were thereby changed from 'mere men' to 'God-men'.[28]

Along with many of his contemporaries, Trine detested organized religion, especially the all-powerful Roman Church. This so-called divine institution had used its power of statecraft to enslave millions to its tenets of belief, provoking persecutions against those who would not subscribe, or dared to take exception to its absolute authority. Under the pretext of the pope's spiritual authority, church fathers had authorized burning, imprisonment, confiscation, torture and death. The long tyranny of the church and its hostility to truth caused Trine and other New Thought advocates to despair of organized religion, seeking instead to educate people to the spiritual message of Jesus alone. Speaking with simple candour and claiming no supernatural powers for himself, Jesus had declared that his sole purpose was to awaken in man the spirit of the living God. He brought no new religion but the simple language of love for one another, and of service. This, remarked Trine, was 'the Living Word'.[29]

Among Trine and other New Thought advocates, religiosity was not understood in the context of an organization, denomination or formally constituted groups, but as a way of thinking. Generally, New Thoughters disdained the fabrications of church polity, viewing it as bereft of the great transcendent truths found in the life and teachings of Jesus. 'Many a student comes from our theological schools so steeped in theological speculations and in denominational dogmas that he hasn't the slightest conception of what the real mission of Jesus was', Trine observed. 'What wonder, then, that the church to which he goes soon becomes a dead shell from which the life has gone, into which those in love with life will no longer enter, a church whose chief concern very soon is, how to raise the minister's stipend?'[30] At the intellectual centre of Trine's beliefs and others in the New Thought movement were the words of Abraham Lincoln, considered one of the most profound religious thinkers in the country even though he was not a member of any particular church. As Lincoln once observed: 'I find difficulty in giving my assent, without mental reservation, to the complicated statements of Christian doctrine which constitute their articles of belief and confessions of faith'.[31]

223

Entering the Silence

The only form of prayer Trine considered effective was that which was meditated alone and in secret. Not until one retired into the quietness of his or her inner being was it possible to feel the vibrations of the Divine Life and become sensitized to the inflowing of its force. Trine called this 'the power of silent demand' and noted that all the great thinkers in the world, including Jesus, spent time in quiet solitude. With it, they 'stilled the outer senses' by coming into harmony with the spiritual vibrations of the Divine Life. Quieting the senses allowed the vibrations, along with their energy, insight and power, to reveal the inner life of the soul, illuminating intuition and placing the individual in touch with the Source of Life. Intuition and spiritual illumination were part of human nature, conjoining body and soul and relating man to the great First Cause, the source of all wisdom.[32]

Trine urged those desiring to elevate their individual capacities to meditate quietly for fifteen to thirty minutes each day. Meditation was the opportunity to 'Send out your earnest desires for whatsoever you will'. If done purposively, 'whatsoever you will, if continually watered by expectation, will sooner or later come to you. All knowledge, all truth, all power, all wisdom, all things whatsoever, are yours . . . All the truly great teachers in the world's history have gotten their powers in this way'. Trine, of course, intended for these 'earnest desires' to be used in the service of mankind and not for personal gain. 'So, unless you are large enough to forget self for the good, for the service of mankind, thus putting yourself on the side of the universal and making it possible for you to give something that will in turn of itself bring fame', he cautioned, the results would prove disappointing. If the ambition was to accumulate great personal wealth, then happiness and satisfaction would ultimately depend on the use and disposition made of it. 'If your object . . . is to pile it up, to hoard it, then neither will come; and you will find it a life as unsatisfactory as one can live'. Practical ethics, or the relationship between Christianity and everyday life, could not be divorced.[33]

The power that transformed thought into material form was a force or magnet which, following the law of attraction, identified and captured those things which the individual most desired. The old Christian adage that godliness implied or condoned personal poverty was mistaken. Poverty, like asceticism, had no basis for existence. Those who were wise used the forces within to open a treasure trove of possibilities. 'Whatever the circumstances', Trine explained, 'you must realize that you have within you forces and powers that you can set into operation that will triumph over any and all apparent or temporary losses. Set these forces into operation and you will then be placing a magnet that will draw to you a situation that may be far better than the one you have lost, and the time may soon come when you will be even thankful that you lost the old one'.[34]

In *What All the World's A-Seeking* (1896), and his widely popular *In Tune With the Infinite* (1897), Trine acknowledged that only when individuals opened themselves to the influx of divine love did they find true peace with the world about them. The challenge was to permit these subtle energies to enter the body's many 'inlets' and to respond positively to them. The mind channelled the in-streaming of these energies, creating a mental atmosphere that surrounded the individual and also other people who came under its influence. Thus, the forces of love, sympathy and kindliness, which were not only ennobling and life-giving to the self, extended to others within their orbit of influence. But the same held true of the forces of hatred, jealousy and fault-finding which not only affected one's own mental state, but others' as well. Thought forces—both good and bad—affected those whose minds and hearts were most susceptible to accepting them.[35]

Everything existed first in thought ('the unseen') before being manifested in the *seen*. In this sense, the *unseen* was *real* and eternal. The *unseen* was the *cause*, while the *seen* (the *effect*), was ever-changing. Thought was an interior force, a creative power which, when directed to a particular channel or form of concentration, became actualized in life, in character or in some material form. 'We are all living, so to speak, in a vast ocean of thought', explained Trine, 'and the very atmosphere around us is continually filled with thought forces that are . . . going out in the form of thought waves'. To the degree that individuals were susceptible to these thought waves, they entered into their lives and, while many such forces were good and opened the soul to the higher impulses, undesirable waves did just the opposite. The mental life of an individual was like a rudder that determined the course taken in the world. This, along with Swedenborg's law of corrrespondences between spiritual and material things, explained how individuals found themselves ruled by either their own thoughts or the thought forces of others.

> The individual existence of man *begins* on the sense plane of the physical world, but rises through successive gradations of ethereal and celestial spheres, corresponding with his ever unfolding deific life and powers, to a destiny of unspeakable grandeur and glory. Within and above every physical planet is a corresponding ethereal planet, or soul world, as within and above every physical organism is a corresponding ethereal organism, or soul body, of which the physical is but the external counterpart and materialized expression. From this etherealized or soul planet, which is the immediate home of our arisen humanity, there rises or deepens in infinite gradations spheres within and above spheres, to celestial heights of spiritualized existence utterly inconceivable to the sense man. Embodiment, accordingly, is two-fold,——the physical being but the temporary husk, so to speak, in and by which the real and permanent ethereal organism is individualized and perfected, somewhat as 'the full corn in the ear' is reached by means of its husk, for which there is no further use. By means of this indestructible ethereal body and the corresponding ethereal spheres of environment with the social life and relations in the spheres, the individuality and personal life is preserved forever.[36]

For Trine, each individual existed for divine self-realization. To the extent that individuals manipulated or trained the things that entered their minds, these became the sum total of their life's experiences, including the power for good or evil. To the extent that they became a channel for the Divine Power, they opened themselves to love and become part of life's great play. As all life was from within out, by taking time to enter the silence each day, the individual came to the conscious realization of the fact that the Divine Life was behind all that existed. This consciousness of God was the condition which individuals strived to live; it was this that the prophets and seers preached and which constituted the message taught by the truly great religions of the world.[37]

A New Christianity

Trine interpreted the *fin de siècle* as a period when the nations of the world seemed at peace with one another. In *The New Alinement of Life, Concerning the Mental Laws of a Greater Personal and Public Power*, he, along with many other New Thought writers at the time, perceived a worldwide religious, philosophical and political renaissance revealing significant new understandings of the laws, inner powers and forces affecting everyday life. Given what he considered was the successful outcome of the World's Parliament of Religions, he noted that philosophy was now more concrete, practical and helpful; that religion was increasingly attentive to the needs of the inner person rather than church polity; and that more and more people were demanding responsible government. Drawing from contemporaries like French philosopher Henri Bergson, German philosopher Rudolf Eucken and William James, Trine pointed out that the academic walls that once contained the world of philosophy were disappearing as people were increasingly interested in the 'use' of a 'philosophy of life' to satisfy their active living. He insisted that Darwin's theory had not been built on materialism but on an intelligible understanding of God's laws. Evolution was 'God-Power' at work in every form of useful activity, lifting everything in its path. This was the great 'Cosmic Plan' perceived and contributed by those who were spiritually open to the Divine and whose lives were directed to the good of the whole.[38] Evolution was the instrumentality through which the Creator carried out His plan. Science and religion were united in both method and spirit in explaining humanity's slow climb out of animality to its destined inheritance. 'The world scarcely *yet* fully appreciates the great service that Darwin has rendered to science, to real religion, and to the general advancement of human thought and progress', Trine wrote.[39]

Trine also celebrated the scepticism resulting from the higher criticism and the findings of archaeology. Both told a story of great changes on the part of thinking men and women who were no longer slaves to church polity. Humanity had finally entered an age of questioning, of longings and of ultimate fulfilment—not for lack of interest in religion but because of the realization that the churches had done little to appeal to the minds and souls of their members. Now, authority must prove itself or fall by the wayside. 'Mighty truths have come to light during the past several decades, and others

227

are rapidly coming', he observed. The world was moving quickly to accept the essentials of Jesus's universal spirit and enjoy the vitalizing power of his simple message. The spirit of religion, not the letter of dogmatic theology, thrilled the modern mind. The Bible and the spirit stood in open contradiction to each other. One voice was given to obedience to the written word, the other to the 'Inward Spirit of Truth and Love'.[40]

Great changes were underway and organized Christianity must either become part of the future, or be left in the past. 'Earnest men seek for a religion built upon a foundation that will make it always in harmony with science', Trine explained, 'for between true science and true religion there never have been and there never can be any discrepancies or contradictions'. If humanity could not find the life-giving teachings of Jesus within the organized churches, it would seek them elsewhere. Unless Christian theology came into alignment with Jesus's teachings, the churches would lack relevance in the modern world. For too long, organized Christianity had clung to its pre-medieval origins. Instead of becoming a leader in truth, it had built a myriad of creeds and dogmas that all but hid the central themes of Jesus's life and teachings. 'To know that we are all partakers of this Universal Divine Life, sons of God and brothers in Christ, that love is the savour of life unto life—this is to love the neighbour as ourselves', Trine taught. This was the centrepiece of true Christian belief. Anything else was the worship of relics from Christianity's past.[41]

Trine recognized a growing spirit of New Christianity (which Swedenborgians called the New Church) among the younger generation of teachers, financiers, legislators and social workers, as well as among some of the most widely read authors, editors and magazine writers. While supportive of their efforts, he cautioned them not to move too fast for fear of alienating the very people they intended to serve. Instead, the New Christianity must draw upon the 'great body of intellectually alive, intellectually honest young men and women who have the Christ spirit of service and who are mastered by a great purpose of accomplishment'. The spirit of Christ was more important than the religion of Christ. The advocates of the New Christianity must 'beware and be wise' in their educational efforts, otherwise those for whom it was intended would be reluctant partners.[42]

For Trine and other spokespersons in the New Thought movement, the New

Christianity had to change from an agency whose purpose was to save souls from hell to one whose purpose was to inspire, direct and build spiritual forces in everyday lives. God as a monster demanding atonement for man's mythical sinfulness and degradation now became a God of love. 'The central point of our existence', Trine explained, 'is divine, and God is incarnated in the whole of humanity'. There was, in fact, an enormous interest in all matters spiritual and a great questioning of organized religion not only among Christians but among religious people throughout the world. 'The old shells are breaking', he announced, 'and things can never again be as they have been'. Christianity had not failed, but its ecclesiasticism had been responsible for inexcusable, brutal and senseless destruction over the ages.[43]

In the theological schools a new and distinctive note was sounding. There was in vogue a new theology which no longer concerned itself with conformity to specific doctrinal issues but rather an open and fearless quest into the teachings of Jesus. 'It is essential that we may the more intelligently distinguish between his own simple hillside teachings, and the strange theories and inventions about him woven by men of fourth-century minds', insisted Trine. Similar accounts were happening in the study of Siddhartha Gautama, the Buddha.[44] 'We are all dwellers in two kingdoms, the inner kingdom, the kingdom of the mind and spirit, and the outer kingdom, that of the body and the physical universe about us'. Since these two kingdoms spelled man's existence, the challenge was finding the right balance between the two. Happy was the individual who realized the essential importance of both, that the origins of life were all from within, and what is inner, would inevitably become the outer.[45]

Health and Well-Being

With all physical life being 'from within out', Trine warned that thoughts such as fear and hatred closed the channels carrying life forces to the body and enabled disease to gain a foothold. Every thought reproduced itself in the body and, while the mind was a natural protector of the body, the wrong mental pictures produced chemical changes dangerous to life. The power of suggestion, the key to the healing process, had been used by physicians since ancient times to activate the patient's life forces. Though cure could be achieved in other ways, permanent healing could only be obtained through a mental process. 'The moment a person realizes his oneness with the Infinite Spirit', explained Trine, 'He then no longer makes the mistake of regarding himself as body, subject to ills and diseases, but he realizes the fact that he is spirit'. In realizing his own supremacy, the individual channelled the appropriate forces to harmonize with his needs.[46] An admirer of mental healer Phineas P Quimby of Maine who, half a century earlier, had introduced suggestion and auto-suggestion as therapeutic agents, Trine saw the importance of this mental agent in healing.[47]

Preventive medicine was one of New Thought's markers of human progress. Health was the natural and normal state of the individual while physical debility, sickness and suffering came through the violation, either on one's own part or on the part of others, of the laws of the universe. Permanent healing came from the life forces within—mental habits that acted on the body's organs and functions. At every moment, habits were formed creating character-building or undesirable thoughts. Thoughts were destiny in that they were parents to the act; the prevailing mental and emotional states were therefore antecedents to character. They became the modus operandi of thought and mind mastery, of habit forming, and character building. Thoughts, in aggregate, either supported or chipped away at physical and mental health.[48]

There would come a time, Trine predicted, when the work of the physician would be to heal the mind as the proper way to heal the body. The physician of the future would be a teacher whose work consisted of keeping patients well rather than treating sickness and disease. 'In the degree that we live in harmony with the higher laws of our being, and so, in the degree that we become better acquainted with the powers of the mind and spirit, will we give less attention to the body,—no less *care*, but less *attention*', he surmised. The body's health and strength of the mind depended on the conscious realization of its association with the spirit. As Trine often remarked, 'God is well and so are you'.[49]

Acting under the guidance of the subjective mind (subconscious), the Life Force became the agency through which the body underwent change. As noted earlier, thoughts, ideas, beliefs and emotions were seeds absorbed by the subconscious where they helped to shape the body. The individual had to determine which of these seeds should form and germinate in the body. Provided the body was strong, healthy and active, the subconscious directed the cell tissues in a positive manner. If, however, the body drifted into destructive patterns, then the subconscious forced the body to respond differently. Here Trine became very specific: 'To think health and strength, to see ourselves continually growing in this condition, is to set into operation the subtlest dynamic force for the externalisation of these conditions in the body that can be even conceived of'. When the body became home to abnormal or false mental and emotional habits, its instability caused the body's cellular structure to grow old and diseased. In this manner, the mind became a silent transformative agency of energy—both good and bad—depending on individual choice. 'Thought is a force, subtle and powerful, and it tends inevitably to produce of its kind', a concept that Henry James, Sr, struggled over a lifetime to explain.[50]

Thought being the 'force', its aggregate habits determined character. Trine called this the *law of the mind* which acted like the reflex nerve system of the body, i.e., 'that whenever one does a certain thing in a certain way it is easier to do the same thing in the same way the next time . . . until in time it comes to pass that no effort is required'. Character represented the sum total habits, formed by thoughts and followed by conscious acts. Character was both life and destiny. 'The great law of the drawing power of the mind', wrote Trine, 'says that like creates like, and that like attracts like'.[51] Here was the very nature of *true virtue*, a belief that Trine shared with James and his sons, as well as with Swedenborg and Jonathan Edwards.

He who comes into this full and living realisation of his oneness with the Divine Life is brought at once into right relations with himself, with his fellow-men, and with the laws of the universe about him. He lives now in the inner, the real life, and whatever is in the interior must necessarily take form in the exterior, for all life is from within out. . . . Thus and thus alone it is that men have become prophets, seers, and saviours; they have become what the world calls the 'elect' of God, because in their own lives they first elected God and lived their lives in His life. And thus it is that to-day men can become prophets, seers, and saviours, for the laws of the Divine Life and the relations of what we term the human life to it are identically the same to-day as they have been in all time past and will be in all time to come.[52]

Christian Socialism

With the popularity of his writings established, Trine turned his attention to a number of social issues that had once consumed his student years at Wisconsin and Johns Hopkins. Increasingly he sided with the so-called 'muckrakers' of the Progressive movement who exposed the problems attendant to unregulated corporate capitalism. By moral right, the wealth created by 'the people' belonged to them, and 'that which belongs to the people morally must be made to belong to them legally and by custom'.[53] Individual health and happiness required wealth to be redistributed on the principle of social justice for all. The same power of mind that transformed the individual was needed to transform society into communities of cooperation and solidarity.

By all accounts, Americans should be a great and prosperous people, uniformly happy and free. Trine noted with disappointment, however, that reality had fallen short of the mark with more than ten million of the nation's working class living in chronic poverty and with increasing numbers dropping into pauperism. Equally disturbing were the actions of private and public charities whose combined yearly handouts of over $200 million were destroying all sense of self-reliance from a once fiercely independent people. Charity did nothing to provide people with work; instead, it concerned itself with 'surface symptoms' and addressed none of the fundamental causes. To his regret, the nation's public and private charities had unwittingly become forces of corruption, gnawing at the soft underbelly of the nation's welfare by carrying blight to everything that they touched. Nearly half of all applicants for charity needed work rather than relief. The lack of employment was the cause of numerous vices, from drunkenness to theft and prostitution. Charity could never replace what was taken away or denied. Social services were not the equivalent of rightful inheritance; they were artificial manipulations in place of justice. Intelligent wage earners should never allow benevolent schemes to take the place of justice. 'There is no donation, however gaudy, that can fill the place of justice', Trine wrote. Justice, not gifts or charity, represented the noblest intentions.[54] The philanthropies of the rich were no substitute for a living wage. 'What may be called the Great Bluff of our time is to put gratuities and benefactions in the place of justice', he warned. 'The attempt of the ruling class to do this is the oldest trick in history'. In spite of the aggressiveness of the rich over the common people, evolution was working itself out and, for the first time in history, he believed the people were in a position to live life on a footing of equality.[55]

With statistics showing an increase in the number of impoverished families, Trine raised the issue of a 'living wage', a concept borrowed from labour organizer John Mitchell of the United Mine Workers of America, who insisted that wages of less than $600 a year kept families in poverty. But the obligation of the business community did not end with the payment of a living wage. Trine also urged the business community to provide sufficient compensation to cover emergencies that impacted every individual and family at some time in their lives. Without it, families were left in dire straits, creating unnecessary poverty among honest hard-working people. With the majority of workers receiving wages amounting to less than $300 per year, families were being forced into a losing struggle, resulting in untold drunkenness, vagrancy and criminality. Aimless and drifting, the nation's poor were losing their self-respect and ambition, ending up in almshouses, prisons, asylums, hospitals and homes for the victims of neglect. With the number of property-less tenants staggeringly high across the nation, with ranges into the 90th percentile in some of the larger cities, the conditions for social unrest were magnifying yearly. Trine warned that the nation was fast approaching a day of reckoning.[56]

In *The Land of Living Men*, published in 1910, Trine described how the nation's working families failed to enjoy civil and economic freedom, happiness and prosperity. Weakened by poverty and private charity, many had sunk into conditions where all initiative and sense of self-reliance were either stifled or lost completely. From the cotton mills of the South to the anthracite mines in the Midwest and the unspeakable urban housing conditions in the Northeast, Trine recounted the growth and uneven distribution of wealth and the contrasts between luxury and poverty. 'Civilization so based cannot continue', he warned, quoting Henry George, and the 'ruins of dead empires' were strewn across history giving witness to that fact. He sounded the alarm of a coming crisis.[57]

America's institutions were in theory democratic and representative, but in reality they were neither. Recognizing the government's shortcomings and the manner in which the tools of government had been captured and held hostage by greed, Trine looked for a common-sense approach that would bring the theory and practice of representative government into alignment. To accomplish this, he encouraged the application of direct legislation through *initiative*, *referendum* and *recall*. By initiative he meant the proposal of a law or statute by petition of a specified percentage of voters; by referendum, he meant a vote by the people on any law passed by the legislature or proposed by the initiative; and by recall, public officials who violated their election pledges could, upon petition of a stipulated number of voters, be retired from office. Trine also advocated for the direct election of the US senators; the institution of an inheritance tax to serve as a weapon against vast private fortunes being used against the greater public welfare; the election of judges; and the creation of a Federal Bureau of Corporations to regulate the methods and aggressions of the trusts and combines to the extent that they were destructive of the people's welfare.[58]

Trine noted that municipal governments in the United States were the most backward in the civilized world, lagging behind Germany, France, England, Norway, Sweden and Belgium. Failing to understand the principle that the people should collectively own that which they collectively created, state and local governments had stood aside while their public service utilities were sold for private gain. While more than two hundred municipalities in Great Britain owned their gas, lighting and power, a practice common on the Continent as well, Americans had surrendered their natural resources to privately owned corporations. Local and state governments had allowed private companies to acquire utilities such as telephone, telegraph, water, gas and railroads at the expense of the public. Recognizing that great accumulations of wealth menaced civil liberties, stifled the freedom of the press, and led to wars abroad and civil unrest at home, Trine warned that corporate greed had become a millstone around the collective necks of the American people, producing poverty, vice, crime, drunkenness and immorality. Unless and until the nation returned to actual representative government, little would change. Democracy had to work in practice as well as in theory or things would get worse.[59]

Trine made frequent reference to the writings of Danish social reformer Jacob A Riis (*How the Other Half Lives*), New York reporter Lincoln Steffens (*Enemies of the Republic* and *The Shame of the Cities*), economist Amos G Warner (*American Charities*), critic and educator John Graham Brooks (*The Social Unrest*), historian and political theorist William Edward H Lecky (*The Political Value of History*) and British sociologist Benjamin Kidd (*Social Evolution*). He also praised the activities of progressive Wisconsin governor Robert La Follette; educator Andrew D White, founder and first president of Cornell University; Illinois governor John Peter Altgeld, advocate of municipal and national ownership and control of all public service utilities and all natural monopolies; mayor Tom L Johnson of Cleveland; and statistician Carroll D Wright, US Commissioner of Labor. He also learned from Henry George (*Progress and Poverty*) that it was 'the people' and their common needs who gave value to the rich franchises operated for private gain and how important it was for government to return them to public ownership. Failing that, these franchises would corrupt the state and municipal governments through bribery, graft and the enrichment of a few. Municipal ownership would put an end to much of the bribery and corruption of public officials. In addition, Trine advocated expanding the Civil Service system and doing away with the political machine as a method of employment.[60]

To achieve these objectives, Trine advocated an alliance of labour unions, brotherhoods and worker federations whose growth and development were signs of positive change for the good of the nation as a whole.[61] In dealing with the nation's social injustices, there was the need for intelligent direction, united action and worker dignity; this included fair wages, healthy living conditions and public education. While admitting that unions had committed errors of judgment during their formative years, Trine felt they were essential to the realization of these goals. He hoped that much of what labour needed to accomplish could be obtained through the political process, buttressed by a strong public school system whose emphasis was on teaching respect for American institutions and the responsibilities of good citizenship. This was the proper route to return the machinery of government back into the rightful hands of 'the people'. Only in this way was it possible to defeat the moneyed corporate interests that created the political machine, throttled representative government and impoverished the nation's hard-working people. A believer in equal opportunity for all and special privileges for none, Trine placed his hope on the 'common people' to find the right balance between the importance of power and the welfare of all.[62]

The Great War and Its Aftermath

Despite Trine's optimism with the changes occurring in religion, philosophy and science, he lamented the wholly 'unchristian' war being fought by the Christian nations in Europe.[63] Believing there were strong sympathies in the United States for both sides in the conflict, he urged his countrymen to assert a sense of 'world-consciousness'. There was a distinction to be made between sympathy and allegiance, Trine wrote, noting that the majority of Americans, including its foreign born, must live up to the expectations of genuine citizenship. Those who could not accept this had no place in American society. He felt that Americans had been too lax in their immigration restrictions, admitting many who had no intention of assimilation. The nation had also been forced to accept many undesirables, some of whom had turned to crime or become dependent on charity. It was essential for the nation's public school system to teach immigrant children the ideals of their new home and its institutions. There was no place for hyphenated citizenship which Trine considered as dangerous to the nation as cancer to the human body.[64]

Trine originally demanded America's isolation from Old World's machinations but came to a far different conclusion by 1917. 'Our period of isolation is over', he announced. 'We have become a world-nation'.[65] He hoped that something might be learned from the war that would prove to be mutually desirable by all the combatants. Perhaps, a permanent 'World's Court' composed of representatives of every nation would take adjudicate those disputes which the contending nations were unable to settle by themselves. Perhaps, too, there might be an 'Allied Army of the Powers' to serve as a police force to enforce the decisions of the World Court. If such changes were established, they would deflate the inflated egos of leaders and serve as a cushion between the world's more belligerent nations.[66]

* * *

A contemplative man, Trine shied from the public's eye, preferring the quiet life of a gentleman farmer, tending to his garden and ruminating about the life of his fellow human beings caught up in the rush of urban living. At his home, Sunnybrae Farm in Croton Landing in New York's Hudson River Valley, he felt at peace exploring empty trails and secluded groves rather than mixing with admiring followers. He spent his final years at Plymouth Place in Claremont, California, where he continued his passion for gardening. Along with his wife Grace Hyde (1874-1972), a poet and author, he remained deeply attuned to nature and the metaphysical side of life. His love of the woods and fields never ended. If anything, he found further illumination in the great sequoias that stood vigil over the Pacific coastline. These old giants, some of which stood three hundred feet in height and fifty or more feet in width were among the oldest living things in the world. Protected by their shade, he contemplated the forces at work in the universe. Trine died in 1958 at the age of ninety-two with bare mention (70 words) of his passing in the *New York Times*. Having written over a dozen books, one of which sold more than two million copies (*In Tune With the Infinite*), it seems remarkable that this Thoreau-like individual asked for no more than what he recommended to his readers: 'To come into the full realization of your own awakened interior powers, is to be able to condition your life in exact accord with what you would have it'.[67] He intended no other legacy.

D T SUZUKI
The Wood Chopper

*Revolutionary in theology, traveler of heaven and hell, champion
of the spiritual world, king of the mystical realm, clairvoyant
unique in history, scholar of incomparable vigor, scientist of
penetrating intellect, gentleman free of worldly taint: all of these
combined into one make Swedenborg. . . . Those who wish to
cultivate their spirit, those who bemoan the times, must absolutely
know of this person.*

(D T Suzuki, *Suedenborugu*, 1913)

Within Western philosophical traditions, Aristotelianism, rather than Platonism, reigned supreme. Its dualism of matter and form not only separated God from creation and the intellect from the senses, but established rationality as civilization's ideal and highest function. In the works of Thomas Aquinas, William of Ockham, Galileo Galilei, Francis Bacon and René Descartes, rationality served the Western mind by transforming its methods, power and influence into notable and sustaining achievements in science and technology. Mystical and docetic advocates emerged from time to time to explore the unmapped and uncertain boundaries of intuition, but the positivist nature of the sciences eschewed any calculus deemed extraneous to the core elements of Aristotelian thinking. Those mystical and intuitive elements that plied the backwaters of Western culture were typically viewed with suspicion, if not outright hostility, and judged to be unproductive, lazy, neglectful, anti-authoritarian and destructive of the purposes of state and society. Inevitably, these traditions deferred to rationality, which triumphantly served as the centrepiece of modernity, valued over all other epistemologies.

Not until the manifestos of Friedrich Nietzsche, the probing questions of Paul Tillich and Martin Heidegger, the seductive themes of D H Lawrence and James Joyce, and the psychiatry of Carl G Jung and Karen Horney, did modernity come face to face with the storied myth of rationality's completeness. Each of these thinkers advocated a less fixed tradition, one which was more subjective and less attached to three-dimensional space. In its place they urged greater reliance on intuition, opposed abstractions, advocated facts over ideas, and preached action as distinct from any final thesis. Their dissatisfaction with Aristotelian-based theology, philosophy and psychology resulted in a reading of more intuitive thinkers such as Emanuel Swedenborg, whose early contributions to science and technology abruptly ended when his eyes opened on a revelatory world of celestial spirits. One of many whom Swedenborg influenced was Daisetsu Teitaro Suzuki, a Zen Buddhist whose books came out of lectures, his lectures out of teaching, and his ideas out of everyday experiences. Over a long lifetime, Suzuki expounded on connections latent in Western esotericism and Buddhist thought, including a transnational appreciation of the works of Swedenborg.

Unlike religious thinkers such as Martin Luther, John Wesley, George Fox and John Calvin, Swedenborg had been known to only a few in the Orient. For those who did recognize his name, his relevance was arguably due to his alleged visits to heaven and hell, conversations with spirits and premonitions of future events. Suzuki, however, discovered in Swedenborg a unique combination of scientific and religious thinking and, with it, a similarity to Buddhism. Rather than view Swedenborg's otherworldly accounts as 'bizarre illusions', he interpreted them as the narratives of an old man attempting to disentangle the mysteries of life and beyond—a mind's eye response to life's paradoxes—using stories that would delight both the child and the adult. Swedenborg's narratives had 'an air of sincerity and honesty about them' which, without embellishment, struck a chord with individuals the world over who were seeking answers to questions that came from the heart. '[O]ne does not have to believe in all of Swedenborg's claims', cautioned Suzuki, 'but one also cannot say that there are not diamonds in the rough'.[1]

During a meeting with religious scholars Henry Corbin and Mircea Eliade in 1954, Suzuki was asked about the similarities he found, if any, between Mahayana Buddhism and Swedenborgianism. He reportedly responded, 'For you Westerners, it is Swedenborg who is your Buddha, it is he who should be read and followed!' He is 'your Buddha of the North'.[2] With the perceptual lens of someone trained as a Zen Buddhist and who had studied America's literary and intellectual history, including the Transcendentalism of Emerson and the pragmatic theory of William James and Charles Sanders Peirce, Suzuki found ideas and concepts in the canon of Swedenborg's writings similar to those already integral to his own belief system and which, in various forms, provided insight and character to his study of human values, ideals and actions.

Daisotsu Toitaro Suzuki (1870 1966)

Daisetsu Teitaro Suzuki, the son of physician Ryojun Suzuki, whose family was a member of the samurai class, was born in 1870 in the city of Kanazawa in the Ishikawa Prefecture north of Tokyo. The youngest of five children, his early years of happy childhood ended with the tragic death of his father when he was six, followed a year later with the death of an older brother, and the financial impoverishment of the family—all of which contributed to his early interest in religion. While studying to become a high school teacher of English and, later as a teacher in a small village school, he began commuting to the Temple Engakuji in Kamakura to train under Zen master Imakita Kosen. Eventually he took up residence at the temple and, following Kosen's death in 1892, continued his study as a lay disciple of Zen master Shaku Soyen who, recognizing Suzuki's facility with the English language, gave him occasional translation projects.[3]

While Buddhism in its more esoteric sense first made contact with American intellectuals like Emerson and Thoreau for whom it became a source of genteel and occult tastes, in Meiji Japan (1868-1912), Zen was introduced by a cadre of university-educated intellectuals seeking to revitalize Buddhism by adopting a rational and scientific religion based on the transcending nature of pure, unmediated, non-rational experience. Considered the only true form of Buddhism, it found receptive support within the Japanese government as well as among a growing number of spiritually adrift intellectuals searching for a more authentic belief system. Zen became a tool of Japanese polity, presenting itself to the West as a living repository of spiritual values capable of absorbing and expounding the most advanced discoveries in science. As explained by Robert Sharf, Zen represented 'the very heart of Asian spirituality, the essence of Japanese culture, and the key to the unique qualities of the Japanese race'.[4] Sharf and Martin J Verhoeven of the so-called 'New Buddhism' school wrote that Suzuki, as well as his teachers, advocated Zen as a way of bringing Japan into the modern world. By comparing Zen to Western monastic thought and culture, they made it respectable to Western intellectuals—an expression of Asian spirituality intended to resonate with Western values and esoteric thinking.[5]

With financial assistance from a family member, Suzuki enrolled at Tokyo Semmon Gakko (Waseda University) and later at Tokyo Imperial University where he studied philosophy and English literature, finding comfort in the writings of the American Transcendentalists, especially Emerson. Suzuki's life changed dramatically, however, when Soyen was invited to present a paper at the World's Parliament of Religions in Chicago in 1893. Because the proceedings were conducted in English, Soyen was required to find a suitable translator to set forth his 'truths' with a view to discovering 'what light Religion has to throw on the great problems of the present age, especially the important questions connected with Temperance, Labor, Education, Wealth and Poverty'.[6] At Soyen's request, Suzuki translated his paper, 'The Law of Cause and Effect, as Taught by Buddha', subsequently printed in John Henry Barrows's two-volume *The World's Parliament of Religions*.[7]

A Rising Star

During Soyen's attendance at the Parliament, he met Paul Carus, author and editor of the Open Court Publishing Company. When the Parliament ended, Carus invited the Zen master to his home in LaSalle, Illinois, where he met Carus's father-in-law, Edward Carl Hegeler, a successful zinc manufacturer who used much of the company's profits to publish and disseminate what he considered to be the key books on philosophy, religion and science. Because Carus considered Soyen's interpretation of Buddhism to be the best example of a modern experiential, scientific and mystical religion, he asked Soyen to provide an introduction to *The Gospel of Buddha*. For this task, Soyen relied again on Suzuki to translate Carus's work for him. This experience, Suzuki's first English-to-Japanese translation, drew him into Carus's intellectual orbit.[8]

Suzuki did not graduate from Tokyo Imperial University; nor did he become a monk. Instead, he became an expert in Zen thought and, in 1896, published *Shin Shukyo Ron* (*A New Theory of Religion*), in which he rejected the idea of a deistic or detached God for a more immanent one. For Suzuki, the universe and its life forms existed under their own power. Life was not a created force; it was a priori. In his intellectual construct, religion and science were essential aspects of true wisdom; they supported each other and neither needed to compete in a struggle for supremacy.[9] In the same year, he wrote an essay titled 'The Zen of Emerson' for the magazine *Zenshu*, offering several examples of how American Transcendentalism aligned with Buddhism. They included the inability to fully express in words the essential nature of spiritual truth; that truth could only be approached through intuition; the acceptance of meditation rather than any logical or empirical process to reach spiritual enlightenment from God within; and finally, the necessity of forgoing 'self' to arrive at spiritual truth.[10] The essay, not unlike Carus's *Karma: A Story of Buddhist Ethics*, explained two fundamental characteristics of Buddhist and Christian teachings: that life exists in the renunciation of one's ego (Matthew 10:39) and that *good* is found in union with God and through God with one another (John 17:21).[11]

Believing that Suzuki showed enormous promise in bringing the traditions of West and East into greater harmony, Soyen encouraged Carus to consider hiring his student to acquire what Palmer Rampell described as 'firsthand insight into American intellectual and spiritual culture'.[12] Carus responded positively to the request and, in 1897, Suzuki joined the Carus household in LaSalle where, among his editorial duties, he assisted Carus with numerous Chinese and Japanese translations including Asvaghosha's *Discourse on the Awakening of Faith in the Mahayana* (1900); *T'ai-Shang Kan-Ying P'ien: Treatise of the Exalted One on Response and Retribution* (1906); the Taoist classic *Lao-Tze's Tao-Teh-King* (1898); *Yin Chih Wen: The Tract of the Quiet Way* (1906); Shaku Soyen's *Sermons of a Buddhist Abbot* (1906); and *Amida-butsu* (1906), a translation into Japanese of Paul Carus's *Amitabha*. He also wrote several articles concerning Eastern thought and culture in the pages of *The Open Court* and *The Monist*, including discussions of the Buddhist concept of *anatman*, or denial of a higher self; the unity of body and soul; positivism; the denial of the annihilation of the soul in nirvana; nirvana as enlightenment; and karma.[13]

In 1905-6, Suzuki served as an interpreter for Soyen during his tour of the United States, after which Suzuki wrote *Outlines of Mahayana Buddhism* (1907) to explain the significance of Zen to the Western world and its relationship with Japanese culture. With his book, translations and knowledge of Western scholarship, Suzuki emerged as one of the best-known scholars on Buddhism. As advocates seeking to bring science and religion under a single roof, Suzuki and Carus believed in their eventual merger. In assessing their relationship, historian Carl Jackson wrote, 'If Suzuki's work had been one of the important bridges to the West's modern understanding of Buddhism, Carus must be accounted one of the chief engineers'. Clearly, Suzuki's years at LaSalle introduced him to a whole new world of opportunity.[14] Proud of his disciple's success in explaining Buddhism to the West, Soyen bestowed on Suzuki the name *Daisetsu*, meaning 'Great Simplicity'.[15]

Over the eleven-year span of his tenure at Open Court, Suzuki gave lectures in San Francisco; visited the Newberry Library in Chicago; requested access from President William Rainey Harper at the University of Chicago to attend John Dewey's lectures; and sought a teaching position at the University of Chicago in the Chinese classics.[16] He also visited Boston where he studied the manuscripts of Emerson and Thoreau, discovering in the former the embodiment of 'spiritual freedom' and, in the latter, an ascetic who best represented a visual image of an 'Americanized Buddha'. Through his study of both men he gained a deeper appreciation of the contemporary American mind and its affinity to Swedenborgianism, Transcendentalism, mental healing and New Thought.[17] Suzuki even met William James and Charles Sanders Peirce, both of whom were developing their respective approaches to pragmatic theory. Suzuki was attracted to pragmatism, introducing it to his former classmate and philosopher Kitaro Nishida who incorporated it in his *Zen no Kenkyu* (1911). As part of his editorial duties, Suzuki corresponded with Peirce, exchanging ideas and concepts common to pragmatic theory and Japanese philosophy. In the works of both James and Peirce, he saw a combined Eastern/Western solution to modernity—a transnational philosophy to liberate society from ideologies and dogmas of all types.[18]

Suzuki also met Albert J Edmunds, a British-American Buddhist and Swedenborgian 'sympathizer' who served as a vital link in the exchange of Japanese and Western occult traditions. A native of Great Britain, Edmunds had emigrated to the United States in 1885 where he worked as a librarian at Haverford College near Philadelphia and as a cataloguer at the Historical Society of Pennsylvania. A Quaker, he dabbled in spiritualism, writing articles for the Society for Psychical Research on Swedenborgianism, Theosophy and related expressions of the occult.[19] He also wrote for the English language periodical *The Light of Dharma* of San Francisco, and collaborated with Masaharu Anesaki in 1905 to publish the *Buddhist and Christian Gospels Now First Compared from the Originals: Being 'Gospel Parallels from Pali Texts'*.[20]

During an eight-day visit to LaSalle in 1903, Edmunds had numerous conversations with Carus, Suzuki and other members of the Open Court Company. His personal journal recounted his encouragement of Suzuki to pursue the study of Swedenborg, a debt later confirmed in 1922 when Suzuki acknowledged that 'It was he [Edmunds] who initiated the present writer into the study of Swedenborgian mysticism'.[21]

Buddha of the North

After leaving LaSalle in 1908, Suzuki made an extended visit to Europe before returning to Japan. He spent time at the Bibliothèque Nationale in Paris studying ancient Chinese manuscripts and travelled to London where officers of the Swedenborg Society commissioned him to translate Swedenborg's *Heaven and Hell* into Japanese. On his return to Japan in 1909, he accepted a chair at Gakushuin University and published *Tenkai to Jigoku* (*Heaven and Hell*), the first Japanese translation of Swedenborg's writings. What made Swedenborg's eschatology credible to the Japanese mind was its broad ecumenical perspective, drawing inspiration from spiritually minded individuals across a spectrum of Christian thinking. In that sense, Swedenborg's approach was strikingly Buddhist, presenting a view of the afterlife that was not of *self* but of a more corporate *Maximus Homo*. That which Swedenborg linked to *proprium* (i.e., love of self and the world) was absent in heaven, replaced by a harmony of ruling loves and tendencies.[22]

In 1910, a year after *Tenkai to Jigoku* was published, Suzuki joined four hundred representatives at the International Swedenborg Congress in London to celebrate the one hundredth anniversary of the founding of the Swedenborg Society. Besides papers and addresses to commemorate the event, there were numerous receptions, presentations and an exhibition of Swedenborgiana displayed at the society's headquarters on Bloomsbury Street.[23] The conference's president, Dr Edward John Broadfield, commented in his opening address that Swedenborg was a 'many-sided' genius who reminded one 'of a great mountain rising from the plain, stately and symmetrical when seen from a distance, on which, as we approach nearer, we see peak rising above peak, and so much grandeur hitherto unsuspected that we find it difficult to make anything like a general survey'.[24]

In 1911 Suzuki married Beatrice Erskine Lane, a Theosophist and Radcliffe graduate in religion and philosophy whom he had met at Gakushuin University. Beatrice had taken courses from William James, Josiah Royce and George Herbert Palmer, and had earned a master's degree and certificate in social work from Columbia University.[25] Lane's knowledge of Swedenborg derived from William James (an early member of the Theosophical Society) whose father, Henry James, Sr, was a well-known Swedenborgian. Beatrice and her mother, Emma Erskine Hahn, were admirers of the Baha'i faith and, along with Suzuki, attended Sarah Farmer's Greenacre retreat in Maine, an intellectual and transnational centre for both New Thought and Baha'i devotees. Following her marriage, Beatrice became a Japanese citizen, a Buddhist scholar in her own right and a popularizer of Zen to the West. Exemplary of her work was *Mahayana Buddhism*, published in 1938, a year before her death.[26]

Suzuki visited England again in 1911 at the invitation of the Swedenborg Society which supported a four-month stay to translate several additional works of Swedenborg into Japanese. These included *The New Jerusalem and Its Heavenly Doctrine* (*Shin Erusaremu to Sono Kyôsetsu*); *Divine Love and Wisdom* (*Shinchi to Shin'ai*); and *Divine Providence* (*Shinryo Ron*). To complete these as well as his earlier *Tenkai to Jigoku*, Suzuki relied on Rudolph L Tafel's three-volume *Documents Concerning the Life and Character of Emanuel Swedenborg* and Latin-to-English translations of Swedenborg.[27] Suzuki also lectured to Society members on the spread of Swedenborgianism in Japan, including the launching of the Japan Swedenborg Society.[28]

In 1913 Suzuki wrote *Suedenborugu*, a biographical overview of Swedenborg's spiritual vision, his character and lifestyle, his views of heaven, love and correspondence, and numerous parallels with Buddhist philosophy. He focused on the Swede's concept of *proprium*; the term *salvation* which meant the 'harmonious unification of belief and action'; the Divine which manifested itself in the form of *wisdom* and *love*; and the actions of life considered ontologically or providentially based (i.e., there was no such thing as a chance universe). Suzuki saw in Swedenborg's writings a basis for countering the moral and spiritual poverty of his homeland. Suzuki learned from both Swedenborg and Carus that true science and true religion were indistinguishable.[29]

In tracing Swedenborg's life from his childhood with its strong religious overtones into his later years as poet, philosopher and man of science, Suzuki recounted the Swede's studies abroad and the ingenious ways he put mathematics, mechanics, mineralogy, chemistry and physics into practice. He took special note of Swedenborg's *Opera Philosophica et Mineralia* (*Philosophical and Mineralogical Works*) and subsequent works, examining the seer's transformation from the world of science to the spiritual realm of the mystic. Suzuki also examined Swedenborg's experience during Easter week in 1744 when, on returning home from church he cried out: 'God's will be done; I am Thine and not mine. God give His grace for this [work]; for it is not mine'.[30] For the next twenty-eight years of his life, explained Suzuki, Swedenborg devoted himself to 'seeing with his spiritual eye the structure, contents, and activities of heaven and hell', explaining in his writings 'as much as the divine will would allow', and believing all the while that he was serving as God's spiritual instrument. Suzuki likened this transformation of Swedenborg into an 'instrument' of God with the Buddhist who turned away from 'self power' to become 'a believer in other-power'. Swedenborg no longer discussed the universe in mathematical terms, having dismissed his scientific ambitions and substituting in their stead a visionary and religious world view. Nevertheless, in both his scientific and religious endeavours there was the ever-present quest to discover the soul and its affections, immortality, and life in the Divine.[31]

Though *Suedenborugu* resembled at times a travelogue of Swedenborg's life and writings, Suzuki dispersed poignant observations that revealed his innermost fascination with the seer. Whether quoting the adage 'Will, namely love, makes the man' from *Heaven and Hell*, or recounting Swedenborg's law of correspondences, his analysis of degrees, or his explanation of the relationship between wisdom and love to the heart and lungs, Suzuki made clear the manifest nature of divine providence in these writings. The same was true for the evil and falsehood in the world, the rationality and freedom of the human mind, the laws of divine providence, or the purpose of creation and the realization of its 'uses'. From his extensive reading, Suzuki learned that it was 'crucial to have a penitent heart and, recognizing one's sins, to accumulate good deeds as befit love and wisdom'.[32]

Unlike nineteenth- and early twentieth-century mediums who claimed extraordinary spiritual faculties, Swedenborg's interaction with the spirit world, according to Suzuki, was unique and incomparable. Swedenborg enjoyed the 'air of a transcendent mystic' who worked and wrote 'under heaven's orders' and who, when he entered a meditative state, lived and acted most frugally, denying himself both food and sleep. Since the spiritual connection between love and understanding was the same as between the heart and lungs, he used the regulation of his breath to advance his understanding. As Suzuki explained, Swedenborg distinguished 'between internal and external, with external breath coming from the mundane world and internal breath from the spiritual world'. This internal breath arose from the true faith of those 'possessed by the spirit'.[33] Swedenborg offered a similar explanation: 'I was thus from the period of childhood able to stop my external breathing and activate only my internal breath, especially by means of absorbing speculations, as otherwise the intense study of truth is scarcely possible'. In the relationship between the breath and the cultivation of mind and body Swedenborg found it possible to converse with spirits and experience inspiration.[34]

In 1924, Suzuki published 'Suedenborugu: Sono Tenkai to Tarikikan' ('Swedenborg's View of Heaven and "Other-Power"'), later republished in *Zen: Miscellaneous Essays* (1927). In it, he remarked that although Swedenborg's religious philosophy was 'unfathomably deep' and sometimes 'seemingly absurd', it nevertheless contained elements that were 'difficult to dismiss'. In particular, *Heaven and Hell* contained 'profound and fascinating' comments regarding the state after death that helped to explain the *self* and its relationship to the Divine and specifically the concept that 'Nothing results from self-power; everything is achieved through the addition of divine power to oneself'. This, Suzuki explained, indicated that Swedenborg's philosophy was remarkably similar to Buddhism; indeed, they were complementary.[35]

Suzuki recounted Swedenborg's philosophical and religious views constructed using the law of correspondences, a law not unlike *Shingon* in Buddhism. While the law in the Western world was based on the biblical belief that 'God created man in his own image' (Genesis 1:27), the *Shingon* teachings unveiled their meaning through songs, stories or events which were understood according to the nature or ability of one's internal acceptance. In Swedenborg's world, true enlightenment could not be achieved through ordinary knowledge; nor could it be perceived independent of divine love and wisdom. Those who believed in self-power would always fail. Self-power was self-love or worldly love which, if pursued, created only hells. The level attained in heaven or hell was proportional to the intensity of self-love and divine love. Each individual was free to make a choice, i.e., free to act according to his or her love. 'Love that flows from the internal originates with the Lord; but when we do not act from this love, we never attain our true life'. The possibilities stemmed from freethinking consciousness granted by the Divine or One.[36]

In both his 1913 biography of Swedenborg and in his 1924 essay, Suzuki examined the similarity of Swedenborg's theological doctrines to those of Buddhism. 'True salvation rests upon a harmonious unity of what one believes with what one does', Suzuki explained. 'Wisdom and Love are the manifestation of the Divine, and Love has more depth and breadth than Wisdom. The Divine Providence reaches into the minutest things of the universe. There must not be any occurrences that happen by accident, but everything is conveyed by the Divine Providence through Wisdom and Love'.[37]

Up until this time in his career, Suzuki had written more on Swedenborg than on Zen. After 1924, however, he discontinued writing about Swedenborg. Described by Andrew Bernstein, Swedenborg 'vanished into the thin air of Buddhahood' as Suzuki searched for universal truths that he felt were more adequately represented in Zen. According to scholars, Suzuki's subsequent writings revealed scant references to Swedenborg except to note on occasion that the two philosophies had similarities, including the law of correspondences, and that the world of Zen, like the 'New Jerusalem', was more poetic than philosophical.[38] As explained by Thomas Tweed, 'we can imagine Suzuki's intellectual development as a series of distinguishable but overlapping phases, each with a different Suzuki emerging as predominant'.[39]

Suzuki, now living in Japan, pursued his Zen interests while carrying with him much of the wisdom he had garnered from his time in Illinois, bringing his earlier study of Swedenborg into his subsequent scholarship. He was able to make Western philosophers and theologians comfortable with Zen due to his knowledge of Swedenborg and the consanguinity between the mystic's search for understanding and the Buddhist's search for enlightenment.[40] At the conclusion of his 1924 essay, Suzuki remarked that, 'There is a great deal I wish to write concerning Swedenborg, but that remains for another day'.[41] In other words, it seems clear that Swedenborg continued to remain relevant to Suzuki's religious and philosophical interests. As the Japanese Swedenborgian Tatsuya Nagashima noted, Swedenborg's writings were solidly in Suzuki's later thinking, calling Suzuki a 'crypto-Swedenborgian'.[42]

The question remains, however, who or what sparked Suzuki's initial interest in Swedenborg? Who acquainted him with the mystic's writings and at whose urging did he agree to spend several years translating and writing about the Swede's thought for Japanese intellectuals? Some believe the catalysts were his wife Beatrice, Paul Carus, Shaku Soyen and perhaps even the 1893 Parliament of Religions. Others have suggested that Suzuki was drawn to Swedenborg because his writings had become 'fashionable currency' among American and European intellectuals, offering spiritual insights that resonated with those who feared the West's self-absorption and technological growth. In his *A Religious History of the American People*, historian Sydney Ahlstrom remarked that Swedenborg's influence had been notable across the American landscape, influencing Transcendentalism, spiritualism, utopian experiments, the free love movement, homoeopathic medicine, Theosophy and New Thought. Therefore, as a student of English literature and a lifelong admirer of Emerson, Suzuki could not have been immune to Swedenborg's influence, particularly as he had no doubt acquainted himself with Emerson's *Representative Men* which included the essay 'Swedenborg; or, the Mystic'.[43] Suzuki could also have discovered Swedenborg in the pages of *The Buddhist Ray* which would have been available to him at the Open Court Company in LaSalle. Published by Herman Vetterling in Santa Cruz, California, it was the first English language periodical devoted to Buddhist religion and philosophy in the United States. Its articles were shared among Japanese Buddhists and sometimes translated and republished in Japanese Buddhist journals.[44]

There were other reasons why Suzuki may have found Swedenborg an appealing subject of study during the eleven years he was living in the United States. Both Suzuki and Swedenborg were intent on building the knowledge base of their respective cultures with information gleaned from neighbouring countries: Swedenborg through studying metallurgy, mining techniques and assessing, and Suzuki with his fascination with Western philosophy and mysticism. Both men sought to live simply and frugally while, at the same time, carrying on an intensive and highly personalized effort to understand the self and its relationship to the *other*. Then too, both had relinquished their efforts to utilize the tools of science and rationality in their search for spiritual truth, choosing instead an intuitive route free from pre-imposed or inadvertent orthodoxies. Finally, both men discovered that spiritual truth came not through ecclesiasticism, rituals, dogmas or other officially condoned systems or structures, but through intuition and ineffability. The vocabulary of inner and outer resonated as they sought to uncover the route to enlightenment.[45]

The most compelling explanation, however, came from Thomas A Tweed at the University of North Carolina at Chapel Hill who suggested in a paper delivered before the World Congress of the International Association for the History of Religions in 2005 that the catalyst for Suzuki's interest in Swedenborg had been none other than Albert J Edmunds. Though not a trained scholar, Edmunds had developed an intense interest in Buddhism and became part of a transnational exchange whose advocates favored a loose blending of Buddhism with the metaphysical traditions of Swedenborg and Theosophy. Representative of late-Victorian occultists, he urged a closer relationship between Christianity and Buddhism, believing their differences to be more contrived than real.[46] 'When this link is recognized, as it is now in the process of being', Edmunds wrote, 'the two great religions of the world, which have hitherto been hostile, will approach each other with respect, and the last obstacle will be removed to the founding of a modern world-religion based upon the facts of science, physical, historical, and psychical'.[47] Edmunds explained that Buddhist beliefs, including the idea of Genesis as a Fall and of Paradise as a spiritual state, had been constructed between the fifth and first centuries before Christ. These myths were then given a Hebrew genesis by Philo Judaeus of Alexandria at the time of Christ, by Origen

251

in the third century, by Jacob Boehme in the sixteenth century, and by Swedenborg in the eighteenth century.[48]

Like Herman Vetterling, Edmunds speculated that the 'ancient Word' referenced by Swedenborg in his *The True Christian Religion*, referred to the esoteric Buddhism of Tibet and Nepal.[49] Swedenborg had claimed conversations with spirits from 'Great Tartary' which suggested the existence of ancient texts that pre-dated both Judaism and Christianity and formed a connection between Christianity and Buddhism. 'Of that ancient Word which existed in Asia before the Israelitish Word', wrote Swedenborg, 'I am permitted to state this new thing, namely, that it is still preserved there among the people who dwell in Great Tartary. In the spiritual world I have talked with spirits and angels from that country, who said that they have a Word, and have had it from ancient times; and that they conduct their Divine worship according to this Word, and that it consists solely of correspondences'.[50]

Comparisons

Suzuki and later scholars noted numerous comparisons between Swedenborgianism and Buddhism.

1) Both Swedenborgianism and Buddhism denied the Cartesian dichotomy of body and mind. Rather than the proverbial 'I think, therefore I am', they substituted 'What I love is what I am'. The goal for each individual was to grow from self-love to no-self, or love of the Divine and of others. The Mahayana Buddhist doctrine of *anatman* ('no self') aligned with Swedenborg's *proprium*. Except for the role of Christ as God-man in Swedenborg, the spiritual constructs of both the Swedenborgian and Buddhist traditions were similar as they led to the influx of love and wisdom that eradicated the self in its encounter with the One.[51]

2) In their denial of subject-object, Swedenborgianism and Buddhism presented the idea of everything existing within. As the Zen master Dōgen explained, 'To study the buddha way is to study the self. To study the self is to forget the self. To forget the self is to be actualized by myriad things. When actualized by myriad things, your body and mind as well as the bodies and minds of others drop away. No trace of realization remains, and this no-trace continues endlessly'. The exercise designed to

remove the *self* from the world was also the objective described by Swedenborg in his *Spiritual Diary*. 'By transforming observed *objects* into *manifestations* of nondual mind', explained David Loy, 'not only the so-called material world but the events of "my" mental activity become more "animated", that is, they gain more of a life of their own, independent of being thought by *me*'.[52]

3) Somewhat analogous to the *anima mundi* of Plato and Indra's net in Buddhism, Swedenborg's *Maximus Homo* formed a universe of which each soul was a microcosm, participating in and exemplifying all its myriad elements. In the Swedenborgian after-world, the face of an individual following natural death became the visible expression of both the internal and external soul. This was simply another way of stating the non-duality of mind and body or subject and object.[53]

4) While the Christian used his freethinking consciousness to receive repentance and resurrection, the Buddhist achieved rebirth through karma. Both, however, placed responsibility on the individual for choices of good or evil and the ensuing consequences. In Swedenborg's explanation of evil and the Buddhist doctrines of *karma* and *samskara*, evil became its own punishment. One's *samskaras* or intentions made a person who he or she was and would be. Intentions became a ruling love, aligning the character or both the spiritual and physical body of the individual. Those *samskaras* that survived death became the self reincarnated in karma.[54]

5) Both denied the efficacy of salvation by good deeds, by faith alone, or by performing rituals. Instead, salvation was achieved through selfless love, i.e., by allowing the spiritual influx to fill what was formerly the 'I' or self, eliminating any dualism between God and man, spirit, and matter. This did not entail the Western sense of asceticism with its denial or renunciation of pleasures; instead, both Swedenborgianism and Buddhism accepted the enjoyment of pleasures as an integral part of divine providence.[55]

6) In the perplexing question regarding free will and divine providence, Swedenborg insisted that human beings acted out of freedom to choose heaven or hell, love or evil. While this response *seemed* to be the result of freedom, it was actually *caused* by the divine will implanted in each according to foreordained desires. Humans became what their habitual actions made them. Realization of this came not by oneself but

through divine providence. Allowing the will and understanding to accept the wisdom and enlightenment of the divine influx was no different than a person in meditation whose selfless joy opened for the sake of the dharma or living a life of love.[56]

7) For Swedenborg, all things existed by divine influx, meaning that all being was 'an image of God in a mirror', received in accordance with its capacity or disposition to love. Both Swedenborgianism and Buddhism considered the ontological self as an illusion, denying as well the separate existence of a Cartesian soul. Negating the subject-object dualism, they viewed each individual as a mirror of his or her ruling love. One is what one loves. 'The activity of love is what gives the sense delight', Swedenborg wrote 'in heaven its activity is with wisdom, and in hell with insanity, but in both cases the activity produces the delight in its subjects'. Each gravitated to that love that mirrored his or her affections. In contradistinction to Descartes, the knower was not separate from the known; the inner and outer were the same. The 'whole'—subject and object—was a unity in space and time.[57]

8) The cornerstone of Swedenborg's revelatory visions was his doctrine of correspondences which had its counterpart in the Buddhist teachings of *Shingon*, meaning that everything perceived in the material world had a counterpart in the invisible or spiritual world. For every outward and visible event there was an inward or spiritual cause. As Swedenborg explained, 'The whole natural world corresponds to the spiritual world, not only the natural world in general but also in every particular. Therefore, whatever in the natural world comes into existence from the spiritual world is said to be in correspondence with it'.[58]

Interestingly, *The Gospel of Thomas*, one of the documents unearthed at Nag Hammadi in Upper Egypt in 1945, presented Jesus and his message as considerably different than found in the canonical gospels of Mathew, Mark, Luke and John. While the latter gospels presented Jesus as the Christ, the son of God, Thomas described Jesus in a more Gnostic fashion, that is, as a teacher of wisdom. In this manner, *The Gospel of Thomas* seemed to align itself more with Zen than with Christianity. As explained by Stephen Morris, 'Thomas offers a more pertinent, more realistic, and more reasonable presentation than do the canonical gospels themselves'. *The Gospel of Thomas* constituted a more primitive form of Jesus's teachings than the canonical gospels and arguably represented 'an early authentic version of the teachings of Jesus, an alternative but legitimate portrayal of what Jesus thought spirituality was all about'.[59] In this respect, both Zen and *The Gospel of Thomas* sought not the worship of Buddha and Jesus but to understand them as teachers of wisdom.[60] For the Buddhist, this was called 'One Mind' and was the all-consuming goal of one's existence, i.e., the quest or search for enlightenment.[61] By contrast, the Jesus of the canonical gospels was not so much seen as a quest but as the journey's end with the expectation of grace. The difference was significant as faith became the centrepiece of canonical Christianity while the existential uncertainty inherent in the search became the centrepiece of *The Gospel of Thomas*. Jesus was not a final answer but the start of a process of self-discovery, a process that Morris considered outside Christian orthodoxy but an essential component in both *The Gospel of Thomas* and in Suzuki's interpretation of Zen Buddhism. The call of both Thomas and Zen was the call to self-knowledge and not, as in Christian orthodoxy, to chronicle the powers of the Son of God.[62]

Zen

Following Soyen's death in 1919, Suzuki and Beatrice moved to Kyoto where he accepted a chair at Otani University, one of the True Pure Land schools known also as Jodo Shinshu, and where they co-founded The Eastern Buddhist Society focusing on Mahayana Buddhism.[63] There, too, they opened a Theosophical Lodge which engaged in both Theosophical and Swedenborgian esotericism and published *The Eastern Buddhist*, an English-language quarterly magazine intended for Western audiences.[64] In 1927, came the first of Suzuki's *Essays in Zen Buddhism*, with additional volumes in 1933 and 1934.[65] These were followed by a burst of publications: *Studies in the Lankavatara Sutra* (1930); *An Index to the Lankavatara Sutra* (1933); *The Training of the Zen Buddhist Monk* (1934); *An Introduction to Zen Buddhism* (1934); *The Gandavyuha Sutra* (with H Idzumi, 1934-6); *Manual of Zen Buddhism* (1935); *Buddhist Philosophy and Its Effects on the Life and Thought of the Japanese People* (1936); *Japanese Buddhism* (1938); and *Zen Buddhism and Its Influence on Japanese Culture* (1938). These, along with his lectures, confirmed Suzuki as Zen's leading voice and interpreter to the Western world. In 1933, the university conferred on him the Doctor of Humane Letters.

Unlike the highly regimented and ritualized practice of traditional Buddhism, Suzuki's approach was that to which Soyen subscribed, namely, the reform group known as *shin bukkyo*, or New Buddhism, with its dual focus on spirituality and building a bridge between Eastern and Western religion and philosophy. Although he initially agreed with Carus regarding the primacy of science and philosophy, he later concluded that there were epistemological impediments causing him to rely on intuition and self-forgetfulness as more effective methods.[66] According to David McMahan in his *The Making of Buddhist Modernism*, Suzuki removed Zen from its more authentic Japanese social, ritual and ethical contexts and reframed it in a combination of German idealism, English Romanticism and American Transcendentalism.[67]

As a pioneer teacher and interpreter of Zen to the West, Suzuki wrote fluently and with authority, using impeccable English. Along with Kaiten Nukariya's *Religion of the Samurai* (1913) and subscribers to *The Eastern Buddhist*, he offered some of the most influential insights into Buddhist philosophy. Though not a priest, his intellectual and practical knowledge of Buddhism was profound, appealing to the inmost consciousness of humanity in its intuitive search for meaning. Zen was 'the art of seeing into the nature of one's own being' through the liberation of the 'creative and benevolent impulses' or energies inherent in each. It opened a 'third eye' to a subject that had long been concealed by ignorance. The very term implied a channel through which coursed all that was true among the world's great religions and philosophies.[68] Zen was the 'ultimate fact of all philosophy and religion' whose vital and inspiring elements moved beyond the intellect with its narrow and dualistic focus on scholasticism and sacerdotalism. It upset this scheme of thought by substituting one in which there existed no logic and no dualistic arrangement of ideas. Turning to paradoxical assertions in the mystic literature of the West, Suzuki expressed himself as 'I myself am heaven and hell', or 'divine darkness' and 'immovable mover'.[69] He also referred frequently to Emerson to express a world stripped of logic and discursive obliquities.[70]

As an essential element of the Mahayana school of Buddhism, Zen served as a channel of enlightenment in life. It was the antipode to logic, addressing the whole mind and not just specific parts or functions. It was also a discipline intended to embrace freedom in all its forms, knowing no limitations and defying any attempt to understand it in abstract. Claiming no sacred books or doctrines, it rejected any special formulation. Nor did it claim any particular monotheistic or pantheistic God as conceived and worshipped by the Judaeo-Christian or Hindu mind. Similarly, it offered no special heaven or lesser abode for those who died.[71] Instead, Zen represented the 'spirit' or inner purity and goodness of an individual that defied both the scientist's microscope and the artist's brush. Elusive and unapproachable using ordinary methods and techniques, Zen became a vast emptiness where, in the deeper self, 'the truth is unfolding itself right before your eye. This is all there is to it—and indeed nothing more!'[72]

Suzuki refused to examine Zen as the topic of philosophical, historical or doctrinal discussion. All such constructions or interpretations were outside the 'living' or unfolding experience of enlightened Buddhahood. 'If a man understands what enlightenment is or really experiences it in himself, he knows the whole secret of the Buddha's superhuman nature and with it the riddle of life and the world', he wrote.[73] Freed from the bondage of intellect, Zen represented the seeking of truth and enlightenment in life, not logic, in facts and not generalizations, in awakened consciousness and not in psychic trances or spiritism.

The basic idea of Zen is to come in touch with the inner workings of our being, and to do so in the most direct way possible, without resorting to anything external or superadded. Therefore, anything that has the semblance of an external authority is rejected by Zen. Absolute faith is placed in a man's own inner being. For whatever authority there is in Zen, all comes from within. This is true in the strictest sense of the word. Even the reasoning faculty is not considered final or absolute. On the contrary, it hinders the mind from coming into the directest communication with itself. The intellect accomplishes its mission when it works as an intermediary, and Zen has nothing to do with an intermediary except when it desires to communicate itself to others. . . . The central fact of life as it is lived is what Zen aims to grasp, and this in the most direct and most vital manner. Zen professes itself to be the spirit of Buddhism, but in fact it is the spirit of all religions and philosophies.[74]

By appealing to experience rather than book knowledge, Suzuki grasped a higher faculty than the intellect to solve life's problems. 'Let the intellect alone', he advised, 'it has its usefulness in its proper sphere, but let it not interfere with the flowing of the life-stream'. Though the intellect explained, analysed, generalized, noted entangling contradictions and systematized logic, Zen marched serenely on its own way or, as the Zen master put it, 'carrying his home-made cane on the shoulder, he goes right on among the mountains one rising above the other'. To understand it was to see two mirrors facing each other with 'no intervening agents', leaving only 'the living, pulsating fact itself'.[75]

The elements considered by Henry James, Sr, Emerson, William James, Charles Peirce and John Dewey as necessary for a union of philosophy and life were remarkably similar to Zen's explanation of pure experience, of means and ends, and the concept of *uses*. Both Suzuki's 'practical' Buddhism (i.e., finding enlightenment while hewing wood or drawing water) and Dewey's *Art as Experience* explained life's meaning not in the form of unapproachable abstractions but as a celebration of the fact that 'life is its own end and answer'. Both taught how to live without the mystery of dualism, that the eternal was now, the supernatural actual, and that all are Buddhas.[76]

Questions concerning Zen nonetheless remain to be answered. Should Zen be considered a religion or a way of living? How much of Zen is tied to formal Buddhist teachings? What Zen precepts are most important? Should there be an alignment between the form and presentation of Zen in the United States and the manner in which Zen is practised in other countries? What does it mean for someone to say he or she is a Zen Buddhist? What makes for an authentic Zen Buddhism?[77]

Pragmatic Wisdom
American pragmatism blossomed in the early decades of the twentieth century. With the work of mathematician Charles Peirce and psychologist William James, it became known as a philosophy of action (i.e., beliefs were tested not by their internal logic

or even their origins, but by their consequences). Ideas, however similar or contrary, were valued for their functional purposes. Through individuals such as the philosopher and educational reformer John Dewey, psychologist Edward Lee Thorndike and philosopher Ralph Barton Perry, pragmatism impacted diverse disciplines—from the humanities and religion to the sciences and social sciences—by creating a pragmatic method and outlook.

There were striking parallels, therefore, within pragmatism, Buddhism and Swedenborgianism. In each, its sponsors were revolting against tradition and intellectualism and seeking to recast old ways of thinking in words that, while new, were also drawn from native roots as well as external sources. Each deprecated absolutism and rigid determinism, distrusted metaphysical system-makers and encouraged adaptation to a changing world. And each was an advocate of 'usefulness' as the proper means of putting their tenets into practice. 'It is a curious fact of history', remarked Eugene Taylor of Harvard, 'that the psychology practiced in India two thousand years ago was more like the psychology taught at Harvard in the 1890's under James than the psychology taught today in academic universities is like the psychology taught in America one hundred years ago'.[78]

As Taylor has documented, both Peirce and James were well versed in Swedenborgianism according to their personal libraries; Harvard Library's records of books charged out to each; the influence of Henry James, Sr on their respective religious sensibilities; their personal correspondence; and references in their published writings.[79] One aspect in particular, Swedenborg's doctrine of use, the principal topic in *Divine Love and Wisdom*, resonated with pragmatic theory. The book considered three particular attributes of the Deity: the Divine of Love, the Divine of Wisdom and the Divine of Use. Since everything in the natural world had it derivation in the spiritual world, Swedenborg explained that 'use' was the purpose of creation. 'All things which have been created by the Lord are uses. They are uses in the order, degree and respect in which they have relation to man, and through man to the Lord from whom they are'. Uses were of three types: for sustaining the body, perfecting the rational and for receiving the spiritual from the Divine.[80] 'Use, therefore, becomes the basic standard by which we read the direction of personality development', Taylor explained. 'The will, which is the receptacle of love, and the understanding, which is the receptacle of wisdom within the person, express themselves in the world through uses'.[81]

By substituting the words 'practical wisdom' for Buddhahood, University of Cincinnati professor Van Meter Ames presented pragmatism as a form of Zen whose philosophy or process consisted of finding wisdom not by escaping the world but finding it in everyday human activity. Buddha was everyman. In both Zen and pragmatism, the emphasis was on the value of life lived for itself and in the moment, and not by measuring or revealing its goodness or badness from an abstraction or afterthought. The immediate experience came first; explanation was ancillary, if at all. 'The first thing was the fact', explained Ames, 'and the belief it fed belonged to it rather than to the theory or theology that followed'. When enlightenment came to the individual, for both the Zen Buddhist and for the pragmatist the event was the same, or as Ames explained, 'something like what William James called a second wind' which instilled an attitude that helped a man to live a life worth having. Life was both a risk and an adventure. The importance was 'not in doing things differently so much as in doing them well and finding them worth doing'. Life was full and good not by any ratiocination that followed the experience, but by the experience itself. Just as the Zen Buddhist understood, so too, did Americans from Emerson to Dewey, that 'life is its own end and answer'.[82]

In pragmatism and in Zen, the aesthetic value came from the enjoyment of the immediate experience which had no other purpose than for its own sake. 'In both', explained Ames, 'intense enjoyment of the immediate is the aim, with realization that it often has to be worked for and waited for, especially if it is to be made widely available and renewable'. Both had the bodhisattva ideal which meant sharing in a love of others instead of a self-centred pursuit of enlightenment. 'Dewey, no less than Zen', Ames insisted, 'denies any purpose beyond that of being absorbed in the business of living'.[83] It was in doing and learning that one arrived at a sense of wholeness.

The Buddhist idea of functionality or practical consequences was also integral to Swedenborg's intent in *Divine Love and Wisdom* where he identified the 'Divine of Love, the Divine of Wisdom, and the Divine of Use'——all of which were the ends of creation. 'All things which have been created by the Lord are uses', Swedenborg wrote, and 'they are uses in the order, degree and respect in which they have relation to man, and through man to the Lord from whom they are'.[84] In removing the existential-ist's sense of alienation and substituting the pragmatist's sense of optimism, and allowing the subject and object to dissolve into the experience, the result was what Suzuki called 'life itself' or *sunyata*. This became the basis for enlightenment—a pre-scientific, non-comprehensible, non-intellectual but practical, aesthetic and satisfying state of human experience or living. It was the pre-analytical act or process of becoming that Ames called the joyful experience of 'oneness and wonder'.[85]

Zen has sometimes been described as chopping wood and carrying water, represent-ing the truth of life not in words, but by living, moving and acting. 'In the actual living of life', Suzuki explained, 'there is no logic, for life is superior to logic'. Zen meant giving up the love and sense of a separate self and living passionately in the moment as if leaving one's internal wholly open to the influx of wisdom and enlightenment. In its practical and disciplinary element, Zen included the notion of work or service. This was at the very core of the Zen monk's education known as the 'Meditation Hall'. The sanctification of work and service prevented Zen 'from deteriorating into quietism or mere intellectual gymnastics'.[86] If life was to be true, it had to be practical, developing all the faculties and having them work harmoniously. While the Christian mystics used prayer, mortification and contemplation to arrive at enlightenment, the Buddhist found it in everyday practical life. Clearly, Zen was not mystical in any Western sense but only in the surprisingly simple, practical and direct approach of *living* life.[87] As Suzuki explained, life should be lived as a 'perfect art' which was self-forgetting and catching life as it flowed, much like a bird flying through the air or a fish swimming in water. The Zen experience was a joyous union of the self with the no-self, or as Christ explained when 'I and my Father are One'. An extraordinarily aesthetic philosophy, it broke through the duality of subject-object in egoless self-abandonment where, in the moment, the self surrendered its will to the will of God.[88]

In his book *Living by Zen*, Suzuki compared 'satori', or enlightenment, to Kierkegaard's leap of faith when the 'vulgar thoughts' of dualism, of subject and object, gave way to a 'superior understanding.[89] Satori, meaning an intuitive and irrational moment, was nonetheless affirmative, the equivalent of suddenly seeing the wonder of ordinary experience, of being born again and rejoicing in the moment. Emerson, Thoreau and Whitman experienced this joyous uncritical and unreflective moment as did the Zen master in the most ordinary affairs of chopping wood, gardening or cooking.[90] Dewey would have considered this experience 'natural and moral . . . active and practical'.[91] Similar to what Jonathan Edwards called *conversion*, what Emerson called the *transparent eyeball*, what William James called *noetic*, or what the Canadian Jesuit Bernard Lonergan identified as *insight*, Zen was an experience that negated any intellectual formulation, logic or reasoning to its existence. French existentialist Albert Camus described it as the emotion Sisyphus felt as he walked back down the mountain.[92] Satori represented a conscious act of understanding—an interior state of enlightenment that left the individual transformed with a largely indescribable but positive attitude toward life and 'otherness'. It connoted a state or possession of understanding that made no distinction between the duality of subject and object but, instead, transcended both with a profound sense of peace, order and unity. Although the experience differed from one individual to another, it produced a heuristic understanding that defied description other than metaphors, likening it to some ineffable and profound liberation of the self.[93]

Similarly, the radical empiricist William James replaced Cartesian dualism with the indivisibility of experience, a single category which he called 'pure experience', meaning that experience is undivided, pre-reflective and devoid of subject and object; it simply *is*. This direct, immediate and intuitive sensation preceded higher levels of consciousness or conceptualization and formed the cornerstone of his empirical philosophy. James's concept corresponded to the Mahayana doctrine of *sunyata*, forming a cross-cultural connection.[94] In both philosophies, the criterion for measuring the validity or truth of an idea was its usefulness when put to work. Ideas were judged by their consequences. There was no meaning or value to an idea without factoring in its use. 'Ideas [which themselves are but parts of our experience] become true just in so far as they help us to get into satisfactory relation with other parts of our existence', wrote James. The test of an idea proceeded from pure sensation, but was true or false based on its effectiveness.[95]

As explained by Ames, this was reason enough to liken Zen to aspects of pragmatism and existentialism even though Zen was typically and inaccurately viewed as enigmatic and Oriental, while pragmatism was considered transparent and American. 'Pragmatism teaches that thought and scientific method are instrumental to the conduct and enjoyment of life', Ames wrote, 'and that life is primarily what it is felt to be in immediate experience'. The importance, therefore, of the here-and-now character of life was a bond between the Zen master and the pragmatist as well as between Zen and existentialism.[96] The Buddhist's path to Zen was through a heuristic intuition that was pre-logical, or what James called 'pure experience'.[97] It represented a union of philosophy with life, a concept as profoundly American as it was Buddhist, linking Henry James, Sr's evolution of consciousness and William James's radical empiricism to Suzuki's 'no-self'. In each, value came in the *doing*, where ends and means combined in the immediacy of the moment. No longer was man spliced into mind and body, body and soul, substance and shadow. There was only the experience, the expression of which was best left to the ideal of bodhisattva, or living beyond the self.[98] For a Westerner, reading Suzuki's *Essays in Zen Buddhism* was equivalent to reading the denial of individuality in the writings of James, Sr; the moral, spiritual, intellectual, practical and psychological journey of his son William; and the spiritual turmoil quieted by Swedenborg's revelatory visions.[99]

In both Zen and Dewey's educational philosophy, direct experience took priority over intellection or logical reasoning. A true Zen follower (or student), was only satisfied when he 'scooped with his own hands the living water of Reality which alone . . . will quench his thirst'.[100] The focus was to 'live within the thing itself and thus to understand it'. Rather than describe a thing from outside, or to talk about it objectively, one needed to achieve an 'inner assimilation or sympathetic merging'.[101] The experience came first and the reasoning followed. Solutions came in life, not in a book.

Columbia University

Following the death of his wife in 1939 and the outbreak of the Second World War, Suzuki went into virtual seclusion, at the conclusion of which he published *The Essence of Buddhism* (1947) and started the English journal *The Cultural East*.

His *Japanese Spirituality*, written in 1944 during the wartime bombings, was translated into English in 1972. Masao Abe, a committed follower of Pure Land Buddhism, hoped that Suzuki would bring the message of Zen to the Western world by remaining in his homeland and translating Zen texts into English.[102] Suzuki, however, chose to take his message of Zen to the West by moving to the United States following the second East-West Philosophers' Conference held in Hawaii in 1949. Accepting an invitation by the Rockefeller Foundation to offer a series of lectures in American universities, he became a visiting professor at the age of eighty at Columbia University where he remained from 1952 until 1958, lodging at the home of Mihoko Okamura on West 94th Street. After retiring from Columbia, Suzuki lectured at Harvard where he helped to found the Cambridge Buddhist Society. Along with Buddhist scholar Alan Watts, he also contributed to the establishment of the Zen Institute in New York and the Zen Center in San Francisco.[103]

During this latter period in his life, Suzuki wrote *The Zen Doctrine of the No-Mind* (1949); *A Miscellany on the Shin Teaching of Buddhism* (1949); *Living by Zen* (1949); *Studies in Zen* (1955); *Zen and Japanese Buddhism* (1958); *Zen and Japanese Culture* (1959); and *Zen Buddhism and Psychoanalysis* (with Erich Fromm and Richard De Martino, 1960). In these publications, Suzuki laid the groundwork for a much richer Buddhist-Christian dialogue. His impact was unprecedented, drawing to his lectures a cadre of disaffected postmodernist students, artists, poets, writers, as well as convert and 'ethnic' Buddhists looking for a more meaningful vision of American society.[104] Suzuki's more notable friends and devotees included composer John Cage; poets Allen Ginsberg and Gary Snyder; writers Jack Kerouac,[105] Aldous Huxley and J D Salinger; psychologists Erich Fromm, Karen Horney and Carl G Jung;[106] British potter Bernard Leach; Trappist Thomas Merton; and existentialist Martin Heidegger. He continued to travel and lecture until his death in 1966 at the age of ninety-four.

The 1960s and 1970s witnessed a virtual pilgrimage of disillusioned middle-class American and European youth in a search for spiritual meaning to their lives. In sojourns to India and Nepal they encountered Tibetan Buddhists who, exiled from their homeland by China, provided a welcome source of spirituality. Some were invited to establish centres and organizations in the UK, the Continent and the United States. Considered to be possessors of true esoteric knowledge, they found a mass market for the West's counterculture consumption that took the form of poetry readings by beat poets; the adaptation of images, words and forms from Hinduism and Buddhism; and charismatic teachers whose guru 'wisdom' was learned by obedient followers.[107]

Mysticism

Mystics have long been the object of curiosity in the West. Depending on the observer's perspective, the experiences are deemed to be intrinsically ineffable or the product of an abnormal psychology. Some of the ferment of mysticism was found in the work of the Transcendental Club (1836), the Free Religious Association (1867), the Theosophical Society (1875), the Harvard Club for the Study of the History of Religions (1891), the World's Parliament of Religions (1893), the Montsalvat School for the Comparative Study of Religion (1894) and the Greenacre Community (1894).[108]

In the era of postmodernism with its crisis of faith in objectivity, a new generation of scientists and philosophers sought to restore intuition to a respectful albeit modest status. Walter T Stace's *Mysticism and Philosophy* (1960), Alfred P Stiernotte's *Mysticism and the Modern Mind* (1959) and Suzuki's *Mysticism: Christian and Buddhist* (1957) revived mysticism's status. Apart from their separate interpretations of the essential nature of the mystical experience, these authors recognized and accepted its universality. For the mystics of the Occident and Orient, experience became a basis of knowledge more relevant and more convincing than any derived from the senses or from reason. The unifying experience was of such intensity and satisfaction that it trumped anything the body and mind achieved in their dual roles.[109]

From the late 1950s until his death in 1966, Suzuki renewed his interest in Christian mysticism, centring not on Swedenborg but on the German monk, theologian and philosopher Meister Eckhart (1260-1327) whom he compared to the followers of the Jodo Shinshu school called *Myokonin*. Suzuki found in the Dominican an individual for whom the act of intuition, born of the will, attained its end not from cognitive reasoning but by knowing itself as it was in itself. In Eckhart, he found someone unburdened by Swedenborg's interstellar wanderings and conversations with angels and other-worldly spirits. This was not to demean the importance of Swedenborg, but rather to identify with a Western esoteric thinker whose mysticism carried less baggage. Unlike Swedenborg, Eckhart's sanity had never been a point of contention.[110] Eckhart did not speak of heavenly spirits or refer to an afterlife; instead, he wrote of human potential and of the discovery of oneself. He provided questions rather than answers, a process rather than an ending, a dialogue rather than doctrines.[111] Suzuki turned from Swedenborg to Eckhart also because of the simplicity of his words and his close similarity with Zen on the topic of self-knowledge. 'To get at the core of God at his greatest', wrote Eckhart, 'one must get into the core of himself at his least, for no one can know God who has not first known himself'. The challenge in finding God was first and foremost to find oneself. Self-knowledge opened the path to knowledge of God. The most direct path to the truth lay in the inner being. This was the path taught by Zen and by Eckhart.[112]

The metaphysical and aesthetic ideas of Eckhart aligned well with the philosophy of the Vedas, Manu and the *Bhagavadgita*. In both *Mysticism: Christian and Buddhist* and in his *Essays in Zen Buddhism, First Series*, Suzuki made a connection between Eckhart and the philosophy of Mahayana Buddhism. He was not alone in his assessment as Ananda K Coomaraswamy, in *Transformation of Nature in Art* (1934), identified Eckhart's sermons as the 'Upanishad of Europe'.[113] Given their parallel beliefs in the Godhead being beyond attribute or description (i.e., 'a Not-Being above Being'); cosmic and personal creation (i.e., the eternality of man's spirit); metaphysics as the way of salvation (i.e., 'the awakening to the oneness of one's true self with the Eternal'); and the illuminative approach to understanding (i.e., 'the purified life must always come before the beatific vision'), the affinities between Eckhart and Eastern philosophy generated considerable interest.[114] Having familiarized himself with the mystical literature of Eckhart, Suzuki concluded: 'I grow firmly convinced that the Christian experiences are not after all different from those of the Buddhist'.[115]

Eckhart's notion of nothingness was reminiscent of the Buddhist concept of *sunyata* in that it was bound up with the overwhelming sense of the oneness of God and man. When he talked of man as pure nothing, Eckhart was saying that man and God were intimately one because God is the creating and sustaining cause of all. If God was being and from him all being came directly, then the Divine was being itself and was thus united to man.[116] Having proposed continuity between Creator and creature, explained theological studies scholar Charlotte Radler, Eckhart maintained that 'the One, as transparent and transcendent nothingness, encompasses and penetrates all' This truth, for Eckhart, underscored his assurance that 'the soul is ontologically rooted in the nothingness of the divine unity and is thus in its deepest essence divine'.[117] This similarity served as an incentive for the conversations Suzuki subsequently had with Trappist monk Thomas Merton.[118]

Thomas Merton

By the mid-twentieth century, the influence of Buddhism on Western Christianity became evident in the popularity of the mystic Thomas Merton and the meditative journey taken by French philosopher and Jesuit Teilhard de Chardin.[119] 'The impact of Suzuki's influence on the West', explained Merton, struck 'in the midst of the existentialist upheaval, at the beginning of the atomic and cybernetic age, with Western religion and philosophy in a state of crisis and with the consciousness of man threatened by the deepest alienation'. Merton discovered in Suzuki a genuine and insightful contributor to psychoanalysis, philosophy and religion. He observed with some disappointment, however, that many of Suzuki's enthusiasts had acquired only a superficial understanding of Zen (a 'froth of Zen') which influenced the popular culture but had little to offer the world of the intellect.[120]

Merton's spirituality, his monastic thought and interest in Eastern religions, followed by his accidental death in 1968, made him a popular topic of discourse among religious thinkers, associating him with Gregory of Nyssa, Johannes Scotus Eriugena, Meister Eckhart, St John of the Cross and other mystics who, believing it impossible to reach God by reason alone, approached God experientially with 'transcending ideas, images, and sense impressions'. This so-called 'negative theology', according to Merton scholar John F Teahan, offered a process termed 'knowing by unknowing', meaning that one attempted to induce a mystical experience for the self rather than assign attributes to God.[121] Merton's affinity to this tradition was noted in his support of intuitive certainty over claims to knowledge predicated on complex reasoning.[122]

In the last years of his life, Merton was drawn to Eastern religions and the affinity between elements in Christian thought and the concept of 'no-mind' in Zen teachings.[123] His use of the term 'emptiness' was certainly distant from mainstream Catholic theology but fitted comfortably into the way Eckhart and other mystics metaphorically expressed the divine essence. Clearly, Merton had formed a rapprochement with Buddhism by what Teahan explained was recognition 'that God is void of substantiality and form, free from discrimination, fully creative yet beyond definition, whether God may, in fact be seen as emptiness'.[124]

Merton read Suzuki's works and communicated with him long before they met. A dialogue between the two men on the 'Wisdom in Emptiness' appeared in *New Directions* magazine in 1961.[125] When the two did finally meet, Merton felt he was with 'someone who, in a tradition completely different from my own, had matured, had become complete, and had found his way'. In Suzuki he found a man in whom Buddhism was truly alive and who could express the Oriental experience in terms understandable to the Western intellect. As Merton explained, Suzuki 'had a remarkable capacity to transpose Zen into the authentic totalities of Western mystical traditions that were most akin to it'. Although Merton had initially felt that Buddhism was 'a very mysterious and confusing jumble of words, images, doctrines, legends, rituals, buildings, and so forth', he came to view it as a great religion containing an 'inner reality' much like he had found in Christianity, Islam and Judaism—a 'direct confrontation with Absolute Being'. For Christianity the engagement was theological and affective through word and love; in Zen it was through insight and emptiness.[126]

While Suzuki considered Eckhart someone whom the West viewed as a 'completely heretical phenomenon', Merton corrected this opinion, explaining that Eckhart actually represented a little-known but orthodox position within Western religious thought. In any event, Merton was comforted in the fact that Suzuki grasped the intuitive nature of Eckhart's ability to understand the mythical and symbolic language and archetypes found in Scripture and the writings of the Church Fathers—a phenomenon that embarrassed many Catholics and had at times troubled Merton himself. Without being a Christian, Suzuki had understood the importance of symbolism. His work, explained Merton, 'remains with us as a great gift, as one of the unique spiritual and intellectual achievements of our time'.[127]

Merton's influence on Christian mysticism is well documented. Less understood, however, is the extent to which Suzuki influenced Merton's understanding of enlightenment. Merton's study of Eastern thought in the latter years of his life resulted in numerous works, including *The Way of Chuang Tzu* (1969); *Asian Journal* (1973); *Mystics and Zen Masters* (1967); and *Zen and the Birds of Appetite* (1968). Each represented an effort to transform Oriental thought into something understandable to the Western mind, a task he found increasingly important. But even beyond this objective were the series of letters between Suzuki and Merton that demonstrated Suzuki's desire to assist Merton in finding enlightenment despite the ominous hurdles imposed by Christianity's theological myths which weighed heavily on his beliefs.[128]

In 1989, the Vatican Congregation for the Doctrine of the Faith reported that, although not considered Christian, the Eastern approach to prayer was not to be rejected out of hand. Although varied forms of meditation sometimes induced psychological states that created a form of self-absorption, its intense experiences sometimes led to authentic levels of consciousness of divine love. In effect, the Vatican gave recognition to a broad range of Oriental meditations that sought to awaken the inner self to the will of God. As Pascaline Coff of the Osage Monastery explained, the experience 'is not only an awareness of our inner self, but, by a gift of intensified faith, we are aware of an experiential grasp of God present within our inner self'.[129] In Christian Scriptures the prescription for this inner journey was set forth with the words: 'Be still and know that I am God' (Psalm 46:10). The stillness of the self brought the individual to the awakening.[130] Practices long shared by early Christians and some of their spiritual traditions could be found as well in Buddhism. As a process of 'consciousness transformation', or realizing 'the awakened heart', much could be learned from Buddhist teachings. Referring to Shantideva's *Guide to the Bodhisattva's Way of Life*, Coff identified numerous similarities between the writings of Buddhist spiritual masters and the early Christian Fathers.[131]

* * *

Given his years in the United States, Suzuki not only grew to appreciate Western-style spirituality through his reading of Swedenborg, but built a bridge between Western and Eastern traditions without distancing himself from his native roots. Like New Thought which blossomed in early twentieth century, he employed sufficient invocations from Emersonianism, Swedenborgianism and the mysticism of Eckhart to make Zen palatable to the spiritual quests of intellectuals worldwide. In effect, there was sufficient kinship with the West's own sojourn into spirituality that Suzuki's philosophy was able to resonate as a positive contribution of Orientalism in the West. For those beginning to think in this manner, it was not too difficult to reflect on Gautama's constant admonishment to his disciples to be their own lamps and to work out their own salvation—a message as relevant to Emerson and Henry James, Sr as it was to Suzuki. Buddha's silence when it came to the question of 'God', suggesting that the very question had no meaning, placed the issue back in the hands of the questioner, thus opening a path to self-deliverance. Reality was to be accepted just as it presented itself without seeking to replace it with hubris concerning God and His role in ensuring life's purpose, if only for His chosen few. Rather than resort to some form of artificial or meaningless existence, a significant number of postmodernists came to see themselves as creators in their own right, working to realize the joy of a fully integrated life. As Emerson remarked in his Divinity School Address: 'It is still true that tradition characterizes the preaching of this country; that it comes out of the memory, and not out of the soul; that it aims at what is usual, and not at what is necessary and eternal; that thus historical Christianity destroys the power of preaching, by withdrawing it from the exploration of the moral nature of man; where the sublime is, where are the resources of astonishment and power'.[132] With these insights and practices, Suzuki liberated the mind from its usual conscious thought patterns, opening a path of inner directedness. Experience rather than faith or reasoned belief offered the most direct path through life's insecurities and paradoxes.

Such as the love is, such is the wisdom, consequently such is the man.
(Emanuel Swedenborg, *Divine Love and Wisdom*, 1763)

Within the rich tapestry that formed the parameters of the nineteenth and twentieth centuries, the individuals in this study served a purpose larger and more meaningful than themselves. While many of their contemporaries were directed by their passions to prophesize a grinding dialectic, these individuals chose to embrace the possibility of change without the accompaniment of destructive appetites and baneful consequences. Even when their efforts were thwarted, they possessed an unshakeable social conscience that, eschewing public melodrama and acrimonious debate, sought to realize an ever higher spirituality for the individual and society.

Having built their beliefs on a combination of intuition and experience, the individuals highlighted in these sketches were noticeably hard-minded in their opinions. Each was steady in purpose and in the practical utility of his views, some of which were admittedly only half-formed aspirations. Daring to be imaginative, they were strikingly sensitive to the ordinances of the Divine as well as to the central issues of the day, including the troubling state of the world and man's place in it. Marked by a curiosity in most things, they sought a synoptic view that included the combination of an all-knowing deity and humanity's participation in the divine plan. Their formulation of man's inner and outer worlds wove a unity of application and purpose to life, nature and society. With divine thought as the model and with intuition illuminating every experience, history contained nothing that was unintended. Though they failed to define society clearly, they regarded its institutions, including its churches, as synonymous with the development of selfhood which hindered man's spontaneity by enforcing a sense of disparity between God and man. Guided by moral intuition and in search of a more lucid explanation of the finer points of eschatology, they pushed at the margins in their openness to change and in their defiance of systematic theology. They were believers who, feeling unsatisfyingly incomplete with the authorized Christian message, sought to engage themselves and their culture in a more ecstatic, sensual experience that was real, conscious and eternal. In their revolt against the Christian legacy, they rejected the notion of original sin and the older religious view of resurrection; instead, they carried an idealized brand of social reform into their spiritual outlook and a view of creation as a process, not a fixed event in time and space. Redemption involved a combination of education, social engagement, reason and moral intuition.

To a person, the individuals in these sketches accepted science and admired evolution, insisting that the physical world possessed a deeper spirituality that pointed to the ultimate merger of man's spirit with the Divine. In their respect for science—both its method and its depiction of the physical world—there was a collective spirit of cooperation and conciliation. When validated, science had a providential design which pointed inevitably to the world's underlying spiritual meaning. As with so many other things, there was a correspondence between nature and an idealistic belief in the reality of spirit. Ultimately, science, religion and morality were one and the same.

Then again, those examined in this study shared a high degree of inquisitiveness, a sense of self-discovery, an exalted belief in human dignity and an artist's power of inspiration. They exuded a freshness of ideas, being confident in their own authenticity and uninhibited in their affection for the richness of unmediated mystical awareness. Seen from a distance, they appeared as fixed stars in a constellation, their brilliance marking a moment of equipoise between their visions and their unbridled appetite to share them with ever-widening audiences. Evident in their writings were themes expressing confident assurance that individual and societal goals were attainable, that benevolence was a common impulse among all classes, that metaphysical speculation was wasteful energy, and that improvement of humankind through individual and communal effort was possible. Given this ebullient sense of history, it is little wonder that their mood was one of optimism, pointing out the inevitability of progress by means of practical 'uses' that no longer required denominational and doctrinal unity

In their world view, the nation was a kind of soul which demanded an awakening or revival. Recognizing issues of broad moral concern, they urged a silent revolution to liberate humankind of its self-love (*proprium*) with its corresponding 'attachments'. In their political ideas, they harboured a reformer's bias based on Swedenborg's doctrine of uses, meaning unity of life and institutions with God through giving and receiving. '[T]he universe was created by God to give existence to uses; and for this reason the universe may be called a theater of uses', wrote Swedenborg.[1] Provided an individual knew the spiritual counterpart of an object or action, he or she was obliged to know its use or utility as well. In this manner did the *Maximus Homo* of Swedenborg become the Divine Society of Henry James, Sr, the associationism of Albert Brisbane, the Brotherhood of Thomas Lake Harris and the Progressivism of Ralph Waldo Trine. Society, conceived in terms of the fellowship of men, ceased to hold Emerson's self-reliant individual as its creative centre but, instead, postulated the fellowship of individuals the *Maximus Homo*—acting as the Divine's redeemed counterpart.

The focus on practical consequences that played so much a part of Swedenborg's doctrine of uses was illustrated in the life of Harris's Brotherhood, Trine's Progressivism, Suzuki's wood chopper and in the secularized world of the pragmatist. For Swedenborg, of course, the doctrine of uses was a method for revealing the spiritual ends of nature, i.e., providing a worldly setting for spiritual development. For the chance universe of the pragmatists, it was a way of bringing individual identity and purpose into realization. While Swedenborg's ardent faith in a transcendent God seemed like a distant star to the pragmatists' concept of a pluralistic universe and trust in the possibilities of scientific inquiry, both evaluated meaning in terms of its functional use.

Common among these sketches was the emerging view of thought governed by purposes that corresponded to individual and societal needs. No longer was it necessary to argue for an exclusive truth or dogma; instead, there was a recognition of common problems and the prospect of kinship among persons of differing races and beliefs. In place of religious dogmatism was an eclectic spiritualism that not only replaced Descartes's dualism of mind and matter with an epistemology that was plastic and variable according to man's place in the world, but also brought Western thought into approximate alignment with the sacred books of the East. Using Swedenborg's ideas not to expound on customs and conventions but as a display of growing discontent with the Western mind's vision of the self, the subjects of these sketches gave play to an idealism that explained humankind in terms of its progressive perfectibility. Devoted to both modern science and philosophy, they viewed human nature as uncorrupted—an image of the Divine. Moulded by natural forces, man had become a complicit partner in the dawning of a new age where God, nature and mind worked in unison to create humanity's redeemed form. Rather than the popular concept of the universe unfolding by chance, God used the growth of consciousness to reunite man with Himself using the acquisition of mind to bring order and purpose to the universe.

ENDNOTES

INTRODUCTION

[1] Peter Gay, *The Enlightenment: An Interpretation: The Rise of Modern Paganism* (New York: Vintage Books, 1966), p. x.

[2] Clarke Garrett, 'Swedenborg and the Mystical Enlightenment in Late Eighteenth-Century England', in *Journal of the History of Ideas*, vol. 45 (1984), pp. 67-81.

[3] Leigh Eric Schmidt, 'The Making of Modern "Mysticism"', in *Journal of the American Academy of Religion*, vol. 71, no. 2 (June 2003), p. 281.

[4] Sydney Ahlstrom, *A Religious History of the American People*, 2nd edn. (New Haven: Yale University Press, 2004), p. 483.

[5] Quoted in Rick Fields, *How the Swans Came to the Lake: A Narrative History of Buddhism in America* (Boulder, co: Shambhala, 1981), p. 67.

[6] Read Tiruvalum Subba Row, *The Philosophy of the Bhagavad-Gita* (Madras: Theosophical Publishing House, 1921); Annie Besant, *Hints on the Study of the Bhagavad Gita* (Benares: Theosophical Publishing Society, 1906); Prem Nath Bazaz, *The Role of the Bhagavad Gita in Indian History* (New Delhi: Sterling Publishers, 1975); J N Farquhar, *Gita and Gospel* (Madras: Christian Literature Society for India, 1903); Eric J Sharpe, 'Western Images of the "Bhagavadgītā" 1885-1985', in *Journal of South Asian Literature*, vol. 23 (1998), pp. 47-57; Eric J Sharpe, 'Protestant Missionaries and the Study of the Bhagavad Gita', in *International Bulletin of Missionary Research*, vol. 6, no. 4 (October 1982), pp. 155-9.

[7] Ralph Waldo Emerson, 'Swedenborg; or, the Mystic', from *Representative Men* (1850), in *The Complete Works of Ralph Waldo Emerson*, vol. IV (Boston: Houghton Mifflin Co., 1876), p. 135.

[8] Charles Carroll Bonney, 'The Genesis of the World's Religious Congresses of 1893', in *New Church Review*, vol. 1 (1894), p. 15.

9   Richard Hughes Seager, *The World's Parliament of Religions: The East/West Encounter, Chicago, 1893* (Bloomington: Indiana University Press, 1995), pp. xxviii-xxix.

CHAPTER ONE

1   Van Wyck Brooks, *New England: Indian Summer 1865-1915* (New York: E P Dutton and Co., 1940), p. 133.

2   William James (ed.), *The Literary Remains of the Late Henry James* (Boston: James R Osgood and Co., 1885), p. 13.

3   Robert Sandeman, *Letters on Theron and Aspasio. Addressed to the Author* (New York: John S Taylor, 1838), pp. 33-4, 73, 76.

4   Read John Walker, *Essays and Correspondence, Chiefly on Scriptural Subjects* (London: Longman, Orme, Brown, Green, and Longman's, 1838); and Jonathan Edwards, *An Essay on the Nature of True Virtue* (London: W Oliver, 1778).

5   Sampson Reed, 'Oration on Genius', in Perry Miller (ed.), *The Transcendentalists: An Anthology* (Cambridge: Harvard University Press, 2001), pp. 50-9.

6   Henry James, Sr, *Society: The Redeemed Form of Man, and The Earnest of God's Omnipotence in Human Nature: Affirmed in Letters to a Friend* (Boston: Houghton, Osgood and Co., 1879), p. 45.

7   Jacqueline E M Latham, 'Henry James Senior's Mrs. Chichester', in *Henry James Review*, vol. 14 (1993), pp. 132-40.

8   Henry James, Sr, *Society: The Redeemed Form of Man*, pp. 48-59, 72.

9   Henry James, Sr, *Substance and Shadow: Or, Morality and Religion in Their Relation to Life: An Essay Upon the Physics of Creation* (Boston: Ticknor and Fields, 1863), pp. 33-4; Henry James, Sr, 'Swedenborg as a Theologian', in *Massachusetts Quarterly Review*, vol. 1 (1848), p. 295; W H Kimball, 'Swedenborg and Henry James', in *Journal of Speculative Philosophy*, vol. 17 (1883), pp. 113-30.

10   John B Wilson, 'Emerson and the "Rochester Rappings"', in *New England Quarterly*, vol. 41 (1968), pp. 248-58.

11   Henry James, Sr, *Lectures and Miscellanies* (New York: Redfield, 1852), pp. 407-10, 418.

12   The manuscript was first published in *Atlantic Monthly*, vol. 54 (1884), pp. 649-62. It has been suggested that Dewhurst could have been intended to depict the real life of Robert White Dunlap, a classmate of James. See Edward Howell Roberts (ed.), *Biographical Catalogue of the Princeton Theological Seminary, 1815-1932* (Princeton, NJ: Trustees, 1939), p. 86. See also Heather L Nadelman, 'Creating an Immortal Life: A Consideration of the Autobiography of Henry James, Sr.', in *The New England Quarterly*, vol. 66 (1993), pp. 247-8.

13 William James (ed.), *The Literary Remains of the Late Henry James*, pp. 125, 127, 138, 140. See also Howard Feinstein, *Becoming William James* (Ithaca, NY: Cornell University Press, 1984), pp. 39-44.

14 William James (ed.), *The Literary Remains of the Late Henry James*, pp. 151, 149, 147.

15 Ibid., pp. 154-7.

16 Ibid., pp. 158-60, 167, 185.

17 Henry James, Sr, *Lectures and Miscellanies*, pp. 378, 384, 306, 390.

18 Frederic Harold Young, *The Philosophy of Henry James, Sr.* (New York: Bookman Associates, 1951), p. 13.

19 Henry James, Sr, *Christianity the Logic of Creation* (London: William White, 1857), pp. 40, 231.

20 Henry James, Sr, *Society: The Redeemed Form of Man*, pp. 41-2.

21 Henry James, Sr, *Moralism and Christianity; Or Man's Experience and Destiny* (New York: J S Redfield, 1850), p. 144.

22 Henry James, Sr, *The Nature of Evil, Considered in a Letter to the Rev. Edward Beecher, D.D. author of 'The Conflict of Ages.'* (New York: Appleton, 1855), pp. 15-16.

23 Henry James, Sr, *The Secret of Swedenborg: Being an Elucidation of His Doctrine of the Divine Natural Humanity* (Boston: Fields, Osgood, and Co., 1869), pp. 77, 81, 97-8.

24 Henry James, Sr, *Letter to a Swedenborgian* (New York: John Allen, 1847), pp. 1-3, 7, 9.

25 Ibid., pp. 10, 11, 19, 24.

26 Henry James, Sr, *Substance and Shadow*, pp. 14, 24-5, 27.

27 Henry James, Sr, *Christianity the Logic of Creation*, p. iv.

28 Henry James, Sr, *Letter to a Swedenborgian*, pp. 11, 13, 19, 24; Frederic Young, *The Philosophy of Henry James, Sr.*, p. 14. Notwithstanding James's view, the American Swedenborgians were becoming an organized sect with some 850 members by 1840 and twenty ministers. Lay leadership was passing into the hands of professional ministers. See Carl Th. Odhner, *Annals of the New Church, 1698-1850* (Bryn Athyn, PA: Academy of the New Church, 1904), pp. 277-8, 566.

29 Henry James, Sr, *Society: The Redeemed Form of Man*, pp. 88-9.

30 Henry James, Sr, *Lectures and Miscellanies*, pp. 392-3.

31 Quoted in William James (ed.), *The Literary Remains of the Late Henry James*, pp. 49, 54-5.

32 Henry James, Sr, *The Nature of Evil*, pp. 41, 46.

33 Henry James, Sr, *Society: The Redeemed Form of Man*, p. 476; Henry James, Sr, 'Religion Old and New', in *The Radical*, vol. 1 (1866), p. 100.

34 Henry James, Sr, *Lectures and Miscellanies*, pp. 147, 154-5, 161, 164, 180.

35 Henry James, Sr, *The Nature of Evil*, pp. 6-7.

36 Henry James, Sr, *Substance and Shadow*, pp. 179, 182.

37 Henry James, Sr, *The Secret of Swedenborg*, pp. iv-vii.

38 Ibid., pp. 6-9.

39 William James (ed.), *The Literary Remains of the Late Henry James*, p. 83.

40 Henry James, Sr, *The Secret of Swedenborg*, pp. 40, 202.

41 Henry James, Sr, *Lectures and Miscellanies*, p. 281.

42 Henry James, Sr, *Moralism and Christianity*, pp. 121, 122, 127.

43 Henry James, Sr, *Substance and Shadow*, pp. 45, 63.

44 Ibid., pp. 147, 154-5; Ralph Barton Perry, 'Religion Versus Morality According to the Elder Henry James', in *International Journal of Ethics*, vol. 42 (1932), pp. 295-6.

45 William James (ed.), *The Literary Remains of the Late Henry James*, pp. 236-7, 311-13.

46 Henry James, Sr, *Society: The Redeemed Form of Man*, p. 74.

47 William James (ed.), *The Literary Remains of the Late Henry James*, p. 272.

48 Clement John Wilkinson, *James John Garth Wilkinson: A Memoir of His Life, With a Selection from His Letters* (London: Kegan Paul, Trench, Trübner and Co., 1911), p. 145.

49 Henry James, Sr, *Moralism and Christianity*, pp. 92-3. See also Victor Hennequin, *Love in the Phalanstery*, tr. with a preface by Henry James, Sr (New York: Dewitt and Davenport, 1849).

50 Henry James, Sr, *What Constitutes the State? A Lecture Delivered Before the Young Men's Association of the City of Albany* (New York: John Allen, 1846), pp. 22, 38.

51 Ibid., pp. 40-4.

52 Henry James, Sr, *Moralism and Christianity*, pp. 39, 80-1, 89.

53 Ibid., pp. 40, 44-5.

54 Henry James, Sr, *Lectures and Miscellanies*, pp. 3-6, 9, 10, 11, 20, 43-4, 45. See George Bancroft, 'The Office of the People in Art, Government, and Religion', in *Literary and Historical Miscellanies* (New York: Harper and Brothers, 1855), pp. 408-35.

55 Henry James, Sr, *The Social Significance of Our Institutions: An Oration Delivered by Request of the Citizens at Newport, R.I., July 4th, 1861* (Boston: Ticknor and Fields, 1861), pp. 11, 9.

56 Henry James, Sr, *Lectures and Miscellanies*, pp. 62-3, 64, 66-9, 72, 92-3.

57 Henry James, Sr, *Society: The Redeemed Form of Man*, p. 226.

58 Paul Jerome Croce, 'Mankind's Own Providence: From Swedenborgian Philosophy of Use to William James's Pragmatism', in *Transactions of the Charles S. Peirce Society*, vol. 43 (2007), p. 499.

59 Henry James, Sr, *Society: The Redeemed Form of Man*, pp. 229-30, 238; William James

(ed.), *The Literary Remains of the Late Henry James*, p. 279. See also Ralph Barton Perry, *The Thought and Character of William James*, 2 vols. (Boston: Little, Brown and Co., 1935), vol. I, p. 17.

[60] Henry James, Sr, *Society: The Redeemed Form of Man*, pp. 298, 239.

[61] Henry James, Sr, *Substance and Shadow*, pp. 454, 459. See also Paul J Croce, 'A Scientific Spiritualism: The Elder James's Adaptation of Emanuel Swedenborg', in Erland J Brock (ed.), *Swedenborg and His Influence* (Bryn Athyn, PA: The Academy of the New Church, 1988), p. 256.

[62] Henry James, Sr, *Christianity the Logic of Creation*, pp. 170, 171, 176, 177.

[63] Henry James, Sr, *Society: The Redeemed Form of Man*, pp. 144-5, 158-9.

[64] William James (ed.), *The Literary Remains of the Late Henry James*, p. 14.

[65] See Daniel Aaron, *Men of Good Hope* (New York: Oxford University Press, 1951); John L Thomas, *Alternative America: Henry George, Edward Bellamy, Henry Demarest Lloyd and the Adversary Tradition* (Cambridge, MA: Harvard University Press, 1983); James T Kloppenberg, *Uncertain Victory: Social Democracy and Progressivism in European and American Thought, 1870-1920* (New York: Oxford University Press, 1986).

[66] Richard Louis Trammell, 'Charles Sanders Peirce and Henry James the Elder', in *Transactions of the Charles S. Peirce Society*, vol. 9 (1973), pp. 202-20; Charles Sanders Peirce, 'Review of the Secret of Swedenborg by Henry James', in *North American Review*, vol. 110 (1870), p. 467.

[67] William James (ed.), *The Literary Remains of the Late Henry James*, pp. 9, 16. See also Austin Warren, *The Elder James* (New York: Macmillan, 1934).

[68] Clinton Hartley Grattan, *The Three Jameses: A Family of Minds* (London: Longmans and Co., 1932), p. 358. See also F O Matthiessen, *The James Family* (New York: Alfred A Knopf, 1947).

[69] R W B Lewis, *The Jameses: A Family Narrative* (New York: Farrar, Straus, Giroux, 1991), p. 38.

[70] See Perry, *The Thought and Character of William James*, vol. I, pp. 26-7; Henry James, Sr, *Christianity the Logic of Creation*, p. 201.

[71] *Letters of Charles Eliot Norton*, ed. M A De Wolfe Howe, 2 vols. (Boston: Houghton Mifflin, 1913), vol. II, p. 379.

[72] Rollo Ogden (ed.), *Life and Letters of Edwin Lawrence Godkin*, 2 vols. (New York: Macmillan and Co., 1907), vol. II, pp. 117-18.

[73] William James (ed.), *The Literary Remains of the Late Henry James*, p. 72.

[74] Larry J Reynolds and Tibbie E Lynch, 'Sense and Transcendence in Emerson, Thoreau, and Whitman', in *The South Central Bulletin*, vol. 39 (1979), pp. 148-51.

75 'I become a transparent eyeball. I am nothing. I see all. The currents of the Universal Being circulate through me; I am part or particle of God'. See Ralph Waldo Emerson, *Nature, Addresses, and Lectures*, ed. Robert E Spiller and Alfred Ferguson (Cambridge: Harvard University Press, 1971), p. 10.

76 'All sound heard at the greatest possible distance produces one and the same effect, a vibration of the universal lyre, just as the intervening atmosphere makes a distant ridge of earth interesting to our eyes by the azure tint it imparts to it': Henry David Thoreau, 'Sounds', in *Walden*, ed. Raymond MacDonald Alden (New York: Longmans, Green, and Co., 1910), p. 103.

77 'How you settled your head athwart my hips and gently turn'd over upon me, / And parted the shirt from my bosom-bone, and plunged your tongue to my bare-stript heart, / And reach'd till you felt my beard, and reach'd till you held my feet': Walt Whitman, 'Song of Myself', in *Leaves of Grass* (Brooklyn, NY: Walter Whitman, 1855), p. 15.

78 Ralph Waldo Emerson, 'Self-Reliance', in *Essays: First Series* (Boston: Phillips, Sampson, and Co., 1857 [1841]), p. 39.

79 Quoted in James Reed, 'Biographical Preface', in Sampson Reed, *Observations on the Growth of the Mind* (Boston: Houghton, Mifflin, and Co., 1889), p. viii; Kenneth Walter Cameron, *Emerson the Essayist* (Raleigh, NC: Thistle Press, 1945), p. 13.

80 Thomas Worcester was invited to become pastor of the Boston Society of the New Church in 1821 and led its New Churchmen for many years, introducing the doctrines of the church and the works of Swedenborg into Massachusetts and Boston society in particular. With Thomas Worcester's appointment as an overseer of Harvard College in 1854 and Harvard's conferring on him the Doctor of Divinity, Swedenborgianism became more or less officially recognized and respected in New England. See Sampson Reed, *A Biographical Sketch of Thomas Worcester, D.D.* (Boston: Massachusetts New Church Union, 1880), pp. 18, 99-100.

81 Clarence Hotson, 'Emerson and the Swedenborgians', in *Studies in Philology*, vol. 27 (1930), pp. 517-18. See Ralph Waldo Emerson, *The Journals of Ralph Waldo Emerson*, ed. E W Emerson and W E Forbes, 10 vols. (Boston: Houghton Mifflin Co., 1909-14), vol. II, p. 25; Sampson Reed, *A Biographical Sketch of Thomas Worcester D.D.*; Sampson Reed, *Observations on the Growth of the Mind* (Boston: Cummings, Hilliard and Co., 1826).

82 Read Guillaume Oegger, *Le Vraie Messie, ou l'Ancien et le Nouveau Testamens examinés d'après les principes de la langue de la nature* (Paris: Felix Locquin, 1829).

83 Ralph Waldo Emerson, *Journals*, vol. II, p. 124. See also Clarence Hotson, 'Sampson Reed, a Teacher of Emerson', in *New England Quarterly*, vol. 2 (1929), pp. 249-77.

84 Charles Eliot Norton (ed.), *The Correspondence of Thomas Carlyle and Ralph Waldo Emerson, 1834-1872*, 2 vols. (London: Chatto and Windus, 1883), vol. I, p. 19.

85   Ibid., pp. 32-3.

86   Ralph Waldo Emerson, *Journals*, vol. III, p. 430.

87   Ralph Waldo Emerson, *The Prose Works of Ralph Waldo Emerson: In Two Volumes* (Boston: Fields and Osgood, 1870), vol. I, p. 91.

88   Oliver Wendell Holmes, *Ralph Waldo Emerson* (Boston: Houghton, Mifflin and Co., 1886), p. 115.

89   Ralph Waldo Emerson, 'The American Scholar: An Address', in *Select Essays and Addresses, Including The American Scholar*, ed. Eugene D Holmes (New York: The Macmillan Co., 1906), pp. 185-208.

90   James Russell Lowell, *The Writings of James Russell Lowell: Literary Essays* (Boston: Houghton, Mifflin, 1892), vol. I, p. 353.

91   Emerson's lecture on Swedenborg, which was repeated numerous times in America and in England, turned out to be a milder presentation than what was eventually published in *Representative Men*. See Clarence Hotson, 'Emerson and the Swedenborgians', pp. 535-6. Between November 1847 and February of 1848, Emerson visited twenty-five towns in England and Scotland, delivering a total of sixty-four lectures covering sixteen different topics, the most popular being 'Domestic Life' and 'Napoleon'. Of the total number of lectures, he delivered 'Swedenborg: the Mystic' only twice, once in Manchester and once in Liverpool. Townsend Scudder, 'A Chronological List of Emerson's Lectures on His British Lecture Tour of 1847-1848', in *PMLA*, vol. 51 (1936), pp. 243-8.

92   Ralph Waldo Emerson, 'Swedenborg; or, the Mystic', from *Representative Men* (1850), in *The Complete Works of Ralph Waldo Emerson*, vol. IV (Boston: Houghton Mifflin Co., 1876), pp. 103-5.

93   Clarence Hotson, 'Emerson's Biographical Sources for Swedenborg', in *Studies in Philology*, vol. 26 (1929), pp. 23-46.

94   Ralph Waldo Emerson, 'Swedenborg; or, the Mystic', p. 125.

95   Ralph Waldo Emerson, *The Complete Works of Ralph Waldo Emerson*, 12 vols. (Boston: Houghton, Mifflin and Co., 1904), vol. VII, p. 290.

96   Ralph Waldo Emerson, 'Worship', in *The Complete Works of Ralph Waldo Emerson*, vol. VI, pp. 208-9.

97   Ralph Waldo Emerson, *Journals*, vol. VIII, pp. 298-9. See also Van Wyck Brooks, *The Flowering of New England* (New York: Dutton, 1936); Van Wyck Brooks, *The Life of Emerson* (New York: Literary Guild, 1932).

98   Ralph Waldo Emerson, 'Swedenborg; or, the Mystic', p. 144.

99   Holmes, *Ralph Waldo Emerson*, p. 201.

100 Ralph Waldo Emerson, *Journals*, vol. X, pp. 198-9.

101 Ibid., vol. IV, p. 491.

102 Ibid., vol. V, p. 477.

103 Ibid., vol. VIII, p. 477.

104 Quoted in Steven Nadler, 'Spinoza the Atheist', at <http://rationalist.org.uk/articles/964/spinoza-the-atheist>, accessed 20 January 2014.

105 Patrick F Quinn, 'Emerson and Mysticism', in *American Literature*, vol. 21 (1950), pp. 408-9.

106 Protap Chunder Mozoomdar, 'Emerson as Seen from India', in F B Sanborn (ed.), *The Genius and Character of Emerson; Lectures at the Concord School of Philosophy* (Port Washington, NY: Kennikat Press, 1971), p. 369.

107 Mozoomdar, 'Emerson as Seen from India', p. 371.

108 Ralph Waldo Emerson, *Journals*, vol. IX, pp. 20-1. See also Peter A Obuchowski, 'Emerson, Evolution, and the Problem of Evil', in *The Harvard Theological Review*, vol. 72 (1979), pp. 150-6.

109 Swami Paramananda, *Emerson and Vedanta* (Boston: The Vedanta Center, 1918), p. 65.

110 Russell B Goodman, 'East-West Philosophy in Nineteenth-Century America: Emerson and Hinduism', in *Journal of the History of Ideas*, vol. 51 (1990), p. 634.

111 Ibid., p. 625. See also Arthur Christy, *The Orient in American Transcendentalism: A Study of Emerson, Thoreau, and Alcott* (New York: Columbia University Press, 1932); Frederic Ives Carpenter, *Emerson and Asia* (Cambridge: Harvard University Press, 1930); Leyla Goren, *Elements of Brahmanism in the Transcendentalism of Emerson*, ed. Kenneth Walter Cameron (Hartford: Transcendental Books, 1977); Dale Riepe, 'Emerson and Indian Philosophy', in *Journal of the History of Ideas*, vol. 28 (1967), pp. 115-22; Carl T Jackson, *The Oriental Religions and American Thought* (Westport: Greenwood Press, 1981); B L Packer, *Emerson's Fall: A New Interpretation of the Major Essays* (New York: Continuum, 1982); Harold Bloom, *Agon: Towards a Theory of Revision* (New York: Oxford University Press, 1982); Julie Ellison, *Emerson's Romantic Style* (Princeton: Princeton University Press, 1984); and Russell B Goodman, *American Philosophy and the Romantic Tradition* (Cambridge: Cambridge University Press, 1990).

112 Russell B Goodman, 'East-West Philosophy in Nineteenth-Century America: Emerson and Hinduism', p. 628. See also Victor Cousin, *Course of the History of Modern Philosophy*, tr. O W Wight, 2 vols. (New York: D Appleton, 1872).

113 See W T Harris, 'Emerson's Orientalism', in F B Sanborn (ed.), *The Genius and Character of Emerson*, pp. 372-85; Charles Malloy, 'An Interpretation of Emerson's "Brahma"', in *Journal of Practical Metaphysics*, vol. 1 (1896), pp. 31-6.

114 See *The Vishnu Purana, A System of Hindu Mythology and Traditions*, tr. H H Wilson (London: J Murray, 1840).

115 Ralph Waldo Emerson, 'Plato; or, the Philosopher', from *Representative Men* (1850), in *The Complete Works of Ralph Waldo Emerson*, vol. IV, pp. 49-52.

116 Perry Miller, 'Jonathan Edwards to Emerson', in *The New England Quarterly*, vol. 13 (1940), pp. 596, 605, 617.

117 René Wellek, 'Emerson and German Philosophy', in *The New England Quarterly*, vol. 16 (1943), p. 62. See also John Smith Harrison, *The Teachers of Emerson* (New York: Sturgis and Walton Co., 1910); F T Thompson, 'Emerson's Indebtedness to Coleridge', in *Studies in Philology*, vol. 23 (1926), pp. 55-76; Charles Eliot Norton (ed.), *The Correspondence of Thomas Carlyle and Ralph Waldo Emerson, 1834-1872*, vol. I, p. 50; F W Holls (ed.), *Correspondence Between Ralph Waldo Emerson and Herman Grimm* (Port Washington, NY: Kennikat Press, 1971).

118 William James (ed.), *The Literary Remains of the Late Henry James*, pp. 298-301.

119 Giles Gunn, 'Henry James, Senior: American Eccentric or American Original?', in *The Journal of Religion*, 54 (1974), p. 238. See Evlyn Barish, *Emerson: The Roots of Prophesy* (Princeton, NJ: Princeton University Press, 1989); Mary K Cayton, *Emerson's Emergence: Self and Society in the Transformation of New England, 1800-1845* (Chapel Hill: University of North Carolina Press, 1989).

120 William James (ed.), *The Literary Remains of the Late Henry James*, pp. 294, 297.

121 Henry James, Sr, 'Emerson', in *Atlantic Monthly*, vol. 94 (1904), p. 740.

122 William T Stafford, 'Emerson and the James Family', in *American Literature*, vol. 24 (1953), pp. 435-6; F O Matthiessen, *The James Family*, p. 428, Oliver Wendell Holmes, *Ralph Waldo Emerson*, pp. 166-70.

123 Quoted in James Elliot Cabot, *A Memoir on Ralph Waldo Emerson*, 2 vols. (Boston: Houghton Mifflin and Co., 1887), vol. I, p. 358. See also Stephen E Whicher, *Freedom and Fate: An Inner Life of Ralph Waldo Emerson* (Philadelphia: University of Pennsylvania Press, 1953); Jonathan Bishop, *Emerson on the Soul* (Cambridge: Harvard University Press, 1964).

CHAPTER TWO

1 John Humphrey Noyes, *History of American Socialisms* (Philadelphia: J B Lippincott and Co., 1870), p. 8.

2 The Owenite communities included: Blue Spring Community in Indiana; Co-Operative Society in Pennsylvania; Coxsackie Community in New York; Forrestville Community in Indiana; Franklin Community in New York; Haverstraw Community in New York; Kendal

Community in Ohio; Macluria in Indiana; New Harmony in Indiana; Nashoba in Tennessee; and Yellow Spring Community in Ohio.

3   These included: Alphadelphia Phalanx, Michigan; Brook Farm, Massachusetts; Brooke's Experiment, Ohio; Bureau Co. Phalanx, Illinois; Clarkson Industrial Association, New York; Clermont Phalanx, Ohio; Columbian Phalanx, Ohio; Garden Grove, Iowa; Goose Pond Community, Pennsylvania; Grand Prairie Community, Ohio; Hopedale, Massachusetts; Integral Phalanx, Illinois; Jefferson Co. Industrial Association, New York; Lagrange Phalanx, Indiana; Leraysville Phalanx, Pennsylvania; Marlboro Association, Ohio; McKean Co. Association, Pennsylvania; Moorhouse Union, New York; North American Phalanx, New Jersey; Northampton Association, Massachusetts; Ohio Phalanx, Ohio; One-mentian Community, Pennsylvania; Ontario Phalanx, New York; Prairie Home Community, Ohio; Raritan Bay Union, New Jersey; Sangamon Phalanx, Illinois; Skaneateles Community, New York; Social Reform Unity, Pennsylvania; Sodus Bay Phalanx, New York; Spring Farm Association, Wisconsin; Sylvania Association, Pennsylvania; Trumbull Phalanx, Ohio; Washtenaw Phalanx, Michigan; Wisconsin Phalanx, Wisconsin.

4   Noyes, *History of American Socialisms*, pp. 14-20.

5   Charles Pellarin, *The Life of Charles Fourier*, tr. Francis Shaw (New York: William H Graham, 1848), pp. 10, 14-16.

6   Pellarin, *The Life of Charles Fourier*, pp. 21-3, 24-6.

7   François Charles Marie Fourier, 'Of Commerce', in *Selections from the Works of Fourier*, tr. Julia Franklin, introd. Charles Gide (London: Swan Sonnenschein and Co., 1901), pp. 91-108.

8   Fourier quoted in David A Zonderman, 'George Ripley's Unpublished Lecture on Charles Fourier', in *Studies in the American Renaissance* (1982), p. 198. See also Arthur O Lovejoy, *The Great Chain of Being: A Study of the History of an Idea* (New York: Harper and Row, 1960).

9   Zonderman, 'George Ripley's Unpublished Lecture on Charles Fourier', p. 193.

10   Fourier, 'Of the Role of the Passions', in *Selections from the Works of Fourier*, p. 66.

11   Jean Baptiste Nacquart's *Traité sur la nouvelle physiologie du cerveau, ou Exposition de la doctrine de Gall sur la structure et les fonctions de cet organe* appeared in 1808; this was followed in 1809 by Gall and Spurzheim's *Recherches sur le système nerveux en général, et sur celui du cerveau en particulier*; and in 1810 by the first two volumes of Gall and Spurzheim's *Anatomie et physiologie du système nerveux en général, et du cerveau en particulier*. The latter work was completed in four volumes in 1819 (volumes 3 and 4 bearing only Gall's name) and appeared in a second edition of six volumes in 1822-5.

12   Zonderman, 'George Ripley's Unpublished Lecture on Charles Fourier', p. 203.

13   Charles Fourier, *The Passions of the Human Soul, and Their Influence on Society and Civilization*, tr. John Morell, introd. Hugh Doherty, 2 vols. (London: Hippolyte Bailliere, 1851), vol. II, pp. 273, 307. See also J Goldstein, *The Post-Revolutionary Self: Politics and Psyche in France, 1750-1850* (Cambridge, MA: Harvard University Press, 2005).

14   Jonathan Beecher, *Charles Fourier: The Visionary and His World* (Berkeley: University of California Press, 1986), p. 166; Albert Brisbane, *Theory of the Functions of the Human Passions, Followed by an Outline View of the Fundamental Principles of Fourier's Theory of Social Science* (New York: Miller, Orton, and Mulligan, 1856), p. 400; Albert Brisbane, 'The American Associationists', in *The United States Magazine and Democratic Review* (February, 1846), pp. 142-8.

15   Pellarin, *The Life of Charles Fourier*, p. 39.

16   See Charles Fourier, *Piéges et charlatanisme des deux sectes Saint-Simon et Owen, qui promettent l'association et le progrès* (Paris: Bossange père, 1831).

17   Pellarin, *The Life of Charles Fourier*, pp. 67-8, 74.

18   *Selections from the Works of Fourier*, p. 41.

19   Pellarin, *The Life of Charles Fourier*, p. 80.

20   Fourier, 'Social Evolution', in *Selections from the Works of Fourier*, pp. 50-2.

21   Fourier, 'Of the Condition of Women', in *Selections from the Works of Fourier*, pp. 77, 80. See also Parke Godwin, *A Popular View of the Doctrines of Charles Fourier, with the Addition of Democracy, Constructive and Pacific* (Philadelphia: Porcupine Press, 1972 [1844]); Victor Hennequin, *Love in the Phalanstery* (New York: Dewitt and Davenport, 1849); Marx Lazarus, *Love vs. Marriage* (New York: Fowlers and Wells, 1852).

22   Fourier, *The Passions of the Human Soul*, vol. I, pp. 151-8, 206, 229.

23   Ibid., vol. II, pp. 252-84.

24   Fourier, 'Of Association', in *Selections from the Works of Fourier*, p. 127.

25   Fourier, 'The Phalanstery', in *Selections from the Works of Fourier*, pp. 137-40, 141-2.

26   Fourier, 'Distribution', in *Selections from the Works of Fourier*, pp. 181-3, 189.

27   Fourier, 'Attractive Labor', in *Selections from the Works of Fourier*, p. 164.

28   Fourier, 'Of Education', in *Selections from the Works of Fourier*, pp. 68-70.

29   Fourier, 'Little Hordes', in *Selections from the Works of Fourier*, pp. 170-5.

30   Fourier, 'Distribution', in *Selections from the Works of Fourier*, p. 183.

31   Fourier, 'Of Manufacturing Production', in *Selections from the Works of Fourier*, pp. 17-19.

32   Fourier, 'Of Agricultural Production', in *Selections from the Works of Fourier*, p. 115.

33   Fourier, 'The Phalanstery', in *Selections from the Works of Fourier*, pp. 143-62.

34   Fourier, 'The Communal Counting-House', in *Selections from the Works of Fourier*, pp. 131-6.

35 Brisbane, *Theory of the Functions of the Human Passions*, pp. 60-1.

36 Fourier, *The Passions of the Human Soul*, vol. I, pp. 104-9.

37 *Selections from the Works of Fourier*, p. 41. See also, Madame Gatti de Gamond, *The Phalanstery: or, Attractive Industry and Moral Harmony* (London: Whittaker, 1841).

38 Carl J Guarneri, 'The Americanization of Utopia: Fourierism and the Dilemma of Utopian Dissent in the United States', in *Utopian Studies*, vol. 5 (1994), p. 73. See also Gilbert Seldes, *The Stammering Century* (New York: Harper and Row, 1965); Van Wyck Brooks, *The Flowering of New England* (New York: E P Dutton, Inc., 1940); Alice Felt Tyler, *Freedom's Ferment* (Minneapolis: University of Minnesota, 1944).

39 *The Phalanx* discontinued its translation of *Quatre Mouvements* and replaced it with *Traité de l'Association Domestique-Agricole* due to its confusing nature, and perhaps because of its eccentricities as well, i.e., Fourier's account of the sexual relations between heavenly bodies.

40 Brisbane, *Theory of the Functions of the Human Passions*, pp. 90-1, 150-7.

41 Albert Brisbane, *A Concise Exposition of the Doctrine of Association, or Plan for a Re-organization of Society* (New York: J S Redfield, Clinton Hall, 1843), pp. 7-8.

42 Read Nicholas V Riasanovsky, *The Teaching of Charles Fourier* (Berkeley, CA: University of California Press, 1969); Albert Brisbane, *Association; Or, A Concise Exposition of the Practical Part of Fourier's Social Science* (New York: AMS Press, 1975 [1843]).

43 Brisbane, *A Concise Exposition of the Doctrine of Association*, pp. 3-4.

44 Brisbane, *Theory of the Functions of the Human Passions*, pp. 14, 19, 37.

45 Read Carl J Guarneri, 'Utopian Socialism and American Ideas: The Origin and Doctrines of American Fourierism, 1832-1848', Ph.D. diss. (Johns Hopkins University, 1979); Richard Norman Pettitt, Jr, 'Albert Brisbane: Apostle of Fourierism in the United States, 1834-1890', Ph.D. diss. (Miami University, 1982); Sterling F Delano, *The Harbinger and New England Transcendentalism: A Portrait of Associationism in America* (Rutherford, NJ: Fairleigh Dickinson University Press, 1983).

46 Carl J Guarneri, 'The Associationists: Forging a Christian Socialism in Antebellum America', in *Church History*, vol. 52 (1983), pp. 36-7; Charles Crowe, *George Ripley, Transcendentalist and Utopian Socialist* (Athens, GA: University of Georgia Press, 1967), pp. 170-83; Marguerite Beck Block, *The New Church in the New World: a Study of Swedenborgianism in America* (New York: Henry Holt and Co., 1932), pp. 153-5.

47 Noyes, *History of American Socialisms*, pp. 15-18.

48 Charles Arthur Hawley, 'Swedenborgianism and the Frontier', in *Church History*, vol. 6 (1937), pp. 203-22.

[49] 'Constitution', in *The Dial*, January, 1842.

[50] Ibid.

[51] Read Charles Crowe, 'This Unnatural Union of Phalansteries and Transcendentalists', in *Journal of the History of Ideas*, vol. 20 (1959), pp. 495-502. See also *Constitution of the Brook Farm Phalanx* (West Roxbury, MA: Brook Farm Phalanx, 1845); J T Codman, *Brook Farm: Historic and Personal Memoirs* (Boston: Arena Pub. Co., 1894); J S Dwight, 'Association', in *The Harbinger*, vol. 6 (1847), p. 170.

[52] Richard Francis, 'The Ideology of Brook Farm', in *Studies in the American Renaissance* (1977), pp. 1-48.

[53] Zonderman, 'George Ripley's Unpublished Lecture on Charles Fourier', p. 185.

[54] Noyes, *History of American Socialisms*, pp. 211-20.

[55] Francis, 'The Ideology of Brook Farm', p. 6.

[56] Charles A Dana, *A Lecture on Association, in Its Connection with Religion* (Boston: Benjamin H Greene, 1844), p. 26.

[57] Ibid., pp. 29, 32.

[58] Ibid., pp. 35-41.

[59] Brisbane, *A Concise Exposition of the Doctrine of Association*, p. 2.

[60] William H Channing, 'Fourier and Swedenborg', in *The Present*, vol. 1 (1844); Parke Godwin, *A Popular View of the Doctrines of Charles Fourier* (New York: J S Redfield, 1844).

[61] Guarneri, 'The Associationists: Forging a Christian Socialism in Antebellum America', p. 39.

[62] Zonderman, 'George Ripley's Unpublished Lecture on Charles Fourier', p. 189. See also Harold Clarke Goddard, *Studies in New England Transcendentalism* (New York: Columbia Press, 1908); J T Codman, *Brook Farm: Historic and Personal Memoirs* (Boston: Arena Pub. Co., 1894); Woodbridge Riley, *American Thought From Puritanism to Pragmatism and Beyond* (New York: Henry Holt, 1915).

[63] Henry James, Sr, 'Reply to New Jerusalem Magazine', in *The Harbinger*, vol. 6 (1847), pp. 54-5.

[64] Ralph Waldo Emerson, 'Fourierism and the Socialists', in *Uncollected Prose, Dial Essays, 1842*, at <http://www.emersoncentral.com/fourierism_and_the_socialists.htm>, accessed 6 September 2013.

[65] Ralph Waldo Emerson, 'New England Reformers', in *Essays: Second Series* (Boston: Phillips, Sampson, and Co., 1855), p. 255.

[66] Kenneth Walter Cameron, *Emerson, Thoreau, and Concord in Early Newspapers: Biographical and Historical Lore for the Scholar and General Reader* (Hartford: Transcendental Books, 1958), p. 28.

[67] Quoted in William H Brock, 'Phalanx on a Hill: Responses to Fourierism in the

Transcendentalist Circle', Ph.D. diss. (Chicago: Loyola University, 1996), at <http://leavesof-grass.org/billbrock/fch00.htm>, accessed 6 September 2013. See also Robert E Burkholder and Joel Myerson, *Emerson: An Annotated Secondary Bibliography* (Pittsburgh: University of Pittsburgh Press, 1985), p. 150.

68 'Constitution', by order of the Central Council, George Ripley, President, 20 May 1845, quoted in Noyes, *History of American Socialisms*, p. 528.

69 William H Channing, 'Appeal to Associationists', 6 June 1846, quoted in Noyes, *History of American Socialisms*, pp. 530-1.

70 Noyes, *History of American Socialisms*, p. 539.

71 Charles Crowe, 'Christian Socialism and the First Church of Humanity', in *Church History*, vol. 35 (1966), pp. 93-106.

72 Parke Godwin, *A Popular View of the Doctrines of Charles Fourier*, p. 106.

73 Hugh Doherty, 'A Reply to the Swedenborgians', in *The Phalanx*, vol. 1, no. 18 (7 September 1844), p. 264.

74 Noyes, *History of American Socialisms*, p. 550.

75 Charles Hempel, *The True Organization of the New Church, as Indicated in the Writings of Emanuel Swedenborg, and Demonstrated by Charles Fourier* (New York: William Radde, 1848), pp. 26, 257.

76 Ibid., pp. 10-12.

77 Ibid., p. 18.

CHAPTER THREE

1 William James, *The Varieties of Religious Experience: A Study in Human Nature* (New York: Modern Library, 1902), p. 13; William B Yeats, *A Vision* (New York: Macmillan Co., 1938), pp. 153-4.

2 Andrew Jackson Davis, *The Magic Staff: An Autobiography of Andrew Jackson Davis* (New York: A J Davis and Co., 1864), p. 247. See also Andrew Jackson Davis, *The Principles of Nature, Her Divine Revelations, and a Voice to Mankind*, 2 vols. (London: John Chapman, 1847).

3 John Humphrey Noyes, *History of American Socialisms* (Philadelphia, PA: Lippincott and Co., 1870), pp. 539, 566-7; Robert W Delp, 'Andrew Jackson Davis: Prophet of American Spiritualism', in *Journal of American History*, vol. 54 (1967), p. 44.

4 Arthur A Cuthbert, *The Life and World-Work of Thomas Lake Harris, Written from Direct Personal Knowledge* (Glasgow: C W Pearce and Co., 1909), pp. 100-10. Known as the 'Apostle Paul' of the Brotherhood, Cuthbert was a faithful disciple, colleague and apologist

who met Harris in 1863 and remained true to him until his death.

5   John Weiss (ed.), *Life and Correspondence of Theodore Parker*, 2 vols. (London: Longman, Green, 1863), vol. I, p. 428.

6   Karl Baron von Reichenbach, *Researches of Magnetism, Electricity, Heat, Light, Crystallization, and Chemical Attraction, in their relation to the vital force*, tr. William Gregory (London: Taylor, Walton and Moberly, 1850), pp. 130, 233, 235.

7   Catherine Albanese, *A Republic of Mind and Spirit: A Cultural History of American Metaphysical Religion* (New Haven: Yale University Press, 2007), p. 156. See also Emanuel Swedenborg, *Heaven and Hell*, tr. George F Dole (West Chester, PA: Swedenborg Foundation, 2000), p. 472 n. 155; John S Haller, Jr, *Swedenborg, Mesmer, and the Mind/ Body Connection: The Roots of Complementary Medicine* (West Chester, PA: Swedenborg Foundation, 2010); R Laurence Moore, 'Spiritualism and Science: Reflections on the First Decade of the Spirit Rappings', in *American Quarterly*, vol. 24 (1972), pp. 474-500; David Robinson, *The Unitarians and Universalists* (Westport, CN: Greenwood Press, 1985).

8   Abel Stevens (ed.), *The National Magazine: Devoted to Literature, Art, and Religion*, vol. I (1852), p. 356; Albanese, *A Republic of Mind and Spirit*, p. 268.

9   Emma Hardinge, *Modern American Spiritualism* (New York: The Author, 1870), pp. 208-13; Noyes, *History of American Socialisms*, pp. 568-70; Cathy Luchetti, *Under God's Spell: Frontier Evangelists, 1772-1915* (San Diego: Harcourt Brace Jovanovich, 1989).

10   Quoted in Moore, 'Spiritualism and Science: Reflections on the First Decade of the Spirit Rappings', p. 480.

11   Cuthbert, *The Life and World-Work of Thomas Lake Harris*, p. 132.

12   Thomas Lake Harris, *An Epic of the Starry Heaven* (New York: Partridge and Brittan, 1855), p. 70.

13   Thomas Lake Harris, *A Lyric of the Morning Land* (New York: Partridge and Brittan, 1854), pp. 30, 52.

14   Thomas Lake Harris *A Lyric of the Morning Land*, p. 66.

15   Quoted in Cuthbert, *The Life and World-Work of Thomas Lake Harris*, p. 359. The name 'Issa', otherwise known as 'Lily' or 'Chrysanthea', was Harris's counterpart.

16   S B Brittan quoted in Thomas Lake Harris, *A Lyric of the Golden Age* (New York: Partridge and Brittan, 1856), p. xv.

17   Thomas Lake Harris, *A Lyric of the Golden Age*, pp. 251-2.

18   Frederic Harold Young, *The Philosophy of Henry James, Sr.* (New York: Bookman Associates, 1951), p. 14.

19   Herbert W Schneider and George Lawton, *A Prophet and a Pilgrim: Being the Incredible*

History of Thomas Lake Harris and Laurence Oliphant; Their Sexual Mysticisms and Utopian Communities Amply Documented to Confound the Skeptic (New York: Columbia University Press, 1942), p. 37.

[20] Thomas Lake Harris, *Arcana of Christianity: An Unfolding of the Celestial Sense of the Divine Word, through Thomas Lake Harris. Part III.—The Apocalypse* (New York: Brotherhood of the New Life, 1867), pp. 11, 16.

[21] Proprium was the worldly and corporeal man separate from the spiritual man; it had no life with the Lord but represented everything that was false, infernal and diabolic. Proprium was the cloud of temptations that were subdued only by worship of the Lord. See Emanuel Swedenborg, *Arcana Caelestia*, tr. John Elliott, 12 vols. (London: Swedenborg Society, 1983-99) §§141, 147-9, 999, 1581, 3812.

[22] Carol G Silver, *Strange and Secret Peoples: Fairies and Victorian Consciousness* (New York: Oxford University Press, 1999), Chapter 1.

[23] W B Yeats, 'Swedenborg, Mediums and the Desolate Places', in *Between Method and Madness— Essays on Swedenborg and Literature*, ed. Stephen McNeilly (London: Swedenborg Society, 2005), p. 4; Cuthbert, *The Life and World-Work of Thomas Lake Harris*, pp. 36-7.

[24] Cuthbert, *The Life and World-Work of Thomas Lake Harris*, pp. 37, 56-7.

[25] Thomas Lake Harris, 'The Fairy', in *The Herald of Life*, vol. 4 (1859), p. 160.

[26] Harris, *Arcana of Christianity. . . Part III.—The Apocalypse*, pp. 309-11, 307-8, 386, 390.

[27] Thomas Lake Harris, *First Book of the Christian Religion* (New York: New Church Publishing Association, 1858); *New Church Tracts: The Ohio Series* (Cincinnati: New Church Brethren in Ohio, 1858).

[28] Its officers included Henry J Newton, Edwin R Kirk, Horatio Foster, James A Requa, George W Smith, James P Rogers, Holman J Hale, Israel A Stone and Edson D Hammond.

[29] Cuthbert, *The Life and World-Work of Thomas Lake Harris*, p. 181.

[30] Quoted in Cuthbert, *The Life and World-Work of Thomas Lake Harris*, p. 173.

[31] Phineas P Quimby, *The Complete Writings*, ed. Ervin Seale, 3 vols. (Marina del Rey, CA: DeVorss, 1988); Haller, *Swedenborg, Mesmer, and the Mind/Body Connection*, pp. 158-66.

[32] Robert McCully, 'Swedenborg in 1746-7', in *The Intellectual Repository and New Jerusalem Magazine*, vol. 18 (1871), pp. 221-30; and 'Swedenborg and Harris', in ibid., pp. 341, 344-5.

[33] See Alex Owen, *The Place of Enchantment: British Occultism and the Culture of the Modern* (Chicago: University of Chicago Press, 2004).

[34] Thomas Lake Harris, 'Regina: A Song of Many Days', in *The Herald of Light*, vol. 4 (1859), p. 105.

[35] 'The Rev. T. L. Harris' Mission in Manchester, England', in *The Herald of Light*, vol. 4 (1860), pp. 252-4.

36   Thomas Lake Harris, *The Millennial Age: Twelve Discourses on the Spiritual and Social Aspects of the Times* (New York: New Church Publishing Association, London: W White, Manchester: J W Farquhar and Nottingham: T Stevenson, 1860); Thomas L Harris, *Modern Spiritualism: Its Truths and Its Errors* (London: W White, 1860); Margaret Oliphant, *Memoir of the Life of Laurence Oliphant and of Alice Oliphant, his Wife*, 2 vols. (New York: Harper and Brothers, 1891), vol. II, p. 3.

37   Thomas Lake Harris, 'Editorial Correspondence', in *The Herald of Light*, vol. 4 (1859), pp. 115-16.

38   Ibid., pp. 116-19.

39   [Thomas Lake Harris], 'The New Church', in *The Herald of Light*, vol. 4 (1860), p. 129.

40   Schneider and Lawton, *A Prophet and a Pilgrim*, pp. 47-8.

41   Thomas Lake Harris, *Arcana of Christianity. . . Part III.—The Apocalypse*, pp. 25-6. See also Timothy L Smith, *Revivalism and Social Reform: American Protestantism on the Eve of the Civil War* (Nashville, TN: Abingdon Press, 1957).

42   Quoted in Noyes, *History of American Socialisms*, p. 583.

43   Mary S Emerson, *Among the Chosen* (New York: H Holt and Co., 1884), pp. 29-30.

44   Thomas Lake Harris, *Arcana of Christianity. . . Part III.—The Apocalypse*, pp. 21, 25-6.

45   Ibid., pp. 20-1.

46   Thomas Lake Harris, *The Breath of God with Man: An Essay on the Grounds and Evidences of Universal Religion* (New York: Brotherhood of the New Life, 1867), pp. 17-18; *Arcana of Christianity. . . Part III.—The Apocalypse*, p. 26.

47   Ibid., p. 14.

48   Margaret Oliphant, *Memoir of the Life of Laurence Oliphant*, vol. II, p. 40.

49   Quoted in Schneider and Lawton, *A Prophet and a Pilgrim*, p. 468.

50   See Thomas Lake Harris, 'The Children of Hymen', in *Herald of Light*, vol. II (1858), p. 307.

51   Hannah Whitall Smith, *Religious Fanaticism, Extracts from the Papers of Hannah Whitall Smith*, ed. Ray Strachey (London: Faber and Gwyer, 1928), pp. 229-39.

52   Schneider and Lawton, *A Prophet and a Pilgrim*, pp. 221-2.

53   Margaret Oliphant, *Memoir of the Life of Laurence Oliphant*, vol. II, pp. 6-7, quotation from vol. I, pp. 212-13.

54   It has been suggested that Laurence first heard of Harris in 1860 and perhaps met him in Japan in 1861. See Margaret Oliphant, *Memoir of the Life of Laurence Oliphant*, vol. II, pp. 1-2.

55   Schneider and Lawton, *A Prophet and a Pilgrim*, p. 96.

56   Read Laurence Oliphant, *Piccadilly a Fragment of Contemporary Biography* (Edinburgh: W Blackwood, 1870).

57   Margaret Oliphant, *Memoir of the Life of Laurence Oliphant*, vol. II, pp. 23-5.

58   See <http://lomitaheights.org/kanaye-nagasawa-fountaingrove-and-paradise-ridge-win-ery/>, accessed 17 March 2014. Included among the original fifteen students were Arinori Mori and Naonobu Samejima who became active in the Meiji Enlightenment Movement on their return to Japan, advocating freedom of religion, secular education and replacement of the Japanese language with English. Mori became the Japanese Ambassador to Washington (1871-3) and later minister of Education. See Andrew Cobbing, *The Japanese Discovery of Victorian Britain* (London: Routledge Curzon, 1998); Ivan Parker Hall, *Mori Arinori* (Massachusetts: Harvard University Press, 1973). See also Jean Libby, 'Paper presented to the American Studies Association annual meeting in November 2006', at <http://www.atozproductions.com/files/The_travels_across_America_with_Arinori_Mori.pdf>, accessed 2 February 2014.

59   Louis Le Grande, 'Thomas Lake Harris', in *The Illustrated American* (16 April 1892), p. 402.

60   Schneider and Lawton, *A Prophet and a Pilgrim*, pp. 155, 190-2.

61   Cuthbert, *The Life and World-Work of Thomas Lake Harris*, p. 192.

62   Robert C Fuller, 'Wine, Symbolic Boundary Setting, and American Religious Communities', in *Journal of the American Academy of Religion*, vol. 63 (1995), p. 511. Read also Thomas Lake Harris, *A Voice from Heaven* (Santa Rosa, CA: Fountain Grove Press, 1879) and Thomas Lake Harris, *The Holy City and the Light Therein* (Santa Rosa, CA: Fountain Grove press, 1880). See also Schneider and Lawton, *A Prophet and a Pilgrim*, pp. 314-22.

63   Interestingly, Harris acknowledged Laurence's marriage to Alice only on condition that they remained celibate and agreed to transfer Alice's property over to Harris.

64   Fountaingrove History Folder, Gaye LeBaron Collection, Special Collections, University Library, Sonoma State University. See also <http://lomitaheights.org/kanaye-nagasawa-fountaingrove-and-paradise-ridge-winery/>, accessed 18 January 2016.

65   Read Thomas Lake Harris, *Declarations of the Divine One-Twain* (Santa Rosa, CA: Fountain Grove Press, 1882); and Thomas Lake Harris, *The Wedding Guest* (Santa Rosa, CA: Fountain Grove Press, 1878).

66   Margaret Oliphant, *Memoir of the Life of Laurence Oliphant*, vol. II, pp. 315-74.

67   Quoted in Mark Bevir, 'The West Turns Eastward: Madame Blavatsky and the Transformation of the Occult Tradition', in *Journal of the American Academy of Religion*, vol. 62 (1994), pp. 754-7.

68   'Blavatsky on Swedenborg', at <http://blavatskyTheosophy.com/blavatsky -on-sweden-borg/>, accessed 6 February 2014. See *The Secret Doctrine* (1897), vol. III, p. 425, vol. II, pp. 701-2; *The Mahatma Letters to A. P. Sinnett* (Theosophical University Press Online

Edition), Letter 48, at <http://www.theosociety.org/pasadena/mahatma/ml-48.htm>, accessed 6 February 2014. There were also references to Swedenborg made by Master Morya and Koot Hoomi, Blavatsky's mysterious Indian Gurus. See *The Mahatma Letters*, Letters 40, 48. See also H P Blavatsky, *The Theosophical Glossary*, ed. G R S Mead (London: Theosophical Publishing Society, 1892), p. 316; H P Blavatsky, *The Key to Theosophy; Being a Clear Exposition, in the Form of Question and Answer, of the Ethics, Science, and Philosophy, for the Study of Which the Theosophical Society has been Founded* (London: Theosophical Publishing Society, 1893), p. 213; and H P Blavatsky, *Isis Unveiled*, 2 vols. (New York: J W Bouton, 1877), vol. I, pp. 306, 580 and vol. II, pp. 73, 470.

[69] See Sir Edwin Arnold, *Light of Asia* at <http://www.urbandharma.org/pdf/lightasia.pdf>, accessed 25 January 2014.

[70] Stephen Prothero, 'Henry Steel Olcott and "Protestant Buddhism"', in *Journal of the American Academy of Religion*, vol. 63 (1995), p. 296.

[71] Henry Steel Olcott, *A Buddhist Catechism, According to the Canon of the Southern Church* (Boston: Estes and Lauriat, 1887), pp. 11-13.

[72] 'Preface', in Henry Steel Olcott, *A Buddhist Catechism*.

[73] Thomas Lake Harris, *The Wisdom of the Adepts. Esoteric Science in Human History* (Fountain Grove, CA: Privately Printed, 1884), pp. v-vi.

[74] Ibid., pp. 180, 187-8.

[75] Ibid., p. v.

[76] Ibid., pp. 23-4.

[77] Ibid., p. 195.

[78] Ibid., p. 205.

[79] Ibid., p. 238.

[80] Ibid., p. 255.

[81] Ibid., p. 263.

[82] Ibid., pp. 265-6.

[83] William Q Judge, 'The Brotherhood of the New Life', in *The Path*, vol. 6 (1892), pp. 346-7.

[84] See *The Open Court* magazine (July 1891), p. 84.

[85] Thomas Lake Harris, *Brotherhood of the New Life: Its Fact, Law, Method and Purpose* (Santa Rosa, CA: Fountaingrove Press, 1891), pp. 1, 4, 10-11, 14, 7.

[86] Thomas Lake Harris, *The New Republic, A Discourse of the Prospects, Dangers, Duties and Safeties of the Times* (Santa Rosa, CA: Fountain Grove Press, 1891), pp. 39, 40.

[87] Thomas Lake Harris, *God's Breath in Man and in Humane Society* (Santa Rosa, CA: The Author, 1891), p. 224.

88   Thomas Lake Harris, *The New Republic*, pp. 3, 5, 6, 8, 18.

89   Ibid., pp. 13, 15, 24-5, 28, 27, 29.

90   Schneider and Lawton, *A Prophet and a Pilgrim*, p. 486.

91   See <http://prwinery.com/index.php/Visit-Us/Nagasawa.html>, accessed 1 December 2014; <http://www.sf.us.emb-japan.go.jp/en/e_m01_01_04.htm>, accessed 2 December 2014; and Gaye LeBaron, *The Japanese 'Baron' of Fountaingrove: A Study of Kanaye Nagasawa and the Japanese Disciples of Thomas Lake Harris* (Santa Rosa, CA: Santa Rosa Junior College, 1976).

CHAPTER FOUR

1   Ralph Waldo Emerson, 'The American Scholar: An Address', in *Select Essays and Addresses, Including The American Scholar*, ed. Eugene D Holmes (New York: The Macmillan Co., 1906), p. 205.

2   Joseph F Kett, *The Formation of the American Medical Profession: The Role of Institutions, 1780-1860* (New Haven: Yale University Press, 1968), p. 153.

3   James Tyler Kent, *Lectures on Homeopathic Philosophy* (Lancaster, PA: Examiner Printing House, 1900), p. 85. Kent taught that the law of similars was the 'law of God'. See James Tyler Kent, *Kent's New Remedies, Clinical Cases, Lesser Writings, Aphorisms and Precepts* (New Delhi: B Jain Publishers, 1994), p. 393.

4   John S Haller, *The History of American Homeopathy: From Rational Medicine to Holistic Health Care* (New Brunswick, NJ: Rutgers University Press, 2009), pp. 9, 21, 46-7.

5   Samuel Hahnemann, *The Organon of Homoeopathic Medicine* (Allentown, PA: Academical Bookstore, 1836), Aphorism 9.

6   Marguerite Beck Block, *The New Church in the New World: A Study of Swedenborgianism in America* (New York: Swedenborg Publishing Association, 1984), pp. 161-2.

7   Samuel Hahnemann, *The Chronic Diseases: Their Specific Nature and Homeopathic Treatment*, tr. Charles Hempel, 5 vols. (New York: William Radde, 1845-6), vol. I, p. iv.

8   Quoted in Alexander Wilder, *History of Medicine: A Brief Outline of Medical History from the Earliest Historic Period with an Extended Account of the Various Sects of Physicians and New Schools of Medicine* (Augusta, ME: Maine Farmer Publishing Co., 1904), p. 329.

9   Constantine Hering, *The Guiding Symptoms of Our Materia Medica*, 10 vols. (Philadelphia: American Homeopathic Publishing Society, 1879-91), vol. I. See also Calvin B Knerr, *A Repertory of Hering's Guiding Symptoms of Our Materia Medica* (Philadelphia: F A Davis Co., 1896).

10   André Saine, 'Hering's Law: Law, Rule or Dogma', from *Simillimum*, vol. VI, no. 4 (April,

1993), at <http://www.homeopathy.ca/articles_det12.shtml>, accessed 2 September 2013.

11   Shirley Reischman, 'Kent and Swedenborg', at <http://hpathy.com/homeopathy-papers/ kent-and-swedenborg/>, accessed 25 August 2013.

12   Clement John Wilkinson, *James John Garth Wilkinson: A Memoir of His Life, With a Selection from his Letters* (London: Kegan Paul, Trench, Trübner and Co., 1911), p. 2.

13   J J G Wilkinson quoted in Frederick H Evans, *James John Garth Wilkinson: An Introduction* (Privately printed by Mrs Frank Claughton Matthews, 1936), pp. 11, 16-18.

14   Letter from Carlyle to J J G Wilkinson, 2 August 1838, in Clement Wilkinson, *James John Garth Wilkinson: A Memoir of His Life*, pp. 34-5.

15   Letter from Carlyle to J J G Wilkinson, quoted in a letter from Wilkinson to his fiancée, 3 October 1839, in Clement Wilkinson, *James John Garth Wilkinson: A Memoir of His Life*, p. 36.

16   J J G Wilkinson, 'Translator's Preface to Part I', in Emanuel Swedenborg, *The Animal Kingdom, Considered Anatomically, Physically, and Philosophically*, tr. J J G Wilkinson, 2 vols. (London: W Newbery, 1843-4), vol. I, pp. vii-xiv.

17   J J G Wilkinson, *Remarks on Swedenborg's Economy of the Animal Kingdom* (London: Walton and Mitchell, 1846), pp. 5-6, 9.

18   Ibid., pp. 11, 12, 13. On the doctrine of correspondence and representation, see Swedenborg, *The Animal Kingdom, Considered Anatomically, Physically, and Philosophically*, tr. J J G Wilkinson, 2 vols. (London: W Newbery, 1843-4), vol. I, p. 451: 'In our Doctrine of Representations and Correspondences, we shall treat of both these symbolical and typical representations, and of the astonishing things which occur, I will not say in the living body only, but throughout nature, and which correspond so entirely to supreme and spiritual things, that one would swear that the physical world was purely symbolical of the spiritual world: insomuch that if we choose to express any natural truth in physical and definite vocal terms, and to convert these terms only into the corresponding spiritual terms, we shall by this means elicit a spiritual truth or theological dogma, in place of the physical truth or precept; although no mortal would have predicted that anything of the kind could possibly arise by bare literal transposition; inasmuch as the one precept, considered separately from the other, appears to have absolutely no relation to it'.

19   J J G Wilkinson, 'Introductory Remarks by the Translator', in Emanuel Swedenborg, *Outlines of a Philosophical Argument on the Infinite and on the Intercourse Between the Soul and the Body*, tr. J J G Wilkinson (London: William Newbery and Boston: O Clapp, 1847), pp. xxvii, xxviii, xxix-xxx.

20   Emanuel Swedenborg, *The Principia; Or, The First Principles of Natural Things*, tr. Augustus Clissold, 2 vols. (London: W Newbery, 1845-6), vol. I, ch. 2, §3, p. 49.

21 Letter from J J G Wilkinson to Mrs Cockerell, 5 May 1890, in Clement Wilkinson, *James John Garth Wilkinson: A Memoir of His Life*, p. 160.

22 Letter from J J G Wilkinson to Mrs Keeley, 21 March 1896, in Clement Wilkinson, *James John Garth Wilkinson: A Memoir of His Life*, p. 170.

23 Letter from J J G Wilkinson to Henry James, Sr, 19 May 1853, in Clement Wilkinson, *James John Garth Wilkinson: A Memoir of His Life*, p. 187.

24 Evans, *James John Garth Wilkinson: An Introduction*, pp. 26, 28, 56, 62.

25 Sue Young, 'James John Garth Wilkinson, 1812-1899', in Sue Young Histories: Biographies of Homeopaths, at <http://sueyounghistories.com/archives/2008/03/20/james-john-garth-wilkinson-and-homeopathy/>, accessed 25 August 2013. Edward Irving Carlyle, 'James John Garth Wilkinson', in Leslie Stephen and Sidney Lee (eds.), *Dictionary of National Biography*, 63 vols. (London: Smith, Elder, and Co., 1885-1900), vol. LXI, pp. 271-2. James's third oldest son, Garth Wilkinson (1845-83) carried the name of his friend. An ardent abolitionist, 'Wilky' fought in the Civil War where he sustained several injuries, and later failed in numerous financial schemes before dying of Bright's disease at the age of thirty-eight.

26 Clement Wilkinson, *James John Garth Wilkinson: A Memoir of His Life*, pp. 51, 67-9. Read J J G Wilkinson, *The Human Body and Its Connexion with Man* (London: Chapman and Hall, 1851).

27 Ralph Waldo Emerson, 'Swedenborg; or, the Mystic', in *The Prose Works of Ralph Waldo Emerson*, 3 vols. (Boston: Houghton, Mifflin and Co., 1881), vol. II, p. 60.

28 Clement Wilkinson, *James John Garth Wilkinson: A Memoir of His Life*, pp. 43, 246; Edward Irving Carlyle, 'James John Garth Wilkinson', pp. 271-2. See also Ralph Barton Perry, *The Thought and Character of William James: As Revealed in Unpublished Correspondence and Notes, Together with His Published Writings* (Boston: Little, Brown, and Co., 1935), pp. 27, 79. Sue Young, 'James John Garth Wilkinson, 1812-1899'.

29 Clement Wilkinson, *James John Garth Wilkinson: A Memoir of His Life*, pp. 13, 42. See also J J G Wilkinson, *Swedenborg Among the Doctors: A Letter to Robert T. Cooper, M.D.* (London: James Speirs, 1895); J J G Wilkinson, *The Human Body and Its Connexion with Man*.

30 Letter from J J G Wilkinson to Henry James, Sr, 8 February 1855, in Clement Wilkinson, *James John Garth Wilkinson: A Memoir of His Life*, p. 255.

31 Quoted from a review of the book in the *New York Daily Tribune* in Clement Wilkinson, *James John Garth Wilkinson: A Memoir of His Life*, p. 82.

32 Sue Young, 'James John Garth Wilkinson, 1812-1899'.

33 Letter from J J G Wilkinson to Henry James, Sr, 14 November 1852, in Clement Wilkinson, *James John Garth Wilkinson: A Memoir of His Life*, p. 250.

34   Clement Wilkinson, *James John Garth Wilkinson: A Memoir of His Life*, p. 93.

35   See J J G Wilkinson, *Unlicensed Medicine; With a Plan of Extending Homoeopathy*, (London: R Theobald, 1855); J J G Wilkinson, *Pasteur and Jenner: An Example and a Warning* (London: William Young, 1881); J J G Wilkinson, *Vaccination as a Source of Small-Pox* (London: London Society for the Abolition of Compulsory Vaccination, 1884); J J G Wilkinson, *The Treatment of Small-pox by Hydrastis Canadensis and Veratrum Viride* (Manchester, 1871); J J G Wilkinson, *The Forcible Introspection of Women for the Army and Navy by the Oligarchy, Considered Physically* (London: F Pitman, 1870); J J G Wilkinson, *A Free State and Free Medicine* (London: F Pitman, 1870).

36   J J G Wilkinson, *War, Cholera, and the Ministry of Health* (Boston: Otis Clapp, and Crosby, Nichols, and Co., 1855), pp. 3, 5-6. Sir Benjamin Hall became President of the General Board of Health in 1854, replacing the unpopular Edwin Chadwick.

37   Ibid., p. 17.

38   Ibid., pp. 23, 24, 28-29.

39   J J G Wilkinson, *Epidemic Man and His Visitations* (London: James Speirs, 1893), pp. 121, 29.

40   J J G Wilkinson, *Swedenborg Among the Doctors*, pp. 4, 5-6, 7, 11.

41   Ibid., pp. 19, 21, 20, 26-8.

42   Ibid., pp. 43-4.

43   J J G Wilkinson, *Improvisations from the Spirit* (London: William White, 1857), pp. 60, 77, 99, 217, 256, 312.

44   Quoted in Clement Wilkinson, *James John Garth Wilkinson: A Memoir of His Life*, pp. 74 5, 90

45   Quoted in Evans, *James John Garth Wilkinson: An Introduction*, p. 71.

46   Letter from J J G Wilkinson to J Thomson, 1 September 1893, in Clement Wilkinson, *James John Garth Wilkinson: A Memoir of His Life*, p. 102.

47   Ibid., p. 103.

48   J J G Wilkinson, *Remarks on Swedenborg's Economy of the Animal Kingdom*, p. 49.

49   Quoted in Clement John Wilkinson, *James John Garth Wilkinson: A Memoir of His Life*, pp. 55, 62.

50   Ibid., pp. 140-1, 142-3, 146-7.

51   See Frederick H Evans, 'James John Garth Wilkinson: An Introduction', in *Homoeopathic World*, vol. 47 (1912), pp. 7-12, 21-2; 70-86; 116-28. The article was later republished as *James John Garth Wilkinson: An Introduction*, pp. 7-8.

52   Ralph Waldo Emerson, 'Literature', in *English Traits* (Boston: James R Osgood and Co., 1876), p. 249.

53 Ralph Waldo Emerson quoted in Evans, *James John Garth Wilkinson: An Introduction*, p. 91.

54 'Matriculation Files', at <http://www.lloydlibrary.org/EMI-1845-1939.pdf>, accessed 25 August 2013.

55 Constantine Rafinesque, *Medical Flora or Manual of the Medical Botany in the United States*, 2 vols. (Philadelphia: Atkinson and Alexander, 1879), vol. I, p. iv.

56 'Eclectic Medical Institute of Cincinnati Matriculation Records', at <http://www.lloydlibrary.org/EMI-1845-1939.pdf>, accessed 30 August 2013. See also John S Haller, Jr, *Sectarian Reformers in American Medicine, 1800-1910* (New York: AMS Press, Inc., 2011), pp. 88-91; John S Haller, Jr, *Medical Protestants: The Eclectics in American Medicine, 1825-1939* (Carbondale, IL: Southern Illinois University Press, 1994), pp. 84-93; John S Haller, Jr, *A Profile in Alternative Medicine: The Eclectic Medical College of Cincinnati, 1845-1942* (Kent, OH: Kent State University Press, 1999), pp. 141-66.

57 Haller, *Medical Protestants*, pp. 178-9. See also Eli Jones, *Reading the Eye, Pulse and Tongue for Indicated Remedy* (East Palestine, OH: Ohio Buckeye Press, 1989); John M Scudder, *Specific Medication and Specific Medicines* (Cincinnati: Wilstach, Baldwin and Co., 1870) and *Specific Diagnosis: A Study of Disease With Special Reference to the Administration of Remedies* (Cincinnati: Wilstach, Baldwin and Co., 1874); Matthew Wood, *The Magical Staff: The Vitalist Tradition in Western Medicine* (Berkeley, CA: North Atlantic Books, 1992), pp. 130-3.

58 'Biography of James Tyler Kent', at <http://www.homeotimes.com/mar09/html/biography.htm>, accessed 26 August 2013.

59 Peter Morrell, 'Kent's Influence on British Homeopathy', at <http://www.homeoint.org/morrell/articles/pm_kent.htm>, accessed 8 November 2013.

60 See Robert Baker (ed.), *The American Medical Ethics Revolution: How the AMA's Code of Ethics Has Transformed Physicians' Relationship to Patients, Professionals, and Society* (Baltimore: The Johns Hopkins University Press, 1999).

61 Kent, *Kent's New Remedies, Clinical Cases, Lesser Writings, Aphorisms and Precepts*, pp. 199-203, 210, 213, 216.

62 Letter dated 21 February 1896 from T P Matthews, in Julian Winston, *The Faces of Homoeopathy: An Illustrated History of the First 200 Years* (Tawa, New Zealand: Great Auk Publishing, 1999), p. 531. Pitcairn also used his fortune to establish the Swedenborgian community at Bryn Athyn, as well as build the community's New Church Cathedral and his residence known as Cairnwood.

63 John S Haller, Jr, *The History of American Homeopathy: The Academic Years, 1820-1935* (New York: Haworth Press, Inc., 2005), pp. 150-2.

64 Kent, *Kent's New Remedies, Clinical Cases, Lesser Writings, Aphorisms and Precepts*, p. 276.

65 Kent, *Lectures on Homeopathic Philosophy*, pp. 77-9.

66 Ibid., pp. 89, 104-5, 108.

67 Kent, *Kent's New Remedies, Clinical Cases, Lesser Writings, Aphorisms and Precepts*, p. 412.

68 Swedenborg, *Angelic Wisdom concerning the Divine Love and Wisdom*, tr. Clifford and Doris Harley (London: Swedenborg Society, 1987), pt. II; and *Arcana Caelestia*, §§5711-26, 8364.

69 Swedenborg, *Arcana Caelestia*, §5726.

70 Ibid., §2930.

71 Swedenborg, *Heaven and Its Wonders and Hell From Things Heard and Seen*, tr. Doris Harley (London: Swedenborg Society, 1992), §§228-31.

72 Denis Demarque, *L'Homoeopathie Médecine de l'Expérience* (Angouleme: Editions Coquemard, 1968), pp. 240-1.

73 Kent, *Lectures on Homeopathic Philosophy*, pp. 19, 21-2, 23.

74 Kent, *Lectures on Homeopathic Philosophy*, p. 23; Kent, *Kent's New Remedies, Clinical Cases, Lesser Writings, Aphorisms and Precepts*, p. 260.

75 Kent, *Kent's New Remedies, Clinical Cases, Lesser Writings, Aphorisms and Precepts*, pp. 228, 238, 291, 310.

76 Kent, *Lectures on Homeopathic Philosophy*, p. 23; Kent, *Kent's New Remedies, Clinical Cases, Lesser Writings, Aphorisms and Precepts*, p. 260.

77 Kent, 'President's Address', in *Transactions of the Society of Homeopathicians*, vol. 4 (1914), p. 7.

78 Kent, 'Aphorisms and Precepts', in *Kent's New Remedies, Clinical Cases, Lesser Writings, Aphorisms and Precepts*, pp. 641-89.

79 Kent, *Lectures on Homeopathic Philosophy*, pp. 29-30.

80 Kent, 'The Development and Formation of the Repertory', in *Transactions of the Society of Homeopathicians*, vol. 4 (1914), pp. 207-10.

81 Margaret L Tyler, 'Kent's Repertory', in *Transactions of the Society of Homeopathicians*, vol. 4 (1914), pp. 291, 295-9.

82 Matthew Wood, *The Magical Staff*, pp. 135-65.

83 Kent, 'President's Address', in *Transactions of the Society of Homeopathicians*, vol. 4 (1914), pp. 3-4.

84 Ibid., p. 4; Kent, *Kent's New Remedies, Clinical Cases, Lesser Writings, Aphorisms and Precepts*, pp. 254, 450-3.

85 Kent, *Lectures on Homeopathic Philosophy*, pp. 56, 57, 154-5, 157-60; Kent, *Kent's New Remedies, Clinical Cases, Lesser Writings, Aphorisms and Precepts*, p. 461.

86 Peter Morrell, 'Homeopathy and Religion', in *The Homeopath*, vol. 2 (1982), pp. 136-8. See also Peter Morrell, 'Homeopathy and Religion (Part II)', at <http://www.homeoint. org/morrell/articles/pm_reli1.htm>, accessed 19 March 2014.

87 Read Margaret Tyler, *Homeopathic Drug Pictures* (London: Homeopathic Publishing Co., 1942).

88 Kent, *Kent's New Remedies, Clinical Cases, Lesser Writings, Aphorisms and Precepts*, p. 257.

89 Read George Vithoulkas, *The Essence of Materia* (New Delhi: B Jain, 1990).

90 Kent quoted in Peter Morrell, 'The Homeopath as Anthropologist or Neutral Observer', at <http://www.homeoint.org/morrell/articles/pm_anthr.htm>, accessed 19 March 2014.

91 Peter Morrell, 'Kent's Influence on British Homeopathy', at <http://www.homeoint.org/ morrell/articles/pm_kent.htm>, accessed 26 August 2013.

92 Kent, *Kent's New Remedies, Clinical Cases, Lesser Writings, Aphorisms and Precepts*, p. 671.

93 Wood, *The Magical Staff*, p. 136.

94 Kent, *Lectures on Homeopathic Philosophy*, pp. 126-43; Julian Winston, *The Faces of Homoeopathy*, p. 167.

95 Francis Treuherz, 'Heclae Larva or the Influence of Swedenborg on Homeopathy', in *The Homeopath*, vol. 4 (1983), pp. 35-53.

96 Peter Morrell, 'Kent's Influence on British Homeopathy', at <http://www.homeoint.org/ morrell/articles/pm_kent.htm>, accessed 26 August 2013.

97 Peter Morrell, 'Homeopathy, Phenomenology and Zen', at <http://www.homeoint.org/ morrell/articles/pm_homan.htm>, accessed 19 March 2014.

CHAPTER FIVE

1 Chicago's financiers included Charles T Yerkes, Marshall Field, Philip Armour, Gustavus Swift, Lyman Gage, and Cyrus McCormick.

2 Charles C Bonney quoted in L P Mercer (ed.), *The New Jerusalem in the World's Religious Congresses of 1893* (Chicago: Western New-Church Union, 1894), pp. 8-9.

3 Ibid., p. 7.

4 Ibid., pp. 4-5 (quoting from Swedenborg's *True Christian Religion*, §8; *Divine Providence*, §§322, 325, 326, 255; and *Heaven and Hell*, §329).

5 Charles C Bonney, 'The World's Parliament of Religions', in *The Monist*, vol. 5, no. 3 (April 1895), pp. 328, 323-4. The committee consisted of the Revd John Henry Barrows, Chair (Presbyterian); Revd Prof. David Swing, Vice Chairman (Independent); Archbishop P A Feehan (Catholic); Bishop William E McLaren (Episcopal); Revd F A Noble (Congregationalist); Revd William M Lawrence (Baptist); Revd F M Bristol (Methodist); Rabbi E G Hirsch (Jewish); Revd A J Canfield (Universalist); Revd Jenkin Lloyd Jones (Unitarian);

Bishop C E Cheney (Reformed Episcopal); Revd M C Ranseen (Swedish Lutheran); Revd John Z Torgersen (Norwegian Lutheran); Revd J Berger (German Methodist); Mr J W Plummer (Quaker); and Revd L P Mercer (Swedenborgian).

6   Mary Eleanor Barrows, *John Henry Barrows: A Memoir. By His Daughter* (Chicago: Fleming H Revell Co., 1894), p. 253.

7   F Max Müller, 'The Real Significance of the Parliament of Religions', in *Arena*, vol. 61 (December 1894), pp. 1-4. See also William Q Judge, 'Theosophy at the World's Fair', in *The Theosophist* (1893), pp. 588-92.

8   Bonney, 'The World's Parliament of Religions', pp. 330-1.

9   Ibid., p. 329.

10   'Letter of Bishop of Canterbury, April 26, 1893', in Jenkin Lloyd Jones (ed.), *A Chorus of Faith as Heard in the Parliament of Religions Held in Chicago, Sept. 10-27, 1893* (Chicago: Unity Publishing Co., 1893), pp. 320-1.

11   A T Pierson, 'The Parliament of Religions: A Review', in *Missionary Review of the World*, vol. 7 (1894), pp. 891-2. See also A T Pierson, 'The Columbian Exposition at Chicago', in *Missionary Review of the World*, vol. 8 (1894), pp. 1-10.

12   Quoted in John Henry Barrows (ed.), *The World's Parliament of Religions: An Illustrated and Popular Story of the World's First Parliament of Religions, Held in Chicago in Connection with the Columbian Exposition of 1893*, 2 vols. (Chicago: Parliament Publishing Co., 1893), vol. I, p. 26.

13   'Rev. A. Cleveland Coxe', in Jones (ed.), *A Chorus of Faith as Heard in the Parliament of Religions*, pp. 323-5. Even today, there are those who consider the Parliament to have been an 'Idolatrous and heretical interreligious abomination' in which 'apostate Catholic bishops, priests, laymen, and pretend Cardinals respected false gods and false religions and prayed in communion with various self-professed non-Catholics, such as Hindus, Buddhists, Apostate Jews, Moslems, Protestants, Schismatics, etc.' This bizarre condemnation by Richard J Ibranyi chastised Archbishop P A Feehan of Chicago, Archbishop Patrick Ryan of Philadelphia, Bishop Cotter of Minnesota, Cardinal James Gibbons of Baltimore, the Catholic Archbishops of America who voted to approve the church's participation in the Parliament, the Revd John J Keane, rector of the Catholic University of America who arranged for a presentation of Catholic doctrine at the Parliament, and Archbishop John Ireland of St Paul who accepted membership on the Advisory Council. Ibranyi even accused Leo XIII of being an 'apostate antipope' for bestowing upon the congress his apostolic benediction. See Richard Joseph Michael Ibranyi, *Idolatrous World's Parliament of Religions of 1893* (New Mexico: Mary's Little Remnant, 2013), pp. 6, 28.

[14] Mary Barrows, *John Henry Barrows: A Memoir*, p. 256. Only afterwards did Pope Leo XIII (1810-1903) oppose any renewal of the cooperative gathering which was proposed for the year 1900 in the city of Bombay. See Francis J Connell, 'Pope Leo XIII's Message to America', at <http://www.catholicculture.org/culture/library/view.cfm?recnum=5230>, accessed 4 April 2014. See also A S Will, *Life of Cardinal Gibbons, Archbishop of Baltimore*, 2 vols. (New York: E P Dutton, 1922), vol. I, p. 569; Walter R Houghton (ed.), *Neely's History of the Parliament of Religions and Religious Congresses at the World's Columbian Exposition* (Chicago: F T Neely, 1893), p. 444.

[15] Quoted in Barrows (ed.), *The World's Parliament of Religions*, vol. I, p. 71. On 20 September, a symposium was held on the relation between science and religion. Those taking part in the discussion were William Dawson, Paul Carus, Adolph Brodbeck, the Revd G T Candlin, Dr Ernest Faber, the Revd Father D'Arby of Paris, Elder B H Roberts of Utah, and Judge Russell of Chicago.

[16] Quoted in Mary Barrows, *John Henry Barrows: A Memoir*, pp. 262, 258.

[17] Barrows (ed.), *The World's Parliament of Religions*, vol. I, pp. 58-9.

[18] Quoted in Mary Barrows, *John Henry Barrows: A Memoir*, pp. 263-7.

[19] Barrows (ed.), *The World's Parliament of Religions*, vol. I, p. 28.

[20] Henry Adams, *The Education of Henry Adams* (New York: Modern Library, 1931), p. 237.

[21] Barrows (ed.), *The World's Parliament of Religions*, vol. II, p. 1581.

[22] Ibid., p. 1572.

[23] Quoted in Robert Elliott Speer, *The Light of the World: A Brief Comparative Study of Christianity and Non-Christian Religions* (West Medford, MA: The Central Committee on the United Study of Missions, 1911), p. 363.

[24] Ibid.

[25] James E Ketelaar, 'Strategic Occidentalism: Meiji Buddhists at the World's Parliament of Religions', in *Buddhist-Christian Studies*, vol. 11 (1991), p. 46.

[26] Mary Barrows, *John Henry Barrows: A Memoir*, p. 271.

[27] Richard Hughes Seager, 'Pluralism and the American Mainstream: The View from the World's Parliament of Religions', in *Harvard Theological Review*, vol. 82:3 (1989), p. 316. See also Reid L Neilson, *Exhibiting Mormonism: The Latter-day Saints and the 1893 Chicago World's Fair* (New York: Oxford University Press, 2011).

[28] Seager, 'Pluralism and the American Manistream: The View from the World's Parliament of Religions', p. 301.

[29] Frank Sewall, 'A Narrative and Critical account of the Parliament of Religions', in Mercer (ed.), *The New Jerusalem in the World's Religious Congresses of 1893*, p. 32.

30   Seager, 'Pluralism and the American Mainstream: The View from the World's Parliament of Religions', p. 317.

31   'Address', in Barrows (ed.), *The World's Parliament of Religions*, vol. I, pp. 67, 68, 74, 75.

32   Quoted in Barrows (ed.), *The World's Parliament of Religions*, vol. I, pp. 80, 93, 94.

33   Frank Sewall, 'A Narrative and Critical account of the Parliament of Religions', p. 48.

34   Barrows (ed.), *The World's Parliament of Religions*, vol. II, p. 1581.

35   Henry Drummond, *The Lowell Lectures on The Ascent of Man* (New York: James Pott and Co., 1899), pp. 342-3.

36   Quoted in Ketelaar, 'Strategic Occidentalism: Meiji Buddhists at the World's Parliament of Religions', p. 44.

37   Quoted in Frank Sewall, 'A Narrative and Critical account of the Parliament of Religions', p. 50.

38   Ketelaar, 'Strategic Occidentalism: Meiji Buddhists at the World's Parliament of Religions', p. 49.

39   Kay Koppedrayer, 'Hybrid Constructions: Swami Vivekananda's Presentation of Hinduism at the World's Parliament of Religions, 1893', in *Religious Studies and Theology*, vol. 23:1 (2004), p. 8.

40   Merwin-Marie Snell quoted in <http://ramakrishnavivekananda.info/vivekananda_biography/07_the_parliament.htm>, accessed 3 January 2014.

41   Swami Vivekananda, *The Complete Works of the Swami Vivekananda*, 9 vols. (Calcutta: Mayavati Memorial Edition, 1915), vol. I, pp. 1-2.

42   Vivekananda, *The Complete Works of the Swami Vivekananda*, vol. I, p. 2.

43   Vivekananda, *The Complete Works of the Swami Vivekananda*, vol. I, p. 2.

44   Koppedrayer, 'Hybrid Constructions: Swami Vivekananda's Presentation of Hinduism at the World's Parliament of Religions, 1893', pp. 19, 21.

45   Vivekananda, 'Why We Disagree, September 15, 1893', in *The Complete Works of the Swami Vivekananda*, vol. I, pp. 2-3.

46   Vivekananda, 'Paper on Hinduism, September 19, 1893', in *The Complete Works of the Swami Vivekananda*, vol. I, pp. 4, 11.

47   Vivekananda, 'Religion Not the Crying Need of India, September 20, 1893', in *The Complete Works of the Swami Vivekananda*, vol. I, pp. 17-18.

48   Vivekananda, 'Address', in *The Complete Works of the Swami Vivekananda*, vol. I, p. 21.

49   Quoted in John W Hanson, *The World's Congress of Religions: The Addresses and Papers Delivered Before the Parliament. And an Abstract of the Congresses Held in the Art Institute, Chicago, Illinois, U.S.A., August 25 to October 15, 1893. Under the Auspices*

of The World's Columbian Exposition (Chicago: W B Conkey Co., 1894), p. 382. See also Anagarika Dharmapala, *Return to Righteousness: A Collection of Speeches, Essays and Letters of Anagarika Dharmapala*, ed. Ananda Guruge (Colombo: Government Press, 1965).

50   Quoted in Barrows (ed.), *The World's Parliament of Religions*, vol. I, pp. 95, 96.

51   Quoted in Hanson, *The World's Congress of Religions*, p. 381.

52   Ibid.

53   Barrows (ed.), *The World's Parliament of Religions*, vol. II, p. 1572.

54   Ketelaar, 'Strategic Occidentalism: Meiji Buddhists at the World's Parliament of Religions', p. 42.

55   Barrows (ed.), *The World's Parliament of Religions*, vol. I, pp. 444-50.

56   Kinza M Hirai, 'Religious Thought in Japan', in *The Arena*, vol. 39 (1893), pp. 259-66. See also Yoshinaga Shin'ichi, 'Suzuki Daisetsu and Swedenborg: A Historical Background', p. 121 in Hayashi Makoto, Otani Eiichi, and Paul L Swanson (eds.), *Modern Buddhism in Japan*, at <https://nirc.nanzan-u.ac.jp/en/files/2014/02/05-Modern-Buddhism-Yoshinaga-on-Suzuki.pdf>, accessed 10 April 2014.

57   Barrows (ed.), *The World's Parliament of Religions*, vol. I, p. 445-6.

58   Ibid., p. 449.

59   Ibid., p. 449.

60   Banriu Yatsubuchi, 'Buddhism', in Barrows (ed.), *The World's Parliament of Religions*, vol. I, pp. 716-21.

61   'Address', in *The Open Court*, vol. IX (1895), pp. 404-5; Barrows (ed.), *The World's Parliament of Religions*, vol. I, pp. 444-50.

62   Mercer (ed.), *The New Jerusalem in the World's Religious Congresses of 1893*, p. 10.

63   Ibid., pp. 72-3, 127.

64   All papers can be found in Mercer (ed.), *The New Jerusalem in the World's Religious Congresses of 1893*, pp. 71-123. They include S M Warren, 'The Soul and Its Future Life'; Lydia Fuller Dickinson, 'The Divine Basis of Co-operation between Men and Women'; Frank Sewall, 'The Character and Degree of the Inspiration of the Christian Scriptures'; Julian K Smyth, 'The Incarnation of God in Christ'; T F Wright, 'Reconciliation Vital, not Vicarious'; and L P Mercer, 'Swedenborg and the Harmony of Religions'.

65   Bonney, 'Address of Welcome', in Mercer (ed.), *The New Jerusalem in the World's Religious Congresses of 1893*, pp. 131-3.

66   Mercer (ed.), *The New Jerusalem in the World's Religious Congresses of 1893*, pp. 10, 133, 136.

67   S M Warren, 'The Soul and Its Future Life', in Mercer (ed.), *The New Jerusalem in the World's Religious Congresses of 1893*, pp. 74-5, 80, 81.

68   Julian K Smyth, 'The Incarnation of God in Christ', in Mercer (ed.), *The New Jerusalem in the World's Religious Congresses of 1893*, pp. 100, 106-7.

69   See John Goddard, 'The Doctrine of the Lord', pp. 181-90; John Presland, 'The Doctrine of Redemption', pp. 190-8; S S Seward, 'The Doctrine of Salvation', pp. 198-205; Howard C Dunham, 'Doctrine of the Future Life', pp. 205-15; John Worcester, 'The Science of Correspondence, and the Word of God', pp. 215-25; and Adolph Roeder, 'The Internal Word in Its Relation to the Religions of the World', pp. 226-39, in Mercer (ed.), *The New Jerusalem in the World's Religious Congresses of 1893*.

70   John Worcester, 'The Science of Correspondence, and the Word of God', in Mercer (ed.), *The New Jerusalem in the World's Religious Congresses of 1893*, pp. 215-25 (quotation from p. 215).

71   See Albinus F Frost, 'The Mission of the New Church to the Gentiles', in Mercer (ed.), *The New Jerusalem in the World's Religious Congresses of 1893*, pp. 311-12.

72   Willard H Hinkley, 'The New Church in America', in Mercer (ed.), *The New Jerusalem in the World's Religious Congresses of 1893*, pp. 278-85.

73   Quoted in Albinus F Frost, 'The Mission of the New Church to the Gentiles', in Mercer (ed.), *The New Jerusalem in the World's Religious Congresses of 1893*, pp. 307, 308, 312. See also Rao Bahadur Dadoba Pandurung, *A Hindu Gentleman's Reflections Respecting the Works of Swedenborg and the Doctrines of the New Jerusalem Church* (London: Swedenborg Society, 1879). See also Emanuel Swedenborg, *Arcana Caelestia*, §§2589-90.

74   Mercer, 'Swedenborg and the Harmony of Religions', in Mercer (ed.), *The New Jerusalem in the World's Religious Congresses of 1893*, p. 123.

75   Barrows quoted in Marcus Braybrooke, 'John Henry Barrows: Producing the First Parliament of Religions', at <http://theinterfaithobserver.org/journal-articles/2012/7/15/john-henry-barrows-producing-the-first-parliament-of-religio.html>, accessed 3 January 2014.

76   Quoted in Marcus Braybrooke, 'The Legacy of the 1893 Parliament of the World's Religions', at <http://theinterfaithobserver.org/journal-articles/2013/3/15/the-legacy-of-the-1893-parliament-of-the-world-religions.html>, accessed 3 January 2014.

77   Examples include the following: 'whatever is good and true in other religious systems is found in full and authoritative form in Christianity' (James S Dennis quoted in Barrows, *The World's Parliament of Religions*, vol. II, p. 1252); 'Despite all that might be said in its favor . . . Buddhism possesses characteristics which clearly indicate that it is not to be the final permanent religion of Japan or of any other country' (M L Gordon quoted in

Barrows, *The World's Parliament of Religions*, vol. II, p. 1293); 'The Catholic religion alone is world-wide and cosmopolitan, embracing all races and nations, and peoples and tongues' (Cardinal Gibbons quoted in Houghton (ed.), *Neely's History of the Parliament of Religions and Religious Congresses*, p. 187).

[78] Examples include the following: 'the potential religious life . . . is not a creed but character' (A M Powell quoted in Houghton (ed.), *Neely's History of the Parliament of Religions and Religious Congresses*, p. 623); 'Back to the primal unity where man appears as a child of God . . . back to this must we go if we will be loyal to our kind' (E L Rexford quoted in Minot J Savage, *The World's Congress of Religions* (Boston: Arena Publishing Co., 1893), p. 242); 'We must not make any distinction between race and race, between civilization and civilization, between creed and creed, and faith and faith' (Shaku Soyen quoted in Barrows (ed.), *The World's Parliament of Religions*, vol. II, p. 1285).

[79] Quoted in Marcus Braybrooke, 'The Legacy of the 1893 Parliament of the World Religions'.

[80] To understand the conflicting nature of the debate read William R Hutchison, *Errand to the World: American Protestant Thought and Foreign Missions* (Chicago: University of Chicago Press, 1987); Marcus Braybrooke, *Inter-Faith Organizations, 1893-1979: An Historical Directory* (Lewiston, NY: Edwin Mellen, 1980); Martin E Marty, *Modern American Religion, Vol. 1: The Irony of It All, 1893-1919* (Chicago: University of Chicago Press, 1986).

[81] See Will Herberg, *Protestant-Catholic-Jew: An Essay in American Religious Sociology* (Garden City, NY: Doubleday, 1955); Paul A Carter, *The Spiritual Crisis of the Gilded Age* (DeKalb: Northern Illinois University Press, 1971), pp. 199-221; Carl T Jackson, *The Oriental Religions and American Thought: Nineteenth-Century Explorations* (Westport, CT: Greenwood, 1981), pp. 243-61; Richard Hughes Seager, 'Pluralism and the American Mainstream: The View from the World's Parliament of Religions', in *Harvard Theological Review*, vol. 82:3 (1989), pp. 301-24; R Laurence Moore, 'Protestant Unity and the American Mission—The Historiography of a Desire', in Moore, *Religious Outsiders and the Making of Americans* (New York: Oxford University Press, 1986), pp. 3-21.

[82] Bonney, 'The World's Parliament of Religions', pp. 339-40.

CHAPTER SIX

[1] Paul Carus, 'Buddhism and Christianity', in *The Monist*, vol. 5 (1894), pp. 99-102 (quotation from p. 100).

[2] Peter N Gregory, 'Describing the Elephant: Buddhism in America', in *Religion and American Culture: A Journal of Interpretation*, vol. 11, no. 2 (2001), p. 233.

3   James E Ketelaar, 'Strategic Occidentalism: Meiji Buddhists at the World's Parliament of Religions', in *Buddhist-Christian Studies*, vol. 11 (1991), p. 40.

4   Winston L King, 'Eastern Religions: A New Interest and Influence', in *The Annals of the American Academy of Political and Social Science*, vol. 387 (1970), p. 67.

5   Donald Harvey Meyer, 'Paul Carus and the Religion of Science', in *American Quarterly*, vol. 14, no. 4 (1962), pp. 597-607.

6   Read Harold Henderson, *Catalyst for Controversy: Paul Carus of Open Court* (Carbondale: Southern Illinois University Press, 1993), pp. 4-21.

7   Paul Carus, 'The Philosophical and Religious Significance of Art', in *Modern Art*, vol. 3 (1895), pp. 50, 52.

8   William H Hay, 'Paul Carus: A Case-Study of Philosophy on the Frontier', in *Journal of the History of Ideas*, vol. 17, no. 4 (1956), pp. 498-510.

9   Paul Carus, *The Religion of Science* (Chicago: Open Court, 1899 [1893]), p. iii; Paul Carus, 'Buddhism and the Religion of Science', in *The Open Court*, vol. X, no. 446 (12 March 1896), p. 4845.

10   Meyer, 'Paul Carus and the Religion of Science', pp. 601-2. See also, Paul Carus, 'The Basis of Ethics and the Ethical Movement', in *The Open Court*, vol. IV, no. 140 (1 May 1890), pp. 2247-8; Paul Carus, 'Ethics and the Cosmic Order', in *The Monist*, vol. 4, no. 3 (1894), pp. 403-16.

11   Carus, *The Religion of Science*, pp. iv-v.

12   Ibid., pp. 12, 20, 32, 24.

13   Paul Carus, *The Dawn of a New Religious Era and Other Essays* (Chicago: Open Court Publishing Co., 1916), pp. 36, 49, 89.

14   Ibid., p. 20.

15   Carus, *The Religion of Science*, pp. 48, 54-5, 59, 60-1.

16   Carus, 'Mysticism', in *The Monist*, vol. 18 (1908), pp. 75, 77, 82.

17   Carus, 'Kant's Significance in the History of Philosophy', in *The Monist*, vol. 12 (1901), pp. 98, 99, 100.

18   Although there is no clear evidence that Carus was introduced to Eastern religions and philosophy during his attendance in the German universities, it remains the case that nineteenth-century German Romanticism had been richly imbued with Indian literature, as evident in the writings of philosopher, theologian and poet Johann Gottfried Herder; German writer and polymath Johann Wolfgang von Goethe; poet, translator and critic August Wilhelm Schlegel; polymath Hermann Grassmann; philosopher Immanuel Kant; philosopher Arthur Schopenhauer; Orientalist and Sanskrit scholar Paul Deussen; and

philologist and Orientalist Max Müller. See Carl T Jackson, 'The Meeting of East and West: The Case of Paul Carus', in *Journal of the History of Ideas*, vol. 29, no. 1 (1968), p. 74; Friedrich Wilhelm, 'The German Response to Indian Culture', in *Journal of the American Oriental Society*, vol. 81:4 (1961), pp. 395-405.

19 [Paul Carus], 'The Religion of Resignation', in *The Open Court*, vol. III, no. 48 (23 January 1890), pp. 2051-2.

20 See Paul Carus, 'Science, a Religious Revelation', an address delivered 19 September 1893 before the World's Congress of Religions at Chicago, in John Henry Barrows (ed.), *The World's Parliament of Religions: An Illustrated and Popular Story of the World's First Parliament of Religions, Held in Chicago in Connection with the Columbian Exposition of 1893*, 2 vols. (Chicago: Parliament Publishing Co., 1893), vol. II, pp. 978-81.

21 Carus, *The Dawn of a New Religious Era and Other Essays*, pp. 24-5, 29.

22 David McMahan, 'Modernity and the Early Discourse of Scientific Buddhism', in *Journal of the American Academy of Religion*, vol. 72 (2004), p. 914.

23 See Arthur Lillie, *Buddha and Early Buddhism* (London: Trübner and Co., 1881); *The Popular Life of Buddha: Containing an Answer to the 'Hibbert Lectures' of 1881* (London: Kegan Paul & Co., 1883); *Buddhism in Christendom, Or, Jesus, the Essene* (London: Kegan Paul, Trench, 1887); *The Cobra Diamond* (London: Ward & Downey, 1890); *The Influence of Buddhism on Primitive Christianity* (London: Sonnenschein & Co., 1893); *Madame Blavatsky and Her 'Theosophy': A Study* (London: Swan Sonnenschein & Co., 1895); *Croquet: Its History, Rules, and Secrets* (London: Longmans, Green, and Co., 1897); *Croquet Up to Date: Containing the Ideas and Teachings of the Leading Players and Champions* (London: Longmans & Co., 1900); *India in Primitive Christianity* (London: Kegan Paul & Co., 1909); *Râma and Homer: An Argument that in the Indian Epics Homer Found the Theme of His Two Great Poems* (London: Kegan Paul & Co., 1912); and *The Gospel according to the Hebrews* (Kessinger Publishing, 2005).

24 See Rudolf Seydel, *Schopenhauers philosophisches System* (Schopenhauer's Philosophical System) (Leipzig, 1857); *Logik oder Wissenschaft vom Wissen* (Logic or Science of Wisdom) (Leipzig, 1866); *Die Religion und die Religionen* (Religion and Religions) (Leipzig, 1872); *Ethik oder Wissenschaft vom Seinsollenden* (Ethics or the Science of What Ought to Be) (Leipzig, 1874); *Das Evangelium von Jesu in seinen Verhältnissen zu Buddha-Sage und Buddha-Lehre* (The Gospel of Jesus in Relation to the Buddha Legend and Teachings) (Leipzig, 1882); *Die Buddha-Legende und das Leben Jesu nach den Evangelien* (The Buddha Legend and the Life of Jesus after the Gospels) (Leipzig, 1884); *Buddha und Christus* (Buddha and Christ) (Breslau, 1884); and *Religion und Wissenschaft. Gesammelte Reden*

und Abhandlungen (Religion and Science. Collected Speeches and Essays) (Breslau, 1887).

25   Carus, 'Buddhism and Christianity', p. 67.

26   Quoted in Carl T Jackson, 'The Meeting of East and West: The Case of Paul Carus', p. 77.

27   Carus, 'Buddhism and the Religion of Science', p. 4845.

28   Carus, 'Buddhism and Christianity', p. 89.

29   Carus, 'Buddhism and Christianity', pp. 83, 86, 87-88.

30   Paul Carus, *The Gospel of Buddha, Compiled from Ancient Records* (Chicago: The Open Court Publishing Co., 1917), pp. v-vii.

31   Shaku Soyen quoted in 'A Japanese Translation of "The Gospel of Buddha" ', in *The Open Court*, vol. IX, no. 391 (21 February 1895), p. 4405.

32   It is ironic that the very Zen doctrines that served Japan's emergence into the modern world, especially in the decades following the Russo-Japanese War of 1905, were the same doctrines that appealed to Western intellectuals such as Paul Carus who was searching for a truly modern religion. As Judith Snodgrass explained, *The Gospel of Buddha* 'presented Buddhism as a religion suited to the modern scientific worldview represented by the west, and most importantly, its Western authorship verified the claims that had been made by Japanese scholars such as Inoue Enryo for some years'. Not Christianity, but Buddhism was the solution to Japan's search for an ideological foundation. When one considers the fact that the book received less than complimentary reviews from the academic world, the question arises as to why the book, which had been written for a Western audience, was so positively received by Japan's Mahayana Buddhists. Was it because of its spiritual instruction, or did it have a strategic importance in the context of Japan's effort to become a modern nation? According to Snodgrass, Japanese Buddhists were aware of the book's shortcomings as an accurate representation of Buddhism. Its importance, however, was in using an authentic Western intellectual to introduce Buddhist ideas 'in a form acceptable by Western standards', to both American and Japanese audiences. See Judith Snodgrass, *'Budda no fukuin*: The Deployment of Paul Carus's *Gospel of Buddha* in Meiji Japan', in *Japanese Journal of Religious Studies*, vol. 25 (1998), p. 328.

33   Paul Carus, *The Dharma or the Religion of Enlightenment: An Exposition of Buddhism*, 4th edn. (Chicago: Open Court Publishing Co., 1898), pp. 3-5.

34   Ibid., pp. 9-11.

35   Ibid., pp. 15, 16, 28.

36   Ibid., pp. 21-2, 25.

37   Ibid., p. 43.

38   Carus, *The Dawn of a New Religious Era and Other Essays*, p. 20.

[39]   Meyer, 'Paul Carus and the Religion of Science', p. 607.

[40]   Martin J Verhoeven, 'The Dharma through Carus's Lens', in Paul Carus, *The Gospel of Buddha: According to Old Records* (Chicago: Open Court, 2004), pp. 1-102.

[41]   Read Joseph Kitagawa (ed.), *Modern Trends in World Religions—Paul Carus Memorial Symposium* (LaSalle, IL: Open Court Publishing Co., 1959).

[42]   Hay, 'Paul Carus: A Case-Study of Philosophy on the Frontier', pp. 498-510; Meyer, 'Paul Carus and the Religion of Science', pp. 597-607.

[43]   Ralph E McCoy (comp.), *Open Court: A Centennial Bibliography, 1887-1987* (LaSalle, IL: Open Court Publishing Company, 1987).

[44]   See <http://sueyounghistories.com/archives/2009/01/16/carl-herman-vetterling-1849-1931/>, accessed 18 March 2014.

[45]   Herman C Vetterling, 'Studies of Swedenborg's Philosophy', in *Theosophist*, vol. 6 (1884), pp. 9-11, 58-61, 238-41, 260-4, 294-7.

[46]   Philangi Dasa, *Swedenborg the Buddhist* (Charleston, SC: Arcana Books, 2003 [1887]), p. xiv.

[47]   Wakoh Shannon Hickey, 'Swedenborg: A Modern Buddha?', in *Pacific World: The Journal of the Institute of Buddhist Studies*, no. 10 (Fall 2008), p. 107. Vetterling's wife was a relative of the Pitcairn family of Pittsburgh which was connected with the Pennsylvania Railroad and with the Pittsburgh Plate Glass Company.

[48]   See Dasa, *Swedenborg the Buddhist*.

[49]   See Swedenborg, *The Spiritual Diary*, vol. V, tr. James F Buss (London: Swedenborg Society, 1902), §6077.

[50]   'Review', in *The Path*, vol. 2, no. 6 (1887), p. 187. See also *The Theosophist* (January, 1888), pp. 258-9.

[51]   Dasa, *Swedenborg the Buddhist*, pp. 338-42.

[52]   The Swedenborgians objected to the book as they perceived it as an esoteric representation of Theosophy.

[53]   Herman C Vetterling, *The Illuminate of Görlitz; or, Jakob Böhme's Life and Philosophy: A Comparative Study* (Leipzig: F A Brockhaus, 1922), pp. 1292-3.

[54]   Paul Carus, 'Spirit or Ghost', in *The Monist*, vol. 12 (1902), pp. 365-403; Carus, 'Mysticism', in *The Monist*, vol. 18 (1908), pp. 75-110. Read also Ann Taves, *Fits, Trances, and Visions: Experiencing Religion and Explaining Experience from Wesley to James* (Princeton, NJ: Princeton University Press, 1999).

[55]   Herman C Vetterling, 'Swedenborg in the Lamasery', in *The Buddhist Ray*, vol. 1, no. 3 (March 1888), p. 22; Dasa, *Swedenborg the Buddhist*, pp. 359-437; Hickey, 'Swedenborg:

A Modern Buddha?', p. 107.

⁵⁶ Thomas A Tweed, 'American Occultism and Japanese Buddhism: Albert J. Edmunds, D. T. Suzuki, and Translocative History', in *Japanese Journal of Religious Studies*, vol. 32, no. 2 (2005), pp. 259-61; Albert J Edmunds, 'Has Swedenborg's "Lost Word" Been Found?', in *Journal of the American Society for Psychical Research*, vol. 7, no. 5 (May 1913), pp. 270-1. Also read Albert J Edmunds and Masaharu Anesaki, *Buddhist and Christian Gospels Now First Compared From the Originals: Being 'Gospel Parallels from Pali Texts'*, 4th edn., 2 vols. (Philadelphia: Innes and Sons, 1908-9).

⁵⁷ Read Stephen Prothero, *The White Buddhist: The Asian Odyssey of Henry Steel Olcott* (Bloomington: Indiana University Press, 1996); Judith Snodgrass, *Presenting Japanese Buddhism to the West: Orientalism, Occidentalism, and the Columbian Exposition* (Chapel Hill, NC: University of North Carolina Press, 2003).

⁵⁸ Gregory, 'Describing the Elephant: Buddhism in America', pp. 237, 241.

⁵⁹ See Barry A Kosmin and Seymour P Lachman, *One Nation Under God: Religion in Contemporary American Society* (New York: Harmony Books, 1993); Martin Baumann, 'Buddhism in the West: Phases, Orders and the Creation of an Integrative Buddhism', in *Internationales Asienforum*, vol. 27, nos. 3-4 (1996), pp. 345-62; Martin Baumann, 'The Dharma Has Come West: A Survey of Recent Studies and Sources', in *Journal of Buddhist Ethics*, vol. 4 (1997), p. 198.

CHAPTER SEVEN

¹ William James, *The Varieties of Religious Experience* (New York: Modern Library, 1902), lectures IV and V, p. 93. See also William James, *Essays on Faith and Morals* (New York: Longmans, Green, and Co., 1949).

² See John S Haller, Jr, *The History of New Thought: From Mind Cure to Positive Thinking and the Prosperity Gospel* (West Chester, PA: Swedenborg Foundation, 2012).

³ See S B Girgus, *The American Self: Myth, Ideology, and Popular Culture* (Albuquerque:University of New Mexico Press, 1981); W M McClay, *The Masterless: Self and Society in Modern America* (Chapel Hill: University of North Carolina Press, 1994); Richard Huber, *The American Idea of Success* (New York: McGraw Hill, 1971); Beryl Satter, *Each Mind a Kingdom* (Berkeley, CA: University of California Press, 1999).

⁴ Read Wendell Thomas, *Hinduism Invades America* (New York: Beacon Press, 1930); Horatio W Dresser, 'An Interpretation of the Vedanta', in *The Arena*, vol. 22 (October 1899), pp. 489-508; Horatio W Dresser, 'Raja Yoga Philosophy', in *The Journal of Practical Metaphysics*, vol. I (July 1897), pp. 294-8.

5   Alfred Whitney Griswold, 'New Thought: A Cult of Success', in *American Journal of Sociology*, vol. 40 (November 1934), p. 313.

6   Ralph Waldo Trine, *The Greatest Thing Ever Known* (New York: Thomas Y Crowell and Co., 1898), p. 54.

7   Ralph Waldo Trine, *The Higher Powers of Mind and Spirit* (New York: Dodge Publishing Co., 1917), p. 20.

8   Quoted in ibid., pp. 169-70.

9   Quoted in Ralph Waldo Trine, *The Land of Living Men* (New York: Dodge Publishing Co., 1910), p. 68.

10 Trine, *The Higher Powers of Mind and Spirit*, pp. 9-10, 20. Read William James, *Principles of Psychology* (New York: H Holt and Co., 1890). See also Ralph Waldo Trine, *On the Open Road: Being Some Thoughts and a Little Creed of Wholesome Living* (New York: Thomas Y Crowell and Co., 1908).

11 Ralph Waldo Trine, *My Philosophy and My Religion* (New York: Dodd, Mead, and Co., 1921), p. 73.

12 Quoted in Trine, *The Higher Powers of Mind and Spirit*, pp. 27, 33. See Emanuel Swedenborg, *Heaven and Hell*, §9.

13 Quoted in Trine, *The Greatest Thing Ever Known*, p. 60.

14 Ralph Waldo Trine, *In Tune With the Infinite: or, Fullness of Peace, Power and Plenty* (New York: Thomas Y Crowell & Company, 1897), p. 65; Trine, *My Philosophy and My Religion*, p. 50.

15 Ralph Waldo Trine, *The New Alinement of Life, Concerning the Mental Laws of a Greater Personal and Public Power* (New York: Dodge Publishing Co., 1913), p. 211.

16 Ralph Waldo Trine, *What All the World's A-Seeking; Or, The Vital Law of True Life, True Greatness, Power, and Happiness* (New York: Thomas Y Crowell, 1896), p. 164.

17 Trine, *In Tune With the Infinite*, p. 181.

18 Ralph Waldo Emerson, *The Selected Writings of Ralph Waldo Emerson*, at <http://www.entheos.com/quotes/by_topic/Ralph+waldo+emerson>, accessed 8 November 2013.

19 Swedenborg, *Arcana Caelestia*, §4223.

20 Trine, *The Greatest Thing Ever Known*, pp. 50-2.

21 Trine, *My Philosophy and My Religion*, pp. 28, 60, 83.

22 Trine, *What All the World's A-Seeking*, pp. 16, 19.

23 Trine, *The Higher Powers of Mind and Spirit*, pp. 25-6.

24 Trine, *The Greatest Thing Ever Known*, pp. 8, 13, 16, 27.

25 Trine, *My Philosophy and My Religion*, pp. 23-5, 62-3, 72.

26 Trine, *In Tune With the Infinite*, pp. 39-40, 108-9, 116.

27 Bergson quoted in Trine, *My Philosophy and My Religion*, p. 39.

28 Trine, *In Tune With the Infinite*, pp. 5-6, 12-13, 15-16, 18.

29 Trine, *The New Alinement of Life*, pp. 24-5, 46, 61.

30 Trine, *The Greatest Thing Ever Known*, pp. 75-6.

31 Quoted in Ralph Waldo Trine, *In the Hollow of His Hand* (New York: Dodd, Mead and Co., 1919), p. 57.

32 Trine, *My Philosophy and My Religion*, pp. 51-3, 69, 71.

33 Trine, *What All the World's A-Seeking*, pp. 49, 53, 58.

34 Trine, *In Tune With the Infinite*, p. 178.

35 Trine, *What All the World's A-Seeking*, pp. 30-5.

36 Trine, *In Tune With the Infinite*, pp. 25-6, 29-30.

37 Ralph Waldo Trine, *Character-Building Thought Power* (New York: Thomas Y Crowell and Co., 1900), pp. 39-40, 42-3.

38 Trine, *The Higher Powers of Mind and Spirit*, p. 176.

39 Trine, *The New Alinement of Life*, pp. 85, 88.

40 Ibid., pp. 70-1, 73, 109, 124.

41 Ibid., pp. 92, 94, 96.

42 Trine, *The Higher Powers of Mind and Spirit*, pp. 130-1, 134.

43 Trine, *In the Hollow of His Hand*, pp. 11-12, 21, 36.

44 Ibid., pp. 42-6.

45 Trine, *The Higher Powers of Mind and Spirit*, p. 3.

46 Trine, *In Tune With the Infinite*, pp. 42-55 (quotation from p. 54).

47 Trine, *In the Hollow of His Hand*, p. 98. See also John S Haller, Jr, *Swedenborg, Mesmer and the Mind/Body Connection: the Roots of Complementary Medicine* (West Chester, PA: Swedenborg Foundation, 2010).

48 Trine, *The New Alinement of Life*, pp. 193, 195, 205-10.

49 Trine, *In Tune With the Infinite*, pp. 82-3, 86.

50 Trine, *The Higher Powers of Mind and Spirit*, pp. 51, 58-9.

51 Trine, *Character-Building Thought Power*, pp. 4-5, 15-16, 27.

52 Trine, *The Greatest Thing Ever Known*, pp. 30-1.

53 Trine, *The Land of Living Men*, p. 142.

54 Ralph Waldo Trine, *In the Fire of the Heart* (New York: McClure, Phillips and Co., 1906), pp. 16-18, 73, 110.

55 Trine, *The Land of Living Men*, p. 88.

56 Trine, *In the Fire of the Heart*, pp. 25-7, 30, 48-9.

57 Trine, *The Land of Living Men*, pp. 59-60.

58 Trine, *In the Fire of the Heart*, pp. 270-1, 274-5.

59 Trine, *The Land of Living Men*, pp. 98, 100-3.

60 Trine, *In the Fire of the Heart*, pp. 135-9. Trine also objected to numerous practices in his lifetime, including hunting for sport, vivisection, the cutting of horse's tails to create the look of an English saddle horse, the slaughter of birds for their feathers in hats, excessive reliance on flesh foods and liquor.

61 Trine, *The Land of Living Men*, p. 143.

62 Trine, *In the Fire of the Heart*, pp. 194, 198-200, 230.

63 Trine, *In the Hollow of His Hand*, p. 17.

64 Trine, *The Higher Powers of Mind and Spirit*, pp. 191, 194-5.

65 Ibid., pp. 209, 226.

66 Trine, *In the Hollow of His Hand*, pp. 214-15.

67 Trine, *In Tune With the Infinite*, title page.

CHAPTER EIGHT

1 D T Suzuki, *Suedenborugu*, in *Swedenborg: Buddha of the North*, tr. Andrew Bernstein (West Chester, PA: Swedenborg Foundation, 1996), pp. 5, 7, 9, 10.

2 Andrew Bernstein, 'Introduction', in Suzuki, *Swedenborg: Buddha of the North*, p. xv. See also <http://www.quantuminteractive.net/quantuminteractive/sd/swedenborg/who-was-swedenborg/swedenborg-influence-on-suzuki.htm>, accessed 5 December 2013.

3 D T Suzuki, 'Early Memories', in Masao Abe (ed.), *A Zen Life: D.T. Suzuki Remembered* (New York: Weatherhill, 1986), pp. 3-9.

4 Robert H Sharf, 'The Zen of Japanese Nationalism', in *History of Religions*, vol. 33, no. 1 (1993), p. 6. See also Peter N Dale, *The Myth of Japanese Uniqueness* (London: Croom Helm, 1986); Nukariya Kaiten, *Religion of the Samurai: A Study of Zen Philosophy and Discipline in China and Japan* (London: Luzac, 1913).

5 Martin J Verhoeven, 'Buddhism and Science: Probing the Boundaries of Faith and Reason', in *Religion East and West: Journal of the Institute for World Religions*, vol. I (June 2001), pp. 77-97; David R Loy, 'Is Zen Buddhism?', in *The Eastern Buddhist*, vol. 28, no. 2 (Autumn 1995), pp. 273-86.

6 Charles C Bonney, 'The Genesis of the World's Religious Congresses of 1893', in L P Mercer (ed.), *The New Jerusalem in the World's Religious Congresses of 1893* (Chicago: Western New-Church Union, 1894), p. 17.

7   Shaku Soyen, 'The Law of Cause and Effect, as Taught by Buddha', in John Henry Barrows (ed.), *The World's Parliament of Religions: An Illustrated and Popular Story of the World's First Parliament of Religions, Held in Chicago in Connection with the Columbian Exposition of 1893*, 2 vols. (Chicago: Parliament Publishing Co., 1893), vol. II, pp. 829-31.

8   Palmer Rampell, 'Laws That Refuse To Be Stated: The Post-Sectarian Spiritualities of Emerson, Thoreau, and D. T. Suzuki', in *New England Quarterly*, vol. 84, no. 4 (December 2011), p. 628; D T Suzuki, 'Introduction: A Glimpse of Paul Carus', in J M Kitagawa (ed.), *Modern Trends in World Religions* (LaSalle, IL: Open Court, 1959), pp. ix-xi; Harold Henderson, *Catalyst for Controversy: Paul Carus of Open Court* (Carbondale: Southern Illinois University Press, 1993), pp. 12-20, 89-117.

9   See Thomas Kirchner, 'D. T. Suzuki's "The Relation of Religion and the State" ', at <http://iriz.hanazono.ac.jp/newhomepage/ronsyu/pdf/tom05.pdf>, accessed 19 February 2015; D T Suzuki, *Shin Shukyo Ron (A New Theory of Religion)* (Kyoto: Baiyo Shoin,1896).

10   Lawrence Buell, *Emerson* (Cambridge: Harvard University Press, 2004), p. 196. See also Yoshinaga Shin'ichi, 'Suzuki Daisetsu and Swedenborg: A Historical Background', p. 127, in Hayashi Makoto, Otani Eiichi and Paul L Swanson (eds.), *Modern Buddhism in Japan*, at <https://nirc.nanzan-u.ac.jp/en/files/2014/02/05-Modern-Buddhism-Yoshinaga-on-Suzuki.pdf>, accessed 10 April 2014.

11   See Paul Carus, *Karma: A Story of Buddhist Ethics* (Chicago: Open Court Publishing Co., 1917).

12   Rampell, 'Laws That Refuse To Be Stated', p. 629; 'Soyen to Carus, December 17, 1895', box 47, folder 46, in Open Court Publishing Company records, Morris Library Special Collections, Southern Illinois University Carbondale.

13   Suzuki's articles for *The Open Court* included: 'Confucius', vol. 13 (November 1899), pp. 644-9; 'The Breadth of Buddhism', vol. 14 (January 1900), pp. 51-3; 'The Seven Gods of Bliss', vol. 21 (1907), pp. 397-406; and 'Fudo-Myowo', vol. 29, no. 712 (September 1915), pp. 513-26; his articles for *The Monist* included: 'Acvaghasha, the First Advocate of the Mahâyâna Buddhism', vol. 10, no. 2 (January 1900), pp. 216-45; 'Lao-Tze and Professor Giles', vol. 11, no. 4 (July 1901), pp. 612-16; 'Giles's *History of Chinese Literature*', vol. 12, no. 1 (October 1901), pp. 116-22; 'The First Buddhist Council', vol. 14, no. 2 (January 1904), pp. 252-82; 'A Brief History of Early Chinese Philosophy', vol. 17, no. 3 (July 1907), pp. 415-50, vol. 18, no. 2 (April 1908), pp. 242-85, and no. 4 (October 1908), pp. 481-509; and 'Buddhism, the Development of Mahayana', vol. 24, no. 4 (October 1914), pp. 565-81.

14   Carl T Jackson, 'The Meeting of East and West: The Case of Paul Carus', in *Journal of the*

History of Ideas, vol. 29, no. 1 (1968), p. 90.

[15] D T Suzuki, *Outlines of Mahayana Buddhism* (New York: Schoken, 1963 [1907]).

[16] 'Suzuki to Carus, September 9, 1897'; 'Suzuki to Carus, February 11, 1899'; 'Suzuki to Carus, March, 1899', in Open Court Publishing Company records, Morris Library Special Collections, Southern Illinois University Carbondale.

[17] Rampell, 'Laws That Refuse To Be Stated', pp. 649, 642.

[18] Eugene Taylor, 'Swedenborgian Roots of American Pragmatism: The Case of D.T. Suzuki', in *Studia Swedenborgiana*, vol. 9, no. 2 (May 1995), at <http://www.shs.psr.edu/studia/index.asp?article_id=129>, accessed 27 January 2014.

[19] Thomas A Tweed, 'American Occultism and Japanese Buddhism: Albert J. Edmunds, D. T. Suzuki, and Translocative History', in *Japanese Journal of Religious Studies*, vol. 32, no. 2 (2005), p. 260; Albert J Edmunds, 'F. W. H. Myers, Swedenborg, and Buddha', in *Proceedings of the American Society for Psychical Research*, vol. 8 (1914), pp. 253-85.

[20] See Albert J Edmunds and Masaharu Anesaki, *Buddhist and Christian Gospels Now First Compared From the Originals: Being 'Gospel Parallels from Pali Texts'*, 4th edn., 2 vols. (Philadelphia: Innes and Sons, 1908-9). The 3rd edition was published in Tokyo by the Yuhokwan Publishing House in 1905.

[21] Tweed, 'American Occultism and Japanese Buddhism', pp. 249-51, 258-9.

[22] See Swedenborg, *Tenkai to Jigoku*, tr. D T Suzuki (Tokyo, 1909).

[23] 'International Swedenborg Congress, London, England', at <http://newchurchhistory.org/funfacts/index7cc7.html?p=547>, accessed 19 November 2013.

[24] Quoted in Suzuki, *Suedenborugu*, p. 11.

[25] Tatsuya Nagashima, 'Foreword', in Suzuki, *Swedenborg: Buddha of the North*, p. ix.

[26] See Adele S Algeo, 'Beatrice Lane Suzuki: An American Theosophist in Japan', in *Quest*, vol. 95, no. 1 (January 2007), pp. 13-17; Tweed, 'American Occultism and Japanese Buddhism', pp. 256-7; Robert P Richardson, 'The Rise and Fall of the Parliament of Religions at Greenacre', in *The Open Court*, vol. XLVI, no. 898 (March 1931), pp. 129-66.

[27] R L Tafel (tr., ed. and comp.), *Documents Concerning the Life and Character of Emanuel Swedenborg*, 3 vols. (London: Swedenborg Society, 1875-7).

[28] See *The One Hundred and Second Report (For the Year 1911-12) of the Swedenborg Society* (London: Swedenborg Society, 1912), pp. 31-4; Yoshinaga Shin'ichi, 'Suzuki Daisetsu and Swedenborg: A Historical Background', p. 129.

[29] Suzuki, *Suedenborugu*, p. 6.

[30] Swedenborg quoted in ibid., p. 25.

[31] Suzuki, *Suedenborugu*, p. 25.

32 Ibid., pp. 30, 35.

33 Ibid., pp. 39-41, 44-5, 51.

34 Quoted in ibid., p. 52. See also Cyriel O Sigstedt, *The Swedenborg Epic: The Life and Works of Emanuel Swedenborg* (New York: Bookman Associates, 1952), pp. 5, 144, 221, 462 (note 374).

35 D T Suzuki, 'Swedenborg's View of Heaven and "Other-Power"', in Suzuki, *Swedenborg: Buddha of the North*, pp. 77-8.

36 Ibid., pp. 81, 83.

37 Suzuki quoted in David Loy, 'The Dharma of Emanuel Swedenborg: A Buddhist Perspective', in *Arcana*, vol. 2, no. 1 (1995), p. 6. A revised version of Loy's essay is reprinted as the 'Afterword' in Suzuki, *Swedenborg: Buddha of the North*, pp. 89-125.

38 Bernstein, 'Introduction', pp. xxx, xv-xvi.

39 Tweed, 'American Occultism and Japanese Buddhism', p. 262.

40 Nagashima, 'Foreword', p. xi.

41 Suzuki, 'Swedenborg's View of Heaven and "Other-Power"', p. 86.

42 Tatsuya Nagashima, 'Daisetsu T. Suzuki, Internationally Known Buddhist: Crypto-Swedenborgian?', in *New Church Life*, vol. 113 (1993), pp. 216-17.

43 Sydney Ahlstrom, *A Religious History of the American People*, 2nd edn. (New Haven: Yale University Press, 2004), p. 483. See also Richard Silver, 'The Spiritual Kingdom in America: The Influence of Emanuel Swedenborg on American Society and Culture, 1815-1860', Ph.D. diss. (Stanford University, 1983); Marguerite Beck Block, *The New Church in the New World: a Study of Swedenborgianism in America* (New York: Henry Holt and Co., 1932).

44 Loy, 'The Dharma of Emanuel Swedenborg', pp. 5-6 (pp. 89-90 in Suzuki, *Swedenborg: Buddha of the North*); Tweed, 'American Occultism and Japanese Buddhism', pp. 255-6.

45 Bernstein, 'Introduction', pp. xx-xxx.

46 Tweed, 'American Occultism and Japanese Buddhism', pp. 249-81.

47 Albert J Edmunds, 'Has Swedenborg's "Lost Word" Been Found?', in *Journal of the American Society for Psychical Research*, vol. 7, no. 5 (May 1913), pp. 270-1. See also Albert J Edmunds, 'Buddhist and Christian Gospels', in *The Open Court*, vol. XIX, no. 592 (September 1905), pp. 538-46.

48 Albert J Edmunds, 'A Buddhist Genesis', in *The Monist*, vol. 14, no. 2 (January 1904), pp. 207-14.

49 See Wakoh Shannon Hickey, 'Swedenborg: A Modern Buddha?', in *Pacific World: The Journal of the Institute of Buddhist Studies*, no. 10 (Fall 2008), pp. 104-6. See also 'Ancient World', in *New Church Messenger*, vol. 80 (1901), pp. 242-3.

50 Emanuel Swedenborg, *True Christian Religion*, tr. John C Ager, 2 vols. (West Chester, PA:

Swedenborg Foundation, 1996), vol. 1, §279.

[51] Emanuel Swedenborg, *Heaven and Hell*, §58.

[52] Dōgen quoted in Loy, 'The Dharma of Emanuel Swedenborg', in Suzuki, *Swedenborg: Buddha of the North*, pp. 95-6. See also Swedenborg, *Heaven and Hell*, §251; Emanuel Swedenborg, *Spiritual Diary*, §§2043-4.

[53] Loy, 'The Dharma of Emanuel Swedenborg', in Suzuki, *Swedenborg: Buddha of the North*, p. 109. See also Swedenborg, *Heaven and Hell*, §§47, 236, 272, 363, 463, 498, 503.

[54] Loy, 'The Dharma of Emanuel Swedenborg', in Suzuki, *Swedenborg: Buddha of the North*, pp. 112-13.

[55] Swedenborg, *Heaven and Hell*, §535.

[56] Emanuel Swedenborg, *Divine Providence*, §§129, 234, 235, Swedenborg, *Divine Love and Wisdom*, §264.

[57] Swedenborg, *Divine Love and Wisdom*, §56; Swedenborg, *Heaven and Hell*, §58; Swedenborg, *True Christian Religion*, vol. 2, §570.5.

[58] Swedenborg, *Heaven and Hell*, §89.

[59] Stephen Morris, 'Buddhism and Christianity: The Meeting Place', in *Buddhist-Christian Studies*, vol. 19, no. 1 (1999), pp. 20, 21.

[60] See Luke 6:40: 'A disciple is not above his teacher, but everyone when he is fully taught will be like his teacher'.

[61] Read D T Suzuki, *Manual of Zen Buddhism* (New York: Grove Press, 1960), p. 93.

[62] Morris, 'Buddhism and Christianity: The Meeting Place', p. 26; D T Suzuki, *Essays in Zen Buddhism, First Series* (New York: Grove Press, 1961), p. 13. Stephen Morris's article showing the parallel teachings of *The Gospel of Thomas* and the Buddhist tradition did not go unnoticed. While he was praised for his insight, he was castigated by his critics who called it a caricature of Christian orthodoxy. John P Keenan, for example, considered it as erroneous to consider Zen (let alone Suzuki's interpretation of Zen) as the 'normative' tradition within Buddhism as it was to single out the texts of Thomas as the normative tradition outside the canonical gospels. To draw conclusions about Buddhism and Christianity on the basis of these singular texts was both 'disingenuous' and 'poor scholarly practice'. For Keenan, the Church took several hundred years before arriving at a 'conciliar definition' of Jesus's divinity and, while Morris contended that the outcome was distinctively different from the extracanonical portrayal of Jesus by Thomas which Morris considered more authentic, the fact remained that Morris was distorting Christianity. It would appear, however, that Keenan's 'polychrome' view of Christianity missed the point made by Morris who was not so much attacking Christian orthodoxy as he was arguing that the formulation of Christology

took a different tack than *The Gospel of Thomas* which, like the Q traditions, preceded the synoptic gospels and, as such, preceded the arm-wrestling that brought Christianity to its politically 'correct' position. For Morris, the God-centred focus of orthodox Christianity on the life of Jesus was not the focus of Thomas, a factor which he found similar to the Zen interpretation of Buddhism. See John P Keenan, 'Critique of "Buddhism and Christianity: The Meeting Place" ', in *Buddhist-Christian Studies*, vol. 19, no. 1 (1999), pp. 35-37.

[63] 'What is Pure Land Buddhism?', at <http://www.religionfacts.com/buddhism/sects/pure_land.htm>, accessed 5 December 2013.

[64] Yoshinaga Shin'ichi, 'Suzuki Daisetsu and Swedenborg: A Historical Background', pp. 113-14

[65] See Lawrence Buell, *Emerson*, pp. 196-7. In deference to his respect for Emerson, Suzuki applied Emerson's first and second series of essays to his own *Essays in Zen Buddhism* in which he described Zen as 'a religion of "self-reliance" ', and acknowledged the importance of the law of correspondences. Suzuki's admiration for Emerson extended over fifty-four years and included references in six of his books. He saw in Emerson and Thoreau an Eastern approach to nature and modernization. See Rampell, 'Laws That Refuse To Be Stated', p. 623. See also Arthur Versluis, *American Transcendentalism and Asian Religions* (New York: Oxford University Press, 1993).

[66] Rampell, 'Laws That Refuse To Be Stated', pp. 626, 633.

[67] David McMahan, *The Making of Buddhist Modernism* (Oxford: Oxford University Press, 2008), p. 125.

[68] Suzuki, *Essays in Zen Buddhism, First Series*, p. 13. See also Suzuki, 'Some Aspects of Zen Buddhism', in *The Eastern Buddhist*, vol. I, nos. 5-6 (1922), pp. 341-2.

[69] Suzuki, *Essays in Zen Buddhism, First Series*, pp. 268-9, 272-3.

[70] Ralph Waldo Emerson, 'Uses of Great Men', in *Representative Men*, quoted in Suzuki, *Essays in Zen Buddhism, First Series*, p. 309.

[71] Suzuki, *Essays in Zen Buddhism, First Series*, pp. 164-8; D T Suzuki, 'What is Zen?', in his *An Introduction to Zen Buddhism* (New York: Grove Press, 1964), pp. 38-47.

[72] D T Suzuki, *An Introduction to Zen Buddhism*, p. 43.

[73] Suzuki, *Essays in Zen Buddhism, First Series*, p. 55.

[74] Suzuki, *An Introduction to Zen Buddhism*, p. 44.

[75] Suzuki, *Essays in Zen Buddhism, First Series*, pp. 19, 20, 23.

[76] Van Meter Ames, 'Zen and American Philosophy', in *Philosophy East and West*, vol. 5, no. 4 (January 1956), pp. 310, 313.

[77] S I Shapiro, 'Contemporary Issues in the Americanization of Zen', in *Buddhist-Christian*

Studies, vol. 11 (1991), p. 269; R Aitken, *Taking the Path of Zen* (San Francisco: North Point Press, 1982); M Van Ames, *Zen and American Thought* (Honolulu: University of Hawaii Press, 1962); C J Beck, *Everyday Zen: Love and Work* (New York: Harper Collins, 1989); R S Ellwood (ed.), *Zen in American Life and Letters* (Malibu, CA: Undena Publications, 1987); P Kapleau, *Zen: Merging of East and West* (New York: Doubleday, 1989); E M Layman, *Buddhism in America* (Chicago: Nelson-Hall, 1976); R M Pirsig, *Zen and the Art of Motorcycle Maintenance* (New York: Bantam, 1975).

78   Quoted in Theodore Benke, 'William James and the Medecine Buddha: The Middle Way of Pragmatism', in *Philosophy East and West* (2000), at <http://theobenke.wordpress.com/>, accessed 10 April 2014. See also Eugene Taylor, 'Psychology of Religion and Asian Studies: The William James Legacy', in *Journal of Transpersonal Psychology*, vol. 10, no. 1 (1978), p. 1; Dale Riepe, 'A Note on William James and Indian Philosophy', in *Philosophy and Phenomenological Research*, vol. 28, no. 4 (June 1968), pp. 587-91; Ralph Barton Perry, *The Thought and Character of William James: As Revealed in Unpublished Correspondence and Notes, Together with His Published Writings* (Boston: Little, Brown, and Co., 1935).

79   See Eugene Taylor, 'Peirce and Swedenborg', in *Studia Swedenborgia*, vol. 6, no. 1 (June 1986) pp. 25-51; Eugene Taylor, *Shadow Culture: Psychology and Spirituality in America* (Washington, DC: Counterpoint, 1999); Eugene Taylor, *The Mystery of Personality: A History of Psychodynamic Theories* (New York: Springer, 2009); Eugene Taylor, *William James on Consciousness Beyond the Margins* (Princeton, NJ: Princeton University Press, 1996); Eugene Taylor and Rob Wozniak (eds.), *Pure Experience: The Response to William James* (Bristol: Thoemmes Press, 1996); Alfred Habegger, *The Father: A Life of Henry James, Senior* (Farrar, Straus and Giroux, New York, 1994); Jeremy Carrette, *William James's Hidden Religious Imagination: A Universe of Relations* (New York: Routledge, 2013).

80   Swedenborg, *Divine Love and Wisdom*, §§327, 331-3. See also Louis G Hoeck, 'Swedenborg's Doctrine of Uses', at <http://www.lastchurch.com/doctrineofuses.html>, accessed 10 April 2014.

81   Eugene Taylor, 'Swedenborgian Roots of American Pragmatism: The Case of D.T. Suzuki', in *Studia Swedenborgiana*, vol. 9, no. 2 (May 1995), at <http://www.shs.psr.edu/studia/index.asp?article_id=129>, accessed 27 January 2014.

82   Van Meter Ames, 'Zen to Mead', in *Proceedings and Addresses of the American Philosophical Association*, vol. 33 (1959), pp. 28, 30-2, 35, 38. See also D C Mathur, 'The historical Buddha (Gotama), Hume, and James on the self: Comparisons and evaluations', in *Philosophy East and West*, vol. 28, no. 3 (July 1978), pp. 254-69; Kamala Kumari, *Notion of Truth in Buddhism and Pragmatism* (Delhi: Capital Publishing House, 1987); Miranda Shaw,

'William James and Yogacara Philosophy: A comparative inquiry', in *Philosophy East and West*, vol. 37, no. 3 (July 1987), pp. 223-44.

83 Ames, 'Zen and American Philosophy', pp. 314, 316.

84 Emanuel Swedenborg, *Divine Love and Wisdom*, §§296, 307, 327.

85 Van Meter Ames, 'Zen and Pragmatism', in *Philosophy East and West*, vol. 4, no. 1 (April 1954), p. 32; Suzuki, *Essays in Zen Buddhism, Second Series* (London: Rider and Company, 1970), p. 220. See also John Dewey, *The Problems of Men* (New York: Philosophical Library, 1946), p. 396.

86 Suzuki, *Essays in Zen Buddhism, First Series*, pp. 299, 316.

87 Suzuki, *An Introduction to Zen Buddhism*, pp. 31-6.

88 Ibid., p. 64.

89 D T Suzuki, *Living by Zen* (Tokyo: Sanseido Press, 1949), p. 49; Van Meter Ames, 'America, Existentialism, and Zen', in *Philosophy East and West*, vol. 1 (1951), p. 36.

90 Read C I Lewis, *An Analysis of Knowledge and Valuation* (LaSalle, IL: Open Court Publishing Co., 1946).

91 John Dewey, 'A Common Faith', in *The Later Works of John Dewey, 1925-1953: Essays, Reviews, Miscellany, and a Common Faith* (Carbondale: Southern Illinois University, 1986), p. 35.

92 See Albert Camus, *The Myth of Sisyphus, and Other Essays* (New York: Knopf, 1955).

93 J Eduardo Perez Valera, 'Toward a Transcultural Philosophy', in *Monumenta Nipponica*, vol. 27 (1972), p. 176; Bernard Lonergan, *Insight* (New York: Philosophical Library, 1963).

94 Miranda Shaw, 'William James and Yogācāra Philosophy: A Comparative Inquiry', in *Philosophy East and West*, vol. 37, no. 3 (July 1987), p. 226; William James, *Essays in Radical Empiricism*, ed. Frederick H Burckhardt, Fredson Bowers and Ignas K Skrupskelis (Cambridge, MA: Harvard University Press, 1976), p. 65.

95 William James, *Pragmatism: A New Name for Some Old Ways of Thinking; Popular Lectures on Philosophy* (New York: Longmans, Green, and Co., 1907), p. 58.

96 Van Meter Ames, 'America, Existentialism, and Zen', p. 35. See also D T Suzuki, *Living by Zen*.

97 William James, 'A World of Pure Experience', in *Journal of Philosophy, Psychology, and Scientific Method*, vol. 1 (1904), pp. 533-43; 561-70. See also Van Meter Ames, 'Zen and Pragmatism', pp. 19-33.

98 See Ames, 'Zen and American Philosophy', pp. 305-20; Eugene I Taylor and Robert H Wozniak, 'Pure Experience, the Response to William James: An Introduction', in Taylor and Wozniak (eds.), *Pure Experience: The Response to William James*, pp. ix-xxxii; D

T Suzuki, *Essays in Zen Buddhism, Third Series* (London: Rider and Co., 1953), pp. 78, 83; William James, *Essays in Radical Empiricism* (New York: Longmans, Green and Co., 1947), p. 193; Eugene Taylor, 'New Light on the Origin of William James's Experimental Psychology', in Michael G Johnson and Tracy B Henley (eds.), *Reflections on the Principles of Psychology: William James After a Century* (Hillsdale, NJ: Lawrence Erlbaum Associates, 1990), p. 34; Charles A Moore (ed.), *Essays in East-West Philosophy: An Attempt at World Philosophical Synthesis* (Honolulu: University of Hawaii Press, 1951).

[99] Suzuki, *Essays in Zen Buddhism, First Series*, pp. 104-7.

[100] D T Suzuki, 'Zen Buddhism', in *Monumenta Nipponica*, vol. 1, no. 1 (January 1938), p. 49.

[101] Ibid., p. 55.

[102] Due to their long affiliation, Abe learned to appreciate Suzuki's method of formulating Zen in a manner understandable to Western thinkers. Accordingly, Abe translated Nishida's *An Inquiry Into the Good* and engaged in significant conversations with Western thinkers of the calibre of Tillich and Heidegger resulting in a much richer Buddhist-Christian dialogue in the ensuing years. See Michiko Yusa, 'Masao Abe: D.T. Suzuki's Legacies and an "Academic Darhma Lineage" in North America', in *Buddhist-Christian Studies*, vol. 28 (2008), pp. 111-13.

[103] Alan Watts was an Anglican priest whose first book on Buddhism, *The Spirit of Zen* (1936) had been due in part to the influence of Suzuki who he had first met in London. During the Second World War, Watts had served as chaplain at Northwestern University north of Chicago before moving to San Francisco where he joined the Los Angeles Vedanta Society. His *The Way of Zen* (1957), *Psychotherapy East and West* (1961) and *The Joyous Cosmology* (1962) became instant gratification for the postmodernist generation beginning to question the objectivity of Western science. Watts was one of those contemporary philosophers who felt that experience and faith rather than reasoned belief provided the path through life's insecurities and paradoxes. His advice was to 'travel light', relinquishing fruitless searches for security and to accept our sensations, feelings and thoughts—the reality of the present—without labelling or pigeonholing them in discrete categories. He explained that Zen's attraction to the Japanese lay in 'the possibility of liberation from self-consciousness' which had been induced into their education. For the West, there were multiple reasons for its growth. 'The appeal of Zen arts to the "modern" spirit in the West, the work of Suzuki, the war with Japan, the itchy fascination of "Zen-stories," and the attraction of a non-conceptual, experiential philosophy in the climate of scientific relativism—all these are involved', he explained. In addition, there was 'our vague disquiet with the artificiality . . . of both Christianity, with its politically ordered cosmology, and technology, with its imperialistic mechanization of a natural world from which man himself feels strangely alien'. For all of these reasons, there

was a disquietude which arose from man's attempt to stand apart from nature in order to control and master it. Alan Watts, 'Beat Zen, Square Zen, and Zen', in *Chicago Review*, vol. 12 (Summer 1958), p. 5. See also Camille Paglia, 'Cults and Cosmic Consciousness: Religious Vision in the American 1960s', in *Arion*, vol. 10, no. 3 (Winter 2003), p. 74; Alan Watts, *The Spirit of Zen: A Way of Life, Work and Art in the Far East*, 3rd edn. (New York: Grove Press, 1960); Alan Watts, *The Way of Zen* (New York: Pantheon, 1957); Alan Watts, *Psychotherapy East and West* (New York: Pantheon Books, 1961); and Alan Watts, *The Joyous Cosmology: Adventures in the Chemistry of Consciousness* (New York: Pantheon Books, 1962).

[104] Joseph M Kitagawa, 'Daisetz Teitaro Suzuki (1870-1966)', in *History of Religions*, vol. 6, no. 3 (February 1967), pp. 265-9. See also Carole Tomkinson (ed.), *Big Sky Mind: Buddhism and the Beat Generation* (New York: Riverhead Books, 1995).

[105] Jack Kerouac's *Dharma Bums* (1958) offered a Beat vision of American society, including a vision of Buddhism as the counterculture alternative to Western Christianity. The quintessential Buddhist, who he moulded into the book character of Japhy Ryder, had all the earmarks of an ancient poet whose disciples (i.e., 'rucksack wanderers') escaped American society by living a semi-monastic life that included drugs, alcohol, tobacco and pliable women. The convert type of Buddhism envisaged by Kerouac was not based on any academic study of Buddhism or even a reflection of Japanese American Buddhism, rather it was a highly subjective vision of what he imagined Buddhism could represent as a counterculture to what he found failing in American society. Individuals, such as the poet Gary Snyder (whom the leading character in Kerouac's *The Dharma Bums* is modelled upon), took Buddhism seriously enough to live monastically in Japan, but most of the Beat generation were borrowers and dabblers, taking enough to feed their counterculture defiance, and brooding over Western culture.

[106] Carl G Jung, the son of a Protestant minister, studied Asian thought in great depth after his break with Freud in 1913. His theory of the collective unconscious drew heavily from the Hindu concept of *samskaras*, meaning the residue of past lifetimes. According to Jung, Zen was one of the exceptional contributions of the Oriental mind whose satori or enlightenment was a matter of 'natural occurrence, of something so very simple that one fails to see the wood for the trees, and in attempting to explain it, invariably says the very thing that drives others into the greatest confusion'. In looking for examples of satori and the release of ego-like consciousness in Western thought beyond that of the Christian mystics, Jung found it in the *Spiritual Exercises* of Ignatius of Loyola and in the transformed man of Nietzsche's *Thus Spake Zarathustra*. Generally, however, he saw it as a highly improbable practice in the Western world whose transmission was neither commendable nor relative

to the conditions of the Western mind. 'Who amongst us would produce such implicit trust in a superior master and his incomprehensible ways? This respect for the greater human personality exists only in the East. Who could boast of believing in the possibility of a transformation experience paradoxical beyond measure; to the extent, moreover, of sacrificing many years of his life to the wearisome pursuit of such an object? And finally, who would dare to take upon himself the authority of a heterodoxical transformation experience?' See C G Jung, 'Foreword', in Suzuki, *An Introduction to Zen Buddhism*, pp. 13, 24.

[107] Read Theodore Roszak, *The Making of a Counter Culture: Reflections on the Technocratic Society and Its Youthful Opposition* (London: Faber and Faber, 1970); Don Morreale (ed.), *Buddhist America: Centers, Retreats, Practices* (Santa Fe: John Muir Publications, 1988); Peter Bishop, *Dreams of Power: Tibetan Buddhism and the Western Imagination* (London: Athlone Press, 1993); Rick Fields, *How the Swans Came to the Lake: A Narrative History of Buddhism in America* (Boston: Shambhala, 1992).

[108] John Findlay, Clark Professor of Metaphysics at Yale, remarked that 'far from being the special possession of peculiar people called mystics, [mysticism] enters into the experience of most men at many times, just as views of the horizon and the open sky enter into most ordinary views of the world'. These so-called great mystics were simply individuals who carried 'to the point of genius an absolutely normal, ordinary, indispensable side of human experience and attitude'. Similarly, the profound nature and expression manifested in Christian mysticism was remarkably similar to that found in the Upanishads and the Buddhist Sutras. It involved an experience of ecstasy that was no more illogical than ordinary beliefs properly expressed. See John Findlay, 'The Logic of Mysticism', in *Religious Studies*, vol. 2 (1967), pp. 146-7, 157. See also W T Stace, *Mysticism and Philosophy* (Philadelphia: Lippincott, 1960).

[109] D T Suzuki, *Mysticism: Christian and Buddhist* (New York: Harper and Brothers, 1957), pp. 53-4. According to British educator and philosopher Stace, there were seven basic traits of mysticism: (1) A unifying vision; (2) An apprehension of One as an inner subjectivity; (3) A sense that what is apprehended is real; (4) A feeling of blessedness and joy; (5) A feeling that what is apprehended is holy; (6) A feeling that what is apprehended is paradoxical; and (7) A feeling that what is apprehended is ineffable and inexpressible. See W T Stace, *Mysticism and Philosophy*; John Findlay, 'The Logic of Mysticism', p. 157.

[110] Suzuki, *Essays in Zen Buddhism, First Series*, p. 126.

[111] Suzuki, *Essays in Zen Buddhism, First Series*, pp. 268-72; 314-62.

[112] Meister Eckhart, *Meister Eckhart: A Modern Translation*, tr. Raymond B Blakney (New York: Harper and Row, 1941), p. 246.

[113] Ananda K Coomaraswamy, *Transformation of Nature in Art* (Cambridge: Harvard

University Press, 1934), p. 61.

[114] Joseph Politella, 'Meister Eckhart and Eastern Wisdom', in *Philosophy East and West*, vol. 15 (1965), pp. 117-33.

[115] Suzuki, *Mysticism: Christian and Buddhist*, p. 20.

[116] Read James M Clark (tr. and ed.), *Meister Eckhart. An Introduction to the Study of His Works* (New York: Thomas Nelson and Sons, 1957); Richard Kieckhefer, 'Meister Eckhart's Conception of Union with God', in *Harvard Theological Review*, vol. 71 (1978), pp. 203-5; Frank Tobin, 'Mysticism and Meister Eckhart', in *Mystics Quarterly*, vol. 10 (1984), pp. 17-24.

[117] Charlotte Radler, 'Losing the Self: Detachment in Meister Eckhart and its Significance for Buddhist-Christian Dialogue', in *Buddhist-Christian Studies*, vol. 26 (2006), pp. 111-12.

[118] Read Reiner Schürmann, *Meister Eckhart: Mystic and Philosopher* (Bloomington: Indiana University Press, 1978); Ueda Shizuteru, ' "Nothingness" in Meister Eckhart and Zen Buddhism with Particular Reference to the Borderlands of Philosophy and Theology', in Frederick Franck (ed.), *The Buddha Eye: An Anthology of the Kyoto School and Its Contemporaries* (New York: Crossroad, 1982), pp. 157-69; David Tracy, *Dialogue with the Other: Inter-Religious Dialogue* (Grand Rapids: Eerdmans, 1990).

[119] Thomas Merton, *Mystic and Zen Masters* (New York: Dell, 1967).

[120] Thomas Merton, 'D.T. Suzuki: The Man and His Work', in Masao Abe (ed.), *A Zen Life: D.T. Suzuki Remembered*, p. 121.

[121] John F Teahan, 'A Dark and Empty Way: Thomas Merton and the Apophatic Tradition', in *The Journal of Religion*, vol. 58 (1978), p. 264. See also Ralph Harper, *The Path of Darkness* (Cleveland: Case Western Reserve University Press, 1968).

[122] Read Thomas Merton, *Thoughts in Solitude* (Garden City, NY: Doubleday and Co., 1968); Thomas Merton, *Mystics and Zen Masters*; Thomas Merton, *New Seeds of Contemplation* (New York: New Directions, 1961); Dennis Q McInerny, *Thomas Merton: The Man and His Work* (Washington, DC: Cistercian Publications, 1974); Patrick Hart (ed.), *Thomas Merton, Monk: A Monastic Tribute* (New York: Sheed and Ward, 1974).

[123] Thomas Merton, *The Ascent to Truth* (London: Hollis and Carter, 1951), p. 26; Merton, *Mystics and Zen Masters*, pp. 221, 242-5.

[124] Teahan, 'A Dark and Empty Way: Thomas Merton and the Apophatic Tradition', pp. 279-81, 285. See also Merton, 'Wisdom in Emptiness', in *Zen and the Birds of Appetite* (New York: New Directions, 1968), pp. 99-138; Merton, *The Climate of Monastic Prayer* (Shannon, Ireland: Irish Universities Press, 1969), p. 128.

[125] D T Suzuki and Thomas Merton, 'The Recovery of Paradise: Wisdom in Emptiness, A

Dialogue: D. T. Suzuki and Thomas Merton', in *New Directions in Prose and Poetry*, vol. 17 (1961), pp. 65-101.

126 Thomas Merton, 'D.T. Suzuki: The Man and His Work', in Masao Abe (ed.), *A Zen Life: D.T. Suzuki Remembered*, pp. 123, 124.

127 Ibid., pp. 125-6. In 1329, Pope John XXII issued *In agro dominico*, condemning Eckhart's teachings, fearing that the University of Paris teacher and preacher might draw the un-educated masses from the pews where they were instructed by the Church's ecclesiastical institutions and their control of saving grace through the sacraments to feel instead the currents of the God directly in some subversive and unmediated experience.

128 Larry A Fader, 'D.T. Suzuki's Contribution to the West', in Masao Abe (ed.), *A Zen Life: D.T. Suzuki Remembered*, p. 98.

129 Pascaline Coff, 'The Inner Journey: Reflections on the Awakening of Mind and Heart in Buddhism and Christianity', in *Buddhist-Christian Studies*, vol. 11 (1991), p. 174.

130 Read Thomas Merton, 'The Inner Experience: Notes on Contemplation', in *Cistercian Studies*, vol. 18, no. 1 (1983), pp. 3-15.

131 Coff, 'The Inner Journey: Reflections on the Awakening of Mind and Heart in Buddhism and Christianity', pp. 184-5; Shantideva, *Guide to the Boddhisattva's Way of Life* (Dharamsala: Library of Tibetan Works and Archives, 1987).

132 Ralph Waldo Emerson, 'Divinity School Address', in *Nature, Addresses, and Lectures*, ed. Robert E Spiller and Alfred Ferguson (Cambridge: Harvard University Press, 1971), p. 87.

RETROSPECTIVE
1 Swedenborg, *True Christian Religion*, vol. 1, §67.

SELECT BIBLIOGRAPHY

Please note this select bibliography comprises works used in the preparation of this book that have not been mentioned in the endnotes, along with works of 'further reading' by the main subjects of the essays in this book. Full bibliographic information for all works cited within this book can be found in the first citation of each work within the endnotes section (pp. 303-66).

Ahlstrom, Sydney, *The American Protestant Encounter with World Religions* (Beloit, WI: Beloit College, 1962).

Aiken, Charles F, *The Dhamma of Gotama the Buddha and the Gospel of Jesus the Christ: A Critical Inquiry into the Alleged Relations of Buddhism with Primitive Christianity* (Boston: Marlier, 1900).

Alcott, A Bronson, *Concord Days* (Boston: Roberts Brothers, 1888).

Alger, William R, *The Poetry of the East* (Boston: Whittemore, Niles, and Hall, 1856).

Almond, Philip C, *The British Discovery of Buddhism* (New York: Cambridge University Press, 1988).

Ameke, Wilhelm, *History of Homoeopathy: Its Origin, Its Conflicts. With an Appendix on the Present State of University Medicine*, tr. Alfred E Drysdale, ed. R E Dudgeon (London: E Gould and Son, 1885).

Anderson, Quentin, *The American Henry James* (New Brunswick, NJ: Rutgers University Press, 1957).

Anonymous, *A Brief History of the Theological Seminary of the Presbyterian Church, at Princeton, New Jersey* (Princeton: John Bogart, 1838).

Armytage, W H G, *Heavens Below: Utopian Experiments in England, 1560-1960* (London: Routledge and Kegan Paul, 1968).

Arnold, Edwin, *The Light of Asia; Or, the Great Renunciation; Being the Life and Teaching of Gautama* (Wheaton, IL: Theosophical Publishing House, 1969 [1879]).

Atkinson, William Walker, *Dynamic Thought; Or, the Law of Vibrant Energy* (Los Angeles: Segnogram, 1906).

——*The Inner Consciousness: A Course of Lessons on the Inner Planes of the Mind, Intuition, Instinct, Automatic Mentation and Other Wonderful Phases of Mental Phenomena* (Chicago: Advanced Thought, 1908).

——*Mind-Power: The Secret of Mental Magic* (Chicago: Advanced Thought, 1912).

Baker, Gregory L, *Religion and Science: From Swedenborg to Chaotic Dynamics* (Jamaica, NY: Solomon Press, 1992).

Beach, Joseph Warren, *The Method of Henry James* (New Haven, CT: Yale University Press, 1918).

Beekman, Lillian G, *Outlines of Swedenborg's Cosmology* (Bryn Athyn, PA: Academy Book Room, 1907).

Benz, Ernst, *Emanuel Swedenborg: Visionary Savant in the Age of Reason* (West Chester, PA: Swedenborg Foundation, 2002).

Bernard, Theos, *Hindu Philosophy* (New York: Philosophical Library, 1947).

Berridge, Edward William, *The Brotherhood of the New Life; An Epitome of the Work and Teaching of Thomas Lake Harris* (Glasgow: C W Pearce and Co., 1896-1917).

Bestor, Arthur, *Backwoods Utopias: The Sectarian Origins and the Owenite Phase of Communitarian Socialism in America, 1663-1829* (Philadelphia: University of Pennsylvania Press, 1950).

Blavatsky, Helena P, *The Secret Doctrine: The Synthesis of Science, Religion, and Philosophy*, 2 vols. (London: Theosophical Publishing, 1888).

Boas, George (ed.), *Romanticism in America* (Baltimore: Johns Hopkins University Press, 1940).

Bozeman, Theodore Dwight, *Protestants in an Age of Science* (Chapel Hill: University of North Carolina Press, 1977).

Braden, Charles Samuel, *These Also Believe: A Study of Modern American Cults and Minority Religious Movements* (New York: The Macmillan Company, 1949).

Brandon, Ruth, *The Spiritualists: The Passion for the Occult in the Nineteenth and Twentieth Centuries* (London: Weidenfeld and Nicolson, 1983).

Braude, Ann, *Radical Spirits: Spiritualism ad Women's Rights in Nineteenth-Century America* (Bloomington: Indiana University Press, 2001).

Braybrooke, Marcus, *Stepping Stones to a Global Ethic* (London: SCM Press, 1992).

Bressler, Ann Lee, *The Universalist Movement in America, 1770-1880* (New York: Oxford University Press, 2001).

Brisbane, Albert, *Association; Or, A Concise Exposition of the Practical Part of Fourier's Social Science* (New York: AMS Press, 1975 [1843]).

——*A Concise Exposition of the Doctrine of Association, or Plan for a Re-organization of Society* (New York: J S Redfield, Clinton Hall, 1843).

——*The European Travel Diaries of Albert Brisbane, 1830-1832: Discovering Fourierism for America*, ed. Abigail Mellen and Allaire Brisbane Stallsmith (Lewiston, NY: Edwin Mellen Press, 2005).

——*General Introduction to Social Sciences Part First.—Introduction to Fourier's Theory of Social Organization* (New York: C P Somerby, 1876).

——*Letters of the American Socialist Albert Brisbane to K. A. Varnhagen von Ense*, ed. Terry H Pickett and Françoise de Rocher (Heidelberg: C Winter, 1986).

——*Philosophy of Money. A New Currency and a New Credit System* (1863).

——*Social Destiny of Man; Or, Association and Reorganization of Industry* (Philadelphia: C F Stollmeyer, 1840).

——*The Social Destiny of Man, or, Theory of the Four Movements by Charles Fourier. Translated by Henry Clapp, Jr with a Treatise on the Functions of the Human Passions. And an Outline of Fourier's System of Social Science by Albert Brisbane* (New York: Robert M Dewitt, 1857).

——*Theory of the Functions of the Human Passions, Followed by an Outline View of the Fundamental Principles of Fourier's Theory of Social Science* (New York: Miller, Orton, and Mulligan, 1856).

——*What is Association?* (New York: J S Redfield, 1843).

Brisbane, Redelia, *Albert Brisbane. A Mental Biography with a Character Study. By His Wife* (New York: Burt Franklin, 1969).

Broomell, Clyde W (ed.), *Divine Healing. The Origin and Cure of Disease. As Taught in the Bible and Explained by Emanuel Swedenborg* (Boston: George H Ellis Co., 1907).

Brown, Slater, *The Heyday of Spiritualism* (New York: Hawthorn Books, 1970).

Buescher, John B, *The Other Side of Salvation: Spiritualism and the Nineteenth-Century Religious Experience* (Boston: Skinner House, 2004).

Burris, John P, *Exhibiting Religion: Colonialism and Spectacle at International Expositions, 1851-1893* (Charlottesville: University Press of Virginia, 2001).

Burton, Katherine, *Paradise Planters: The Story of Brook Farm* (London: Longmans, Green and Co., 1939).

Bynum, W F, and Roy Porter (eds.), *Medical Fringe and Medical Orthodoxy, 1750-1850* (London: Croom Helm, 1987).

Campbell, Anthony, *Two Faces of Homoeopathy* (London: Robert Hale, 1984).

Campbell, Bruce F, *Ancient Wisdom Revived: A History of the Theosophical Movement* (Berkeley: University of California Press, 1980).

Carus, Paul, *Buddhism and Its Christian Critics* (Chicago: Open Court Publishing Co., 1897; new and revised edition, 1905).

——*The Dawn of a New Religious Era and Other Essays* (Chicago: Open Court Publishing Co., 1916).

——*The Dharma or the Religion of Enlightenment: An Exposition of Buddhism*, 4th edn. (Chicago: Open Court Publishing Co., 1898).

——*The Gospel of Buddha, Compiled from Ancient Records* (Chicago: The Open Court Publishing Co., 1917).

——*Karma: A Story of Buddhist Ethics* (Chicago: Open Court Publishing Co., 1917).

——*The Religion of Science* (Chicago: Open Court, 1899 [1893]).

——*The World's Parliament of Religions and the Religious Parliament Extension* (Chicago: Open Court Publishing Co., 1896).

Chappell, Vere, *Sexual Outlaw, Erotic Mystic: The Essential Ida Craddock* (San Francisco: Red Wheel/Weiser, 2010).

Christy, Arthur E (ed.), *The Asian Legacy and American Life* (New York: John Day, 1942).

Clark, Jerome, *Hidden Realms, Lost Civilizations, and Beings from Other Worlds* (Detroit: Visible Ink, 2010).

Clarke, James Freeman, *Ten Great Religions: An Essay in Comparative Theology* (Boston: Houghton, Mifflin, 1895 [1871]).

Close, Stuart, *The Genius of Homeopathy: Lectures and Essays on Homeopathic Philosophy* (New Delhi: B Jain, 1993).

Cook, Francis H, *Hua-yen Buddhism: The Jewel Net of Indra* (University Park, PA: Pennsylvania State University Press, 1977).

Cooke, George Willis, *Unitarianism in America* (Boston: American Unitarian Association, 1910).

Coulter, Harris L, *Divided Legacy. A History of the Schism in Medical Thought*, 3 vols. (Richmond, CA: North Atlantic Books, 1975-82).

Cox, Robert S, *Body and Soul: A Sympathetic History of American Spiritualism* (Charlottesville, VA: University of Virginia Press, 2003).

Cranston, Sylvia, *H.P.B.: The Extraordinary Life and Influence of Helena Blavatsky, Founder of the Modern Theosophical Movement* (New York: Putnam's, 1994).

Croce, Paul Jerome, *Science and Religion in the Era of William James, Volume One:*

Eclipse of Certainty, 1820-1880 (Chapel Hill: University of North Carolina Press, 1995).

Dasa, Philangi (pseud. Herman C Vetterling), *Swedenborg the Buddhist; or, the Higher Swedenborgianism, Its Secrets and Thibetan Origin* (Los Angeles: The Buddhist Swedenborgian Brotherhood, 1887; repr. Charleston, SC: Arcana Books, 2003).

Davis, Andrew Jackson, *The Harmonial Man; Or, Thoughts for the Age* (Boston: Bela Marsh, 1853).

DeJong, J W, *A Brief History of Buddhist Studies in Europe and America* (Delhi: Sri Satguru Publications, 1987).

Dingle, Herbert, *Swedenborg as a Physical Scientist* (London: Swedenborg Society, 1938).

Dombrowski, James, *The Early Days of Christian Socialism in America* (New York: Columbia University Press, 1937).

Doyle, Arthur Conan, *The History of Spiritualism* (Amsterdam: Fredonia Book, 2003).

Dresser, Horatio, *A History of the New Thought Movement* (New York: Thomas Y Crowell Co., 1919).

Duban, James, *The Nature of True Virtue: Theology, Psychology, and Politics in the Writings of Henry James, Sr., Henry James, Jr., and William James* (Madison, NJ: Fairleigh Dickinson University Press, 2001).

Duss, John, *The Harmonists: A Personal History* (Philadelphia: Porcupine Press, 1972).

Eastman, Arthur M, *Life and Reminiscences of Dr. Constantine Hering* (Philadelphia: Published by the Family for Private Circulation, 1917).

Edmonds, John W, and George T Dexter, *Spiritualism*, 2 vols. (New York: Partridge and Brittan, 1853-5).

Edwardes, Michael, *East-West Passage: The Travel of Ideas, Arts and Inventions between Asia and the Western World* (New York: Taplinger Publishing Co., 1971).

Ekirch, Arthur A, *The Idea of Progress in America, 1815-1860* (New York: Columbia University Press, 1944).

Eliade, Mircea (ed.), *The Encyclopedia of Religion*, vol .13 (New York: Macmillan, 1987).

Ellwood, Robert, *Alternative Altars: Unconventional and Eastern Spirituality in America* (Chicago: University of Chicago Press, 1979).

Emerson, Ralph Waldo, *The Complete Works of Ralph Waldo Emerson*, 12 vols. (Boston: Houghton, Mifflin and Co., 1904).

—*English Traits* (Boston: James R Osgood and Co., 1876).

—*Essays: First Series* (Boston: Phillips, Sampson, and Co., 1857 [1841]).

—*Essays: Second Series* (Boston: Phillips, Sampson, and Co., 1855).

—*The Journals of Ralph Waldo Emerson*, ed. E W Emerson and W E Forbes, 10 vols.

(Boston: Houghton Mifflin Co., 1909-14).

—*Nature, Addresses, and Lectures*, ed. Robert E Spiller and Alfred Ferguson (Cambridge: Harvard University Press, 1971).

—*The Prose Works of Ralph Waldo Emerson: In Two Volumes* (Boston: Fields and Osgood, 1870).

—*Representative Men* (1850), in *The Complete Works of Ralph Waldo Emerson*, vol. IV (Boston: Houghton Mifflin Co., 1876).

—*The Selected Writings of Ralph Waldo Emerson*, ed. Brooks Atkinson (New York: Modern Library, 1950).

—*Select Essays and Addresses, Including The American Scholar*, ed. Eugene D Holmes (New York: The Macmillan Co., 1906).

Evans, Warren Felt, *The Divine Law of Cure* (Boston: H H Carter and Co., 1881).

—*Esoteric Christianity and Mental Therapeutics* (Boston: H H Carter and Karrick, 1886).

—*The Primitive Mind-Cure* (Boston: H H Carter and Co., 1885).

Faivre, Antoine, and Wouter J Hanegraaff (eds.), *Western Esotericism and the Science of Religion* (Leuven: Peeters, 1998).

Fenollosa, Ernest F, *East and West: The Discovery of America and Other Poems* (New York: Crowell, 1893).

Fourier, Charles, *Charles Fourier's the Phalanx, or Journal of Social Science* (New York: Burt Franklin, 1967).

—*Design for Utopia: Selected Writings of Charles Fourier*, tr. Julia Franklin (New York: Schocken Books, 1971).

—*Harmonian Man: Selected Writings of Charles Fourier*, ed. Mark Poster (Garden City, NY: Doubleday, 1971).

—*The Hierarchies of Cuckoldry and Bankruptcy*, tr. Geoffrey Longnecker (Cambridge, MA: Wakefield Press, 2011).

—*The Passions of the Human Soul, and Their Influence on Society and Civilization*, tr. John Morell, introd. Hugh Doherty, 2 vols. (London: Hippolyte Bailliere, 1851).

—*Piéges et charlatanisme des deux sectes Saint-Simon et Owen, qui promettent l'association et le progrès* (Paris: Bossange père, 1831).

—*Political Economy Made Easy. A Sketch, Exhibiting the Various Errors of Our Present Political Arrangements* (London: Sherwood, 1828).

—*Selections from the Works of Fourier*, tr. Julia Franklin, introd. Charles Gide (London: Swan Sonnenschein and Co., 1901).

—*Social Science: The Theory of Universal Unity* (New York: American News Co., 1900).

——*The Theory of the Four Movements*, ed. Gareth Stedman Jones and Ian Patterson, tr. Ian Patterson (New York: Cambridge University Press, 1996).

——*Theory of Social Organization* (New York: C P Somerby, 1876).

——*The Utopian Vision of Charles Fourier: Selected Texts on Work, Love, and Passionate Attraction*, tr. and ed. Jonathan Beecher and Richard Bienvenu (Columbia, MO: University of Missouri Press, 1983).

Frothingham, Octavius Brooks, *Transcendentalism in New England: A History* (Philadelphia: University of Pennsylvania Press, 1972).

Gabriel, Ralph Henry, *The Course of American Democratic Thought* (New York: The Ronald Press, 1940).

Gevitz, Norman (ed.), *Other Healers: Unorthodox Medicine in America* (Baltimore: Johns Hopkins University Press, 1988).

Golemba, Henry L, *George Ripley* (Boston: Twayne, 1977).

Guarneri, Carl J, *The Utopian Alternative: Fourierism in Nineteenth-Century America* (Ithaca, NY: Cornell University Press, 1991).

Gypser, K-H (ed.), *Kent's Minor Writings on Homeopathy* (Heidleberg: Haug, 1987).

Hall, T C, *The Religious Background of American Culture* (Boston: Little, Brown and Co., 1930).

Handy, Robert T, *A Christian America: Protestant Hopes and Historical Realities* (New York: Oxford University Press, 1984).

Hanegraaff, Wouter J, and Jeffrey John Kripal (eds.), *Hidden Intercourse: Eros and Sexuality in the History of Western Esotericism* (New York: Fordham University Press, 2011).

Hanson, John W, *The World's Congress of Religions. The Addresses and Papers Delivered Before the Parliament. And an Abstract of the Congresses Held in the Art Institute, Chicago, Illinois, U.S.A., August 25 to October 15, 1893. Under the Auspices of The World's Columbian Exposition* (Chicago: W B Conkey Co., 1894).

Harding, William, and Carl Bode (eds.), *The Correspondence of Henry David Thoreau* (New York: New York University Press, 1958).

Haroutunian, Joseph, *Piety Versus Moralism* (New York: Henry Holt and Co., 1932).

Harris, Thomas Lake, *Aims and Issues of the New Church* (Glasgow: James Fowler, 1863).

——*Appendix to the Arcana of Christianity. The Song of Satan: a series of poems originating with a society of infernal spirits, and received during temptation-combats* (New York: New Church Publishing Association, 1858).

——*The Arcana of Christianity; an Unfolding of the Celestial Sense of the Divine Word through T. L. Harris. Part I.—Genesis* (New York: New Church, 1858).

——*Arcana of Christianity: An Unfolding of the Celestial Sense of the Divine Word, through Thomas Lake Harris. Part III.—The Apocalypse* (New York: Brotherhood of the New Life, 1867).

——*Battle Bells* (Santa Rosa, CA: Fountain Grove Press, 1891).

——*The Breath of God with Man: An Essay on the Grounds and Evidences of Universal Religion* (New York: Brotherhood of the New Life, 1867).

——*Bridal Hours: Lyrical Utterances of the Two-in-One.* (Santa Rosa, CA: Fountain Grove Press, 1878).

——*Brotherhood of the New Life: Its Fact, Law, Method and Purpose* (Santa Rosa, CA: Fountaingrove Press, 1891).

——*Conversation in Heaven: A Wisdom Song* (Santa Rosa, CA Fountain Grove Press, 1894).

——*Declarations of the Divine One-Twain* (Santa Rosa, CA: Fountain Grove Press, 1882).

——*An Epic of the Starry Heaven* (New York: Partridge and Brittan, 1855).

——*Extemporaneous Sermons: Preached in the Marylebone Institute, London, in the Year 1860*, ed. Thomas Robinson (Manchester: Ratcliffe & Co., 1879).

——*First Book of the Christian Religion* (New York: New Church Publishing Association, 1858).

——*God's Breath in Man and in Humane Society* (Santa Rosa, CA: The Author, 1891).

——*The Golden Child; A Daily Chronicle*, 5 vols. (Santa Rosa, CA: Privately Printed, 1878).

——*The Great Republic: A Poem of the Sun* (New York and London: Brotherhood of the New Life, 1867).

——*The Holy City and the Light Therein* (Santa Rosa, CA: Fountain Grove Press, 1880).

——*Hymns of Spiritual Devotion for the New Christian Age*, 2 vols. (New York: New Church Publishing Association, 1861).

——*Hymns of the Two-in-One: for Bridal Worship in the Kingdom of the New Life* (Salem-on-Erie, NY: Brotherhood of the New Life, 1876).

——*In Dawnrise: A Song of Songs* (Privately Printed, 1896).

——*The Joy Bringer: Fifty Three Melodies of the One-in-Twain* (Santa Rosa, CA: Fountaingrove, 1886).

——*Juvenile Depravity and Crime in Our City* (New York: C B Norton, 1850).

——*Lecture on Spiritual Manifestations, Past, Present, and Future, Delivered in the People's Theater, Saint Louis* (Boston: George C Rand, 1853).

——*The Lord: the Two-in-One, Declared, Manifested and Glorified* (Salem-on-Erie, NY: Brotherhood of the New Life, 1876).

——*The Luminous Life* (Santa Rosa, CA: Privately Printed, 1882).

——*Lyra Triumphalis. People Songs: Ballads and Marches* (Santa Rosa, CA: Fountaingrove Press, 1891).

——*A Lyric of the Golden Age* (New York: Partridge and Brittan, 1856).

——*A Lyric of the Morning Land* (New York: Partridge and Brittan, 1854).

——*The Marriage of Heaven and Earth: Verified Realities* (Glasgow: C W Pearce & Co., 1903).

——*The Millennial Age. Twelve Discourses on the Spiritual and Social Aspects of the Times* (New York: New Church Publishing Association, London: W White, Manchester: J W Farquhar and Nottingham: T Stevenson, 1860).

——*Modern Spiritualism: Its Truths and Its Errors* (London: W White, 1860).

——*The Narrow Way of Attainment. Being a series of eight lectures delivered before the Boston Society Esoteric* (Applegate, CA: Esoteric Pub. Co., 1895).

——*The New Church: Its Spirit, Scope and Mission. A Lecture. Delivered in the Cairo Street Schoolroom, Warrington* (Manchester: Johnson and Rawson, 1860).

——*The New Jerusalem, the Crown of Churches and the Glory of the World. A Sermon, preached on Wednesday, March 14th, 1860, in the Mechanics' Hall, Nottingham* (London: William White, 1860).

——*The New Republic, A Discourse of the Prospects, Dangers, Duties and Safeties of the Times* (Santa Rosa, CA: Fountain Grove Press, 1891).

——*The Power and Glory of the Church of Christ. A Sermon* (London: William White, 1860).

——*Regina: A Song of Many Days* (London: William White, 1860).

——*Second Book of Fragments* (Santa Rosa, CA: Fountaingrove Press, 1897).

——*The Song of Theos: A Trilogy* (Glasgow: C W Pearce & Co., 1903).

——*Star-Flowers, A Poem of the Woman's Mystery* (Santa Rosa, CA: Fountaingrove, 1886-7).

——*The Triumph of Life* (Glasgow: C W Pearce & Co., 1903).

——*Truth and Life in Jesus; Sermons Preached in the Mechanics' Institution, Manchester, 1859* (London: William White, 1860).

——*Veritas, A Word-Song* (Glasgow: C W Pearce & Co., 1910).

——*A Voice from Heaven* (Santa Rosa, CA: Fountain Grove Press, 1879).

——*The Wedding Guest* (Santa Rosa, CA: Fountain Grove Press, 1878).

——*White Roses for the Pall*, 2 vols. (Glasgow: C W Pearce & Co., 1910).

——*The Wisdom of Angels* (New York: New Church Publishing Association, 1857).

——*The Wisdom of the Adepts. Esoteric Science in Human History* (Fountain Grove, CA: Privately Printed, 1884).

Hatch, Nathan O, *The Democratization of American Christianity* (New Haven, CT: Yale

University Press, 1989).

Hearn, Lafcadio, *Gleanings in Buddha-Fields: Studies of Hand and Soul in the Far East* (Tokyo: Tuttle, 1971 [1897]).

Hempel, Charles J, *Organon of Specific Homoeopathy; or, an Inductive Exposition of the Principles of the Homoeopathic Healing Art, Addressed to Physicians and Intelligent Laymen* (Philadelphia: Rademacher and Sheek, 1854).

Hering, Constantin, *A Concise View of the Rise and Progress of Homoeopathic Medicine*, tr. Charles F Matlack (Philadelphia: The Hahnemannean Society, 1833).

——*Domestic Physician* (Philadelphia: Rademacher, 1845).

Hindmarsh, Robert, *Rise and Progress of the New Jerusalem Church in England, America, and Other Parts*, ed. Edward Madeley (London: Hodson and Son, 1861).

Hoover, Dwight W, *Henry James, Sr. and the Religion of Community* (Grand Rapids, MI: William B Eerdmans Pub. Co., 1969).

Hort, Gertrude M, Richard Basil Ince, and William Perkes Swainson, *Three Famous Occultists: Dr. John Dee, Franz Anton Mesmer, and Thomas Lake Harris* (London: Rider and Co., 1939).

Houghton, Walter R (ed.), *Neely's History of the Parliament of Religions and Religious Congresses at the World's Columbian Exposition* (Chicago: F T Neely, 1893).

Howe, Daniel Walker (ed.), *Victorian America* (Philadelphia: University of Pennsylvania Press, 1976).

Huc, Evariste Régis, *Recollections of a Journey through Tartary, Thibet, and China, during the years 1844, 1845, and 1846*, 2 vols. (New York: Appleton, 1852).

Inada, Kenneth K, and Nolan P Jacobson (eds.), *Buddhism and American Thinkers* (Albany: State University of New York Press, 1984).

Inagaki, Hisao, *A Dictionary of Japanese Buddhist Terms* (Union City, CA: Heian International, 1989).

James, Henry, Jr, *Notes of a Son and Brother* (New York: Charles Scribner's Sons, 1914).

James, Henry, Sr, *Christianity the Logic of Creation* (London: William White, 1857).

——*The Church of Christ Not an Ecclesiasticism: A Letter of Remonstrance to a Member of the Soi-Disant New Church*, 2nd edn. (London: W White, 1856).

——*The Gospel Good News to Sinners* (New York: Scatcherd and Adams, 1838).

——*Lectures and Miscellanies* (New York: Redfield, 1852).

——*Letter to a Swedenborgian* (New York: John Allen, 1847).

——*Moralism and Christianity; Or Man's Experience and Destiny* (New York: J S Redfield, 1850).

——*The Nature of Evil, Considered in a Letter to the Rev. Edward Beecher, D.D. author of 'The Conflict of Ages.'* (New York: Appleton, 1855).

——*The Secret of Swedenborg: Being an Elucidation of His Doctrine of the Divine Natural Humanity* (Boston: Fields, Osgood, and Co., 1869).

——*The Social Significance of Our Institutions: An Oration Delivered by Request of the Citizens at Newport, R.I., July 4th, 1861* (Boston: Ticknor and Fields, 1861).

——*Society: The Redeemed Form of Man, and The Earnest of God's Omnipotence in Human Nature: Affirmed in Letters to a Friend* (Boston: Houghton, Osgood and Co., 1879).

——*Substance and Shadow: Or, Morality and Religion in Their Relation to Life: An Essay Upon the Physics of Creation* (Boston: Ticknor and Fields, 1863).

——*What Constitutes the State? A Lecture Delivered Before the Young Men's Association of the City of Albany* (New York: John Allen, 1846).

James, William, *The Will to Believe, and Other Essays in Popular Philosophy* (New York: Longmans, Green, and Co., 1897).

——(ed.), *The Literary Remains of the Late Henry James* (Boston: James R Osgood and Co., 1885).

Jones, Eli, *Definite Medication* (Boston: The Therapeutic Publishing Co., 1911).

——*Reading the Eye, Pulse and Tongue for Indicated Remedy*, ed. Wade Boyle (East Palestine, OH: Ohio Buckeye Press, 1989).

Jonsson, Inge, *Emanuel Swedenborg*, tr. Catherine Djurklou (New York: Twayne Publishers, 1971).

Kant, Immanuel, *Kant on Swedenborg: Dreams of a Spirit-Seer and Other Writings*, ed. Gregory R Johnson (West Chester, PA: Swedenborg Foundation, 2002).

Kapleau, Philip (ed.), *The Three Pillars of Zen: Teaching, Practice, and Enlightenment* (Tokyo: Weatherhill, 1965).

Kellogg, Julia, *Philosophy of Henry James: A Digest* (New York: John W Lovell Co., 1883).

Kellogg, Samuel Henry, *The Light of Asia and the Light of the World: A Comparison of the Legend, the Doctrine, and the Ethics of the Buddha with the Story, the Doctrine, and the Ethics of Christ* (London: Macmillan, 1885).

Kent, James Tyler, *Kent's Comparative Repertory of the Homeopathic Materia Medica* (New Delhi: B Jain Publishers, 2006).

——*Kent's Minor Writings on Homoeopathy*, ed. K-H Gypser (Heidelberg: Karl F Haug Publishers, 1987).

——*Kent's New Remedies, Clinical Cases, Lesser Writings, Aphorisms and Precepts* (New

Delhi: B Jain Publishers, 1994).

—*Lectures on Homoeopathic Materia Medica*, 2nd edn. (Philadelphia: Boericke and Tafel, 1911).

—*Lectures on Homeopathic Philosophy* (Lancaster, PA: Examiner Printing House, 1900).

—*Repertory of the Homoeopathic Materia Medica* (London: Homoeopathic Book Service, 1986).

—*Sexual Neuroses* (St Louis: Maynard and Tedford, 1879).

—*What the Doctor Needs to Know in Order to Make a Successful Prescription* (Calcutta: P K Ghosh, 1957).

Kerr, Howard, and Charles L Crow (eds.), *The Occult in America: New Historical Perspectives* (Urbana, IL: University of Illinois Press, 1983).

King, William Harvey (ed.), *History of Homeopathy and Its Institutions in America: Their Founders, Benefactors, Faculties, Officers, Hospitals, Alumni, etc., With a Record of Achievement of Its Representatives in the World of Medicine*, 4 vols. (New York: Lewis Publishing Co., 1905).

Kitagawa, Joseph M, *The History of Religions: Understanding Human Experience* (Atlanta, GA: Scholars Press, 1987).

Knerr, Calvin B, *Life of Hering* (Philadelphia: The Magee Press, 1940).

Kuhn, Alvin Boyd, *Theosophy: A Modern Revival of Ancient Wisdom* (New York: Henry Holt, 1930).

Kurtz, Edward T, Sr, *Brocton and Portland* (Charleston, SC: Arcadia Publishing, 2007).

Lamm, Martin, *Emanuel Swedenborg: The Development of His Thought*, tr. Tomas Spiers and Anders Hallengren (West Chester, PA: Swedenborg Foundation, 2000).

Lancaster, Clay, *The Japanese Influence in America* (New York: Walton H Rawls, 1963).

Leonard, George, *Walking on the Edge of the World: A Memoir of the Sixties and Beyond* (Boston: Houghton Mifflin, 1988).

Lowell, Percival, *The Soul of the Far East* (Boston: Houghton Mifflin, 1888).

Macintosh, Douglas Clyde, *The Problem of Religious Knowledge* (New York: Harper and Brothers, 1940).

Mack, Charles S, *Philosophy in Homoeopathy: Addressed to the Medical Profession and to the General Reader* (Chicago: Gross and Delbridge, 1890).

McCully, Richard, *The Brotherhood of the New Life and Thomas Lake Harris* (Glasgow: J Thomson, 1893).

Matthiessen, F O, *American Renaissance: Art and Expression in the Age of Emerson and Whitman* (New York: Oxford University Press, 1941).

Melton, J Gordon, *The Encyclopedia of American Religions* (Wilmington, NC: McGrath Publishing Co., 1978).

Mercer, L P (ed.), *The New Jerusalem in the World's Religious Congresses of 1893* (Chicago: Western New-Church Union, 1894).

Miller, Robert Gibson, and James Tyler Kent, *A Synopsis of Homoeopathic Philosophy* (New York and Delhi: B Jain, 1995).

Moseley, James G, Jr, *Complex Inheritance: The Idea of Self-Transcendence in the Theology of Henry James, Sr., and the Novels of Henry James* (Missoula, MT: American Academy of Religion and Scholars Press, 1975).

Müller, F Max, *Selected Essays on Language, Mythology and Religion*, 2 vols. (London: Longmans, Green, and Co., 1881).

Murphet, Howard, *Hammer on the Mountain: Life of Henry Steel Olcott, 1832-1907* (Wheaton, IL: Theosophical Publishing House, 1972).

Myren, Ann, and Dorothy Madison (eds.), *Living at the Source: Yoga Teachings of Vivekananda* (Boston: Shambhala Publications, 1993).

Northop, F S C, *The Meeting of East and West* (New York: The Macmillan Co., 1946).

Olcott, Henry Steel, *Old Diary Leaves: The History of the Theosophical Society, Third Series, 1883-87* (Adyar, Madras: Theosophical Publishing House, 1972).

Oldenburg, Hermann, *Buddha: His Life, His Doctrine, His Order*, tr. William Holy (London: Williams and Norgate, 1882).

Oliphant, Laurence, *Masollam; A Problem of the Period*, 3 vols. (Edinburgh: Blackwood, 1886).

Peiris, William, *Edwin Arnold: Brief Account of His Life and Contribution to Buddhism* (Kandy, Sri Lanka: Buddhist Publication Society, 1970).

Persons, Stow, *Free Religion: An American Faith* (New Haven: Yale University Press, 1947).

Pettit, Norman, *The Heart Prepared: Grace and Conversion in Puritan Spiritual Life* (New Haven: Yale University Press, 1966).

Podmore, Frank, *Modern Spiritualism: A History and a Criticism*, 2 vols. (London: Methuen and Co., 1902).

Potter, Karl H, *Presuppositions of India's Philosophies* (Englewood Cliffs, NJ: Prentice-Hall, 1963).

Prebish, Charles S, *American Buddhism* (North Scituate, MA: Duxbury, 1979).

Rhys Davids, Thomas William, *Buddhism: Its History and Literature* (New York: G P Putnam's, 1896).

—*Buddhism: Being a Sketch of the Life and Teachings of Gautama, the Buddha*

(London: Society for Promoting Christian Knowledge, 1890).

Rosenstone, Robert A, *Mirror in the Shrine: American Encounters with Meiji Japan* (Cambridge, MA: Harvard University Press, 1988).

Rothstein, William, *American Physicians in the Nineteenth Century: From Sects to Science* (Baltimore: Johns Hopkins University Press, 1972).

Rydell, Robert W, *All the World's a Fair: Visions of Empire at American International Exhibitions, 1876-1916* (Chicago: University of Chicago Press, 1984).

Sangharakshita, Bhikkhu, *Angarika Dharmapala: Biographical Sketch* (Kandy: Buddhist Publication Society, 1964).

Schneider, Herbert W, *A History of American Philosophy* (New York: Columbia University Press, 1946).

—*Religion in 20th Century America* (Cambridge, MA: Harvard University Press, 1952).

Schürmann, Reiner, *Meister Eckhard: Mystic and Philosopher* (Bloomington: Indiana University Press, 1978).

Seldes, Gilbert, *The Stammering Century* (New York: The John Day Company, 1927).

Silver, Ednah C, *Sketches of the New Church in America* (Boston: Massachusetts New Church Union, 1920).

Sorokin, Pitirim, *Social Philosophies of an Age of Crisis* (Boston: Beacon Press, 1950).

Stanley, Michael, *Emanuel Swedenborg: Essential Readings* (Wellingborough: Aquarian Press, 1988).

Stiernotte, Alfred P (ed.), *Mysticism and the Modern Mind* (New York: Liberal Arts Press, 1959).

Strouse, Jean, *Alice James: A Biography* (Boston: Houghton Mifflin Co., 1980).

Suzuki, Daisetsu Teitaro, *A Brief History of Early Chinese Philosophy* (London: Probsthain and Co., 1914).

—*Buddha of Infinite Light* (Boston: Shambhala Publications, 1998).

—*Essays in Zen Buddhism, First Series* (New York: Grove Press, 1961).

—*Essays in Zen Buddhism, Second Series* (London: Rider and Company, 1970).

—*Essays in Zen Buddhism, Third Series* (London: Rider and Co., 1953).

—*The Essence of Buddhism*, 2nd edn. (London: Buddhist Society, 1947).

—*The Field of Zen: Contributions to the Middle Way, the Journal of the Buddhist Society* (New York: Harper and Row, 1970).

—*An Introduction to Zen Buddhism* (New York: Grove Press, 1964).

—*Japanese Buddhism* (Tokyo: Board of Tourist Industry, 1938).

—*Living by Zen* (Tokyo: Sanseido Press, 1949).

——*Manual of Zen Buddhism* (New York: Grove Press, 1960).

——*Mysticism: Christian and Buddhist* (New York: Harper and Brothers, 1957).

——*On Indian and Mahayana Buddhism*, ed. Edward Conze (New York: Harper and Row, 1968).

——*Outlines of Mahayana Buddhism* (New York: Schoken, 1963 [1907]).

——*Shin Buddhism* (New York: Harper and Row, 1970).

——*Shin Shukyō Ron (A New Theory of Religion)* (Kyoto: Daiyo Shoin,1896).

——*Suedenborugu*, in *Swedenborg: Buddha of the North*, tr. Andrew Bernstein (West Chester, PA: Swedenborg Foundation, 1996).

——*Zen and Japanese Buddhism* (Tokyo: Japan Travel Bureau, 1958).

——*Zen and Japanese Culture* (Princeton, NJ: Princeton University Press, 1959).

——*Zen Buddhism: Selected Writings of D.T. Suzuki*, ed.William Barrett (Garden City, NY: Doubleday and Co., 1956).

——*The Zen Doctrine of No-Mind: The Significance of the Sutra of Hui-neng* (York Beach, ME: Samuel Weiser, 1969).

——(with Erich Fromm and Richard De Martino), *Zen Buddhism and Psychoanalysis* (New York: Harper & Row, 1960).

Swainson, William P, *Thomas Lake Harris and His Occult Teaching* (London: William Rider and Son, 1922).

Swank, Scott Trego, 'The Unfettered Conscience. A Study of Sectarianism, Spiritualism, and Social Reform in the New Jerusalem Church', Ph.D. diss. (University of Pennsylvania, 1970).

Swedenborg, Emanuel, *Angelic Wisdom concerning the Divine Love and Wisdom*, tr. Clifford and Doris Harley (London: Swedenborg Society, 1987).

——*The Animal Kingdom, Considered Anatomically, Physically, and Philosophically*, tr. J J G Wilkinson, 2 vols. (London: W Newbery, 1843-4).

——*Arcana Caelestia*, tr. John Elliott, 12 vols. (London: Swedenborg Society, 1983-99).

——*Conjugial Love*, tr. John Chadwick (London: Swedenborg Society, 1996).

——*Divine Providence,* tr. William Dick and E Pulsford (London: Swedenborg Society, 1988).

——*The Economy of the Animal Kingdom, Considered Anatomically, Physically, and Philosophically*, tr. Augustus Clissold, 2 vols. (London: W Newbery, 1845-6).

——*Heaven and Its Wonders and Hell From Things Heard and Seen*, tr. Doris Harley (London: Swedenborg Society, 1992).

——*Heaven and Hell*, tr. George F Dole (West Chester, PA: Swedenborg Foundation, 2000).

——*The New Jerusalem and Its Heavenly Doctrine*, tr. Rudolph L Tafel (London:

Swedenborg Society, 1993).

—*Outlines of a Philosophical Argument on the Infinite and on the Intercourse Between the Soul and the Body*, tr. J J G Wilkinson (London: William Newbery and Boston: O Clapp, 1847).

—*The Principia; Or, The First Principles of Natural Things*, tr. Augustus Clissold, 2 vols. (London: W Newbery, 1845-6).

—*The Spiritual Diary*, 5 vols. (London: Swedenborg Society, 1883-1902), vol. V, tr. James F Buss.

—*True Christian Religion*, tr. John C Ager, 2 vols. (West Chester, PA: Swedenborg Foundation, 1996).

Swift, Lindsay, *Brook Farm: Its Members, Scholars, and Visitors* (New York: Macmillan and Co., 1900).

Toksvig, Signe, *Emmanuel Swedenborg: Scientist and Mystic* (New Haven: Yale University Press, 1948).

Transactions of the International Swedenborg Congress, Held in Connection with the Celebration of the Swedenborg Society's Centenary, London, July 4 to 8, 1910 (London: Swedenborg Society, 1912).

Trine, Ralph Waldo, *Character-Building Thought Power* (New York: Thomas Y Crowell and Co., 1900).

—*Every Living Creature or Heart-Training through the Animal World* (New York: Thomas Y Crowell and Co., 1899).

—*The Greatest Thing Ever Known* (New York: Thomas Y Crowell and Co., 1898).

—*The Higher Powers of Mind and Spirit* (New York: Dodge Publishing Co., 1917).

—*In the Fire of the Heart* (New York: McClure, Phillips and Co., 1906).

—*In the Hollow of His Hand* (New York: Dodd, Mead and Co., 1919).

—*In Tune With the Infinite: or, Fullness of Peace, Power and Plenty* (New York: Thomas Y Crowell & Company, 1897).

—*The Land of Living Men* (New York: Dodge Publishing Co., 1910).

—*The Man Who Knew; how he brought the good news that the kingdom of God is within us, and we may put ourselves in tune with the centre of life* (New York: The Bobbs-Merrill Co., 1936).

—*My Philosophy and My Religion* (New York: Dodd, Mead, and Co., 1921).

—*This Mystical Life of Ours: a book of suggestive thoughts for each week through the year* (New York: T Y Crowell and Co., 1907).

—*The New Alinement of Life, Concerning the Mental Laws of a Greater Personal and*

Public Power (New York: Dodge Publishing Co., 1913).

——*On the Open Road: Being Some Thoughts and a Little Creed of Wholesome Living* (New York: Thomas Y Crowell and Co., 1908).

——*The Power that Wins: Henry Ford and Ralph Waldo Trine in an Intimate Talk on Life* (Indianapolis: Bobbs-Merrill Co., 1929).

——*Thoughts I Met on the Highway: Words of Friendly Cheer from 'The Life Books'* (New York: Dodge Publishing Co., 1912).

——*Through the Sunlit Year: a book of suggestive thoughts for each day through the year from the writings of Ralph Waldo Trine* (New York: Dodd, Mead and Co., 1919).

——*What All the World's A-Seeking; Or, The Vital Law of True Life, True Greatness, Power, and Happiness* (New York: Thomas Y Crowell, 1896).

——*The Winning of the Best* (New York: Dodge Publishing Co., 1912).

——*The World's Balance-Wheel* (New York: Dodd, Mead, and Co., 1920).

Trobridge, George, *Swedenborg: Life and Teaching* (London: Swedenborg Society, 1974).

Tweed, Thomas A, *The American Encounter with Buddhism, 1844-1912: Victorian Culture and the Limits of Dissent* (Chapel Hill, NC: University of North Carolina Press, 1992).

Urquhart, W S, *The Vedanta and Modern Thought* (London: Humphrey Milford, 1928).

Vetterling, Carl Herman, *The Illuminate of Görlitz; or, Jakob Böhme's Life and Philosophy: A Comparative Study* (Leipzig: F A Brockhaus, 1922).

——(pseud. Philangi Dasa), *Swedenborg the Buddhist; or, the Higher Swedenborgianism, Its Secrets and Thibetan Origin* (Los Angeles: The Buddhist Swedenborgian Brotherhood, 1887; repr. Charleston, SC: Arcana Books, 2003).

Villeneuve, Crispian, *Rudolf Steiner in Britain: A Documentation of His Ten Visits* (Forest Row: Temple Lodge, 2009).

Vithoulkas, George, *The Science of Homeopathy* (New York: Grove Press, 1980).

Waterfield, Robin, *Hidden Depths: The Story of Hypnosis* (London: Macmillan, 2002).

Welbon, Guy, *The Buddhist Nirvana and Its Western Interpreters* (Chicago: University of Chicago Press, 1968).

Welch, Claude, *Protestant Thought in the Nineteenth Century*, 2 vols. (New Haven, CT: Yale University Press, 1972-85).

Wilkinson, James John Garth, *The Affections of Armed Powers: A Plea for a School of Little Nations* (London: James Speirs, 1897).

——*The African and the True Christian Religion, his Magna Charta. A Study in the Writings of Emanuel Swedenborg* (London: James Speirs, 1892).

——*The Book of Edda Called Voluspa: A Study in Its Scriptural and Spiritual*

Correspondences (London: James Speirs, 1897).

—*The Combats and Victories of Jesus Christ* (London: James Speirs, 1895).

—*Compulsory Vaccination, Its Wickedness to the Poor* (London: F Pitman, 1873).

—*Emanuel Swedenborg: A Biography* (London: W Newbery, 1849; 2nd edn. London: James Speirs, 1886).

—*Epidemic Man and His Visitations* (London: James Speirs, 1893).

A Free State and Free Medicine (London: F Pitman, 1870).

—*The Forcible Introspection of Women for the Army and Navy by the Oligarchy, Considered Physically* (London: F Pitman, 1870).

—*The Greater Origins and Issues of Life and Death* (London: James Speirs, 1885).

—*The Homoeopathic Principle Applied to Insanity: A Proposal to Treat Lunacy by Spiritualism* (London: William White, 1857).

—*The Human Body and Its Connexion with Man* (London: Chapman and Hall, 1851).

—*Improvisations from the Spirit* (London: William White, 1857).

—*Isis and Osiris in the Book of Respirations: Prophecy in the Churches. In the Word, God with Us. The Revelation of Jesus Christ* (London: James Speirs, 1899).

—*The New Jerusalem and the Old Jerusalem. The Place and Service of the Jewish Church Among the Aeons of Revelation. With Other Essays* (London: James Speirs, 1894).

—*Oannes According to Berosus: A Study in the Church of the Ancients* (London: James Speirs, 1888).

—*On Human Science, Good and Evil, and Its Works; and on Divine Revelation and Its Works and Sciences* (London: James Speirs, 1876).

—*On the Cure, Arrest, and Isolation of Small Pox by a New Method; and on the Local Treatment of Erysipelas, and all Internal Inflammations: with a Special Chapter on Cellulitis, and a Postscript on Medical Freedom* (London: Leath and Ross, 1864).

—*Our Social Health. A discourse delivered before the London 'Ladies' Sanitary Association,' February 28, 1865* (Boston: S Welles Cone, 1865).

—(pseud. John Lone) *Painting with Both Hands; or, the Adoption of the Principle of the Steroscope in Art, as a Means to Binocular Pictures* (London: Chapman and Hall, 1856).

—*Pasteur and Jenner: An Example and a Warning* (London: William Young, 1881).

—*A Popular Sketch of Swedenborg's Philosophical Works: Read Before the Swedenborg Association, June 3, 1847* (London: William Newbery, 1847).

—*Remarks on Swedenborg's Economy of the Animal Kingdom* (London: Walton and Mitchell, 1846).

——*Revelation, Mythology, Correspondences* (London: James Speirs, 1887).

——*Science for All. A Lecture Delivered Before the Swedenborg Association, March 25, 1847* (London: William Newbery, 1847).

——*Small-Pox and Vaccination* (London: F Pitman, 1871).

——*The Soul is Form and Doth the Body Make: The Heart and Lungs, the Will and the Understanding. Chapters in Psychology* (London: James Speirs, 1890).

——*Swedenborg Among the Doctors. A Letter to Robert T. Cooper, M.D.* (London: James Speirs, 1895).

——*The Treatment of Small-pox by Hydrastis Canadensis and Veratrum Viride* (Manchester, 1871).

——*Unlicensed Medicine; With a Plan of Extending Homoeopathy*, (London: R Theobald, 1855).

——*The Use of Glanderine and Farcine in the Treatment of Pulmonary and Other Diseases* (London: William White, 1857).

——*Vaccination as a Source of Small-Pox* (London: London Society for the Abolition of Compulsory Vaccination, 1884).

——*Vaccination Tracts* (London: William Young, 1877-9).

——*War, Cholera, and the Ministry of Health* (Boston: Otis Clapp, and Crosby, Nichols, and Co., 1855).

Winchell, Wallace, 'The Mystical Experience of Thomas Lake Harris: The Seer as a Creator of His Own Visionary World', Ph.D. diss. (Hartford Seminary Foundation, 1976).

Wolf, William J, *Thoreau: Mystic, Prophet, Ecologist* (Philadelphia: Pilgrim, 1974).

Yamaski, Taiko, *Shingon: Japanese Esoteric Buddhism* (Boston, MA: Shambhala, 1988).

Ziolkowski, Eric J (ed.), *A Museum of Faiths: Histories and Legacies of the 1893 World's Parliament of Religions* (Atlanta: Scholars Press, 1993).

INDEX